K.DUNN

A Foundation in Business Accounting

A Foundation in Business Accounting

Richard S Giles

Bournemouth & Poole College

Stanley Thornes (Publishers) Ltd

First published in 1991 by:
Stanley Thornes (Publishers) Ltd
Old Station Drive
Leckhampton
CHELTENHAM GL53 0DN
England

British Library Cataloguing in Publication Data

Giles, R. S. (Richard S.)
A foundation in business accounting.
1. Great Britain. Business firms. Accounting
I. Title
657.0941

ISBN 0–7487–0559–7

Typeset by Tech-Set, Gateshead, Tyne & Wear.
Printed and bound in Singapore by Chong Moh Offset Printing Pte Ltd

Contents

Part IV The evaluation of financial statements and further issues

Preface

A Foundation in Business Accounting adopts a modern approach, suitable for the study of accounting in the 1990s and takes a more practical look at computer-based accounting.

The book is targeted at students on their first course of accounting studies. It could also be suitable for the small businessman who requires a clear and practical understanding of his accounts. It should be useful to students reading for their first level degree/diploma business study courses and professional courses, as a background reader.

Each chapter begins with some question objectives, followed by an introduction. The main volume of each chapter is treated as relevantly and directly as possible. Each chapter is concluded with a brief summary outlining major points. Many examples and solutions have been provided throughout the text to facilitate learning. Five projects are also provided for assignment work in the Projects chapter.

The text uses both the traditional and running balance methods of ledger recording. As far as is necessary for a book at this level, it conforms to the requirements laid down in the 1985 Companies Act. Most of the accounts therefore, relating to financial statements are in the vertical style, conforming to Format No.1.

Permission has kindly been granted to include questions from various examination bodies, associations and organisations.

A Foundation in Business Accounting covers the course content and structure of the following syllabuses relating to financial accounting:

RSA	Royal Society of Arts (stages I and II)
GCSE	General Certificate of Secondary Education
LCC	London Chamber of Commerce (levels I and II)
AAT	Association of Accounting Technicians (preliminary and intermediate levels)
CIOB	Chartered Institute of Bankers (Foundation)
ACCA	Chartered Association of Certified Accountants (Foundation)
CIMA	Chartered Institution of Management Accountants (Foundation)
ICM	Institute of Commercial Management.

In addition to these courses, the book covers, to a large extent, the basic accounting material required for other examinations, including GCE 'A' level and first year degree courses.

The book looks at accounting with a modern and up-to-date approach and includes the relevant legislation relating to the Companies Acts 1985 and 1989, at the time of publication.

Acknowledgements

I would like to take this opportunity to thank both students and staff of the Business Studies and Computing Department at Bournemouth & Poole College for their guidance and assistance and in particular, John Capel. My other colleagues include Christine Freer, Douglas Lewis, Rod Pearce, Graham Whitehall and also some former colleagues, Mervyn Bright, now in private practice, and David Balfour (Stafford College).

In addition I would like to express my thanks to the examining boards who have kindly granted permission to use their past papers and to Microsoft Ltd for the use of the *Pegasus* software in the computer-based accounting sections.

Richard S Giles

PART I, CHAPTER

1 Accounting information

- *Why do different types of business organisations such as sole traders, partnerships and limited companies, need accounting information?*
- *What are the five accounting groups?*
- *What are the responsibilities of an accounts office and that of the accountant?*

Introduction

What is accounting? Why is accounting so necessary to all types of businesses whether they are large or small?

Accounting information is as essential to the small retailer on the street corner as it is to any large organisation such as Sainsbury's or Tescos.

Whether the business is in the private or public sector (Government owned), makes little difference. Businesses need accounting information to make them run more efficiently. Without this information, many businesses would not be able to operate.

It is essential to know what money is coming into, and what money is going out of, a business. What it is earning and what it is spending. A major function of accounting is to ensure that financial records are kept on a day-to-day basis and from this data, a set of accounts can be prepared.

Why are accounts needed? The purpose of keeping a set of accounts may be summarised below.

Keeping financial records

Keeping a set of accounting records provides the business with essential details such as the income it earns, the expenses it incurs, the financial resources it has, the debts it owes, the customers who owe it money and many other vital pieces of information. A set of accounts will provide accurate details of all the financial transactions of the enterprise.

Preparing financial statements

The information derived from keeping financial records can be used to prepare the business's financial statements such as the profit and loss account and the balance sheet.

The business's profit or loss for the period can be calculated to see how successful it has been and a statement can be prepared to show the financial position of the business in terms of how it is financed and what its resources are.

Controlling the business

Accounting not only deals with historical records of the business's financial transactions, it can also be dynamic in the sense that it may be used to plan ahead, to forecast results and to provide sound control of the business overall. Businesses can use accounting records to help them prepare budgets concerning the planning of sales, production, running expenses, cash flow, profits and anything else which will help the owners and management of businesses make better and more informed decisions.

Financial information is recorded in the books of a business, where the *ledger* is a system which is used to provide the day-to-day details of recording transactions. These transactions form the accounts of the business.

Some business organisations may record a great number of accounts because of the nature and size of their enterprise. However, irrespective of the size of a business or the number of accounts it operates, there are only *five* groups of accounts. These groups are:

assets, liabilities, capital, revenue and *expenses.*

The accounts office of a business has the key function of recording all financial information on a day-to-day basis. Accounts are recorded in the ledger. Increasingly, the computer is playing a significant part in the recording of accounts. Many accounting packages are available to facilitate the recording process including customers' and suppliers' accounts, stock control, payroll, invoicing and many other aspects of the business.

Why do people go into business? People want to go into business for different kinds of reasons. Many feel it is a challenge and want to use their initiative. It may be a little daunting, exciting and a bit of an adventure. Others simply want to be their own boss; they may be fed up with working for someone else.

For most businesses, the principal motive for operating as an enterprise, is to make profits. A sole trader, a business owned by one person, will not need to share its profits. A partnership will need to distribute its profits in accordance with the partnership agreement. A company may distribute some of its profits to shareholders in the form of dividends.

Who needs accounting information?

Many different types of people need and want accounting information either on a day-to-day basis or that provided by financial statements like the profit and loss account and the balance sheet.

The owners of an enterprise will want to measure the success of their business. This applies equally to sole traders, partnerships or shareholders of limited companies. These different types of owners want to know how profitable their business is and whether their investment is likely to prosper.

The creditors of an enterprise will want to know specifically whether a business is in a position to be able to repay its debts. In other words, whether or not it has sufficient *liquidity* to do so. Creditors can assess a business's liquidity from the figures prepared in the balance sheet.

The taxation authorities will want to assess the tax liability of a business, that is, on the profits calculated in the financial year. The profit and loss account and the balance sheet will be of interest to them.

The management of organisations, particularly of limited companies, will want to have all kinds of financial information at their fingertips, for example sales and purchase figures, bank and cash details, customer and supplier numbers. From this information, more effective control of business resources is achieved, better decisions are concluded and the overall performance of a business may be evaluated. Sound planning for the future can be prepared from the financial information gathered and recorded.

Potential investors will also be interested in a business's performance. They will need to know the financial performance of a company for the purpose of deciding whether or not to risk their investment. Will the company be successful and provide them with dividends, ensuring that their capital will increase through the value of their shares?

The five accounting groups

Accounting has *five* distinct groups of accounts, irrespective of the number of accounts recorded in a business. These groups are:

assets
liabilities
capital
revenue
expenses.

Assets are described as things of value *owned* by a business, that is, its resources in the shape of premises, equipment, motor vehicles, stock, cash, etc.

Liabilities are described as the debts of the business, the things of value *owed* to its creditors for stock, loans, overdrafts, mortgages, unpaid bills, etc.

Capital represents the owner's interest in the business. The owner is seen as a *separate* entity from the business in that personal interest is kept separate from business interest. The owner's worth in the business is calculated from the difference between assets and liabilities. Thus:

$$\text{Capital} = \text{Assets} - \text{Liabilities}$$

If the business assets were valued at £1000 and its liabilities at £800, the owner's net worth in the business would be £200.

Capital may be represented by a sole trader (one-person business), a partnership (two to 20 partners' capital) or by the shareholders of a limited company where there is no limit to the number of shareholders who invest capital.

Revenue refers to the income earned by a business in selling its goods or services. Other forms of revenue may come from the receipt of bank interest, commission, discount, rent or other earnings.

Expenses refers to the goods and services paid for or incurred by the business in the pursuit of its revenue, that is, wages, salaries, purchases of goods, and overheads such as light, heat, insurance, rates and advertising.

These groups of accounts are recorded in the ledgers of the business. The ledgers record the financial transactions of the business so that a historical sequence of events is developed in the shape of accounts. From these accounts, the financial statements of the business are prepared for the purpose of finding out how the business is performing.

Is the business successful or not? Whether the business is large or small, owned by a single person or a cast of thousands, each organisation needs to know if the business is performing to a satisfactory level.

The accounts office

The Accounts Manager

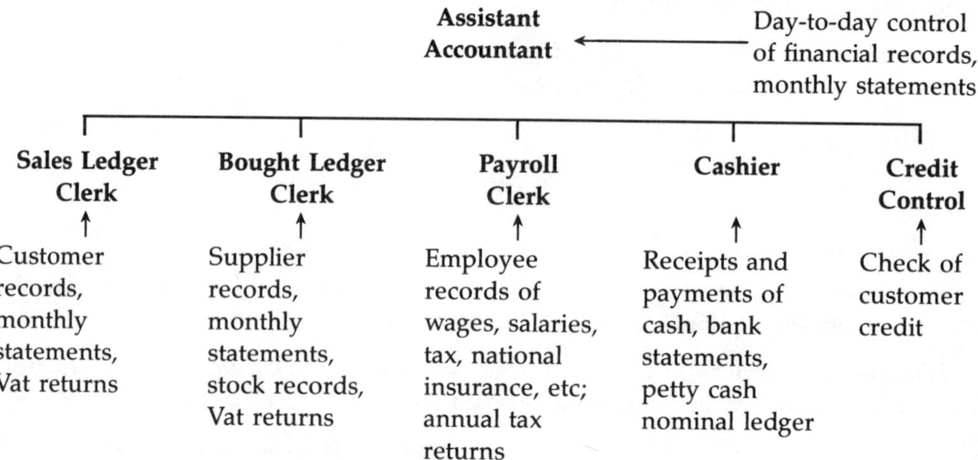

The accurate, day-to-day recording of financial transactions is one of the most important functions of an accounts office.

The sales and bought ledger clerks are responsible for customer and supplier accounts respectively. Documents such as invoices and credit notes, and evidence of payment will be the 'raw materials' from which the accounting information will be recorded.

The cashier is responsible for banking and cash transactions and also receiving and checking bank statements to see if entries match the business's records. He or she may also be responsible for the nominal ledger which records all accounts except customers' and suppliers' – the responsibility of the sales and bought ledger clerks. A junior accounts clerk may be delegated with the responsibility of being in charge of all petty cash expenses.

The payroll clerk is responsible for the calculation of the business's wages and salaries paid to its employees. This will include payments for bonuses and overtime, the appropriate deductions for tax and national insurance, and other payments stopped from pay.

Many businesses need to keep accurate records of stock for the purpose of knowing when to reorder the next batch before stocks fall too low. It is important to carry the optimum level of stock because if too much is purchased, it may tie up cash required for other purposes, or if too little is bought, stock levels could soon run out and valuable orders lost.

The credit controller is responsible for ensuring that customers are creditworthy and can pay their bills on time. If customers delay their payments, this can lead to liquidity problems for the business, that is, the business can become short of immediately accessible funds to meet its debts.

The management of the office will have overall control of the accounting staff and be responsible for ensuring that records are maintained accurately and the accounts are thoroughly up-to-date. The accountant and his assistant will be responsible for the preparation of the accounting statements, such as the profit and loss account and the balance sheet. They will also be responsible for the preparation of budgeting, that is, planning ahead for the purpose of ensuring that sufficient cash resources will be available to meet future payments and also to help control patterns of expenditure for the departments within the organisation.

Computers are playing a key role in the recording of financial transactions in many accounting offices. Computer software is available and programs may be purchased to record all the accounts of the business such as payroll, stock control, sales and bought ledgers. The accounts clerk types in the data on a keyboard rather than writing down the information as in a manual system.

The accountant in practice

The work of a provincial accountant is often complex and varied yet it can be very interesting and not at all desk bound as many people might imagine.

Many clients need to be visited at their place of work and need all sorts of financial advice, particularly on aspects such as taxation, mortgages, loans and overdraft facilities, and how to raise further capital.

There are a wide range of different business enterprises down a typical high street, sole traders, partnerships and companies, and all need the services of an accountant at some time, even if it is only at the end of the financial period to prepare the profit and loss account and balance sheet. Clients may include dentists and doctors, hotel and catering businesses, retail and wholesale organisations, manufacturing firms, pubs and places of entertainment, and many other ventures. This provides a variety of work, mostly of an interesting nature.

The range of services a practice can offer would include:

- preparation of accounts for different types of businesses such as sole traders, partnerships and companies;
- the audit of accounts for companies;
- taxation advice (income tax, capital gains tax, Vat);
- financial consultancy and management accounting including budgets and projections of profit;

a general book-keeping service including payroll preparation;
advice on the sale and purchase of businesses;
advice on the raising of new capital;
investment, pension and insurance guidance;
tax planning.

This is by no means an exhaustive list of services. Some accountants may specialise in bankruptcies and liquidations, others may specialise in a particular line of business such as hotel and catering or the medical profession. The field of accounting is one of the most varied and interesting in the financial world.

Summary

1 Accounting is one of the most important aspects in business because it provides financial information to those persons who need to know how the business is performing.

2 A record of accounts explains what is happening in the business in terms of its resources, its debts, its revenue and its expenses. These accounts are recorded in what is called the ledger system.

3 Financial statements can be prepared from the accounts to find out how well the business has performed. Was it a success or did it perform badly? The profit and loss account and the balance sheet represent the two major accounting reports.

4 There are *five* major groups in accounting, irrespective of the number of accounts recorded. These are assets, liabilities, capital, revenue and expenses.

5 The accounts office is responsible for the recording of financial information. Ledger clerks are appointed to record the transactions into the books of account. The accountant is responsible for day-to-day control of the office and for ensuring that the financial reports are prepared as and when they are required.

The accountant in practice can have one of the most varied and interesting jobs in the financial world.

QUESTIONS

1 Why is it important for businesses to record financial information? Does this also apply to the small business?

2 Financial statements may be prepared from a set of accounts. What statements are these?

3 A business may have thousands of accounts in its books. How many groups of accounts could these be organised into? Give a brief description of each group.

4 What is the ledger used for in accounting?

5 What could be considered a key function in an accounts office? In modern offices the staff would most probably be using a computer program to record financial information. What software is available to record this information?

CHAPTER

2 Sources of capital

- ***What are the various sources of finance needed to start a business?***
- ***How do these sources relate to the owner's capital and that capital which is borrowed?***

Introduction

When a business commences at the outset, the size of its initial capital will influence the size of the business itself. The larger the finance available at the start of a business, it follows that the business is likely to be larger.

A public limited company (plc) that can invite the public to purchase its shares via a prospectus, has the greatest potential to raise capital having no restriction as to the amount of capital it can ask shareholders to buy. For example, when Imperial Metal Industries plc began its life in 1978, it offered 123 million shares at 60 p each, raising a vast sum to begin its business operations. On the other hand, a small sole trader wanting to set up his or her own business, may require a moderately small sum of capital to start off the enterprise. Perhaps a van and a few thousand pounds in the bank may be sufficient.

The major sources of finance are:

owner's capital
borrowed capital
debenture issues
profits
creditors.

The owner's capital

To start any kind of business venture requires money either in cash or other asset form such as a motor vehicle, premises, equipment, etc. The initial value of the owner's assets will be recorded as his initial capital invested in the business at the date the business commences.

If a person begins a venture with £2000 in the bank and a vehicle valued at £1000, the initial owner's capital will be worth £3000. This is referred to as the owner's *net worth*.

Capital	=	Assets
(Net worth)		Bank £2000 + Vehicle £1000
£3000		

If the business is successful and makes profits, some of which are retained in the enterprise, then capital will increase over the years. Losses have the effect of reducing capital. Therefore, capital comparisons are important from year to year, to see whether the owner's capital has increased or decreased.

Borrowed capital (or loan capital)

Banks and building societies are a major source of borrowing. This may be in the form of overdrafts, short and longer-term loans and mortgages.

Loans in the short term (less than 12 months) are regarded as current liabilities and are generally used to finance day-to-day expenditure such as wages, salaries, rent, rates, stock purchases, etc. The business may have arranged overdraft facilities with the bank for the purpose of ensuring that adequate cash resources are available to pay for these expenses. Interest is charged on a daily basis, usually a few percentage points above the bank's base rate. If the base rate is 12 per cent, the bank may charge about 14 per cent or 15 per cent interest on the overdraft balance.

Borrowed capital is part of the business's liabilities. If the business arranged a £3000 loan with a local bank, the equation above could be extended to read:

Capital	=	Assets	−	Liabilities
£3000		Bank £5000	−	Loan £3000
		Vehicle £1000		

$$C = A - L$$

or

$$A = C + L$$

$$£6000 = £3000 + £3000$$

This is known as the *accounting equation*. The accounting equation will be illustrated further in Chapter 3.

Debenture issues

Debentures are also part of an enterprise's loan capital and are therefore liabilities. They are issued by public limited companies as a means of raising the financial assets of a company without resorting to either issuing more capital in the form of shares or finding alternative sources of borrowing.

Bought and sold on the Stock Exchange, debentures are marketable securities like shares. Their value is determined by the interest rates paid on the debenture stock as compared with current rates of interest available at the time. They are issued for a specific period of time, paying a fixed rate of interest, for example, ten year stock at 9 per cent. This means that a company is prepared to pay 9 per cent interest per annum for ten years on every £100 of stock. After the ten years, the stock matures and is said to be redeemable – the company buys back its stock. Some debentures are irredeemable which means that although interest is still paid, the stock is never 'matured'.

Debentures are usually secured liabilities on the assets of a business, often known as mortgage debentures. The debenture holders can be paid from the proceeds of the sale of assets should the business be liquidated (bankrupt).

Debentures are similar to the Government's gilt-edged securities offered on the Stock Exchange at fixed interest rates over a specific time period.

Note that an issue of shares is part of a company's equity and represents share capital. Debentures are part of a company's long-term liabilities and represent loan capital. They usually have some priority in being paid first, before other creditors, if a company is liquidated.

Profits

One of the most positive and sure ways to expand a business is to plough back a proportion of its profits into the enterprise each financial year. IBM Computers did this for at least the first seven years of business, retaining virtually all its profits, paying nothing in dividends to its shareholders, but expanding its field of operations with the extra finance coming from its profits. Profits retained in the business can further its growth and at the same time, increase the equity of the owner's investment.

Many companies plough back their profits into what is called their *reserves* and in this way are able to expand into very large organisations. The major banks like Barclays and Lloyds plough millions into their reserves and are then able to expand their operations world wide.

Creditors

Trade creditors supply businesses with stock or services. Some organisations that order large stocks can take advantage of the free finance available, that is, the period of credit they are given before the stock is paid for. Supermarkets like Sainsbury's are able to order vast supplies of stock on a number of months' credit thereby securing an important source of short-term finance.

Other sources

There are other sources of finance available. In 1981, the Government started the Loan Guarantee Scheme designed to help new business ventures particularly in hi-tech industries. The Government also sponsors venture capital under the Investors in Industry scheme for specific long-term projects in industry which may take time to become profitable.

Businesses may also lease assets rather than buy them. This is a form of rental rather than purchase and allows the business to find alternative uses for the finance it has available. A lease is a chargeable expense against profits, helping to reduce tax payments.

Summary

1 There are five major sources of capital available to finance a business:
   the owner's capital
   borrowed capital
   debentures
   profits
   creditors.

2 The owner's capital is known as the *net worth* – representing the owner's equity in the business. The accounting equation can emphasise what the owners of a business are worth:

Capital = Assets – Liabilities

3 All forms of borrowing, short or long-term, are listed under the business's liabilities.

4 Profits which are ploughed back into a business help it to expand and grow. Losses will reduce the business's capital, that is, its equity.

5 The Government can also sponsor some forms of loan capital as seen in the Loan Guarantee Scheme and Investors in Industry.

QUESTIONS

1 How does the initial capital invested in a business influence its size?

2 Make a list of the finance available recorded under a business's liabilities.

3 What is the accounting equation? How is it related to what the owners are worth in the business?

4 What is the distinct difference between a share and a debenture?

5 Where would a business arrange short-term finance? For which purposes would this normally be used?

6 What is meant by the term 'owner's equity'? What type of owners are found in the business world?

CHAPTER

3 The balance sheet

- *Why is the balance sheet an important financial statement?*
- *Which groups of accounts are used to prepare the balance sheet?*
- *What is the accounting equation?*

Introduction

The two major financial statements in business are the balance sheet and the profit and loss account. These are prepared to illustrate a business's financial performance over a period of time, normally once a year. However, for management purposes, the statements may be required more frequently, perhaps monthly or quarterly, to help evaluate business performance.

The accounts of the business are balanced off at the appropriate time and then used to prepare the statements. Assets, liabilities and capital accounts form the basis of the balance sheet. Revenue and expense accounts are matched together for the purpose of calculating the business's profit or loss and are used to prepare its profit and loss account. (The profit and loss account is covered in Chapter 4.)

The balance sheet

The balance sheet lists the business's assets, liabilities and capital accounts in order to give its overall financial position at any given time in terms of its resources (assets) and the financing of its resources (capital and liabilities).

The balance sheet can emphasise what the owners are worth in the business in terms of the accounting equation:

$$\text{Capital} = \text{Assets} - \text{Liabilities}$$

For example, if a business has assets worth £300 000 and liabilities of £100 000, the owners are worth £200 000.

$$\begin{aligned} \text{Capital} &= \text{Assets} &- \text{Liabilities} \\ £200\,000 &= £300\,000 &- £100\,000 \end{aligned}$$

The alternative accounting equation emphasises the worth of the business and its financing:

Assets	=	Capital	+	Liabilities
£300 000	=	£200 000	+	£100 000

The balance sheet may be prepared in *two* formats:

Vertically, emphasising Assets − Liabilities = Capital, or
Horizontally, emphasising Assets = Capital + Liabilities

The first format will be used predominantly throughout this text because it is used widely in all types of business enterprises and its form of presentation makes comparisons with other years easier.

Example

The following information represents the assets, liabilities and capital of Craythorne & Co Ltd as at 1 January 1989:

	£	£
ASSETS:		
Premises	150 000	
Equipment	40 000	
Vehicles	10 000	200 000
Stock	55 000	
Debtors	30 000	
Bank	10 000	
Cash	5 000	100 000
		300 000
LESS LIABILITIES:		
Trade creditors	40 000	
Short-term loan	8 000	
Bills outstanding	2 000	50 000
Mortgage on premises		50 000
		100 000
CAPITAL:		
150 000 @ £1 shares	150 000	
Retained profits	50 000	200 000

Assets	− Liabilities	=	Capital
£300 000	− £100 000	=	£200 000

The business is worth £300 000 on paper which is financed by the combination of the shareholders' capital and profits, and the liabilities. The shareholders' net worth is £200 000, representing their equity in the business.

Types of assets and liabilities

There are two main types of *assets:*

Fixed assets represent the more or less permanent assets of the business. They are not normally for resale. Examples include premises, fixtures and fittings, furniture, equipment and motor vehicles.

Investments of a long-term nature may also be included. The purchase of stocks and shares in other companies or property investment are some examples.

These fixed assets are what is termed *tangible* because they can be seen. Some assets are *intangible* because they cannot be seen. Goodwill is one of the latter and represents the good name or reputation of the business which could be valuable if it is sold.

Current assets represent those types of assets which are used for trading purposes. They constantly change in value, circulating between stock, cash, bank and debtors. They are also referred to as *trading* or *circulating* assets. These assets are more liquid than fixed assets because they can be converted to cash more readily.

There are two main types of *liabilities*:

Long-term liabilities refer to the repayment of debt for more than 12 months, described in the balance sheet as creditors payable after 12 months. They are also known as *deferred* liabilities. Examples include mortgages, and loans and hire-purchase repayments longer than 12 months. Debentures are also long-term.

Current liabilities represent the debts of the business which are repayable within 12 months. Examples include trade creditors, bills oustanding, bank overdrafts, and short-term loans repayable within 12 months.

Types of capital

Capital represents the net worth of the owner and is the difference between assets and liabilities as indicated in the accounting equation. In the balance sheet it is listed under the 'Financed by' section. In a limited company, the capital is represented by its share capital and retained profits (reserves). A sole trader's finance would be represented by his or her capital, profit and any deductions for drawings (personal takings in cash or stock). A partnership would be represented by each of the partner's capital and current accounts (personal accounts).

The balance sheet of Craythorne & Co Ltd illustrates types of assets and liabilities.

Craythorne & Co Ltd –
Balance sheet as at 1 January 1989

	£	£	£
FIXED ASSETS			
Premises	150 000		
Equipment	40 000		
Motor vehicles	10 000		200 000

(Continues)

	£	£	£
CURRENT ASSETS			
Stocks	55 000		
Debtors	30 000		
Bank	10 000		
Cash	5 000	100 000	
less			
CURRENT LIABILITIES			
Trade creditors	40 000		
Short-term loan (12 months)	8 000		
Bills accrued	2 000	50 000	
Net current assets			50 000
Capital employed			250 000
less			
DEFERRED LIABILITIES			
Mortgage on premises			50 000
Net assets			200 000
FINANCED BY			
Shareholders' capital:			
150 000 @ £1 ordinary shares	150 000		
Retained profits	50 000		200 000

NOTES

1 Net current assets

Also referred to as *working capital* and is calculated by deducting current liabilities from current assets:

Net current assets = Current assets − Current liabilities

£50 000 = £100 000 − £50 000

Every organisation needs to have *adequate working capital* for the purpose of being able to meet current debts and to be in a position to trade comfortably. A business does not want to be pressed by its creditors to meet payment on demand. There must be sufficient cash or liquid resources to be converted to cash to satisfy the payment of creditors.

2 The current ratio

Also referred to as the *working capital ratio* and is calculated by dividing current assets by current liabilities.

$$\text{Current ratio} = \frac{\text{Current assets}}{\text{Current liabilities}} = \frac{£100\,000}{£50\,000} = 2:1$$

A current ratio of 2 : 1 is considered adequate for working capital needs. Every £2 of current asset covers £1 of current debt. The minimum ratio should not fall below 1 : 1 otherwise the business is said to be *insolvent* and therefore not in a position to cover its current debts. Creditors pressing for payment could force the business into liquidation (bankruptcy).

3 **Capital employed**
This refers to the employable capital in the business as represented by its fixed assets added to its working capital, that is, its net current assets.

Capital employed	=	Fixed assets + Net current assets
£250 000	=	£200 000 + £50 000

Changes in the balance sheet

The occurrence of financial transactions will change the balance sheet figures. The ledger is used to record transactions although it is possible to see their effect in the balance sheet.

Example (from Craythorne & Co Ltd)

1 Debtors pay off £10 000 from their accounts by cheque.
2 More stock is bought on credit terms from the firm's suppliers (creditors) £5000.
3 The outstanding bills are paid off by cash £2000.

Result:				*Balance* £
1	Debtors	decrease	£30 000 − £10 000	20 000
	Bank	increase	£10 000 + £10 000	20 000
2	Stock	increase	£55 000 + £5 000	60 000
	Creditors	increase	£40 000 + £5 000	45 000
3	Bills	decrease	£2 000 − £2 000	—
	Cash	decrease	£5 000 − £2 000	3 000

As a result of these changes:

	£	£	£
CURRENT ASSETS			
Stock		60 000	
Debtors		20 000	
Bank		20 000	
Cash		3 000	
		103 000	
less			
CURRENT LIABILITIES			
Trade creditors	45 000		
Short-term loan	8 000		
Bills due	—	53 000	
Net current assets			50 000

Irrespective of the number of transactions that occur, the balance sheet should always balance because of the *dual aspect* of each transaction recorded. This is the principle of double-entry recording which is dealt with in Chapter 5.

Example

The following information relates to the accounts of Freddie Smith, a sole trader in the retailing business, as at 31 March 1989.

	£	
Premises	51 000	
Fixtures, fittings	1 000	
Equipment	3 500	
Vehicle	4 500	.... Fixed assets
Stock	3 730	
Debtors	3 490	
Cash	200	.... Current assets
Bank overdraft	1 505	
Creditors	4 500	
Bills due	55	
Loan (short-term)	360	.... Current liabilities
Loan (long-term)	41 000	.... Deferred liabilities
Capital (1/4/88)	18 000	
Year's profit	5 000	
Personal drawings	3 000	.... Financed by

REQUIRED

1 Prepare a balance sheet in both vertical and horizontal formats for Freddie, as on 31 March 1989.

2 Show the accounting equation figures representing the business's resources as financed by its owner and liabilities.

3 Briefly comment on Freddie's ability to pay off his current debts.

1 VERTICAL PRESENTATION

Freddie Smith –
Balance sheet as at 31 March 1989

	£	£	£
FIXED ASSETS			
Premises	51 000		
Fixtures, fittings	1 000		
Equipment	3 500		
Vehicle	4 500		60 000
CURRENT ASSETS			
Stock	3 730		
Debtors	3 490		
Cash	200	7 420	
less			
CURRENT LIABILITIES			
Bank overdraft	1 505		
Creditors	4 500		
Bills due	55		
Loans (short-term)	360	6 420	
Net current assets			1 000
Capital employed			61 000
less			
DEFERRED LIABILITIES			
Loan (long-term)			41 000
			20 000
FINANCED BY			
Capital (1/4/88)	18 000		
+ Profit	5 000	23 000	
− Drawings		(3 000)	20 000

Accounting equation

Capital	=	Assets	−	Liabilities
£20 000	=	£67 420	−	£47 420

The owner's capital (Freddie Smith's) equals the difference between the business's assets and liabilities. In this case £20 000 represents the net worth of the owner which equals £20 000 in net assets.

2 HORIZONTAL PRESENTATION

Freddie Smith –
Balance sheet as at 31 March 1989

FIXED ASSETS	£	£	DEFERRED LIABILITIES	£	£
Premises	51 000		Loan		41 000
Fixtures, fittings	1 000				
Equipment	3 500		CURRENT LIABILITIES		
Vehicle	4 500	60 000	Creditors	4 500	
			Bank overdraft	1 505	
			Bills due	55	
CURRENT ASSETS			Loan (short-term)	360	6 420
Stock	3 730				
Debtors	3 490		CAPITAL (1/4/88)	18 000	
Cash	200	7 420	+ Profit	5 000	
				23 000	
			− Drawings	(3 000)	20 000
		67 420			67 420

Accounting equation

Assets	=	Capital	+	Liabilities
£67 420	=	£20 000	+	£47 420

The business resources of £67 420 are financed by the owner's capital of £20 000 and the liabilities (or external debt) of £47 420.

3 FREDDIE'S WORKING CAPITAL

Working capital	=	Current assets	−	Current liabilities
£1000	=	£7420	−	£6420

Freddie has barely sufficient liquidity to meet his short-term debt. He has a current ratio of 1.16 : 1 which is scarcely above the minimum 1 : 1 and he is therefore in danger of becoming insolvent. The financing of Freddie's business is mainly in the hands of his liabilities which are about 2.4 times greater than his own capital in the business.

The business equation (or profit equation)

It is possible to calculate the business profit for the year from consecutive balance sheets, without giving details of revenue and expenses. Information required for the calculation is:

a) the change in net assets ($A - L$) from one financial period to the next,
b) the personal drawings for the year of the owner, and
c) any further capital invested by the owner within the financial period.

$$P = NA + D - NC$$

where P = Profit; NA = Net asset change; D = Drawings; and NC = New capital.

Example

1 January 1989	$C = A - L$	
	£1000 = £1500 − £500	
31 December 1989	£1750 = £3000 − £1250	
		Drawings for year £2250
	$P = NA + D - NC$	New capital £1000
	£2000 = £750 + £2250 − £1000	

Check:

	£
Capital (1/1/89)	1 000
+ Profit	2 000
	3 000
+ New capital	1 000
	4 000
− Drawings	(2 250)
Capital (31/12/89)	1 750

Summary

1 The balance sheet represents the business's assets, liabilities and capital at any given point in time. It shows the business's financial position in terms of its resources (assets) and financing of the resources (capital and liabilities).

2 The accounting equation may emphasise:

the owner's net worth: $C = A - L$, or

the business's worth: $A = C + L$

3 Assets may be divided into fixed and current. Fixed assets are more permanent and less liquid than current assets. The trading or circulating assets refer to current assets.

4 Liabilities may be divided into current or long-term (deferred). Creditors to be paid within 12 months are current and those debts longer than 12 months are long-term.

5 Net current assets (or working capital) should be adequate for any type of organisation for the purpose of meeting its current debts. It is calculated by deducting current liabilities from current sales. The current ratio should be about 2 : 1 and should not fall below 1 : 1, otherwise the business is said to be insolvent, that is, it is not in a position to be able to pay its current debts.

6 The business equation may be used to calculate the business profit. $P = NA + D - NC$. It should equal the profit calculated if expenses were deducted from revenue, as in the trading and profit and loss account.

QUESTIONS

1 The following information relates to the accounts of Janet Robertson, as on 31 December 1990:

	£
ASSETS:	
Plant and machinery	7 875
Motor van	8 350
Equipment	1 875
Stocks	51 450
Debtors	2 421
Cash	904
LIABILITIES:	
Creditors	20 170
Bank overdraft	14 212
Loan account (five years)	11 460
Hire-purchase finance (five years)	9 293
CAPITAL:	
Capital: J Robertson (1/1/90)	15 000
Net profit for year	4 000
Drawings	1 260

REQUIRED:

a) Prepare the balance sheet of J Robertson as on 31 December 1990, showing working capital. (Working capital = Current assets − Current liabilities.)
b) Note the value of stocks. What could be the significance if the demand for Robertson's goods declined?

2 The following information relates to the financial position of J Jones on 1 January:

	£
Debtors	4 900
Creditors	3 350
Bank overdraft	4 200
Bank loan (ten years)	12 500
Premises	28 000
Equipment and tools	6 500
Motor vehicle	5 200
Stocks	4 950
Cash	500

REQUIRED:

a) Calculate the capital of the owner, J Jones, as on 1 January.
b) Prepare the Balance Sheet of J Jones, as on 1 January.
c) Show the accounting equation from the owner's view, as on 1 January.

3 The financial position of Freddy Smith as on 30 June was as follows:

	£
Premises	60 000
Furniture, fixtures	6 500
Equipment	4 450
Motor van	2 150
Stock	3 800
Debtors	1 225
Creditors	3 540
Bank	1 420
Cash	200
Hire-purchase finance (12 months)	850
Customs & Excise (Vat owing)	355
Mortgage on premises	35 000
Freddy's drawings	5 000
Freddy's profit	10 000
Freddy's capital	35 000

REQUIRED:

a) Prepare the balance sheet of Freddy Smith as on 30 June. Show his working capital as part of the presentation.
b) Calculate his working capital ratio (current assets/liabilities).
c) What proportion of Freddy's total assets are trading assets?

4 The following figures relate to the financial affairs of Mary Jones as on 1 June 1990:

	£
Premises	58 000
Machinery and equipment	15 000
Motor van	5 500
Office furniture	2 500
Stock	5 000
Debtors	2 500
Cash in hand	500
Creditors	3 475
Bank overdraft	3 525
Bills due	1 000
Mortgage	25 000
Bank loan (five years)	10 000
Capital	40 000
Profits	7 000

REQUIRED:

a) Prepare the balance sheet of M Jones as on 1 June 1990.
b) Show the accounting equation emphasising the owner's net worth.
c) Has Jones sufficient funds to meet her current debts?

5 The balance sheet of J Robertson as on 31 December is as follows:

ASSETS	£	CAPITAL	£	£
Plant and machinery	787	J Robertson (1/1)	?	
Motor vans	835	Net loss	385	
Tools and equipment	187	Drawings	291	
Stocks	5 145			
Debtors	242	LIABILITIES		
Cash	90	Loan account (eight years)		1 146
		Hire-purchase finance (three years)		929
		Creditors		2 017
		Bank overdraft		1 421
	7 286			7 286

REQUIRED:

a) Calculate J Robertson's capital on 1 January.

b) Prepare the balance sheet of J Robertson in the vertical method showing the amount of working capital.
c) What kind of trading year do you consider Robertson has had? Make a brief comment.

6 Ann Clarke began her business enterprise on 1 June with a motor vehicle valued at £1500 and a bank account balance of £4000.

During June, her initial business transactions were:
a) Bought equipment for £2575 by cheque.
b) Stock was purchased on credit terms from Robson for £900.
c) Also purchased stock by cheque for £345.
d) Paid Robson on account, £500.
e) Paid for some furniture, by cheque, £250.
f) Purchased further stocks on credit terms from Robson, £230.
g) Final transaction for June was to arrange a bank loan over three years, £2000.

REQUIRED:
a) Prepare a balance sheet for Ann as on 30 June to show the effect of these transactions. Include in your presentation, the working capital. Calculate the working capital ratio.
b) Show the accounting equation as on 30 June from Ann's view.

7 The following information was extracted from the books of R S Williams on 31 December 1990:

	£
Bank overdraft	1 107
Debtors	4 518
Creditors	2 653
Stock	2 659
Capital: R S Williams (1/1/90)	10 000
Drawings	2 250
Premises	7 350
Fixtures and fittings	1 165
Motor van	808
Equipment	2 000
Long-term loan (ten years)	4 000
Net profit for year	2 990

The owner, R S Williams, invested a further £2000 in the business on 31 December 1990, essentially to clear his bank position.

REQUIRED:
a) Prepare the balance sheet of R S Williams, as on 31 December 1990 after his further investment of £2000.
b) Calculate the working capital ratio of the business. Would you consider it reasonable?

(RSA adapted)

8 The information below relates to the summarised balance sheets of R D Andrews:

	Year 1	*Year 2*	*Year 3*
	£	£	£
Stock	800	1 040	2 920
Debtors	740	700	700
Bank/cash	440	300	—
Premises	16 000	16 000	16 000
Other fixed assets	1 300	1 300	1 380
	19 280	19 340	21 000
Capital	18 000	18 220	19 180
Bank overdraft			1 020
Creditors	1 280	1 120	800
	19 280	19 340	21 000

REQUIRED:

a) Calculate the working capital of R D Andrews at the end of each year.
b) Calculate the working capital ratio correct to one decimal place.
c) Which of the three years do you consider R D Andrews is best able to meet his current debts? Explain why.

(RSA)

9 On 1 January 1990, the accounting equation of C Freer was:

$$\text{Capital} = \text{Assets} - \text{Liabilities}$$
$$£10\,000 = £28\,000 - £18\,000$$

On 31 December 1990 it was:

$$£15\,000 = £39\,000 - £24\,000$$

C Freer introduced new capital of £2000 during the year and total drawings for the year to 31 December were £8500.

REQUIRED:

By use of the appropriate business equation, calculate C Freer's profit for the year ended 31 December 1990.

10 Redraft the balance sheet below of Harry Smith as at 30 June in vertical form: it is a poor presentation which needs adjustment.

Capital		£	*Assets*	£
H Smith		12 000	Premises	25 500
Liabilities			Motor vehicles	4 500
Loan from Frank		24 000	Drawings of Harry	1 000
Overdraft		1 505	Office equipment	3 000
Creditors	4 500		Cash	100
- Debtors	3 490	1 010	Stocks	3 780
Gas bill due		55	Fixtures and fittings	1 050
Hire-purchase on vehicles outstanding (6 months)		360		
		38 930		38 930

ALSO REQUIRED:

a) A brief comment regarding the extent of liabilities in relation to Harry's own capital. The loan from Frank is over a period of five years.
b) An opinion as to whether Harry's cash resources are adequate.
c) A comment on Harry's capital tied up in fixed assets relative to capital tied up in his trading assets (current assets).
d) Show the accounting equation illustrating $C = A - L$.

(Institute of Bankers)

CHAPTER

4 The profit and loss account

- *Why is the profit and loss account an important financial statement?*
- *Which groups of accounts are used to prepare it?*
- *What information does the profit and loss account and the balance sheet provide?*

Introduction

This financial statement is prepared for the purpose of calculating the business's profit or loss for the period, whether it is monthly, quarterly, half yearly, yearly or any other time period. Businesses need to prepare financial statements at least once in the financial year, for tax purposes. The profit and loss account is the abbreviated name for the trading and profit and loss account.

In preparing the business's trading and profit and loss account, revenue accounts are matched against expense accounts. If revenue is greater than expenses, a *profit* is made. If expenses are greater than revenue, a *loss* is the result.

To make profits is one of the most fundamental aspects of business life. Success in business is equated with profits but failure is reflected if losses occur.

From the five groups of accounts (assets, liabilities, capital, revenue and expenses), the first three make up the balance sheet leaving revenue and expenses to be matched in the trading and profit and loss account.

The trading account

This section of the statement is used to match sales with the cost of sales for the purpose of calculating the business's *gross profit*.

Gross profit = Sales − Cost of sales

Example

If a motor vehicle cost £5000 and is sold for £8000 the gross profit equals £3000. (Sale price less purchase price.)

The cost of sales, in most most cases, is a combination of stock beginning + purchases − stock end. This will be shown in more detail later in Chapter 16.

The profit and loss account

This part of the statement is used to calculate the *net profit* by deducting all other expenses against the gross profit. Any other income earned by the business (other than sales) is added to profit.

Net profit = Gross profit − Other expenses + Other income

If, when selling the motor vehicle, other expenses include advertising, repairs and a proportion of overhead costs, amounting in total to £1500, and the business earned a further £500 from a commission on other business, then

Net profit	= Gross profit	− Other expenses	+ Other income
£2000	= £3000	− £1500	+ £500

The purpose of the trading and profit and loss account is to list the business's revenue and expense accounts, deducting expenses from revenue to calculate the gross and net profit of the enterprise.

Example

The following information represents the accounts of P Jackson as on 28 February 1989:

	Debit £	*Credit* £
ASSETS		
Premises	12 000	
Fixtures, furniture, fittings	2 000	
Equipment	3 000	
Unsold stock (28/2/89)	805	
Debtors	875	
Bank/cash	2 855	
LIABILITIES		
Mortgage		8 000
Bank loan (two years)		2 000
Creditors		1 435
CAPITAL P Jackson (1/2/89)		10 000
Drawings: P Jackson	100	
REVENUE		
Sales		3 085
Commission received		30

(Continues)

	Debit	Credit
	£	£
EXPENSES		
Wages (part-time)	375	
Light and heat	220	
General expenses	20	
Cost of sales	2 300	
	24 550	24 550

REQUIRED:

1 Prepare P Jackson's trading and profit and loss account for the month ended 28 February 1989.

2 Prepare P Jackson's balance sheet as on the same date. Show net current assets as part of the presentation and calculate his current ratio.

P Jackson –
Trading and profit and loss account
for the month ended 28 February 1989

		£
SALES		3 085
– COST OF SALES		2 300
Gross profit		785
– EXPENSES		
Wages	375	
Light and heat	220	
General expenses	20	615
		170
+ OTHER REVENUE		
Commission received		30
Net profit		200

NOTE

Asset and expense accounts are listed on the left-hand column. This is known as the *debit* side. Liability and capital accounts are listed on the right-hand column and this is known as the *credit* side.

Why is this the case? Debit and credit entries are associated with the ledger and this will be revealed in Chapter 5.

P Jackson –
Balance sheet as at 28 February 1989

	£	£	£
FIXED ASSETS			
Premises	12 000		
Fixtures and fittings	2 000		
Equipment	3 000		17 000
CURRENT ASSETS			
Stock	805		
Debtors	875		
Bank	2 855		
Cash	—	4 535	
less			
CURRENT LIABILITIES			
Creditors		1 435	
Net current assets (working capital)			3 100
			20 100
less			
DEFERRED LIABILITIES (long-term)			
Mortgage	8 000		
Bank loan	2 000		10 000
			10 100
FINANCED BY			
Capital: P Jackson	10 000		
+ Net profit	200		
	10 200		
– Drawings	100		10 100

NOTES

1 The net profit of £200 is transferred from the profit and loss account to the owner's capital account. Profits increase the net worth of the owner.

2 Drawings represent the owner's personal expenses, not associated with the business expenses and are a reduction from capital. If drawings exceed net profit, the net worth of the owner will decrease.

3 It is important to see whether the owner's net worth is increasing or decreasing over the financial periods, particularly in relation to the business's liabilities.

4 The presentation of the financial statements is shown *vertically* and will be the standard format in this text.

Example

The following information continues the exercise of P Jackson. The accounts for the year ended 31 December 1989 were as follows:

	Debit	*Credit*
	£	£
Premises	12 000	
Fixtures, furniture and fittings	2 400	
Equipment	4 800	
Unsold stock (31/12/89)	2 420	
Debtors	1 150	
Creditors		5 010
Bank/cash		2 800
Mortgage on premises		7 150
Bank loan		1 950
Capital (1/1/90): P Jackson		10 000
Drawings: P Jackson	2 330	
Sales		48 850
Cost of sales	32 420	
Wages	8 280	
Motor expenses	3 624	
Light and heat	2 100	
Rates and insurance	3 400	
Advertising	456	
Telephone and stationery	295	
General expenses	485	
Commision received		400
	76 160	76 160

REQUIRED:

1 Prepare the trading and profit and loss account for the year ended 31 December 1989.
2 Calculate the working capital and briefly comment on P Jackson's trading results.

P Jackson –
Trading and profit and loss account
for the year ended 31 December 1989

	£	£
SALES		48 850
LESS COST OF SALES		32 420
Gross profit		16 430

(Continues)

	£	£
LESS EXPENSES		
Wages	8 280	
Motor expenses	3 624	
Light and heat	2 100	
Rates and insurance	3 400	
Advertising	456	
Telephone and stationery	295	
General expenses	485	18 640
		(2 210)
PLUS OTHER REVENUE		
Commission received		400
Net loss for the year		(1 810)

P Jackson –
Balance sheet as on 31 December 1989

	£	£	£
FIXED ASSETS			
Premises	12 000		
Fixtures, furniture and fittings	2 400		
Equipment	4 800		
	19 200		19 200
CURRENT ASSETS			
Stock (31/12/89)	2 420		
Debtors	1 150	3 570	
LESS CURRENT LIABILITIES			
Creditors	5 010		
Bank overdraft	2 800	7 810	
Net current liabilities	(0.46)		(4 240)
			14 960
LESS LONG-TERM LIABILITIES			
Mortgage	7 150		
Bank loan	1 950		9 100
			5 860

(Continues)

	£	£	£
FINANCED BY			
Capital	10 000		
Less net loss	(1 810)	8 190	
Less drawings		2 330	5 860

NOTES

1 The results show that it was not a financially successful year for P Jackson. He suffered a net loss of £1810 and was also insolvent on 31 December. His working capital ratio of 0.46 : 1 indicates that he is poorly placed to meet his short-term financial commitments.

2 P Jackson's equity (his net worth in the business) has fallen from £10 000 capital at the beginning of the year to £5860 at the end, as a result of the net loss and drawings for personal use.

If the business is not turned round in the following financial period, he could well be out of business.

Summary

1 The purpose of this statement is to calculate the business's profit or loss in the accounting period under review.

2 The trading part of the account shows the gross profit while the profit and loss section shows the net profit.

3 Gross profit = Sales − Cost of sales

Net profit = Gross profit − Other expenses + Other income

4 The preparation of the business's trading and profit and loss account and its balance sheet indicates the business's profit or loss and its financial position.

5 Assets and expenses are listed on the left (debit) and capital, liabilities and revenue on the right (credit) when the accounts are prepared. This is covered later in Chapter 5.

QUESTIONS

1

Trial balance –
Jenkins Jeans Co Ltd
31 March 1990

	Dr	*Cr*
	£	£
Premises	65 000	
Equipment and machines	5 000	
Motor vehicle	3 750	
Cost of sales	10 700	
Bank	1 255	
Petty cash	100	
Debtors	4 450	
Creditors		6 525
Mortgage on premises		30 000
Sales		21 650
Stock (31/3/90)	3 455	
Commission earned		1 155
Gross wages	4 765	
Light and heat	150	
Telephone, insurance	225	
Petty cash expenses	300	
General overheads	1 180	
Capital		41 000
	100 330	100 330

REQUIRED:

Prepare the trading and profit and loss account of the company for the month ending 31 March 1990. Prepare a balance sheet as on that date. Show working as part of the presentation.

2 The following is the trial balance of B Forbes as at 31 December 1989. Draw up a set of final accounts for the year ended 31 December 1989.

	Debit	*Credit*
	£	£
Sales		229 200
Cost of sales	143 000	
Wages	28 400	
Rent and rates	5 200	
Post and telephone	2 150	
Insurance	1 850	
Printing and stationery	980	

(Continues)

	Debit	*Credit*
	£	£
Sundry expenses	2 150	
Debtors	11 800	
Creditors		4 200
Fixtures and fittings	8 100	
Motor vans	7 900	
Long-term loan		18 000
Drawings	14 200	
Bank/cash	1 800	
Capital		16 630
Stock (31/12/89)	40 500	
	268 030	268 030

REQUIRED:

a) Prepare a trading and profit and loss account for the year ended 31 December 1989.
b) Prepare a balance sheet as at 31 December 1989.

3 The following trial balance was extracted from the accounts of J Harries on 31 December 1989.

	Debit	*Credit*
	£	£
Sales		200 000
Cost of sales	104 500	
Rent and rates	11 000	
Heat and light	2 150	
Wages	29 850	
Printing and stationery	2 250	
Interest on loan	1 000	
Misc. expenses	650	
Drawings	11 800	
Premises	50 000	
Fixtures and fittings	4 500	
Motor vehicles	6 000	
Debtors	8 400	
Bank	1 200	
Cash	300	
Creditors		5 200
Loan from Smith (more than 12 months)		10 000
Capital		29 900
Stock (31/12/89)	11 500	
	245 100	245 100

REQUIRED:

a) Prepare a trading and profit and loss account for the year ended 31 December 1989.
b) Prepare a balance sheet as at 31 December 1989.

4 R James drew up the following trial balance as at 31 November 1989. You are to draft the trading and profit and loss account for the year to 31 November 1989 and a balance sheet as at that date.

	Debit £	*Credit* £
Capital		20 500
Loan from Robbins (more than 12 months)		16 000
Drawings	12 360	
Cost of sales	73 100	
Motor van	17 100	
Sales		148 000
Debtors and creditors	8 200	6 300
Motor expenses	3 150	
Rent and rates	6 250	
Postage and telephone	1 440	
Wages and salaries	28 340	
Insurance	1 210	
Sundry expenses	990	
Bank/cash	430	
Fixtures and fittings	14 270	
Interest on loan	1 760	
Advertising	9 400	
Stock (30/11/89)	12 800	
	190 800	190 800

5

Trial balance –
Jenkins Jeans Co Ltd
31 March 1990

	Dr £	*Cr* £
Premises	53 150	
Equipment and machines	4 000	
Motor vehicle	4 750	
Cost of sales	4 700	
Bank (overdraft)		8 022
Petty cash	200	
Debtors, creditors	4 050	4 785
Mortgage on premises		32 450
Bank loan (five years)		4 725
Sales		11 850
Bills due		248
Gross wages	5 025	
Light and heat	72	

(Continues)

	Dr	*Cr*
	£	£
Telephone, insurance	105	
Petty cash expenses	148	
General overheads	800	
Directors' fees	500	
Stock (31/3/90)	4 580	
Share capital		20 000
	82 080	82 080

REQUIRED:

a) Prepare the trading and profit and loss account of the company for the month ended 31 March 1990. Prepare a balance sheet as on that date. Show working capital as part of the presentation.
b) Calculate the appropriate accounting ratio to measure working capital.

6 The following information is taken from the accounts of Rachel Lee, a businesswoman buying and selling a range of goods:

Trial balance of R Lee as on 30 June 1990

	£	£
Motor vehicle	8 750	
Premises	36 900	
Stock (30/6/90)	8 605	
Cost of sales	55 725	
Sales		120 344
Rent received		1 782
Rates and insurance	1 395	
Salaries	18 346	
Overheads	14 385	
Creditors		6 755
Debtors	7 400	
Bank		2 045
Cash	400	
Drawings	10 420	
Capital		31 400
	162 326	162 326

REQUIRED:

Prepare Rachel Lee's trading and profit and loss account for the year ended 30 June 1990 and a balance sheet as on that date.

Show net current assets as part of the presentation and calculate the working capital ratio. Has Rachel Lee sufficient working capital to cover her debts?

5 The ledger system

- *What is the underlying principle when recording ledger accounts?*
- *How many different types of ledgers could be used?*
- *What are the two basic methods which could be used to record accounts?*
- *Why is the trial balance a useful device?*

Introduction

The ledger is used to record the financial transactions of a business. These records should be in date order and other than sales, the accounts are normally recorded at cost, that is, the cost price of the goods or services incurred.

The recording process is based on the principle of double entry and is regarded as the book-keeping function of accounting. Every transaction has *two* aspects of equal value to record and both these aspects must be recorded, otherwise incomplete information will occur in the accounts and they will fail to balance.

Many businesses need more than a single ledger to record accounting information. Three distinct ledgers may be in use:

the *sales ledger* records customers' accounts,
the *purchase ledger* records suppliers' accounts,
the *nominal ledger* records miscellaneous accounts such as expenses, revenue, assets and liabilities.

Some businesses may have numerous customers and suppliers and it makes sense to isolate these into their own ledgers. In the examples which follow, only the nominal ledger will be used to record transactions because only a few debtors' and creditors' accounts will be used. Note that the purchase ledger is also known as the *bought ledger* and that the nominal ledger is also known as the *general ledger*.

The dual aspect of recording transactions

Every financial transaction has *two* aspects to be recorded. For example,

Bought a motor van on credit £4500 from Zaroff's Garage . . .

'On credit' refers to payment being delayed until a later time. A record is made in the ledger at the time of the credit and, of course, when payment is made. Which two accounts are affected?

Motor van (asset) £4500 in value.
Zaroff's (liability) £4500 in value.

The principle of double entry relates to the fact that one account will be debited with £4500 and its corresponding account will be credited with the same value.

Rule applied

If an asset is increased, it is a debit entry. If an asset is decreased, it is a credit entry.

The opposite relates to a liability account.
If a liability is increased, it is a credit entry. If a liability is decreased, it is a debit entry.

Nominal ledger

Date	*Details*	*Debit* £	*Credit* £	*Balance* £	
Motor van account					
1/10	Zaroff's	4500		4500 Dr	(Asset +)
Zaroff's account					
1/10	Motor van		4500	4500 Cr	(Liability +)

NOTES

1 Under details, the name of the corresponding account is recorded as a means of cross-reference to each account.

2 A debit or credit simply refers to either an increase or decrease to the account depending on what type of an account it is. Assets and liabilities have already been categorised. What of the other three groups? Expenses are dealt with in the same way as assets. Capital and revenue accounts are dealt with in the same way as liabilities.

The following matrix will help you to decide which account will need to be a debit entry and which corresponding account will require a credit entry.

Recording accounts

Accounting group	**Type of balance* Dr or Cr**		**To increase the account**	**To decrease the account**
Assets	Debit		Debit	Credit
Expenses	Debit		Debit	Credit
Liabilities		Credit	Credit	Debit
Capital		Credit	Credit	Debit
Revenue		Credit	Credit	Debit

NOTE

*'Balance' of an account is the *difference* in value between the debit and credit entries.

Example of transactions in the books of Craythorne & Co Ltd

Craythorne & Co uses the modern *running balance method* of recording its transactions, that is, in the same way as shown on the previous page with debit, credit and balance columns side by side. With this method, the balance of any account is known immediately after the transaction is recorded.

	Transaction	*Action*
1	Sold Freddie Smith, a customer, £5000 goods on credit.	Dr F Smith (asset +) Cr Sales (revenue +)
2	Bought goods from Tom Jones, a supplier, £2500 on credit.	Dr Purchases (expense +) Cr T Jones (liability +)
3	Freddie Smith pays £1500 on account.	Dr Bank (asset +) Cr F Smith (asset −)
4	Craythorne & Co send a cheque to Jones, £500 on account.	Dr T Jones (liability −) Cr Bank (asset −)
5	Cash sales paid into bank £250.	Dr Bank (asset +) Cr Sales (revenue +)

Craythorne's ledger

Date	*Details*	*Debit* £	*Credit* £	*Balance* £
F Smith account				
1/10	Balance			—
5/10	Sales	5 000		5 000 Dr
27/10	Bank		1 500	3 500
T Jones account				
1/10	Balance		*	—
8/10	Purchases		2 500	2 500 Cr
28/10	Bank	500		2 000
Sales account				
1/10	Balance			—
5/10	Smith		5 000	5 000 Cr
9/10	Bank		250	5 250
Purchases account				
1/10	Balance			—
8/10	Jones	2 500		2 500 Dr
Bank account				
1/10	Balance			—
9/10	Sales	250		250 Dr
27/10	Smith	1 500		1 750
28/10	Jones		500	1 250

NOTES

1 For simplicity, each account has commenced with an opening 'nil' balance shown as a dash.
2 *The double-entry aspect of each transaction has been recorded. For example, 8/10 Jones Cr £2500, Purchases Dr £2500.
3 The balance of each account is the *difference* in value between debits and credits.
4 This method of recording transactions is known as the *running balance*. The following pages will illustrate both the traditional and running balance styles of ledger.

The trial balance

The trial balance is an arithmetical check of the double-entry system. Have both aspects of every transaction been recorded accurately? For every debit entry, is there an equal value for its corresponding credit?

The trial balance may be drawn up at any time to check the accuracy of the recording process. The trial balance figures may be recorded in the nominal ledger.

Are the accounts in Craythorne's ledger correct?

Craythorne & Co Ltd –
Trial balance as on 31 October

Account	*Dr* £	*Cr* £
Smith	3 500	
Jones		2 000
Sales		5 250
Purchases	2 500	
Bank	1 250	
	7 250	7 250

The total debits equal the total credits, therefore the accuracy of the double-entry principle has been maintained. The trial balance will fail to balance if both aspects of a transaction are not recorded.

The traditional style of recording ledger accounts

The diagram overleaf represents the traditional style of ledger headings where the page is separated in the middle, giving the ledger its two sides. This format represents a 'T' shape of recording accounts.

Debit entries are recorded on the left-hand side and credit entries on the right-hand side:

Debit			*Credit*		
Date	*Details*	*Amount* £	*Date*	*Details*	*Amount* £

Name of the account

NOTES

1 The traditional 'T' accounts have two sides, the left is for recording all debit entries, the right for recording all credit entries.
2 The name (or title) of each ledger account is best entered in the centre of the page.
3 In the details column, the name of the corresponding account is recorded as a means of cross-reference.

Example: the traditional method of recording

The following information relates to an example exercise concerning another retailer, P Jackson, who commenced business activities on 1 June, by depositing £20 000 into a business bank account. The accounting equation on this date is:

Capital	=	Assets	− Liabilities
£20 000	=	Bank £20 000	− £0

P Jackson – the recording of assets, liabilities and capital in the ledger

Date	*Transactions*		*Debit* £	*Credit* £
June 1	P Jackson commenced business by depositing £20 000 into the business bank account		Bank a/c £20 000	Capital a/c £20 000
5	P Jackson paid the following by cheque:			
	Equipment	£8 000	Equipment a/c £8 000	Bank a/c £8 000
	Premises	£4 000 (Deposit)	Premises a/c £4 000	Bank a/c £4 000
	Fixtures and fittings	£2 000	Fixtures and fittings a/c £2 000	Bank a/c £2 000

(Continues)

Date	*Transactions*	*Debit* £	*Credit* £
5	Obtained a building society mortgage from the Abbey Building Society, £10 000, to pay the balance on the premises	Premises a/c £10 000	Building society a/c £10 000
7	Obtained a bank loan from his bank for £3 000 (at 15% rate) over five years	Bank a/c £3 000	Bank loan a/c £3 000
	Total debits and credits	£47 000	£47 000

The ledger of P Jackson

Debit			*Credit*		
Date	*Details*	*Amount* £	*Date*	*Details*	*Amount* £
		Bank account			
June 1	Capital	20 000	June 5	Equipment	8 000
June 7	Bank loan	3 000	June 5	Premises	4 000
			June 5	Fixtures	2 000
		Capital account			
			June 1	Bank	20 000
		Equipment account			
June 5	Bank	8 000			
		Premises account			
June 5	Bank	4 000			
June 5	Abbey Bld Soc	10 000			
		Abbey Building Society account			
			June 5	Premises	10 000
		Bank loan account			
			June 7		3 000
		Fixtures and fittings account			
June 5	Bank	2 000			

NOTE

With this method of recording, it is necessary to periodically 'balance off' each account in order to find the actual balance. In the above example there is a debit balance of £9000 on the bank account (debits have totalled £23 000, credits have totalled £14 000, a difference of £9000).

Balancing off the accounts in the ledger

The procedure to be adopted is as follows:

1 Enter 'balance c/d' (carried down) on the lesser value of the two sides.

2 This will make both sides equal in total. The totals should appear on the same horizontal line and be double underscored.

3 Once the totals have been entered, the word 'balance b/d' (brought down) is entered under the total, on the opposite side of the account, i.e. this will be the balance at that time.

4 As regards the frequency of balancing off much depends on the volume of transactions. Once per month is the acceptable minimum.

The balancing of P Jackson's bank account and premises account is as follows:

Debit			*Credit*		
		Bank account			
		£			£
June 1	Capital	20 000	June 5	Equipment	8 000
June 7	Bank loan	3 000	June 5	Premises	4 000
			June 5	Fixtures	2 000
			June 8	Balance c/d	9 000
		23 000			23 000
June 9	Balance b/d	9 000			
		Premises account			
June 5	Bank	4 000			
June 5	Abbey Bld Soc	10 000			
		14 000			

NOTE

Where entries appear only on one side of an account as is the case with the premises account these need only be sub-totalled – do not underscore.

Recording the sales and purchases of goods

The value of any unsold stock is regarded as a current asset to the business. At the end of a financial period, there is usually a stock-taking time when the value of any unsold stock is assessed. The value of unsold stock is normally at its cost price and the closing value of stock at the end of one financial period is, in fact, the opening value of stock in the following period.

Any purchases of goods which occur throughout the financial period are recorded in a *purchases account*, (not stock). Any sales of goods which occurs throughout the financial period are recorded in a *sales account*, (not stock). This will be in evidence as the example of P Jackson's accounts continues.

P Jackson – The recording of revenue and expenses in the ledger

Date	*Transactions*	*Debit* £	*Credit* £
June 10	Bought goods (for resale) £2 000, cheque	Purchases a/c £2 000	Bank a/c £2 000
10	Bought goods (for resale) £3 000 on credit from E Gray	Purchases a/c £3 000	E Gray a/c £3 000
12	Sold goods to J Clark, £1 000, on credit	J Clark a/c £1 000	Sales a/c £1 000
13	Cash sales, £1 840 to bank	Bank a/c £1 840	Sales a/c £1 840
14	Paid rent by cheque, £400	Rent a/c £400	Bank a/c £400
15	Paid wages by cheque, £520	Wages a/c £520	Bank a/c £520
18	Paid stationery by cheque, £280	Stationery a/c £280	Bank a/c £280
20	Sold goods by cheque, £1 800	Bank a/c £1 800	Sales a/c £1 800
24	Bought goods £2 600, by cheque	Purchases a/c £2 600	Bank a/c £2 600
27	From J Clark, received cheque £700	Bank a/c £700	J Clark a/c £700
29	Paid by cheque, E Gray, £2 000	E Gray a/c £2 000	Bank a/c £2 000
30	Paid by cheque, wages £540	Wages a/c £540	Bank a/c £540
30	Sold goods to Clark £1 320, on credit	J Clark a/c £1 320	Sales a/c £1 320
	Total debits and credits	£18 000	£18 000

The ledger of P Jackson

Debit			*Credit*		
Date	*Details*	*Amount* £	*Date*	*Details*	*Amount* £
		Bank account			
June 8	Balance b/d	9 000	June 10	Purchases	2 000
13	Sales	1 840	14	Rent	400
20	Sales	1 800	15	Wages	520

(Continues)

Debit			*Credit*		
Date	*Details*	*Amount* £	*Date*	*Details*	*Amount* £
27	J Clark	700	18	Stationery	280
			24	Purchases	2 600
			29	E Gray	2 000
			30	Wages	540
			30	Balance c/d	5 000
		13 340			13 340
July 1	Balance b/d	5 000			
		Capital account			
			June 1	Bank	20 000
		Equipment account			
June 5	Bank	8 000			
		Premises account			
June 5	Bank	4 000			
	Abbey Bld Soc	10 000			
		14 000			
		Abbey Building Society account			
			June 5	Premises	10 000
		Bank loan account			
			June 7	Bank	3 000
		Fixtures and fittings account			
June 5	Bank	2 000			
		Purchases account			
June 10	Bank	2 000			
11	E Gray	3 000			
24	Bank	2 600			
		7 600			
		E Gray account (Creditor)			
June 29	Bank	2 000	June 11	Purchases	3 000
30	Balance c/d	1 000			
		3 000			3 000
			July 1	Balance b/d	1 000

(Continues)

Debit			Credit		
Date	*Details*	*Amount* £	*Date*	*Details*	*Amount* £
		Sales account			
			June 12	J Clark	1 000
			13	Bank	1 840
			20	Bank	1 800
			30	J Clark	1 320
					5 960
		J Clark account			
June 12	Sales	1 000	June 27	Bank	700
30	Sales	1 320	30	Balance c/d	1 620
		2 320			2 320
July 1	Balance b/d	1 620			
		Rent account			
July 14	Bank	400			
		Wages account			
June 15	Bank	520			
30	Bank	540			
		1 060			
		Stationery account			
June 18	Bank	280			

P Jackson – Trial balance as on 30 June

	Debit £	*Credit* £
Bank	5 000	
Capital		20 000
Equipment	8 000	
Premises	14 000	
Abbey Building Society		10 000
Bank loan		3 000
Fixtures and fittings	2 000	
Purchases	7 600	
E Gray (Creditor)		1 000
Sales		5 960

(Continues)

	Debit £	*Credit* £
J Clark (Debtor)	1 620	
Rent	400	
Wages	1 060	
Stationery	280	
	39 960	39 960

The running balance method of recording ledger accounts

Example: the running balance method of recording

Transactions

June	1	M Walker commenced a retail business by depositing £10 000 into a business bank account.
	2	Paid for fixtures and fittings by cheque, £2400.
	2	Bought goods for resale, paying by cheque, £1800.
	2	Bought further goods on credit, £2000, from R Davies.
	3	Paid rent by cheque, £100.
	4	Paid stationery by cheque, £150.
	5	Received £1000 cheque for sale of goods.
	12	Paid rent by cheque, £100.
	14	Bought further goods on credit £1100 from R Davies.
	17	Received £790 for sale of goods.
	18	Paid rent by cheque, £100.
	24	Sold goods on credit to H Smith, £600.
	25	Paid rent by cheque, £100.
	27	Sold goods on credit to H Smith, £500.
	28	Paid salaries, £1000 by cheque.
	29	Paid R Davies, £1400 cheque, on account.
	30	Paid for further fixtures and fittings £410, by cheque.

REQUIRED:

1 Record the above transactions in the ledger of M Walker, using the running balance method of recording.
2 Prepare a trial balance as on 30 June.

NOTE

Check all transactions carefully to ensure that a *double entry* is recorded for each. For example,

June 1	Bank account	Dr	£10 000		
	Capital account			Cr	£10 000
June 2	Fixtures and fittings account	Dr	£2 400		
	Bank account			Cr	£2 400

Ledger – M Walker

Date		*Details*	*Dr* £	*Cr* £	*Balance* £	
Bank account						
June	1	Capital	10 000		10 000	Dr
	2	Fixtures		2 400	7 600	
	2	Purchases		1 800	5 800	
	3	Rent		100	5 700	
	4	Stationery		150	5 550	
	5	Sales	1 000		6 550	
	12	Rent		100	6 450	
	17	Sales	790		7 240	
	18	Rent		100	7 140	
	25	Rent		100	7 040	
	28	Salaries		1 000	6 040	
	29	R Davies		1 400	4 640	
	30	Fixtures		410	4 230	
Capital account						
June	1	Bank		10 000	10 000	Cr
Fixtures and fittings account						
June	1	Bank	2 400		2 400	Dr
	30	Bank	410		2 810	
Purchases account						
June	2	Bank	1 800		1 800	Dr
	2	R Davies	2 000		3 800	
	14	R Davies	1 510		5 310	
R Davies account						
June	2	Purchases		2 000	2 000	Cr
	14	Purchases		1 510	3 510	
	29	Bank	1 400		2 110	
Rent account						
June	3	Bank	100		100	Dr
	12	Bank	100		200	
	18	Bank	100		300	
	25	Bank	100		400	
Stationery account						
June	4	Bank	150		150	Dr

(Continues)

Date	Details	Dr £	Cr £	Balance £
Sales account				
June 5	Bank		1 000	1 000 Cr
17	Bank		790	1 790
24	H Smith		600	2 390
27	H Smith		500	2 890
H Smith account				
June 24	Sales	600		600 Dr
27	Sales	500		1 100
Salaries account				
June 28	Bank	1 000		1 000 Dr

M Walker – trial balance as at 30 June

	Dr £	Cr £
Bank	4 230	
Capital: M Walker		10 000
Fixtures and fittings	2 810	
Purchases	5 310	
R Davies (supplier)		2 110
Rent	400	
Stationery	150	
Sales		2 890
H Smith (customer)	1 100	
Salaries	1 000	
	15 000	15 000

NOTE

The totals agree, so that it is reasonably certain that the double-entry principle of recording has been adhered to and that there are no errors. (It is possible for the trial balance totals to agree, even with errors, as will be seen in Chapter 26.)

The running balance or the traditional style of recording?

The majority of computerised accounting systems produce ledger accounts which are consistent with the running balance method of recording accounts (see Chapter 9). Bank statements are also presented in this format, showing a continuous running balance in the final right-hand column.

Whichever method is adopted to record ledger transactions, makes no difference to the final balance, as long as the double-entry principle is strictly adhered to.

In the traditional style of recording, debits are separated from credits by the centre line of the page. In the teaching of accounting, most institutions tend to adopt this method for the purpose of communicating the double-entry principle. Students should be conversant with either method.

The advantage of the running balance method is that, after each transaction, the balance is calculated giving an immediate update of the account. With the traditional method, you need to go through the process of balancing off each account at frequent intervals, to find the balance as it currently stands.

NOTES

1 In the illustrated examples only a single ledger was used. In P Jackson's ledger, his nominal ledger, he had only a single debtor and a single creditor.

The main purpose of dividing the ledger is that it will be easier to cope with greater volumes of transactions, particularly if there is a sizeable number of debtors and creditors, in which case separate ledgers will be required for debtors (the sales ledger) and for creditors (the bought or purchases ledger).

2 **Personal accounts** – the accounts of debtors and creditors, that is, the individual accounts of customers and suppliers, for sales and purchases on credit, are the personal accounts of the business.

3 **Nominal accounts** – these represent impersonal accounts of the business, that is, the revenue and expense accounts such as rent, wages, salaries, sales and purchases.

4 **Real accounts** – these refer to the tangible assets of the business, the resources such as premises, equipment, fixtures, fittings, stock, bank and cash.

Nominal and real accounts are recorded in the nominal ledger.

Summary

1 The ledger is used to record the everyday financial transactions of a business. These transactions are processed into accounts.

2 Each transaction has a dual aspect based on the principle of double-entry recording, that is, for every debit entry there is a corresponding credit.

3 A debit or credit simply relates to either an increase or decrease in an account depending in which group the account lies. A *balance* in an account is the difference in value between the debit and credit entries.

4 Recording the accounts may be in either the running balance method or traditional method of entry. The former is considered the modern or more versatile and is in a format which looks like a bank statement, the balance being struck after each transaction. The latter more traditional style, has debits on the left-hand side and credits on the right. It has the disadvantage that the immediate balance is not apparent.

5 The three distinct types of ledger refer to the sales ledger (debtors), the bought ledger (creditors) and the nominal ledger (all other accounts).

6 The nominal ledger records the nominal (revenue and expense) accounts of the business and also the real accounts (the tangible assets). The sales and bought ledgers record the individual personal accounts of the business.

QUESTIONS

1 Which of the following accounts have debit balances? Which of them have credit balances? Tick which you think is the appropriate column for each account.

Account	*Debit*	*Credit*
Premises		
Fixtures and fittings		
Creditors		
Debtors		
Bank overdraft		
Sales		
Cash		
Capital		
Bank loans		
Wages		
Purchases		
Mortgage		

2 Balance the following accounts at the end of the month and bring down the balances where you think it is appropriate.

Jack Jones account

		£			£
1/1	Bank	500	1/1	Balance b/d	1 200
31	Bank	1 850	20	Purchases	1 000
			28	Purchases	500

Bank account

1/1	Balance b/d	500	1/1	J Jones	500
7	Sales	750	5	Rent	250
14	Sales	540	7	General expenses	345
21	Sales	650	15	R Green	1 200
28	Sales	535	20	Light and heat	340
			27	J Jones	1 850

(Continues)

	£			£
	Sales account			
		1/1	Balance b/d	2 300
		7	Sales	750
		14	Sales	540
		21	Sales	650
		28	Sales	535

3 The ledger account balances on 30 June of Hannah Smith were:

	£
Stock	1 500
Bank (Dr)	6 610
Plant and equipment	8 000
Motor vehicle	3 500
Sales	4 190
Purchases	1 760
Wages	2 230
Rent	1 130
General expenses	960
Debtors	1 910
Creditors	2 500
Bank loan	3 120
Interest due on loan	110
Capital account: Hannah Smith	17 680

REQUIRED:

Prepare the trial balance of H Smith as on 30 June.

4 The following information relates to the books of David Novel:

July	1	Commenced business with a capital of £2000 represented in his bank account.
	2	Bought goods on credit from Tom Smith, £2500.
	14	Cash sales into bank, £750.
	15	Paid purchases by cheque, £500.
	17	Paid rent by cheque, £125.
	18	Paid gas, electricity by cheque, £80 (light and heat account).
	21	Cash sales into bank, £600.
	25	Sold goods to R Baker on credit, £200.
	26	Paid cheque to Tom Smith on account, £500.
	27	Bought further goods from Tom Smith on credit, £1000.
	28	Cash sales into bank, £625.
	30	R Baker paid £100 on account, by cheque.
	30	Paid for general expenses, £80 cheque.
	30	Paid for advertising, £35 cheque.
	30	Bought a second-hand motor van, £500 by cheque.

REQUIRED:

Enter the above transactions in the ledger of David Novel for the month of July and extract a trial balance as on 31 July.
In all ledger exercises, choose either the traditional or running balance method of recording.

5 Complete the columns to show the effect of the transactions of Roberta David. The first is done for you.

a) Commenced business with a motor vehicle (£600) and a bank account of £1500.
b) Bought a new motor van on credit, XYZ £1800.
c) Bought office furniture, paying by cheque £300.
d) Paid £500 to XYZ account.
e) Took out a loan from Barclays, £2500.
f) Bought equipment for cash, £1500.
g) Won £500 on the races and put it into the business!
h) Sold the motor vehicle for £600 to J Briggs on credit.

	Capital		*Assets*		*Liabilities*	
	Dr (£)	*Cr (£)*	*Dr (£)*	*Cr (£)*	*Dr (£)*	*Cr (£)*
a)		2100	600 1500			

REQUIRED:

After completing the above entries, show the accounting equation, giving the value of capital, assets and liabilities.

6 Complete the columns to show the effect of the transactions of Sam Jackson. Again, the first is done for you.

a) Bought goods on credit from Tom Dooley, £400.
b) Cash sales, £750.
c) Cash purchases, £650.
d) Paid salaries, £120 by cheque.
e) Paid gas and electricity, £35 cheque.
f) Sold goods to R Baker on credit £85.
g) Received £60 commission on a sale.
h) Paid £150 to Tom Dooley.
i) Bought more goods from Tom, £360.
j) Cash sales, £670.
k) R Baker paid £50 on account.
l) Paid the Echo £15 for advertising.

	Assets		*Liabilities*		*Revenue*		*Expenses*	
	Dr (£)	*Cr (£)*	*Dr (£)*	*Cr (£)*	*Dr (£)*	*Cr (£)*	*Dr (£)*	*Cr (£)*
a)				400			400	

REQUIRED:

Which of the above entries would *not* go in the profit and loss account?

7 The following information refers to the accounts of Ann Rogers, a retailer on the high street:

Balances on 1 May:

		£
Debtors:	R David (Dr)	500
	L Jones (Dr)	230
Creditors:	J Robert (Cr)	150
	G Andrew (Cr)	200
Bank account (Dr)		270
Capital account (Cr)		650

Transactions occurring during the month of May

May 3	Sold goods to R David £300 on credit.
3	Sold goods to L Jones £250 on credit.
3	Bought goods on credit from J Robert, £600.
5	Bought goods on credit from G Andrew, £850.
10	R David settled his account balance as on 1 May, sending a cheque £500.
12	Sent a cheque £150 to J Robert and £200 to G Andrew.
15	Paid for shop rent, £300 cheque.
17	Paid assistant's wages, £125 cheque.
20	L Jones sent a cheque £200 on account.
25	Sold goods to L Jones on credit, £180.
27	General overheads paid by cheque, £70.
28	Bought goods on credit from J Robert, £50.
30	Sold goods to R David, £280 on credit.
31	Bought some shop equipment on credit from Joe Brown, £750.

REQUIRED:

a) Enter all the above information in the ledger of Ann Rogers for the month of May.
b) Extract a trial balance as on 31 May.

8 The trial balance of Ken Stevens on 30 April 1984 was as follows:

Ken Stevens –
Trial balance as at 30 April 1984

	Dr £	*Cr* £
Sales		20 750
Purchases	13 170	
General expenses	4 972	
Fixtures	2 500	
K Gibson	1 130	
T Lowe		700

(Continues)

	Dr £	*Cr* £
Bank	1 720	
Drawings	2 800	
Capital		7 228
Stock	2 386	
	28 678	28 678

During the month of May the following transactions took place:

1 May	Bought goods on credit from T Lowe, £85.
2 May	Sold goods on credit to K Gibson, £105.
18 May	Banked cash sales £400.
20 May	K Gibson paid £680 by cheque in part settlement of his account.
26 May	Paid general expenses by cheque, £97. Sent a cheque value £300 to T Lowe in part settlement of his account.
28 May	Paid general expenses by cheque, £275.
30 May	Withdrew £300 from the bank for his own use.

REQUIRED:

a) Open the accounts at 1 May 1984.
b) Record the transactions directly in the accounts by means of double entries. Do *not* use subsidiary books.
c) Extract a trial balance at 31 May 1984.

(RSA)

9 The following are the balances in the ledger of J Stamp, a sole proprietor, as at 31 July 1986.

	Dr £	*Cr* £
L Brain (Debtor)	200	
S Round (Debtor)	400	
A Wells (Creditor)		500
Heating and lighting	600	
Printing and stationery	500	
Rent and rates	900	
Wages	5 400	
Vehicle	1 500	
Equipment	600	
Discount allowed and received	300	200
Purchases	8 400	
Sales		13 000
Bank	500	
Capital		5 600
	19 300	19 300

During August the following transactions took place:

i) Cash sales for the month amounted to £3100.
ii) Cash purchases for the month amounted to £1600.
iii) Credit sales were:
  9/8/86 £300 to L Brain and £200 to S Round
  26/8/86 £150 to L Brain and £250 to S Round
iv) Credit purchases from A Wells were:
  10/8/86 £400
  21/8/86 £600
v) Other payments by cheque were:
  7/8/86 £50 Rent
  9/8/86 £90 Stationery
  15/8/86 £70 Electricity
  31/8/86 £700 Wages
vi) On 2/8/86 L Brain settled his outstanding balance.
vii) On 19/8/86 S Round paid £350 on account.
viii) On 2/8/86 J Stamp paid A Wells the outstanding balance.

TASKS

a) Open up the ledger accounts as at 31 July 1986.
b) Enter up all the August transactions, using the running balance method of recording.
c) List the balances in the form of a trial balance.

NOTE:

All cash received is paid into the bank and all payments have been made by cheque.
(Institute of Commercial Management)

10 Tick which ledger you think the following accounts ought to be recorded:

Account	**Nominal ledger**	**Sales ledger**	**Bought ledger**
Jackson's (supplier)			
Sales			
Purchases			
Rent			
T Smith (customer)			
Bank			
Capital			
Cash			
Mark's (supplier)			
Wages (R Jones)			
Premises			
Motor van			

Make a list of the above accounts into three categories:

Nominal accounts Real accounts Personal accounts.

CHAPTER

6 The sales journal

- *What are the journals used for?*
- *How many different types are there?*
- *What is the function of the sales journal?*
- *From what sources of information can the sales journal be prepared?*

Introduction

The major function of journals is to record credit transactions relating to sales, purchases, sales returns (returns inward) and purchases returns (returns outward). The same type of transactions of a daily and routine nature can be recorded together. For example, a batch of sales invoices can be listed by their invoice number and in date order and key information such as customers' names, account numbers, sales values, Vat and total sums due, are extracted. Daily, weekly or even monthly figures (depending on the number) can then be totalled and details posted to the appropriate ledgers.

It may appear that in modern systems of accounting, particularly where computers are used, that the journal's function has become obsolete. This is not really the case. Someone needs to classify a batch of invoices in some sort of order. The invoices must be checked for accuracy and a total of the day's or week's figures should be calculated as a check *prior* to posting to the ledgers. These figures could be entered on a control sheet that goes with the batch of invoices. This is a function called *journalising*, that is, preparing information from business documents before ledger posting.

There are five major journals:

1 *Sales journal:* records all sales on credit to customers. Figures are extracted from the invoices sent to customers.
Posting to the sales ledger and nominal ledger.
2 *Purchases journal:* records all purchases on credit from suppliers. Figures are extracted from the invoices received from suppliers.
Posting to the purchases ledger and nominal ledger.
3 *Returns inward journal:* records all returns or allowances relating to customers. Figures are extracted from the credit notes sent to customers.
Posting to the sales ledger and nominal ledger.

4 *Returns outward journal:* records all returns or allowances relating to suppliers. Figures are extracted from the credit notes received from suppliers.
Posting to the purchases ledger and nominal ledger.
5 *The journal:* used for those type of transactions which occur outside the scope of the above journals. For example, correcting errors (refer to Chapter 27).

The accounting system

The recording of financial transactions is the basis of preparing accounts. Financial transactions basically fall into one of two categories: either by cash or on credit terms. The journals may be used to organise the credit transactions and a cash book system used for cash or bank transactions. Information from these 'prime entries' can then be posted to the ledgers.

The trial balance is used as a checking device to ensure that the principle of double entry is recorded for every transaction. Finally, from these records, accounting statements are prepared to show the business's profit or loss and financial position.

Recording of financial transactions.

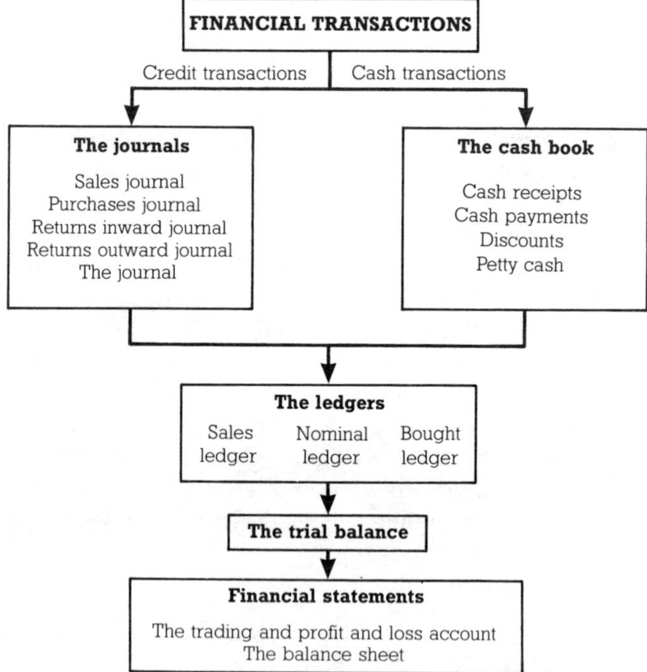

Value Added Tax (Vat)

Vat is a charge on goods and services in the UK and represents an indirect source of taxation to the Government. Business people who are Vat registered, that is, they have received a certificate of registration from the Customs & Excise Department, are given their registration number and tax periods. They are obliged to pay output tax (Vat collected on sales) and have the right to deduct input tax (Vat paid on purchases, fixed assets or expenses).

The Vat account is normally settled on a quarterly basis. For example, if a business collected £400 Vat (outputs) in a quarterly period and paid £350 Vat (inputs) on purchases and expenses, the balance owed to Customs & Excise would be £50 for that tax period.

The current standard rate of tax charged on goods and services is 15 per cent. However, traders who have a relatively low turnover (sales) per year, need not be registered as a taxable person. The actual turnover figure can fluctuate each year as decided by the Chancellor in his spring budget. At the outset of the 1990s this was £25 400 per annum. Any business having a turnover less than this need not keep Vat records and is, therefore, exempt.

Businesses exempt

Firms which are exempt from tax do not keep records for Vat purposes. They do have to pay Vat for purchases (inputs) but cannot charge Vat to their customers (outputs). They are disadvantaged because they cannot reclaim Vat inputs from Customs & Excise. Besides businesses with a small turnover, insurance companies, banks and postal services are also exempt. Some small businesses can register for Vat purposes if they wish, but then they would have to do all the Vat paperwork which is involved, in the same way as for any business which is Vat registered.

Businesses zero-rated

Firms which are Vat zero-rated are registered traders with Customs & Excise and have the advantage of being able to reclaim input tax on their purchases, but do not charge Vat on their sales. Food (but not catering), publishing, building construction and medicines are some of the businesses in this category. A Vat account is recorded and claims are made to Customs & Excise on the Vat these businesses have been charged.

A *debit* balance in the Vat account means that more inputs of tax have been paid than outputs. Customs & Excise owe the outstanding balance to the business and therefore in the balance sheet it would be shown as a current asset. A *credit* balance in the Vat account means the reverse. A sum is owed to Customs & Excise and will be shown as a current liability in the balance sheet.

The simplified sales journal (without Vat)

The details for the sales journal will be taken directly from the invoice. The double entry is:

Debit the debtor's account; *Credit* the sales account.

Example

Enter the following customers into a sales journal for the month of June and then post to the ledger. Assume a 'nil' balance in the customer's account at the beginning of the month.

Date	*Customer's name*	*Invoice no.*	*Amount* £	
1/6	C Taylor	2801	800	Dr customer's a/c
4/6	M Johnson	2802	200	Dr customer's a/c
19/6	M Johnson	2803	300	Dr customer's a/c
23/6	C Taylor	2804	120	Dr customer's a/c
		Cr Sales a/c:	1 420	

POSTING TO LEDGER

		Debit £	*Credit* £	*Balance* £	
C Taylor account					
1/6	Sales	800		800	Dr
23/6	Sales	120		920	
M Johnson account					
4/6	Sales	200		200	Dr
19/6	Sales	300		500	
Sales account					
30/6	Debtors		1 420	1 420	Cr

The sales invoice

Below is an invoice sent from R Pearce to one of his customers, C Taylor.

INVOICE
R Pearce Sports Proprietor

To: C Taylor
24 Boscombe Dve
Bournemouth

VAT Reg: 76 48424 23
Invoice No: INV/2802

Date: 4th June 1989
Your Order Ref: 30 May
Dispatch Date: 4 June 89
Terms: 10% Trade
Carriage Paid

Code number	*Qty*	*Description*	*Unit price £*	*Total price £*	*Less trade* £*	*Net value £*
C25	20	Slazenger cricket bats	10	200	20	180
C31	4	Cricket balls	5	20	—	20
X42	2	Professional goal and nets	330	660	66	594
		Extras				6

E&OE

TOTAL NET: £800
VAT @ 15%: £120

Delivery Address: as above
Payment within 28 days of invoice date

TOTAL VALUE: £920

NOTES

*Trade discount refers to a deduction to the customer allowing him to buy the goods at a reduced price. It is normally given to people who are traders. A cash discount is offered to customers to encourage them to pay their accounts promptly.

Sales procedure

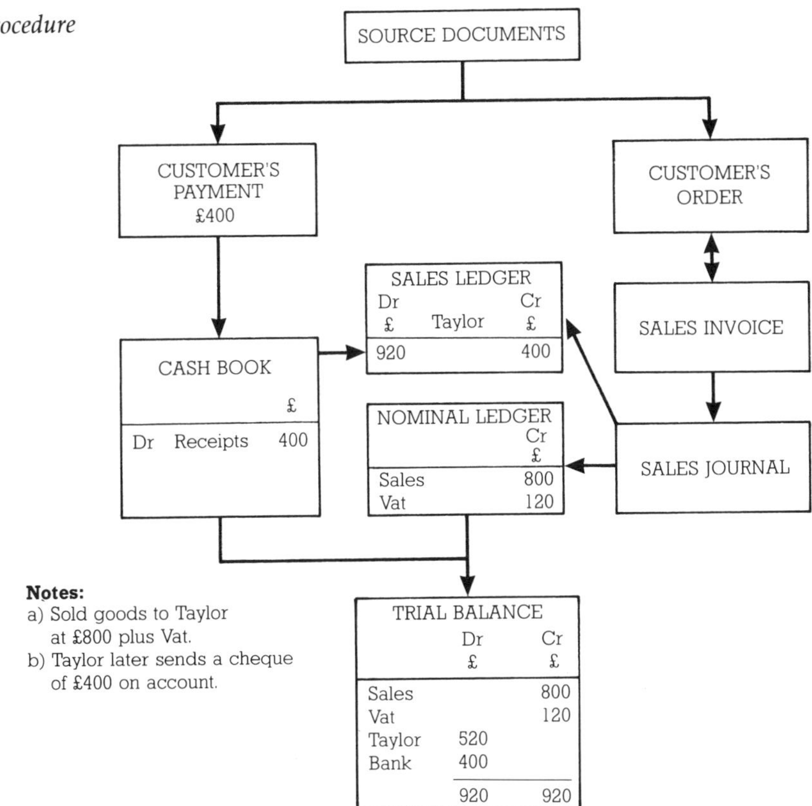

Notes:
a) Sold goods to Taylor at £800 plus Vat.
b) Taylor later sends a cheque of £400 on account.

NOTE

Vat refers to value added tax. This is an indirect source of taxation charged by the Government on many of our goods and services. The current rate is 15 per cent. If Vat is added to sales, it is referred to as 'output' tax and when added to purchases, it is 'input' tax. Vat is usually paid to the Customs & Excise Department each quarter and the sum paid by a business is the difference between the sum collected on sales and the sum paid for on purchases.

The sales journal (with Vat)

Details for entry to the sales journal will be extracted from the sales invoice sent to customers. A control sheet, showing the key figures of the invoices sent, may in itself, be a form of journal. Generally, the details extracted from the invoice are:

Date of sale
Invoice number
Customer's name
Customer's account number
The net sales values
Vat (if charged)
The total value of the invoice.

This information could be directly fed into a computer system. Chapter 9 will demonstrate the procedure where a computer program is used for the input of invoice data. An example of an invoice is on page 62 and figures have been extracted for the entry to the sales journal below.

The sales journal of R Pearce

Date	*Customer's name and account no.*		*Invoice no.*	*Net sales account* £	*Vat account* £	*Total value* £
1/6	C Taylor	S12	2801	800	120	920 Dr
4/6	M Johnson	S08	2802	200	30	230 Dr
19/6	M Johnson	S08	2803	300	45	345 Dr
23/6	C Taylor	S12	2804	120	18	138 Dr
				1 420	213	1 633
				Cr Sales	Cr Vat	

Posting to ledgers

Sales ledger

		Debit £	*Credit* £	*Balance* £
C Taylor account S12				
1/6	Sales	800		800 Dr
1/6	Vat	120		920
23/6	Sales	120		1 040
23/6	Vat	18		1 058
M Johnson account S08				
4/6	Sales	200		200 Dr
4/6	Vat	30		230
19/6	Sales	300		530
19/6	Vat	45		575

Nominal ledger

		Debit £	*Credit* £	*Balance* £
Sales account N25				
30/6	Debtors		1 420	1 420 Cr
Vat account N30				
30/6	Debtors		213	213 Cr

NOTE

The double entry:

1 *Debit* each debtor's account (in the sales ledger) with sales + Vat.

2 *Credit* the total value of sales (in the nominal ledger) to sales account; the total value of Vat (in the nominal ledger) to Vat account.

Sales, Vat and the use of the sales ledger control account

On 1 July, the balances in the books of R Pearce were:

Sales ledger:	£		*Nominal ledger:*	£
Lewis	100 Dr		Sales account	1 420 Cr
Smith	250 Dr		Vat account	213 Cr
Kings	150 Dr		Sales ledger control	2 133 Dr
Taylor	1 058 Dr			
Johnson	575 Dr			
	2 133			

During the month of July, sales invoices were sent to the following customers:

	Invoice no.	*Date*	*Net sales*	+ *Vat (15%)*
			£	£
Lewis	2805	4/7	200	
Smith	2806	8/7	300	
Lewis	2807	12/7	120	
Kings	2808	15/7	340	
Smith	2809	21/7	100	
			1 060	

Cheques were received from customers at the end of the month for the following:

	£	£
Lewis	400	
Smith	500	
Kings	100	
Taylor	500	
Johnson	—	1 500

THE SALES LEDGER CONTROL ACCOUNT

This represents a total account of all debtors listed in the sales ledger (£2133). It may be used as a cross-checking device and as a measure of control, that is, a check can be made to ensure that the individual balances totalled in the sales ledger equal the sales ledger control account balance.

The sales journal of R Pearce for July SJ6

Date	*Customer's name and account no.*		*Invoice no.*	*Net sales account* £	*Vat account* £	*Total value* £	
4/7	Lewis	S10	2805	200	30	230	Dr
8/7	Smith	S11	2806	300	45	345	Dr
12/7	Lewis	S10	2807	120	18	138	Dr
15/7	Kings	S09	2808	340	51	391	Dr
21/7	Smith	S11	2809	100	15	115	Dr
				1 060	159	1 219	
				Cr Sales	Cr Vat	Dr Sales control	

Sales ledger

		*Folio**	*Debit* £	*Credit* £	*Balance* £
D Lewis account S10					
1/7	Balance				100 Dr
4/7	Sales	SJ6	200		
	Vat		30		330
12/7	Sales	SJ6	120		
	Vat		18		468
30/7	Bank	C8		400	68
D Smith account S11					
1/7	Balance				250 Dr
8/7	Sales	SJ6	300		
	Vat		45		595
21/7	Sales	SJ6	100		
	Vat		15		710
30/7	Bank	C8		500	210
B Kings account S09					
1/7	Balance				150 Dr
15/7	Sales	SJ6	340		
	Vat		51		541
30/7	Bank	C8		100	441
C Taylor account S12					
1/7	Balance				1 058 Dr
30/7	Bank	C8		500	558
M Johnson account S08					
1/7	Balance				575 Dr

*Folio Cross-refer to the journal or cash book page number.

THE SCHEDULE OF DEBTORS FOR JULY

	£	£
Lewis	68	
Smith	210	
Kings	441	
Taylor	558	
Johnson	575	1 852*

*The total value of debtors, £1852, must cross-check with the sales ledger control account in the nominal ledger. If the figures do not match, an error has been made either in the sales ledger or the control account. The error must be located and corrected.

Nominal ledger

		Folio	Debit £	Credit £	Balance £
Sales account N42					
1/7	Balance				1 420 Cr
30/7	Debtors	SJ6		1 060	2 480
Vat account N50					
1/7	Balance				213 Cr
30/7	Debtors	SJ6		159	372
Sales ledger control account N40					
1/7	Balance				2 133 Dr
30/7	Sales and Vat	SJ6	1 219		3 352
	Bank	C8		1 500	1 852*
Bank account (extract from cash book)					
30/7	Debtors		1 500		1 500 Dr

Summary

1 The journals are subsidiary books or books of first entry. They are used to record credit transactions taken from source documents like the invoice or credit note.

2 Journals facilitate the double-entry system by summarising and classifying the routine credit transactions relating to sales, purchases and returns.

3 The five major journals are: sales, purchases, returns in, returns out and the journal. The journal is dealt with in Chapter 27.

4 The sales journal lists all invoices to customers and facilitates posting to the sales and nominal ledgers. The sales control account can be used as a cross-checking device between the schedule of debtors and the control account.

QUESTIONS

1 The following represents the sales invoices of R Jones for the month of June 1990:

	Customer's account	*Invoice no.*	*Value £*
2/6	Gibbs, P	4535	360
5/6	Walton, G	4536	400
9/6	Doe, M	4537	700
15/6	Slater, G	4538	420
20/6	Gibbs, P	4539	280
25/6	Doe, M	4540	100

No Vat is charged, the items being wholesale vegetables.

REQUIRED:

a) Prepare the sales journal for the month of June.
b) To which ledger are the above accounts posted? On which side of the customer's account do they appear?
c) Where is the total value for the month posted? On which side of the account does it appear? Why?

2 On 1 July, the sales ledger balances of G Grant were:

	£	
Goldney, P	220	Dr
Woods, B	150	Dr
Capel, J	400	Dr
Carlton, R	300	Dr
	1 070	

In the nominal ledger, the sales ledger control account on the same date verified the debtor's schedule of £1070 Dr.

Sales invoices sent to customers for July were:

	Customer's account	*Invoice no.*	*Value £*	*+ Vat (15%) £*
5/7	Goldney	4005	360	+15%
9/7	Capel	4006	160	+15%
14/7	Carlton	4007	100	+15%
18/7	Capel	4008	180	+15%
17/7	Woods	4009	240	+15%
25/7	Carlton	4010	200	+15%

On 30 July, Goldney, Capel and Carlton settled their account balances as on 1 July, by cheque.

REQUIRED:

a) The sales journal for the month of July.
b) The preparation of the sales and nominal ledger accounts (including control).

3 Invoice 4242 from R Pearce to I Creese is shown below. Answer the questions below from the view of R Pearce, the Sports Ltd proprietor.

<table>
<tr><td colspan="5">Vat reg.</td><td colspan="3">R Pearce
Sports Ltd

Telephone 69455</td><td colspan="2">Invoice
No. 4242</td></tr>
<tr><td>Area
16</td><td colspan="3">Customer order details
0/15672 2.MAY.88</td><td colspan="2">Fwd</td><td>Date
25.5.88</td><td>Account no.
H1452</td><td>Invoice no.
184285</td><td>Page
no.</td></tr>
<tr><td colspan="4">Invoice address
I Creese
Loxley Dve
Broadstone</td><td colspan="6">Consignee</td></tr>
<tr><td>Code
451</td><td>Qty
10</td><td colspan="3">Description
Tennis sets</td><td colspan="2">Price
£8.20</td><td>Goods value</td><td>Vat rate %
15.00</td><td>Vat</td></tr>
<tr><td colspan="7">Total goods</td><td></td><td></td><td></td></tr>
<tr><td colspan="7">Total Vat</td><td></td><td>←</td><td></td></tr>
<tr><td colspan="7">Invoice total</td><td></td><td></td><td></td></tr>
<tr><td colspan="10">Terms: 20% trade discount</td></tr>
</table>

REQUIRED:

a) Calculate the value of the invoice. The unit price of one tennis set is £8.20 excluding the 20 per cent trade discount.
b) In which journal would the figures from the above invoice be entered? How are the figures posted to the ledgers?
c) R Pearce uses control accounts. For what purpose are they used?

4 The following information represents the sales journal of J Durham for May 1990:

Customer account	*Invoice*	*Product 'A'*	*Product 'B'*	*Vat (15%)*
		£	£	£
R Jones	3651	60	20	
S Smith	3652	280	40	
T Brown	3653	400	100	
R Jones	3654	100	60	

REQUIRED:

a) Complete the sales journal for May, calculating the appropriate sum for Vat.

b) The opening balances in J Durham's sales ledger were:

		£
1/5	Jones	250
1/5	Smith	345
1/5	Brown	675

Enter these in the sales ledger and then post the above journal entries. Make up your own dates.

c) Post the information above to the appropriate ledgers and use the control account. Prepare separate sales accounts for each product.

d) Prepare a schedule of debtors and ensure the total matches the sales ledger control account.

5 The following information relates to the accounts of Jenkins Jeans Ltd as on 1 January 1990:

CURRENT ASSETS		
Stock		1 000
Debtors:		
Davies	800	
Smith	450	1 250
Bank		750
		3 000
CURRENT LIABILITIES		
Creditors:		
Harries	1 250	
Brown	250	1 500

REQUIRED:

Enter the above accounts in the books of Jenkins Jeans Ltd using sales and purchases ledgers for personal accounts and the nominal ledger for all other accounts, as on 1 January 1990.

During the month of January, the following invoices were sent to customers:

	Name	*Invoice*	*Amount* £	*Sales*	*Code*
5/1	Davies	2334	200 +15%	S161	(clothing)
12/1	Smith	2335	80 +15%	S162	(equipment)
17/1	Davies	2336	120 +15%	S162	(equipment)
21/1	Forbes (new)	2337	400 +15%	S163	(misc)
28/1	Smith	2338	300 +15%	S161	(clothing)
30/1	Forbes	2339	160 +15%	S163	(misc)

REQUIRED:

a) The sales journal for January. Use separate columns to analyse the sales type.
b) Post the individual sales totals to the nominal ledger.
c) Prepare the sales ledger accounts for each customer.

CHAPTER

7 The purchases journal

- *What is the function of the purchases journal?*
- *How does cash discount affect the calculation of Vat?*

Introduction

When invoices are received from suppliers following the purchase of goods, the purchasing department needs to check the details against the original purchase requisition to ensure that the terms, conditions and price are as agreed.

The goods received in stores also need to be checked to ensure that all aspects are in order in terms of quantity, type and condition of goods. When these details are verified, the invoices received may then be sent to the accounts department for recording in the appropriate ledgers.

Credit notes are used when returns or allowances are made against invoices and have the effect of reducing the balance of a supplier's account. Credit notes from suppliers represent returns outward and details need to be checked against the original invoice to verify value, trade and cash discounts, and Vat. When these are verified, the note is passed to accounts for ledger recording.

Monthly statements from suppliers of goods or services, summarise the transactions between the buyers and sellers. Statements received from suppliers (creditors) must be checked against the details of the supplier's account in the bought ledger, before any payment is made.

A supplier's invoice

Below is an invoice from a supplier of R Pearce (sports shop proprietor). The essential details taken from the invoice for the purpose of entry to the purchases journal include:

Date	12 July
Supplier	Slazenger Sports
Account no.	S65
Invoice no.	334597
Net purchase	£240.00
Vat	£34.20
Total creditor's account	£274.20

Slazenger Sports

Denby, Wakefield,
West Yorks

Vat Reg. 144 9842 84
Telephone 0204 664555
Telex 669944 88

R Pearce
77 Penhill Rd
Penhill
Poole

Account no. S65

Your order no.	Dispatch	Consignment: carriage paid	Invoice 334597	Invoice date 12 July 1990

Quantity	*Code no.*	*Details*	*Price*	*Goods value*	*Trade (20%)*	*Net value*
			£	£	£	£
20	Z238	Tennis rackets (Snr)	15	300	60	240

Total goods (net)	240.00
Vat*	34.20
	274.20

Terms: Cash discount 5% within 30 days

NOTE

*Vat: If cash discount is offered to buyers (for prompt payment) the discount (£12) is deducted from the net value of goods for the purpose of Vat calculation:

Total goods (net)	£240	
Less cash discount	12	£228.00
Vat charge 15%		34.20

Only if the invoice is paid within the time specified can the customer deduct the £12 discount offered.

Purchases procedure

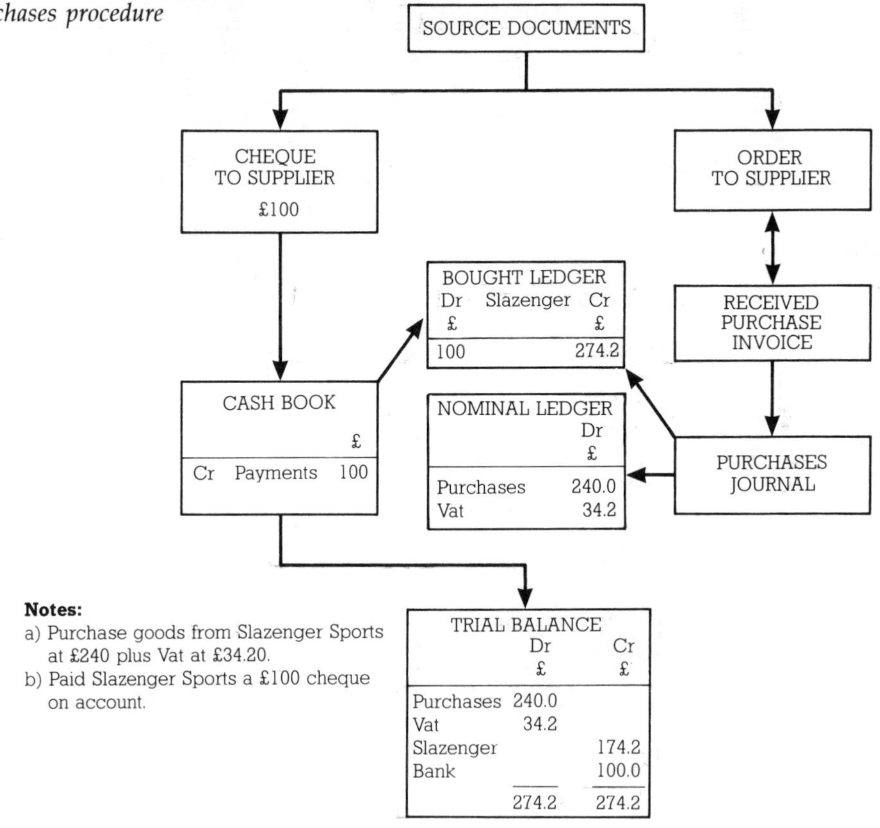

A simplified purchases journal (without Vat)

The details for the purchases journal will be taken directly from the invoice received from suppliers. The double entry is:

Debit the purchases account
Credit the creditor's account.

Example

Enter the following suppliers into a purchases journal for July and then post to the ledger. Assume a 'nil' balance in the supplier's account at the beginning of the month.

Date	*Supplier's name*	*Invoice no.*	*Amount* £	
12/7	Slazenger Sports	334597	240	Cr Supplier's a/c
15/7	Metre	78568	400	Cr Supplier's a/c
23/7	Slazenger Sports	379442	280	Cr Supplier's a/c
25/7	Auto Sports	2121	600	Cr Supplier's a/c
		Dr Purchases a/c:	1 520	

Posting to the ledger

		Debit	Credit	Balance
		£	£	£
Slazenger Sports account				
12/7	Purchases		240	240 Cr
23/7	Purchases		280	520
Metre account				
15/7	Purchases		400	400 Cr
Auto Sports account				
25/7	Purchases		600	600 Cr
Purchases account				
30/7	Creditors	1 520		1 520 Dr

The information from the invoice could be directly fed into a computer program. Chapter 9 will demonstrate the procedure where such a program could be used for the input of invoice data. The example below continues with the business of R Pearce, sports shop proprietor.

The purchases journal of R Pearce, sports shop proprietor (with Vat)

Date	*Supplier's name and account no.*		*Invoice no.*	*Net purchases account*	*Vat account*	*Total value*
				£	£	£
12/7	Slazenger Sports	P65	334597	240	34.20	274.20 Cr
15/7	Metre	P60	78568	400	60.00	460.00 Cr
23/7	Slazenger Sports	P65	379442	280	39.90	319.90 Cr
25/7	Auto Sports	P55	2121	600	90.00	690.00 Cr
				1 520	224.10	1 744.10
				Dr Purchases	Dr Vat	

Posting to the ledgers

Bought ledger (B/L)

		Debit	Credit	Balance
		£	£	£
Slazenger Sports account P65				
12/7	Purchases		240.0	
	Vat		34.2	274.2 Cr
23/7	Purchases		280.0	
	Vat		39.9	594.1

(Continues)

		Debit	Credit	Balance
		£	£	£
Metre account P60				
15/7	Purchases		400.0	
	Vat		60.0	460.0 Cr
Auto Sports account P55				
25/7	Purchases		600.0	
	Vat		90.0	690.0 Cr

Nominal ledger (N/L)

		Debit	Credit	Balance
		£	£	£
Purchases account N35				
30/7	Creditors	1 520.00		1 520.0 Dr
Vat account N30				
30/7	Creditors	224.10		224.1 Dr

NOTE

The double entry:

1 Credit each creditor's account (in the B/L) with purchases + Vat.
2 Debit the total value of purchases (in the N/L) to the purchases account (excluding Vat). Debit the total value of Vat (in the N/L) to the Vat account.
3 The purchases ledger is commonly known as the bought ledger and vice versa. The text will tend to use the term, bought ledger, for the accounts of suppliers.

Purchases, Vat and the use of the bought ledger control account

On 1 August, the balances in the books of R Pearce were:

Bought ledger:	£	*Nominal ledger:*	£
Slazenger Sports	594.1 Cr	Purchases account	2 840.0 Dr
Metre	460.0 Cr	Vat account	147.9 Cr
Auto Sports	690.0 Cr	*Bought ledger control	1 744.1 Cr
International	—		
	1 744.1		

During the month of August, purchase invoices were received from the following suppliers:

	Invoice no.	Date	Net purchases (+ Vat)
			£
Metre	88735	5/8	400
Metre	88956	10/8	860
International	444497	21/8	600
Auto Sports	3765	27/8	200

At the end of August, cheques were sent to the following:

	£	£
Slazenger Sports	250	
Metre	1 000	
Auto Sports	500	1 750

NOTE

***The bought ledger control account**

This account represents a total account of all creditors in the bought ledger (£1744.10). It is used as a cross-checking device and as a measure of control, that is, a check can be made to make sure that the individual balances of the bought ledger are verified with the bought ledger control account. The control accounts are not part of the double entry, but are used to cross-check the accuracy of the personal ledgers.

REQUIRED:

1 Prepare the purchases journal for the month of August.
2 Record all the appropriate details in the ledgers of R Pearce.

The purchases journal of R Pearce for August PJ8

Date	*Supplier's name and account no.*	*Invoice no.*	*Net purchases account* £	*Vat account* £	*Total value* £	
5/8	Metre	88735	400	60	460	Cr
10/8	Metre	88956	860	129	989	Cr
21/8	International	444497	600	90	690	Cr
27/8	Auto Sports	3765	200	30	230	Cr
			2 060	309	2 369	
			Dr Purchases	Dr Vat	Dr Bought control	

Bought ledger

		Folio	*Debit* £	*Credit* £	*Balance* £
Slazenger Sports account P65					
1/8	Balance				594.1 Cr
30/8	Bank	C9	250		344.1
Metre Sports account P60					
1/8	Balance				460.0 Cr
5/8	Purchases	PJ8		400	
	Vat			60	920.0
10/8	Purchases	PJ8		860	
	Vat			129	1 909.0
30/8	Bank	C9	1 000		909.0

(Continues)

		Folio	Debit £	Credit £	Balance £
Auto Sports account P55					
1/8	Balance				690.0 Cr
27/8	Purchases	PJ8		200	
	Vat			30	920.0
30/8	Bank	C9	500		420.0
International account P70					
1/8	Balance				—
21/8	Purchases	PJ8		600	
	Vat			90	690.0 Cr

The schedule of creditors for August:

	£	£
Slazenger Sports	344.1	
Metre	909.0	
Auto Sports	420.0	
International	690.0	2 363.1*

NOTE

*Needs to be verified with the bought ledger control account in the nominal ledger.

Nominal ledger

		Folio	Debit £	Credit £	Balance £
Purchases account N35					
1/8	Balance				1 520.0 Dr
30/8	Creditors	PJ8	2 060		3 580.0
Vat account N30					
1/8	Balance				147.9 Cr
30/8	Creditors	PJ8	309		161.1 Dr
Bought ledger control account N45					
1/8	Balance				1 744.1 Cr
30/8	Purchases and Vat	PJ8		2 369	4 113.1
30/8	Bank	C9	1 750		2 363.1
Bank account (extract from cash book)					
30/8	Creditors			1 750	1 750 Cr

NOTE

The balances between the schedule of creditors and the bought ledger control account agree (£2363.1). The double-entry aspect is therefore verified. When the trial balance is prepared, the control account balances will be entered to represent the total of debtors and creditors.

Debit:	Purchases account	£2 060
	Vat account	309
Credit:	Each creditor account (purchase + Vat)	
	B/L control account £2369	

Summary

1 The purchases journal lists all invoices from suppliers and facilitates posting of information to the purchases (bought) and nominal ledgers.

2 The bought ledger control account can be used as a cross-checking device between the schedule of creditors and the control account. If the two balances fail to agree, the checking of records in both sets of ledgers and journal must take place until the errors are found, then corrected.

3 Vat – If a cash discount is offered by a supplier of goods, to encourage the prompt payment of accounts, the discount may be deducted from the value of goods for the purpose of Vat calculation only. This will marginally reduce the chargeable Vat.

4 Vat is an indirect tax under the control of HM Customs & Excise Department. Currently, most of our goods and services are charged at a standard rate of 15 per cent. Some goods and services are either zero rated or exempt from tax, which means that the 15 per cent rate is not charged.

QUESTIONS

1 The following supplier's invoices were received by R Pearce, for September:

		Invoice no.	*Value* £	*Vat* £
7/9	Slazenger	84552	480	72
12/9	Auto	5553	100	15
15/9	Slazenger	84995	500	75
23/9	Metre	2333	320	48
29/9	Auto	6541	400	60

REQUIRED:

a) Prepare the purchases journal for the month of September.
b) Which ledger are the individual accounts posted? On which side of the account?
c) How are the totals of this journal posted?

2 The details of an invoice received by R Pearce were as follows:

From: Sports Ltd
10 Cricket bats; Code 55; Unit price £22 each.

Trade discount	25 per cent
Cash discount	5 per cent (if paid within 28 days)
Vat	15 per cent

REQUIRED:

a) Calculate the net value of the invoice (including Vat).
b) If the facts are recorded in the books of R Pearce, which ledgers would be used?

3 Suppliers' account balances on 1 September in the books of R Pearce were:

	£	
Metre	800	Cr
Auto	500	Cr
Dunlop	420	Cr
B/L control a/c	1 720	Cr

In September, Pearce bought on credit:

		Invoice	£
8/9	Metre	2775	1 200 + Vat
12/9	Auto	7884	680 + Vat
17/9	Auto	8552	600 + Vat
23/9	Dunlop	11447	300 + Vat

On 30 September, Pearce sent cheques to:

	£
Metre	1 000
Auto	1 000
Dunlop	420

REQUIRED:

a) The purchases journal for September.
b) The bought ledger accounts for each supplier (or purchases ledger).
c) The bought ledger control account, as it would appear in the nominal ledger.
d) The purchases and Vat accounts in the nominal ledger. (Commence each with a zero balance.)

4 The following sales and purchases were made by Smithers during the month of May 1986.

5 May	Sold three desks the list price of which was £150 each on credit to Ace Furnishings. Trade discount was given at the rate of $33\frac{1}{3}$ per cent.
10 May	Sold two dining suites list price £360 each less trade discount of 25 per cent on credit to Comfy Chair Co.
18 May	Purchased the following goods on credit from The Top Woodworkers: 24 kitchen chairs list price £12 each, trade discount 25 per cent; 12 wall cupboards list price £10 each, trade discount 20 per cent.

All transactions are subject to Vat at 15 per cent and cash discount is neither given nor received.

In addition to the above, Smithers *received an invoice* for £110 on 20 May from Jones. This was for shop fittings supplied for use within the business and charged Vat at 15 per cent.

REQUIRED:

a) Calculate the net value of the invoice in each of the four instances mentioned above.
b) Write up the sales account, purchases account, shop fittings and Vat account for the month of May. Your Vat account should show the amount owing to/by the Customs & Excise as at 31 May 1986.

(RSA)

5 The undermentioned credit purchases were made on 1 July 1988.

	List price
	£
Royal Engineering Co	1 400
Preston Builders Ltd	1 700
Edward & Smith Co	1 300

The first two companies give a trade discount of 25 per cent off the list price. Edward & Smith give 20 per cent trade discount. All purchases are subject to 15 per cent Vat.

REQUIRED:

a) Write up the purchases day book showing net price, Vat and the total charged to each customer.
b) When posting to the appropriate ledgers, state how the accounts would be posted from the day book.

(RSA adapted)

6 The following supplier's invoices were received by R Pearce, for October:

		Invoice no.	*Value* £	*Vat*
10/10*	Slazenger	94555	460	+ 15%
14/10	Metre	3342	300	+ 15%
17/10	Auto	6553	220	+ 15%
22/10	Auto	6589	120	+ 15%
24/10	Slazenger	98993	500	+ 15%
27/10	Metre	3873	360	+ 15%
29/10	Auto	7541	400	+ 15%

REQUIRED:

a) Prepare the purchases journal for the month of October.
*Note that Slazenger allows a cash discount of 5 per cent on their invoices and this affects Vat calculations.

b) Post the relevant details to the purchases and nominal ledgers. Commence each account with a zero balance. Open the appropriate control account.

Pearce paid the following cheques to his suppliers on 30 October:

	£
Slazenger	500
Metre	250
Auto	250

7

Purchases day book – ABC Company

Date	*Supplier*	*Invoice no.*	*Men's shoes* £	*Women's shoes* £	*Children's shoes* £	*Vat* £	*Total creditor* £
3/2	Footwear Ltd	F2236	120			18.00	138.00
6/2	FH&W	08476			95	14.25	109.25
7/2	Country Casual	14279		75		11.25	86.25
14/2	Footwear Ltd	F2239	210			31.50	241.50
16/2	FH&W	08979			190	28.50	218.50
21/2	Footwear Ltd	F2240	525			78.75	603.75
28/2	Jones Leather	26011		270		40.50	310.50
			855	345	285	222.7	1 707.75

How would the following entries be posted to the ledgers?

a) Each supplier's account is credited with the total sum. Yes/No?

b) The total sum of men's, women's and children's shoes is debited/credited to the purchases account of each category?

Purchases account		
(Men's)	£855	Dr/Cr
(Women's)	£345	Dr/Cr
(Children's)	£285	Dr/Cr
Vat account	£222.75	Dr/Cr
Purchase control account	£1707.75	Dr/Cr

c) Assuming that each creditor's account is a zero balance on 1 February, post the information from the day book to the purchases ledger.

8 The credit purchases of stock for January were as follows:

Date	*Supplier account*	*Invoice no. received*	*Gross purchases* £	*Net purchases* £	*Vat* £	*Total* £
Jan 5	Underwood Mills Ltd	3046	1 000	800	114.00	
7	Illingworth & Edwards	29851	1 200	960	136.89	
10	Milburn & Harris Ltd	4367	500	425	62.16	
15	Underwood Mills Ltd	4768	380	304	43.32	
20	Illingworth & Edwards	34420	530	424	68.42	
25	Snow Material Supplies	2321	240	204	29.84	

Check the accuracy of the invoices before totalling the columns. Underwood Mills Ltd and Illingworth & Edwards give 20 per cent trade discount and offer 5 per cent cash discounts. Milburn & Harris and Snow Supplies give 15 per cent trade discount and offer 5 per cent cash discounts.

REQUIRED:

a) Total the columns across and down after checking the accuracy of the Vat calculations. Correct any which may be inaccurate.
b) Which of the above figures would be posted to the nominal ledger and to which accounts?

BTEC National

CHAPTER

8 The returns journal

- *What are the functions of the returns inward and returns outward journals?*
- *From what source document are they prepared?*
- *Why is a statement sent to customers?*

Introduction

The source document relating to returns or allowances made to customers is the credit note. If goods are returned from buyers to sellers for any reason such as damage, shoddy work, being the wrong type or are unwanted, the credit note is raised by the seller and sent to the buyer.

On receipt of a credit note, it is checked for accuracy, including any discounts, Vat and the final total. Details may then be recorded in the appropriate ledgers.

The journals are:

The returns inward journal: for returns or allowances, made to customers. Credit notes are sent to customers (sales returns).

The returns outward journal: for returns or allowances from suppliers. Credit notes are received from suppliers (purchases returns).

The credit note

A credit note sent from Slazenger Sports to R Pearce is shown on page 86.

Example: The returns outward journal

During the month of August, R Pearce sent goods back to two of his suppliers, Slazenger Sports and Metre. The returns outward journal recording these returns is shown below:

Returns outward journal of R Pearce

RO4

Date	*Supplier's account*	*Credit note no.*	*Returns outward account* £	*Vat account* £	*Total value* £
4/8	Slazenger	8957	48	6.84	54.84 Dr
25/8	Metre	43335	50	7.50	57.50 Dr
			98	14.34	112.34
			Cr Returns out a/c	Cr Vat a/c	Dr Bought control a/c

Bought ledger

		Folio	*Debit* £	*Credit* £	*Balance* £
Slazenger Sports account P65					
1/8	Balance				594.10 Cr
4/8	Returns out	RO4	48.00		
	Vat		6.84		539.26
Metre account P60					
1/8	Balance				460.00 Cr
25/8	Returns out	RO4	50.00		
	Vat		7.50		402.50

Nominal ledger

		Folio	*Debit* £	*Credit* £	*Balance* £
Returns outward account N44					
1/8	Balance				—
30/8	Creditors	RO4		98.00	98.00 Cr
Vat account N50					
1/8	Balance				147.90 Cr
30/8	Creditors	RO4		14.34	168.24
Bought ledger account N45					
1/8	Balance				1 744.10 Cr
30/8	Returns and Vat		112.34		1 631.76

NOTE

The double entry:

1 Debit: each creditor's account with returns and Vat (bought ledger)
Bought ledger control account £112.34.

2 Credit: returns outward account £98.00
Vat account £14.34.

Slazenger Sports

CREDIT NOTE

Denby, Wakefield,
West Yorks

R Pearce
77 Penhill Rd
Penhill
Poole

Vat Reg. 144 9842 84
Telephone 0204 664555
Telex 669944 88

Credit in respect of

Goods Return √
Shortage —
Errors —
Allowances —

Invoice no. 334597
Date 12/7/90

Order no.

Credit note no. C/8957
Date 4/8/90

Quantity	Code no.	Details	Price	Goods value	Trade (20%)	Net value
4	Z238	Tennis R	15	60	12	48.00
		Vat				6.84
		Total credit:				54.84

Returns inward and outward procedure

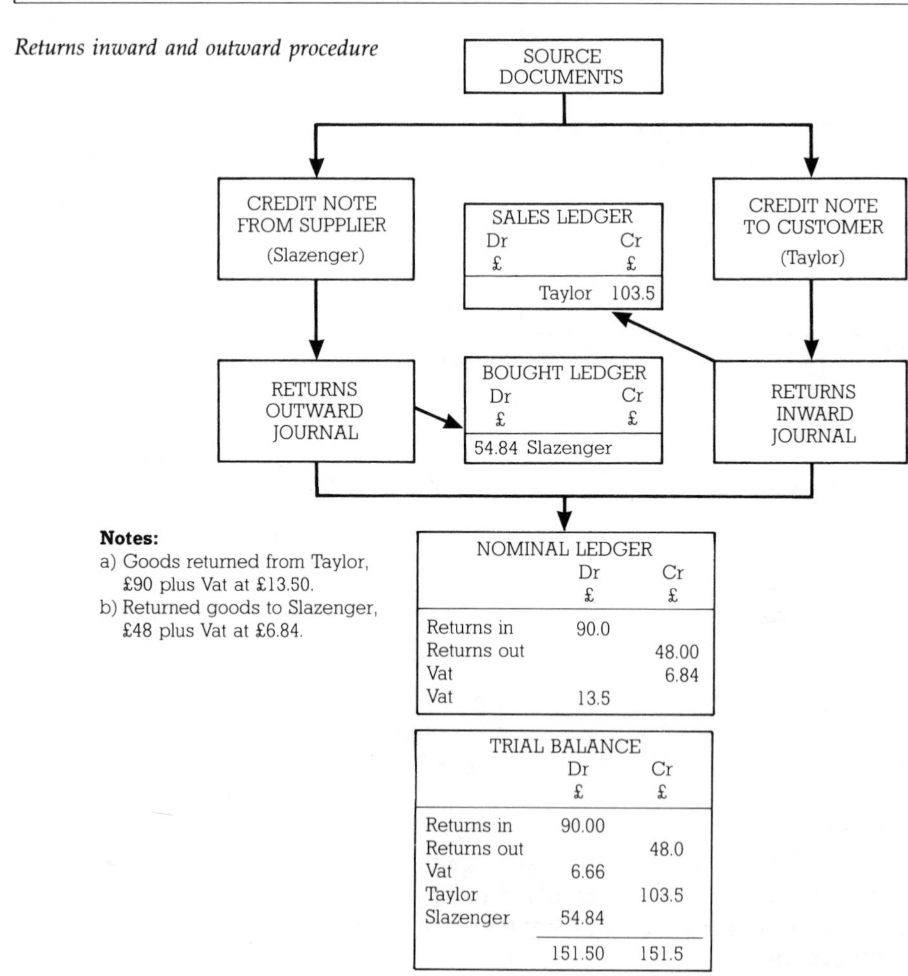

Notes:

a) Goods returned from Taylor, £90 plus Vat at £13.50.
b) Returned goods to Slazenger, £48 plus Vat at £6.84.

Example: The returns inward journal

During the month of August, R Pearce had goods returned to him from two of his customers, Taylor and Johnson because the goods were flawed. The returns inward journal is prepared from the credit notes raised by Pearce and is shown below:

RI2

Date	*Customer's account*	*Credit note no.*	*Returns inward account* £	*Vat account* £	*Total value* £
15/8	C Taylor S12	545	90	13.5	103.5 Cr
23/8	M Johnson S08	546	100	15.0	115.0 Cr
			190	28.5	218.5
			Dr Returns inward a/c	Dr Vat a/c	Cr Sales control a/c

Sales ledger

		Folio	*Debit* £	*Credit* £	*Balance* £
C Taylor account S12					
1/8	Balance				558.0 Dr
15/8	Returns in			90.0	
	Vat			13.5	454.5
M Johnson account S08					
1/8	Balance				575.0 Dr
23/8	Returns in	RI2		100	
	Vat			15	460.0

Nominal ledger

		Folio	*Debit* £	*Credit* £	*Balance* £
Returns inward account N41					
1/8	Balance				—
30/8	Debtors	RI2	190.0		190.00 Dr
Vat account N50					
1/8	Balance				147.90 Cr
30/8	Creditors	RO4		14.34	168.24
30/8	Debtors	RI2	28.5		133.74
Sales ledger control account N40					
1/8	Balance				1 852.00 Dr
30/8	Returns in	RI2		190.0	
	Vat			28.5	1 633.50

NOTE

The double entry:

1 Credit: each debtor's account with returns and Vat (sales ledger)
Sales ledger control account £218.50.

2 Debit: returns inward account £190.00
Vat account £28.50.

The statement of account

Statements of account are sent to customers giving details of the current transactions which have occurred between buyer and seller. It is a statement which reminds customers of their outstanding debt. In the example below, R Pearce sends a prepared statement of account to his customer, C Taylor. The final balance due should, of course, cross-check with Taylor's account in the sales ledger.

Statement of account

R Pearce
Sports Proprietor
77 Penhill Road
Penhill
Poole

Vat Reg. 76 48424
Telephone: 4455

To: C Taylor
24 Boscombe Drive
Bournemouth

Account no. S12

Date	*Details*	*Debit*	*Credit*	*Balance*
		£	£	£
1/7	Balance b/f			1 058.0
30/7	Cheque – Thank you		500.0	558.0
15/8	C/N 545		103.5	454.5
3/9	Invoice no. 2955	200		
	Vat	30		684.5
5/9	Balance due			684.5

Summary

1 The returns inward journal lists all returns from customers and facilitates posting to the sales and nominal ledgers.

2 The returns outward journal lists all returns to suppliers and facilitates posting to the purchases and nominal ledgers.

3 The credit note is the source document for returns. A credit note sent to customers is the basis of recording returns inward. A credit note received from suppliers is the basis of recording returns outward.

4 Credit notes have the effect of reducing the value of a debtor's account for returns inward and reducing the value of a creditor's account for returns outward.

5 A statement of account is sent to customers, usually monthly, to itemise what is owed.

QUESTIONS

1 R Pearce returned goods to his suppliers in September and received the following credit notes:

		Credit note no.	*Value* £	*Vat* £
15/9	Slazenger	C44	60	9
22/9	Auto	C80	20	3
29/9	Metre	C14	100	15

REQUIRED:

a) Prepare the returns outward journal for the month of September.
b) How are the individual accounts posted?
c) How are the totals of the journal posted?

2 R Pearce received goods which had been returned by his customers during September. He sent them the following credit notes:

		Credit note no.	*Value* £	*Vat* £
14/9	D Lewis	C13	60	9
22/9	D Smith	C14	120	18
28/9	C Taylor	C15	20	3

REQUIRED:

a) Prepare the returns inward journal for September.
b) How are the individual accounts posted?
c) How are the totals of the journal posted?

3 Creditors' balances in the books of R Pearce on 1 October were:

	£
Slazenger	885 Cr
Auto	350 Cr
Metre	638 Cr

Balances in Pearce's nominal ledger on 1 October were:

	£
Returns outward account	980 Cr
Vat account	224 Cr
Bought ledger control account	1 873 Cr

R Pearce received the following credit notes during October:

			Credit note
12/10	Slazenger	£60 + Vat	C79
25/10	Metre	£30 + Vat	C185
29/10	Auto	£84 + Vat	C26

REQUIRED:

a) The returns outward journal for the month of October.
b) The bought ledger accounts of the three creditors.
c) The nominal ledger accounts as listed above.

4 Debtors' balances on 1 October in the books of R Pearce were:

	£
D Lewis	680 Dr
D Smith	1 020 Dr
C Taylor	420 Dr

Balances found in Pearce's nominal ledger on 1 October were:

	£
Returns inward account	775 Dr
Vat account	224 Cr
Sales ledger control account	2 120 Dr

R Pearce sent credit notes to customers who had returned goods to him during October:

			Credit note no.
4/10	D Smith	£44 + Vat 15%	C16
13/10	D Lewis	£20 + Vat 15%	C17
28/10	C Taylor	£36 + Vat 15%	C18

REQUIRED:

a) The returns inward journal for October.
b) The sales ledger accounts of the three debtors.
c) The nominal ledger accounts as listed above.

5 D Withers is a wholesaler. The following *credit* transactions took place during the month of May. Enter each transaction in the appropriate book of original entry, total for the month and post to the purchases, sales, returns and Vat accounts in the ledger.

All amounts given are before the addition of Vat, which is to be taken as 15 per cent. All trade purchases are allowed a trade discount of 20 per cent, not yet taken into account in the figures given below. Trade discount is *not* allowed on any sales.

			£
May	1	Purchased stock from T Smithers Ltd	400
	3	Sold stock to W Wilkin	350
	4	Sold stock to T Wilson	300
	11	Returned stock bought on 1 May to T Smithers Ltd	50
	12	Purchased stationery for office use from Paper Co Ltd	150
	14	Purchased office furniture from Office Supplies Ltd	400
	20	T Wilson returned stock	20
	29	Sold stock to W Wilkin	170
	29	Purchased stock from T Smithers Ltd	150

REQUIRED:

a) The appropriate journals for the month of May.
b) The posting of all relevant accounts to the nominal ledger only.

(RSA)

6 On 1 June personal accounts in J Smith's ledger had the following balances:

	£	
R Morton	175	Cr
W Pierce	184	Cr
L Appleby	150	Dr
T Shuttleworth	210	Dr
M Vincent	145	Dr

The following transactions took place during the month of June

			£
June	3	Sold goods on credit to T Shuttleworth	150
	4	Sold goods on credit to M Vincent	210
	8	Bought goods on credit from R Morton	470
		Paid R Morton by cheque	175
	9	T Shuttleworth settled his account to date by cheque	
	11	Bought goods on credit from W Pierce	197
	12	Returned goods to R Morton	10
		Sold goods on credit to L Appleby	240
		Sold goods on credit to T Shuttleworth	160

(Continues)

		£
15	L Appleby returned goods	10
	Returned goods to W Pierce	15
19	Paid W Pierce by cheque	184
25	L Appleby paid by cheque	150
26	Sold goods on credit to M Vincent	310
29	Bought goods on credit from W Pierce	180
	Sold goods on credit to T Shuttleworth	160
30	M Vincent returned goods	14
	Paid W Pierce by cheque	182

From the information given above write up the *personal accounts* in J Smith's ledger. To obtain full marks the accounts should be of the three-column type, with columns headed Dr, Cr and balance. The amount of the balance on each account should be calculated afresh after each entry in the account.

Note Day books and nominal ledger accounts are *not* required.
Vat is not charged.

(RSA)

7 Lesley Dawson commenced business on 1 January 1987 with capital of £30 000. She put £28 000 into a business bank account and kept the remainder in a cash account as cash in hand. During the first two weeks in January the following business transactions occurred:

January	1	Credit purchases: Green & Co £4000; Black & Co £2500.
	2	Purchased fixtures and fittings £6200, paying by cheque.
	5	Paid by cheque £56, advertising in the local paper.
	6	Paid rent six months in advance, £6000 by cheque.
	7	Cash sales, £400. Credit sales: Redhill & Co, £3500.
	8	Wages paid by cheque, £86.
	9	Paid insurance premium for 12 months £400, by cheque.
	12	Credit purchases: Green & Co, £3000.
	13	Paid postage and stationery by cash, £38.
	14	Withdrew cash, £500, for personal use.
	15	Paid Green & Co 50 per cent of his outstanding balance.
	15	Wages paid by cash, £84.
	16	Cash sales, £880. Credit sales: Redhill & Co £4600; Shaw Ltd £2100.
	17	Redhill & Co send a cheque £5000 on account.

REQUIRED:

a) Prepare the sales and purchases journals for the period to 17 January 1987. Post to the appropriate ledgers.
b) Open appropriate ledger accounts for the business, recording the above transactions. Extract a trial balance as on 17 January 1987.
c) Why is it necessary to have more than a single ledger system for different types of business organisations?

CHAPTER

9 Computer-based accounts: sales and purchases ledger programs

- *Why are computers used in the recording of financial information?*
- *What do printouts (hard copies) from computers look like?*
- *Is the information different from that of manual ledger systems?*

Introduction

There are many different computer hardware systems in use in accounts offices. Some companies may have large, powerful mainframe systems provided by organisations such as IBM, ICL, Honeywell and Dec. These systems will use software packages (programs which tell the computer what to do) which will be used by different sections of the company for different functions. These may include research, development, production and, of course, accounting. Other companies may have a network of microcomputers (personal computers) used solely by the accounts department and will probably use accounting software to assist them in various ways including recording ledger accounts, stock control, payroll, invoicing and costing.

There are many companies producing microcomputers for an expanding market, some of the leaders in this field include Acorn, Amstrad, Apple, Commodore and Philips. The mainframe suppliers like IBM and ICL also produce their own models.

The range of software programs tailored specifically to the accountant is large. These include packages, which basically provide the same functions; to improve the recording, storage and retrieval of information. Many of these packages have the distinct advantage of being fully integrated, that is, the package can link up with several programs such as invoicing and sales ledger, stock control and purchase/sales processing, and job costing with the payroll function.

The competition to provide software for accounting is highly intensive. Some popular packages on the market are *Pegasus* (one of the principal leaders), *Plusmark*, *Sage* and *Tetra*. These provide a wide range of packages which tend to start with separate 'modules', for example, the sales and purchases ledgers. Users can gradually build up a system until a fully integrated network is developed where computers virtually talk to each other in the supply of information and analysis. *Lotus* and *Microsoft Excel* tend to specialise in what are called *spreadsheet* packages and both the *Lotus 1-2-3* and *Excel* programs are highly popular in industry and commerce particularly for budgeting, analysis and graphics. Chapter 25 examines the use of spreadsheets in more detail.

Many software companies tend to produce programs which are specifically in harmony (compatible) with a particular machine system. For example, *Sage* is IBM compatible and *Pegasus* is RM Nimbus compatible.

The microcomputer

The diagram below relates to the hardware, that is, the computer itself and other peripherals such as the printer and disk drive. It includes the following components:

1 The computer screen which provides the visual display of the program and data.

2 The keyboard, very much like that of the typewriter, but having a number of extra keys to provide further computer functions.

3 The computer disk drive where the disks are loaded onto the computer, which enables it to operate a program. Some have single drives and it may be necessary to first load the program to operate a function such as sales, then the data disk to input specific data such as customers and invoices, etc. Some have double drives enabling the program disk and the data disk to be used simultaneously.

The computer network

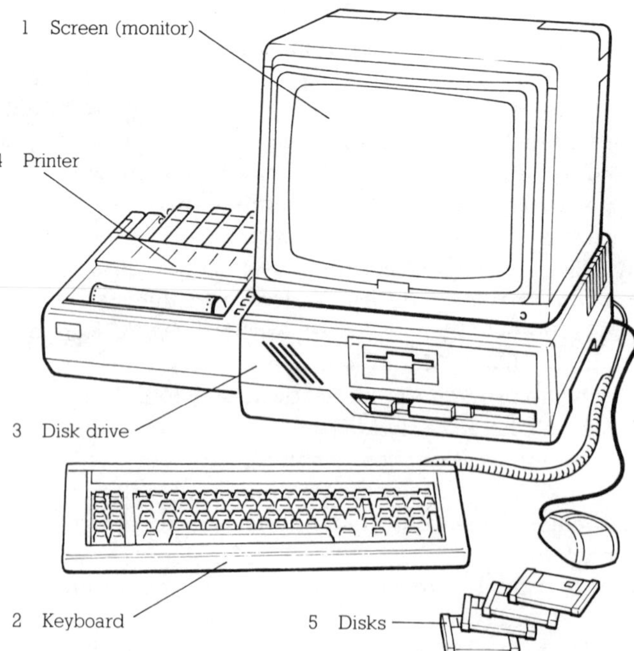

4 The printer, which has the obvious function of printing the information (called hard copies) required for business documents such as invoices and customer statements, and also the printouts of individual accounts.

5 The program and data disks. Currently, there are two basic types of floppy disk, the $5\frac{1}{4}''$ and the $3\frac{1}{2}''$ diameter disks. The program disk gives the computer its precise instructions. The data disks are used for the input of specific information relating to the program used.

The sales and purchases ledger programs

The accurate recording of financial transactions on a day-to-day basis is one of the most important functions in accounting.

The use of computers in all kinds of different businesses, small and large, has helped to modernise and update the system of record keeping. The routine, repetitive transactions may easily be recorded, updated, classified and recalled instantly when required. Management and owners of businesses can be provided with the information they want at the press of a button. Significantly, this information may be printed out and analysed to provide the essential data such as:

How much is owed to creditors and when do they need to be paid?
How much do customers owe and do they pay regularly?
Is sufficient cash coming in?
Which products sell best?
How much is spent on overheads?
How much is spent on the payroll?
Is there sufficient stock available?

These are the type of questions management need to answer in order to keep a sound control of the business and to help them to make the right decisions.

Where businesses use computers for the input of financial information, it is necessary to have the right software to provide them with the information that is required.

Software refers to program disks which are designed for the computer to carry out precise instructions relating to the field of work required, for example, sales, purchases and nominal ledgers, payroll, stock control, etc.

The program disk is loaded into the computer's memory to run the appropriate file, for example, sales ledger, and then a data disk may be used to store the relevant information of that file. For the sales ledger program, this would be all the information relating to customers.

Loading data onto the computer

Data refers to the day-to-day financial transactions which occur in business. For example, if a batch of invoice copies to customers require entry to the sales ledger, the sales ledger program would be called from the appropriate file or menu and a data disk would already be in the computer's disk drive awaiting the facts and figures to be loaded into the computer's memory and relayed to the relevant customer accounts.

The computer is likely to have a printer attached to its network and a whole range of important printouts can be provided, including statements, individual accounts, list of accounts, analysis of accounts, stock records and payroll details, depending on the facilities provided by the program.

The sales ledger program

An accounting program may either be part of a network system or linked to a mainframe, where it may be conveniently called upon the screen when required, by simply pressing the appropriate command key. Or, it may be necessary to load a program disk which includes the program instructions to run a particular function, such as the sales or purchases ledgers. A data disk will be used to record the program and the information stored on it.

Once a disk is loaded onto the computer, the operator will choose which file or menu is required. There may be several files on an accounting package and the computer may require an identifying letter or number, for example, '1' may be the code for the sales ledger program, '2' for the purchase ledger.

Programs in business usually operate on what is called a *menu* system, that is, the user is given a number of choices or functions to use. The user will choose a particular function and press the relevant key in order to get started. For example, in the programs shown in this section, the Jenkins Jeans Co Ltd displays the following main menu:

1. Sales Ledger
2. Purchase Ledger
3. Nominal Ledger
4. Stock Control
5. Payroll
6. Invoicing
7. Costing
8. Terminate

Select and Press Number Required

The first function we need is the sales ledger, therefore the number 1 would be pressed on the keyboard. The sub-menu of the sales ledger would then be displayed:

MENU: SALES LEDGER

1. Ledger Transactions
2. Period End
3. Analysis of Sales
4. Reports

Select and Press Number Required

The most frequently used function would be number 1, Ledger Transactions, which would give a list of further options to operate such as entering invoices, credit notes and receipts.

The function Period End may be used to end a financial period and sales turnover maybe zeroed to commence a new period. The customers' balances are not zeroed of course, the balance being brought forward.

The Analysis of Sales function may be particularly useful to those types of businesses which want to know which stocks are moving and which may be slow. They may want an analysis of sales geographically, by department or by sales executives. Sales may easily be coded for this purpose.

The fourth function, Reports may be used to indicate batches of sales over periods of time or any other statistical information provided by a particular program.

The general features of a reasonable sales ledger program would include:

a facility to store a large number of accounts;
details of each debtor's records;
individual customer turnover to date;
automatic processing to the nominal ledger, thereby completing the double entry;
sales journal;
Vat analysis;
credit control limits for customers;
aged debtors analysis;
receipts analysis and details of discounts;
customer statements.

Most of the above items would be available for printout and this gives computer-based accounting a further edge. Not only can this information be stored on a small disk, it can be retrieved instantly and a copy output on the printer whenever the information is required – unbeatable over a manual system any time. In large organisations the use of computerised information is essential for management and helps them in their daily decision making.

If the user selected function number 1 of the sales ledger menu, Ledger Transactions, a further menu would appear, giving an additional list of options:

MENU: LEDGER TRANSACTIONS

1. Accounts Up-Date
2. Ledger Posting
3. Invoice & Credit Note Listing
4. Receipts & Adjustments
5. Customer Accounts
6. Customer Statements
7. Aged Debtors List
8. List of Accounts
9. Outstanding Debtors Total
10. Terminate

Select and Press Number Required

The Ledger Transactions function would be used daily to enter details relating to customers. Examples of these functions are shown as hard copies in the exercise relating to Jenkins Jeans Co Ltd on pages 101–3. The facilities that each of the options provide is summarised overleaf:

1 **Accounts Up-Date:** The screen would show information such as:

*ACCOUNT NUMBER	NAME & ADDRESS
S001	J. DAVIES 14 Highfield Road Broadstone

COMMENT	CREDIT LIMIT	CODE
Tele. 554788	4 000	S

*Cursor flashing

The cursor is awaiting an instruction from the user and in this case it is flashing over the account number and is waiting for the operator to enter the relevant number. If the account is new, the computer will state 'New Account' and await further input. If the account is an existing one, all other relevant information will be displayed on screen (as above).

2 **Ledger Posting:** The cursor on the screen would prompt which account was required and then the details of the customer would be displayed automatically:

ACCOUNT NUMBER	DATE	TYPE	REFERENCE	VALUE	VAT/DISC.	PERIOD
S001	1/1/90	A	Open/Bal	800		1
J. DAVIES						

In the above example, the opening balance of a customer, J Davies, has been entered. Under 'TYPE', the letter 'A' signifies the appropriate code to enter an opening balance. The letter 'I' could signify invoice, the letter 'C' credit note, and so forth. Once details of any transaction are entered, the sales ledger file is automatically updated and may be viewed when required.

3 **Invoice & Credit Note Listing:** This function lists the invoice and credit notes for any given period, for example, a day, a week, a month, or longer. In the printout, the month's invoices and credit notes are listed. This detail would be the same as that given in the sales day book:

Sales:	£1 040
Vat	£156
Total Debtors	£1 196

4 **Receipts & Adjustments:** This function allows the operator to list the receipts and adjustments for the period required as with the invoice and credit note listing. In the printout, totals are shown for:

Receipts:	£1 510
Discounts	£40
Adjustments:	£1 250 (opening balances)

5 **Customer Accounts:** This function is used to display, either on screen or printout, the details of each customer's account. All transactions to the debtor are shown, including:

date of entries
invoice and credit note numbers
cheque numbers
discounts given
the age of the debt in months.

This function is used frequently to check records of individual customers and will be an important check on credit control. How much does the customer owe? Account No. S001 (Davies) has a current debt of £299. When did he last pay his account? Does he pay in reasonable time? These are important questions which need answers in order to keep adequate control of customer accounts. The speed of debt collection is vital to a business's cash flow and working capital.

6 **Customer Statements:** If a customer's statement needs to be printed and sent, this function will give details of the account as found in option number 5 above.

7 **Aged Debtors List:** This function may be viewed on screen or as a printout, as shown in the example. The balance of each customer is indicated and 'aged' according to how old the debt is. In the printout, all the debts are listed as 'current', the total debt being £896. This figure should equal the sales ledger control account as in the nominal ledger. The credit limit and telephone numbers of each customer are also printed for convenience.

8 **List of Accounts:** This function gives a list of the customer accounts required. In the printout, the three accounts of Jenkins Jeans are listed, also indicating the turnover to date, credit limit and telephone number of each customer. Code 'S' can refer to the geographical area the customer comes from.

9 **Outstanding Debtors Total:** This function will display on screen the outstanding debt owed by the total debtors. It should equal the total amount given in option number 7 and is used as a quick check on how much customers owe; it should also equal the sales ledger control account balance.

Total Debtors = £896

10 **Terminate:** This function returns the operator to the main sales ledger menu.

An example of the computer-based accounts of Jenkins Jeans Co Ltd is presented as a set of printouts on pages 103–7.

a) The first set of printouts all refer to the sales ledger program of Jenkins Jeans Co Ltd. The company has only three customers at present:

J. Davies	S001
F. Smith	S002
B. Forbes	S003

Each of these debtors have been entered in the sales program and all relevant details such as opening balances, invoices and receipts have been input.

b) The second set of printouts relate to the purchases ledger program, the company having three suppliers:

J. Harries	P001
D. Brown	P002
R. James	P003

Each of these suppliers have been entered in the purchase program and all relevant details have been input. Both the sales and purchases ledgers have a basic analysis of sales and purchases:

S161 and P161 refer to clothing
S162 and P162 refer to equipment
S163 and P163 refer to miscellaneous goods.

By including these codes, Jenkins Jeans Co Ltd will be able to analyse instantly how both sales and purchases are moving for these categories.

c) The final section of this exercise relates to Chapter 10 and emphasises the nominal ledger program which concludes with the company's trial balance.

Computer-based accounts – input of information

Situation

The following information relates to the accounts of Jenkins Jeans Co Ltd as on 1 January 1990:

Balance Sheet as on 1 January 1990

	£	£
FIXED ASSETS		
Furniture and equipment	4 500	
Motor vehicle	4 000	8 500

(Continues)

		£	£
CURRENT ASSETS			
Stock		1 000	
Debtors			
Davies	800		
Smith	450	1 250	
Bank		750	
		3 000	
CURRENT LIABILITIES			
Creditors:			
Harries	1 250		
Brown	250	1 500	
Net current assets			1 500
			10 000
FINANCED BY			
Capital:			10 000

TASK A:

Enter the above accounts in the books of Jenkins Jeans Co Ltd using sales and purchases ledgers for personal accounts and the nominal ledger for all other accounts, as on 1 January 1990.

During the month of January, the following invoices were sent to customers:

	Name	*Invoice*	*Amount £*	*Sales code*
5/1	Davies	2334	200 +15%	S161 (clothing)
12/1	Smith	2335	80 +15%	S162 (equipment)
17/1	Davies	2336	120 +15%	S162 (equipment)
17/1	Forbes (new)	2337	400 +15%	S163 (misc.)
28/1	Smith	2338	300 +15%	S161 (clothing)

Invoices received from suppliers during the month of January were:

	Name	*Invoice*	*Amount £*	*Purchase codes*
11/1	Harries	8875	360 +15%	P161 (clothing)
17/1	Brown	33391/4	120 +15%	P163 (misc.)
25/1	Harries	9320	400 +15%	P162 (equipment)
28/1	James (new)	1212	160 +15%	P161 (clothing)

Credit note sent to customer:

24/1	Davies	c/n 42	60 +15%	S162 (equipment)

TASK B:

Prepare the sales and purchases day books for the month of January. The credit note may be included in the sales day book as a negative figure.

If computer-based accounts are to be prepared, give each account an appropriate account number and also ensure that the opening customer and supplier balances are entered in the sales and purchases ledger programs.

Account numbers to be used:

Sales ledger		*Purchases ledger*	
S001	J. Davies	P001	J. Harries
S002	F. Smith	P002	D. Brown
S003	B. Forbes	P003	R. James

Cheques received during January were:

	Name	*Amount* (£)
28/1	Davies	760 (discount allowed £40).
30/1	Smith	500 on account.
30/1	Forbes	250 on account.
31/1	Cash sales	3 220 (into bank). (Vat £420 included)

Cheques paid during January were:

	Name	*Amount* (£)
25/1	Harries	1 000 on account.
28/1	Brown	235 (discount received £15).
30/1	Wages	400
30/1	Overheads	500

TASK C:

Post all cheques received and paid to their appropriate accounts in the personal and nominal ledgers. If computer-based accounts are prepared, enter all debtors' and creditors' details in their respective sales and purchases ledger programs. If a nominal ledger program is used, give an appropriate ledger account for the nominal accounts: sales, purchases, Vat, discounts, wages and overheads.

TASK D:

Prepare a schedule of debtors and creditors for the month of January. If control accounts are used, these should verify the totals of the schedules.

Extract a trial balance as on 31 January 1990.

Nominal ledger account numbers

A001	Furniture and equipment
A002	Motor vehicles
C001	Sales ledger control
C002	Purchases ledger control
C005	Bank
D680	Capital
E134	Wages
E135	Overheads
E645	Discount allowed
L696	Vat inputs
L697	Vat outputs
P161	Purchases (clothing)
P162	Purchases (equipment)
P163	Purchases (miscellaneous)
P360	Discount received
R161	Stock (balance sheet)
S161	Sales (clothing)
S162	Sales (equipment)
S163	Sales (miscellaneous)

The sales ledger program printouts

Printouts from ledger transactions are as follows:

Option No. 3: Invoices and credit note listing;
Option No. 4: Receipts and adjustments;
Option No. 5: Customer accounts;
Option No. 7: Aged debtors list;
Option No. 8: List of accounts; and
Main sales ledger menu – Option No. 3: Sales analysis.

Option No. 3: Invoice and credit note listing

Jenkins Jeans Co. Ltd.

01.01.90 S/L Invoices & Credit Notes (To Date) Page 1

A/c	Date	Type	Reference	Value	Goods	VAT	
S001	05.01.90	Invce	2334	230.00	200.00	30.00	J. Davies
S002	12.01.90	Invce	2335	92.00	80.00	12.00	F. Smith
S001	17.01.90	Invce	2336	138.00	120.00	18.00	J. Davies
S003	01.01.90	Invce	2337	460.00	400.00	60.00	B. Forbes
S002	28.01.90	Invce	2338	345.00	300.00	45.00	F. Smith
S001	24.01.90	Cnote	c/n	−69.00	−60.00	−9.00	J. Davies
Total Invoices				1 265.00	1 100.00	165.00	
Total Cr. Notes				−69.00	−60.00	−9.00	
Total				1 196.00	1 040.00	156.00	

Note: acts as the Sales Journal

Option No. 4: Receipts and adjustments

Jenkins Jeans Co. Ltd.

01.01.90 S/L Receipts & Adjusts (To Date) Page 1

A/c	Date	Type	Reference	Value	Period	
S001	01.01.90	Adjust	open/bal	800.00	1	J. Davies
S002	01.01.90	Adjust	open/bal	450.00	1	F. Smith
S001	28.01.90	Recpt	chq345678	−760.00	1	J. Davies
S001	28.01.90	Discnt	chq345678	−40.00	1	J. Davies
S002	30.01.90	Recpt	chq234567	−500.00	1	F. Smith
S003	30.01.90	Recpt	chq234123	−250.00	1	B. Forbes

Total Discounts	−40.00
Total Receipts	−1 510.00
Total Refunds	.00
Total Adj – Contras	.00
Total Adj – Bad Debts	.00
Total Adj – Write Offs	.00
Total Adj – Misposts	.00
Total Adj – Discounts	.00
Total Adj – Interest	.00
Total Adj – Sundry	1 250.00
Total	−300.00

Option No. 5: Customer accounts

J. Davies Account S001 01 Jan 1990
14 Highfield Rd.
Broadstone T/Over 260/Jan Cr. Lim 4000
Interest Rate 0.00%

Date	Type	Reference	Status	Debit	Credit	Balance
01.01.90	Adjust	open/bal	Jan	800.00		
05.01.90	Invoice	2334		230.00		
17.01.90	Invoice	2336		138.00		
24.01.90	Cr. Note	c/n			69.00	
28.01.90	Receipt	chq345678	Jan		760.00	
28.01.90	Discnt	chq345678	Jan		40.00	

3 Months +	2 Months	1 Month	Current	Total
.00	.00	.00	299.00	299.00

Note: indicates the turnover (£260) for the month (exc. vat)
Credit Limit £4000

F. Smith
224 Ashley Rd.
Poole

Account S002 | 01 Jan 1990
T/Over 380/Jan | Cr. Lim 4000
Interest Rate 0.00%

Date	Type	Reference	Status	Debit	Credit	Balance
01.01.90	Adjust	open/bal	Jan	450.00		
12.01.90	Invoice	2335		92.00		
28.01.90	Invoice	2338		345.00		
30.01.90	Receipt	chq234567	Jan		500.00	

3 Months +	2 Months	1 Month	Current	Total
.00	.00	.00	387.00	387.00

B. Forbes
15 Christchurch Rd.
Bournemouth

Account S003 | 01 Jan 1990
T/Over 400/Jan | Cr. Lim 4000
Interest Rate 0.00%

Date	Type	Reference	Status	Debit	Credit	Balance
01.01.90	Invoice	2337		460.00		
30.01.90	Receipt	chq234123	Jan		250.00	

3 Months +	2 Months	1 Month	Current	Total
.00	.00	.00	210.00	210.00

Option No. 7: Aged debtors list

Jenkins Jeans Co. Ltd.

01.01.90 Aged Debtors List Page 1

A/c	3 Months +	2 Months	1 Month	Current	Total	Cr. Limit
S001	.00	.00	.00	299.00	299.00	4 000
.Davies			000 554788*			
S002	.00	.00	.00	387.00	387.00	4 000
.Smith			000 667744			
S003	.00	.00	.00	210.00	210.00	4 000
.Forbes			000 554433			
Total	.00	.00	.00	896.00	896.00	

*Customer's telephone number

Option No. 8: List of accounts

S001	J. Davies	000 554788	
	14 Highfield Rd.	Code S	
	Broadstone	Type B	
		Cr. Limit	4 000
		T/Over	260/Jan
S002	F. Smith	000 667744	
	224 Ashley Rd.	Code S	
	Poole	Type B	
		Cr. Limit	4 000
		T/Over	380/Jan
S003	B. Forbes	000 554433	
	15 Christchurch Rd.	Code S	
	Bournemouth	Type B	
		Cr. Limit	4 000
		T/Over	400/Jan

Note: Code S indicates 'southern' trader
Type B indicates 'balance' brought forward each month
Telephone numbers and credit limits included
Turnover per month excludes Vat

Sales ledger menu – Option No. 3: Sales analysis

Jenkins Jeans Co. Ltd.

01 Jan 90 Sales Analysis Input Page 1

Code	Type	VAT	Value	A/c	Date	Reference
S L697	I	0	30.00	S001	05.01.90	2334
S S161	I	1	200.00			
S L697	I	0	12.00	S002	12.01.90	2335
S S162	I	1	80.00			
S L697	I	0	18.00	S001	17.01.90	2336
S S162	I	1	120.00			
S L697	I	0	60.00	S003	01.01.90	2337
S S163	I	1	400.00			
S L697	I	0	45.00	S002	28.01.90	2338
S S161	I	1	300.00			
S L697	C	0	−9.00	S001	24.01.90	c/n
S S162	C	1	−60.00			

(Continues)

Jenkins Jeans Co. Ltd.

01 Jan 90 Sales Analysis Page 1

Cust. Type	Product	Value	
S	L697	156.00	Vat
S	S161	500.00	Clothing
S	S162	140.00	Equipment
S	S163	400.00	Miscellaneous
Total		1 196.00	

The purchases ledger program

This program operates in an almost identical way to the sales ledger program and is used to record the individual suppliers of a business, giving details of purchases, returns, payments, and any other information which relates to creditors.

The control of purchasing is a key management function. All purchases must be bought and paid for at the right time, at the right quantity and quality, and at the right price. Management needs to have up-to-date information about all its suppliers. How long will they wait before payment? What discounts do they offer? Who is the person to contact in the event of queries?

The amount of money a business spends on its stock can be a major expenditure and therefore affects its cash flow and working capital. Has the business sufficient cash resources to pay its creditors on time?

A good computer program can provide the up-to-the-minute information management needs, including:

- a facility to store a large number of accounts;
- details of supplier's records;
- supplier turnover;
- printouts of the purchases journal;
- Vat analysis;
- automatic processing to the nominal ledger;
- analysis of purchases, payments and discounts;
- aged creditors analysis;
- a link-up to stock control.

The options available on the purchases ledger program are virtually the same as those of the sales program and the sub-menu, Ledger Transactions, is the one most frequently in use:

MENU: LEDGER TRANSACTIONS

1. Accounts Up-Date
2. Ledger Posting
3. Invoice & Credit Note Listing
4. Payments & Adjustments
5. Supplier Accounts
6. Aged Creditors List
7. List of Accounts
8. Outstanding Creditors Total
9. Terminate

Select and Press Number Required

The ledger transactions function would be used on a daily basis to record details relating to suppliers' accounts. Each of the options are summarised below:

1 **Accounts Up-Date**. The screen would display the following:

ACCOUNT NUMBER	NAME & ADDRESS
P001	John Harries 156 Ashly Road Parkstone Poole

SETTLEMENT DAYS	DISCOUNT RECEIVED	DAYS BEFORE SETTLEMENT	CREDIT LIMIT	CODE
30	5%	4	4 000	S

In the above example, P001 refers to the supplier, John Harries. This creditor allows 5 per cent cash discount if payment is made within 30 days and the cheque should be arranged to be paid within four days of the 30-day limit. The supplier has allowed a credit limit of up to £4000 at present. The Code 'S' signifies that the supplier is located in the South of England.

2 **Ledger Posting.** This function is used perhaps the most frequently, the cursor * flashing on screen would prompt the operator for the number of the account required. P001 would bring the details of J Harries on screen:

ACCOUNT	DATE	TYPE	REFERENCE	VALUE	VAT/DISC.	PERIOD
P001	11/1/90	I	8875	414	54	1
J. Harries						

In this example, Jenkins Jeans has purchased £414 of goods of which £54 is Vat. Under 'Type' the letter 'I' signifies that an invoice is to be entered, the invoice number is also to be entered under the heading 'Reference'.

Printouts of the purchases ledger program include the following:

3 **Invoice & Credit Note Listing.** The details of this function would be the same as for the purchases day book:

	£
Purchases	1 040
Vat	156
Total creditors	1 196

4 **Payments & Adjustments.** This function allows the operator to list all payments and adjustments for the period required. Totals are shown for:

	£	
Payments:	1 235	
Discounts:	15	
Adjustments:	1 500	(opening balances)

5 **Supplier Accounts**. All transactions relating to the creditor are shown, including:

date of entries
purchase invoices and credit notes
cheque numbers and payments
discounts received
the age of the amount due in months.

This is a function used frequently to check that payments are made on time and valuable discounts taken if they are available. For example, J Harries is owed £1124, all in the current month. If 30 days are allowed, then payment need not be made until February.

6 **Aged Creditors List**. The balance of each creditor is indicated and 'aged' according to the age of the amount due. In the printout, the total due for payment is all under the current month, £1446. This figure should equal the balance of the purchases ledger control account in the nominal ledger. The number of days on invoice (30), discount (5 per cent) and the days before cheque payment (4) are also shown.

7 **List of Accounts.** This provides a list of the supplier accounts required. Jenkins has only three of them at present. Details of supplier turnover, credit limit, settlement terms and code are also indicated.

8 **Outstanding Creditors Total.** This is not provided as a printout but the outstanding debt due to suppliers will be shown on screen and can also serve as a check with the purchase ledger control account.

Total creditors = £1446.

9 **Terminate.** This terminates the sub-menu and returns the operator to the main purchases ledger menu.

All input data can be validated by the system and any errors corrected by pressing appropriate keys.

The purchases ledger program printouts

Printouts from ledger transactions are as follows:

Option No. 3: Invoices and credit note listing;
Option No. 4: Payments and adjustments listing;
Option No. 5: Supplier accounts;
Option No. 6: Aged creditors list;
Option No. 7: List of accounts; and
Main purchases ledger menu – Option No. 3: Purchase analysis.

Option No. 3: Invoice and credit note listing

Jenkins Jeans Company Ltd.

01.01.90 P/L Invoices & Credit Notes (Today's) Page 1

A/c	Date	Type	Reference	Value	Goods	VAT	
P001	11.01.90	Invce	8875	414.00	360.00	54.00	J. Harries
P001	25.01.90	Invce	9320	460.00	400.00	60.00	J. Harries
P002	17.01.90	Invce	33391/4	138.00	120.00	18.00	D. Brown
P003	28.01.90	Invce	1212	184.00	160.00	24.00	R. James
Total Invoices				1 196.00	1 040.00	156.00	
Total Cr. Notes				0.00	0.00	0.00	
Total				1 196.00	1 040.00	156.00	

Note: acts as the Purchases Journal

Option No. 4: Payments and adjustments listing

Jenkins Jeans Company Ltd.

01.01.90 P/L Receipts & Adjusts (Today's) Page 1

A/c	Date	Type	Reference	Value	Period	
P001	01.01.90	Adjust	O/Balance	1 250.00	1	J. Harries
P001	25.01.90	Paymnt	Chq. 222222	−1 000.00	1	J. Harries
P002	01.01.90	Adjust	O/Balance	250.00	1	D. Brown
P002	28.01.90	Paymnt	Chq. 222223	−235.00	1	D. Brown
P002	28.01.90	Discnt	Chq. 222223	−15.00	1	D. Brown

(Continues)

A/c	Date	Type	Reference	Value	Period
Total Discounts				−15.00	
Total Payments				−1 235.00	
Total Refunds				0.00	
Total Adj – Contras				0.00	
Total Adj – Write Offs				0.00	
Total Adj – Misposts				0.00	
Total Adj – Discounts				0.00	
Total Adj – Sundry				1 500.00	
Total				250.00	

Option No. 5: Supplier accounts

J. Harries
156 Ashly Road
Parkstone
Poole

Account P001 — 01 Jan 1990

T/Over 760/Jan — Cr. Lim 4000

Date	Type	Reference	Status	Debit	Credit	Balance
01.01.90	Adjust	O/Balance	Jan		1 250.00	
11.01.90	Invoice	8875			414.00	
25.01.90	Invoice	9320			460.00	
25.01.90	Payment	Chq. 222222	Jan	1 000.00		

3 Months +	2 Months	1 Month	Current	Total
0.00	0.00	0.00	1 124.00	1 124.00

Note: indicates the turnover (£760) for the month (exc. vat)
credit limit £4000

D. Brown
55 The Broadway
Broadstone
Poole

Account P002 — 01 Jan 1990

T/Over 120/Jan — Cr. Lim 3000

Date	Type	Reference	Status	Debit	Credit	Balance
01.01.90	Adjust	O/Balance	Jan		250.00	
17.01.90	Invoice	33391/4			138.00	
28.01.90	Payment	Chq. 222223	Jan	235.00		
28.01.90	Discnt	Chq. 222223	Jan	15.00		

3 Months +	2 Months	1 Month	Current	Total
0.00	0.00	0.00	138.00	138.00

R. James
184 Old Wareham Road
Corfe Mullen
Wimborne

Account P003 | 01 Jan 1990

T/Over 160/Jan | Cr. Lim 3000

Date	Type	Reference	Status	Debit	Credit	Balance
28.01.90	Invoice	1212			184.00	

3 Months +	2 Months	1 Month	Current	Total
0.00	0.00	0.00	184.00	184.00

Option No. 6: Aged creditors list

Jenkins Jeans Company Ltd.

01.01.90 Aged Creditors List Page 1

A/c	3 Months +	2 Months	1 Month		Current	Total	Cr. Limit
P001	0.00	0.00		0.00	1 124.00	1 124.00	4 000
J. Harries		30	5.00%		4 Days		
P002	0.00	0.00		0.00	138.00	138.00	3 000
D. Brown		30	6.00%		4 Days		
P003	0.00	0.00		0.00	184.00	184.00	3 000
R. James		30	5.00%		4 Days		
Total	0.00	0.00		0.00	1 446.00	1 446.00	

Note: discount % (5% and 6%)
30 day invoices, 4 days before time expires for payment

Option No. 7: List of accounts

P001	J. Harries	30 5.00%		4 Days
	156 Ashly Road	Code S		
	Parkstone	Type B		
	Poole	Cr. Limit	4 000	
		T/Over	760/Jan	

(Continues)

P002	D. Brown	30 6.00%		4 Days
	55 The Broadway	Code S		
	Broadstone	Type B		
	Poole	Cr. Limit	3 000	
		T/Over	120/Jan	
P003	R. James	30 5.00%		4 Days
	184 Old Wareham Road	Code S		
	Corfe Mullen	Type B		
	Wimborne	Cr. Limit	3 000	
		T/Over	160/Jan	

Note: Code S indicates 'southern' trader
Type B indicates 'balance' brought forward each month
30 day invoices, discounts at 5 and 6%
4 days before payment is made
Credit limits and turnover (exc. vat) included

Purchases ledger menu – Option No. 3: Purchase analysis

Jenkins Jeans Company Ltd.

01 Jan 90 Purchase Analysis Input Page 1

Code	Type	VAT	Value	A/c	Date	Reference
S L696	I	0	54.00	P001	11.01.90	8875
S P161	I	1	360.00			
S L696	I	0	18.00	P002	17.01.90	33391/4
S P163	I	1	120.00			
S L696	I	0	60.00	P001	25.01.90	9320
S P162	I	1	400.00			
S L696	I	0	24.00	P003	28.01.90	1212
S P161	I	1	160.00			

(Continues)

Jenkins Jeans Company Ltd.

01 Jan 90	Purchase Analysis			Page 1
Suppl. Type	Product	Value		
S	L696	156.00	Vat	
S	P161	520.00	Clothing	
S	P162	400.00	Equipment	
S	P163	120.00	Miscellaneous	
Total		1 196.00		

Summary

1 Computer-based accounting programs are readily available to help businesses automate the recording of transactions and also to provide management with instant information to help them make better decisions.

2 Computer-based accounts gives immediate access to any section of information required. They give up-to-the-minute analysis of key accounting areas, for example, sales, purchases, stock, etc.

3 Computers save time and help a business to monitor and control information more easily and efficiently.

4 Most good software packages are user friendly, that is, they are easy for the operator to understand and use.

5 Computer systems are operated from menus displayed on the screen from a program. Selections are made by pressing the appropriate key to obtain the function needed. The sales and purchase programs may have many features all of which are designed to give immediate access to specific details when required.

6 Irrespective of which system is used, an accounting program will tend to give the same type of options which offer features designed to provide flexibility and a wide range of functions. Nearly all computer companies which produce software programs, offer separate modules, such as sales or purchases ledgers, which can be steadily built upon to make a fully-integrated network of accounting packages.

7 The presentation of details on either screen or hard copy will generally appear the same for most packages. Some of them will vary in the way accounts are visually presented. For example, in the sales ledger, the customers account may appear as:

MENU: SALES LEDGER

CUSTOMER ACCOUNTS:

Account No. S001 Account: J. Davies

Date	Reference	Details	Value	Debit	Credit
010190	Balance			800	
050190	2334	S161	200		
	vat	L697	30	230	
170190	2336	S162	120		
	vat	L697	18	138	
240190	c/n42	S162	60		
	vat	L697	9		69
280190	234566	C005	760		
	disc.	E645	40		800

Amount Outstanding: £299
Credit Limit: £4 000
Turnover this period: £260
Current Debt: £299
Other Debt:

QUESTIONS

1 Briefly describe the parts which make up the computer's hardware.

2 What is computer software? What kind of software is available in accounting?

3 Briefly explain why more large businesses tend to use computer programs rather than the traditional manual methods of recording financial information.

4 A computer program often works by a menu system. What is a menu in computer language? Give an example to illustrate your answer.

5 If you have access to a computer system and an accounting program, try to input the data from an appropriate journal question from the previous chapters.

6 Which type of businesses would not really benefit from the use of a business program?

7 In the printouts of the sales ledger program, check the following:

a) the function of option 3 (invoice and credit notes) and how it relates to the sales journal;
b) the function of option 5 (customer accounts) and how the information compares with a manual recording in the sales ledger;
c) the significance of option 7 (aged debtors) and its usefulness to management;
d) the function of option 3 (sales analysis) and the importance of having sub-totals for each sales category.

CHAPTER

10 Computer-based accounts: the nominal ledger program

- *What kind of information can a nominal ledger program provide?*
- *How can it assist management to make decisions?*

Introduction

The nominal ledger is at the heart of all accounting information. It gives details of all the accounts of the business, with the exception of individual debtors and creditors which are to be found in the sales and purchases ledgers. However, the nominal ledger will have the totals of these in the two control accounts, the sales and purchases ledger control.

Business management relies heavily on the speed of its accounting data in a form which is easily comprehensive and meaningful. It is therefore of importance to management to have a program which may be relied upon to retrieve and reorganise facts and figures from accounting records so that they can be assessed quickly and evaluated in order to make management more efficient and profitable.

There are a number of software packages available on the market which provide excellent programs incorporating many valuable features, including the preparation of final accounts (the trading and profit and loss account and the balance sheet), budgeting for both monthly and annual figures, and departmental analysis. *Pegasus*, *Sage* and other software accounting programs, generally include all these facilities.

The use of a good and reliable program ensures that immediately the last transaction has been entered into the system, management has its reports up-to-date. By merely pressing the right keys, the trial balance and the final accounts, at any given time, can be prepared and printouts (hard copies) run off as required.

General features

The features overleaf are often standard for a nominal ledger program in many software packages and include the following:

facility for large storage of accounts;
automatic double entry with each transaction;
integration with sales and purchases ledgers;
integration with other accounting packages – invoicing, stock control, payroll, etc.;
listing of nominal accounts;
automatic trial balance;
automatic final accounts;
printouts (hard copies) for individual accounts, listing transactions, trial balance, final accounts;
budget reports.

The accounting packages generally provide very sound business control systems. As long as the operator keys in the raw data precisely, the computer takes over and instantly updates the relevant accounts giving access to any information which is required.

Working a nominal ledger disk

A computer program will display only what information is fed into it and therefore an operator must still take absolute care when inputting data from any source document, for example, an invoice or credit note. If the input is right, then the output will be right. The program should provide an instant flow of information when required.

The nominal ledger program is loaded onto the computer's disk drive in the same way as with the sales and purchase ledger programs discussed in the last chapter. The date should be entered when the screen prompts and there may also be a requirement to supply a password code to get into the system. The data on the disk may hold important and confidential business information and may only be accessible to those who have authority to access it.

Once the date and the appropriate file letter or number has been entered, the system's main menu should appear on screen. Many software programs generally have these features:

MENU:

1. Sales Ledger	5. Payroll
2. Purchase Ledger	6. Invoicing
3. Nominal Ledger	7. Costing
4. Stock Control	8. Terminate

Select and Press appropriate
No. Required

To enter the nominal ledger option number 3 would be pressed. Once the nominal ledger file is on screen, it may then demand the password to be entered before further procedure is possible. Assuming we have the right codeword, the nominal ledger menu would appear:

MENU: Nominal Ledger

1. Ledger Transactions
2. Period End
3. Sales & Purchases Analysis
4. Special Reports

Select and Press appropriate
No. Required

The options are explained as follows:

1 **Ledger Transactions.** This option is the most frequently used on a day-to-day basis and will be discussed after outlining the other three options below.

2 **Period End.** This function is used to 'zeroise' the accounts at the end of a financial period. The new period will then commence with nil opening balances. Any outstanding balances therefore, will require opening entries to commence the new financial period.

3 **Sales & Purchases Analysis.** On some systems, it may be necessary to have a function which will transfer the information from the sales and bought ledgers and integrate it with the nominal ledger. By using this function, it will confirm that all entries relating to the personal ledgers will be transferred to the appropriate nominal accounts, that is, to sales, purchases, Vat, bank and the control accounts. The sales and purchases ledgers may either be operated independently, or integrated with the nominal ledger.

4 **Special Reports.** This option will give, either on screen or on printout, the financial reports, that is, the profit and loss account and the balance sheet. The significant point is that immediately after any transaction is entered, the financial statements will be updated instantly to give management the on-the-spot information they require.

The first option is used more frequently than the others. On pressing number 1, Ledger Transactions, the menu will appear on screen:

MENU: Nominal Ledger
Ledger Transactions

1. Accounts Up-date
2. Journal Entries
3. List Transactions
4. Account Enquiries
5. Trial Balance
6. List of Accounts
7. Terminate

Select and Press Appropriate
No. Required

If all transactions relating to the sales and purchases ledgers are required to be transferred to the nominal ledger as part of an integrated system, then on some systems it will be necessary to confirm the transfer by operating the sales and purchases analysis (option number 3), on the main nominal ledger menu.

It may be that information is required either on screen or on printout. If a printout is needed, the prompt on the screen will indicate the printer is available and the necessary key to be pressed, for example, the space bar.

Examples

1 **Accounts Up-date.** The same procedure applies here as is the case with the sales and purchases ledgers. The cursor prompts the operator to enter the account number required, or if it is a new account to allocate a new account number and the name of the new account.

Acc No.	Account Name
C005	BANK ACCOUNT
Budget	**Report Code**
£15 000	B05

Budget: There may be a budget figure allocated to each account. In the case of the bank account, a sum of £15 000 has been allocated for overdraft facilities.

Report Code: This may be used to identify certain aspects of where the account is to be placed in relation to the financial reports. For example:

P: to be placed in profit and loss account;

B: to be placed in the balance sheet.

If any details are to be changed concerning any account, then this option will be used.

2 **Journal Entries.** This function is to be used to enter any transaction relating to any account other than individual debtors or creditors which are listed in the sales and purchases ledgers. All transactions must follow strictly the double-entry principle, commencing with debit entries first and then the corresponding credit entries. The respective accounts will then be updated once the return key is pressed. In the example below, the entry refers to Jenkins Jeans Co Ltd, as illustrated in the program:

Date	Input By	Narrative
31/01	RG	Cash Sales to Bank

Acc No.	Account Name	Debit	Credit	Comments
C005	Bank a/c	3 220		Sales & Vat
S161	Sales a/c		2 800	Bank
L697	Vat a/c		420	Bank
END				

All the nominal transactions for the day can be entered using this option. All debit figures must equal all credit figures. If the totals do not match up, the computer will not accept the entry and will make some rather unpleasant warning sounds. It is usual to type the word 'End' in the account number column to indicate to the system that the final entry has been made. When the return key is pressed, the entries will be verified and all appropriate accounts will be updated. The ESC key will return the operator back to the 'Ledger Transactions' menu.

3 List Transactions. This option allows the operator to either view on screen or take a printout of the transactions for the day or for any longer period required.
The screen will display:

1st Entry	Last Entry
1	5

To examine all the transactions stored to date, press the return key in each box. In the Jenkins Jeans Co Ltd program, there are five entries relating to transactions.

4 Account Enquiries. This option allows the operator to either view on screen or take a printout of any nominal ledger account. The account number is entered where the screen prompts, then it will indicate:

Acc No.

R161

STOCK ACCOUNT
Hard Copy? Y/N

If 'no' is requested the account will appear on screen.
If 'yes' is requested the printer will be activated and a printout is produced.

5 **The Trial Balance.** This option allows the operator to view or take a printout of the trial balance, as up-to-date as the last transaction entered and instantly accessible. The accounts in the example are listed according to their code number groups:

A = assets
C = control and bank accounts
E = expenses
L = liabilities and capital accounts
P = purchases accounts
S = sales accounts

6 **List of Accounts.** The same procedure applies as in option number 3. The prompt on screen will require the operator to enter the appropriate account numbers required or if the return key is pressed in each box all the accounts will be listed. A printout may be taken if required.

7 **Terminate.** This allows the operator to return to the main menu of the nominal ledger.

The following represent some of the printouts taken of various nominal ledger functions. They relate to the accounts of Jenkins Jeans Co Ltd and are a continuation of the exercise in Chapter 9.

The nominal ledger program printouts

Printouts from ledger transactions are as follows:

Option No. 2: Journal Entries;
Option No. 4: Account Enquiries;
Option No. 5: The Trial Balance;
Option No. 6: List of Accounts.

Option No. 2: Journal entries (1 to 5)

Jenkins Jeans Co Ltd.

01.01.90 Transaction List Page 1

Entry 1 01.01.90 Type = Journal

		Dr	Cr
A001	Furniture & Equipment	4 500.00	
A002	Motor Vehicles	4 000.00	
R161	Stock (Balance Sheet)	1 000.00	
C001	Sales Ledger Control	1 250.00	
C005	Bank	750.00	
C002	Purchases Ledger Control		1 500.00
D680	Capital		10 000.00
Input By RG		11 500.00	11 500.00

(Continues)

Entry 2 31.01.90 Type = Journal

		Dr	Cr	
C005	Bank	3 220.00		sales
S161	Sales (clothing)		2 000.00	bank
S162	Sales (equipment)		800.00	bank
L697	VAT Outputs		420.00	bank
Input By RG		3 220.00	3 220.00	
Grand Total				
		14 720.00	14 720.00	

Note: 1. Opening Entries as per Balance Sheet
2. Cash Sales into Bank

Jenkins Jeans Co Ltd.

01.01.90 Transaction List Page 1

Entry 3 31.01.90 Type = Journal

		Dr	Cr	
E134	Wages	400.00		bank
E135	Overheads	500.00		bank
C005	Bank		900.00	wages & overheads
Input By RG		900.00	900.00	

Entry 4 31.01.90 Type = Journal

		Dr	Cr	
C001	Sales Ledger Control	1 196.00		sales & vat
S161	Sales (clothing)		500.00	
S162	Sales (equipment)		140.00	
S163	Sales (miscellaneous)		400.00	
L697	VAT Outputs		156.00	
C005	Bank	1 510.00		receipts
E645	Discount allowed	40.00		discount
C001	Sales Ledger Control		1 550.00	
Input By RG		2 746.00	2 746.00	
Grand Total				
		3 646.00	3 646.00	

(Continues)

Note: 3. Payments for Wages & Overheads by cheque
4. Transfer of Entries from Sales Ledger Program
Check with Sales Ledger Options Nos. 3 & 4

Jenkins Jeans Co Ltd.

01.01.90 Transaction List Page 1

Entry 5 31.01.90 Type = Journal

		Dr	Cr	
P161	Purchases (clothing)	520.00		
P162	Purchases (equipment)	400.00		
P163	Purchases (miscellaneous)	120.00		
L696	VAT Inputs	156.00		
C002	Purchases Ledger Control		1 196.00	purch. & vat
C002	Purchases Ledger Control	1 250.00		
C005	Bank		1 235.00	payments
P360	Discount Received		15.00	discount
Input By RG		2 446.00	2 446.00	
Grand Total		2 446.00	2 446.00	

Note: 5. Transfer of Entries from Purchase Ledger Program
Check with Purchase Ledger Options Nos. 3 & 4

Option No. 4: Account enquiries

Furniture & Equipment Account A001 01 Jan 1990

Date	Entry	Type	Input By	Dr	Cr	Comment
01.01.90	1	Journal	RG	4 500.00		
		Account Total		4 500.00		

Motor Vehicles Account A002 01 Jan 1990

Date	Entry	Type	Input By	Dr	Cr	Comment
01.01.90	1	Journal	RG	4 000.00		
		Account Total		4 000.00		

(Continues)

Sales Ledger Control — Account C001 — 01 Jan 1990

Date	Entry	Type	Input By	Dr	Cr	Comment
01.01.90	1	Journal	RG	1 250.00		
31.01.90	4	Journal	RG	1 196.00		sales & vat
31.01.90	4	Journal	RG		1 550.00	
		Account Total		896.00		

Purchase Ledger Control — Account C002 — 01 Jan 1990

Date	Entry	Type	Input By	Dr	Cr	Comment
01.01.90	1	Journal	RG		1 500.00	
31.01.90	5	Journal	RG		1 196.00	purch. & vat
31.01.90	5	Journal	RG	1 250.00		
		Account Total			1 446.00	

Bank — Account C005 — 01 Jan 1990

Date	Entry	Type	Input By	Dr	Cr	Comment
01.01.90	1	Journal	RG	750.00		
31.01.90	2	Journal	RG	3 220.00		sales
31.01.90	3	Journal	RG		900.00	wages & overheads
31.01.90	4	Journal	RG	1 510.00		receipts
31.01.90	5	Journal	RG		1 235.00	payments
		Account Total		3 345.00		

Capital — Account D680 — 01 Jan 1990

Date	Entry	Type	Input By	Dr	Cr	Comment
01.01.90	1	Journal	RG		10 000.00	
		Account Total			10 000.00	

VAT Inputs — Account L696 — 01 Jan 1990

Date	Entry	Type	Input By	Dr	Cr	Comment
31.01.90	5	Journal	RG	156.00		
		Account Total		156.00		

VAT Outputs Account L697 01 Jan 1990

Date	Entry	Type	Input By	Dr	Cr	Comment
31.01.90	2	Journal	RG		420.00	bank
31.01.90	4	Journal	RG		156.00	
		Account Total			576.00	

Discount Received Account P360 01 Jan 1990

Date	Entry	Type	Input By	Dr	Cr	Comment
31.01.90	5	Journal	RG		15.00	discount
		Account Total			15.00	

Stock (Balance Sheet) Account R161 01 Jan 1990

Date	Entry	Type	Input By	Dr	Cr	Comment
01.01.90	1	Journal	RG	1 000.00		
		Account Total		1 000.00		

Purchases (clothing) Account P161 01 Jan 1990

Date	Entry	Type	Input By	Dr	Cr	Comment
31.01.90	5	Journal	RG	520.00		
		Account Total		520.00		

Purchases (Equipment) Account P162 01 Jan 1990

Date	Entry	Type	Input By	Dr	Cr	Comment
31.01.90	5	Journal	RG	400.00		
		Account Total		400.00		

Purchases (miscellaneous) Account P163 01 Jan 1990

Date	Entry	Type	Input By	Dr	Cr	Comment
31.01.90	5	Journal	RG	120.00		
		Account Total		120.00		

Sales (clothing) Account S161 01 Jan 1990

Date	Entry	Type	Input By	Dr	Cr	Comment
31.01.90	2	Journal	RG		2 000.00	bank
31.01.90	4	Journal	RG		500.00	
		Account Total			2 500.00	

Sales (equipment) Account S162 01 Jan 1990

Date	Entry	Type	Input By	Dr	Cr	Comment
31.01.90	2	Journal	RG		800.00	bank
31.01.90	4	Journal	RG		140.00	
		Account Total			940.00	

Sales (miscellaneous) Account S163 01 Jan 1990

Date	Entry	Type	Input By	Dr	Cr	Comment
31.01.90	4	Journal	RG		400.00	
		Account Total			400.00	

Wages Account E134 01 Jan 1990

Date	Entry	Type	Input By	Dr	Cr	Comment
31.01.90	3	Journal	RG	400.00		bank
		Account Total		400.00		

Overheads Account E135 01 Jan 1990

Date	Entry	Type	Input By	Dr	Cr	Comment
31.01.90	3	Journal	RG	500.00		bank
		Account Total		500.00		

Discount allowed Account E645 01 Jan 1990

Date	Entry	Type	Input By	Dr	Cr	Comment
31.01.90	4	Journal	RG	40.00		discount
		Account Total		40.00		

Option No. 5: The trial balance

Jenkins Jeans Co Ltd.

01.01.90 Summary Trial Balance Page 1

		Dr	Cr
A001	Furniture & Equipment	4 500.00	
A002	Motor Vehicles	4 000.00	
C001	Sales Ledger Control	896.00	
C002	Purchases Ledger Control		1 446.00
C005	Bank	3 345.00	
D680	Capital		10 000.00
E134	Wages	400.00	
E135	Overheads	500.00	
E645	Discounts allowed	40.00	
L696	VAT Inputs	156.00	
L697	VAT Outputs		576.00
P161	Purchases (clothing)	520.00	
P162	Purchases (equipment)	400.00	
P163	Purchases (miscellaneous)	120.00	
P360	Discount Received		15.00
R161	Stock (Balance Sheet)	1 000.00	
S161	Sales (clothing)		2 500.00
S162	Sales (equipment)		940.00
S163	Sales (miscellaneous)		400.00
Grand Totals		15 877.00	15 877.00

Option No. 6: List of accounts

Jenkins Jeans Co Ltd.

01.01.90 Nominal Accounts Page 1

A/c	Account Name	Budget	Report Code
A001	Furniture & Equipment	0	B01
A002	Motor Vehicles	0	B02
C001	Sales Ledger Control	0	B03
C002	Purchases Ledger Control	0	B04
C005	Bank	0	B05
D680	Capital	0	B06
E134	Wages	0	P01
E135	Overheads	0	P02
E645	Discount allowed	0	P03

(Continues)

L696	VAT Inputs	0	B07
L697	VAT Outputs	0	B08
P161	Purchases (clothing)	0	P04
P162	Purchases (equipment)	0	P05
P163	Purchases (miscellaneous)	0	P06
P360	Discount Received	0	P07
R161	Stock (Balance Sheet)	0	B09
S161	Sales (clothing)	0	P08
S162	Sales (equipment)	0	P09
S163	Sales (miscellaneous)	0	P10
X998	Sales Suspense	0	B11
X999	Purchases Suspense	0	B10

Summary

1 The nominal ledger is central to all accounting information. If it is to help management (including owners) make sound decisions, all accounts must be thoroughly up-to-date and easily accessible.

2 A nominal ledger program should provide management with a flow of information which is easy to use and instantly available, including the preparation of financial reports either on screen or printout (hard copy).

3 A nominal ledger program may be part of an integrated package which not only includes the sales and bought ledgers, but also stock control, wages, invoicing and any other aspect which may help the organisation in keeping its records, either to be viewed on screen or taken as printouts.

4 The accuracy of keeping records still lies with the operator. The input of information must be 100 per cent accurate, otherwise the computer will store incorrect information. However, all input will automatically follow the double-entry principle and if figures do not match up, the program will have its own method of letting the user know.

5 The nominal ledger program, as with most software packages, operates on a system of menus. That is, a list of options are available to the operator for the purpose of using a wide range of different functions. An operator should be fully conversant with the options available and know what each can do and also how they integrate within the program as a whole.

QUESTIONS

1 What type of functions are available on a nominal ledger program?

2 What facility is used to record day-to-day transactions and in which menu does this occur? Give some examples.

3 How may details from the sales and purchases ledgers be transferred to the nominal ledger?

4 Check the exercise of Jenkins Jeans Co Ltd fully by linking Chapters 9 and 10. For example, the balance sheet should reflect journal entry number 1. Make sure all transactions are followed through on the printouts, concluding with the trial balance.

5 Which function would be used if the financial statements were required, after the trial balance had been prepared?

6 When operating option 2 (journal entries), check how the daily transactions are recorded, adopting the double-entry principle. If debit entries fail to equal credit entries, how might the computer respond?

7 Is the presentation of the nominal accounts in the program used any different from that of a manual system?

CHAPTER

11 The cash book

- *What function does the cash book provide?*
- *How does it assist in ledger posting?*
- *How can a modified cash book assist management?*

Introduction

The cash book is an extension of the nominal ledger and is used to record all transactions relating to the cash or bank accounts. If an organisation has many cash or banking transactions, it may be an improvement in the accounting system to separate these from the mainstream transactions of the nominal ledger and enter them into some form of cash book.

The cash book records receipts and payments relating to the cash and bank accounts. The receipts are entered on the left-hand side of the book (debit) and payments on the right-hand side (credit):

(Dr)	*Receipts*			*Payments*		*(Cr)*
	Cash	*Bank*			*Cash*	*Bank*
	£	£			£	£

Recording: debit – cash or bank increases (asset +);
credit – cash or bank decreases (asset −).

A further facility which can be used in the design of a cash book is to have columns to record cash discounts. If a cash discount is offered to customers to encourage them to pay their accounts more promptly, the discount taken by customers can be recorded at the same time their payment is made.

Example: debit side of cash book

D Smith (debtor) sends a cheque of £200 to settle his account of £210.

	Discount allowed	*Cash account*	*Bank account*
	£	£	£
D Smith	10		200

Example: credit side of cash book

R Pearce sends a cheque of £675 to International, receiving a £15 discount for prompt settlement of account:

	Discount received	*Cash account*	*Bank account*
	£	£	£
International	15		675

The division between cash and credit transactions

A business needs to record transactions on credit in two stages:

1 at the point of sale or purchase;
2 at the point when cash/bank is received or paid.

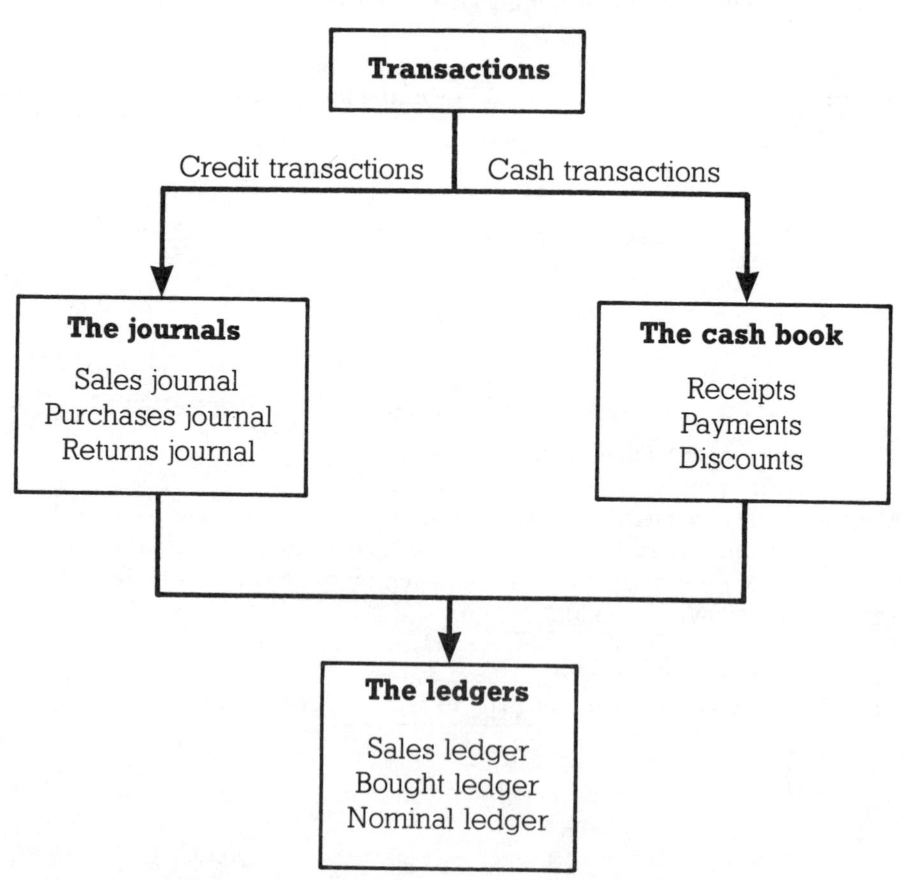

Example of cash book transactions

R Pearce recorded the following transactions during the month of August:

1/8	Balances brought forward, cash £200, bank £1925 (Dr).
5/8	Paid general expenses, cheque £50.
6/8	Cash sales, £420.
6/8	Personal drawings (R Pearce) £120 cash.
7/8	D Smith settles his account, £200 cheque, discount £10.
10/8	Southern Electricity bill paid by cheque, £43.
12/8	General expenses, cheque £50.
13/8	Cash sales, £345.
13/8	Drawings, £120 cash.
15/8	Southern Gas, £85 cheque.
19/8	From B Kings, cheque £420, in settlement of debt, £441.50.
20/8	Drawings, £120 cash.
20/8	Cash sales, £410.
21/8	Paid cash, £800, into bank. (Contra entry, credit cash £800, debit bank £800.)
23/8	Paid for stationery, £25 cash.
26/8	General expenses, cheque £50.
27/8	Cash sales, £450.
27/8	Drawings, £120 cash.
28/8	British Telecom (telephone), £67 cheque.
30/8	Payments to creditors (by cheque): Slazenger Sports £250 Metro Sports £1000 Auto £500
31/8	Paid International £675 cheque, discount received, £15.
31/8	Drawings, £150 cash.

REQUIRED:

1. Prepare the cash book of R Pearce for the month of August. Bring down the cash and bank balances on 1 September.
2. Post the personal accounts of debtors and creditors to their respective accounts in the sales and bought ledgers.
3. Post other accounts relating to sales, expenses and drawings to their respective accounts in the nominal ledger.
4. Post the totals of discount allowed and received to the nominal ledger.

NOTES

In order to complete the double-entry aspect of recording for each transaction, the debit entries of the cash book are posted to the credit side of their respective ledger accounts; the credit entries are posted to the debit side of their respective ledger accounts. The two discount totals remain on the same side because only a tally of the totals are recorded (the double entry is already completed when entries are posted to personal accounts).

The cash book of R Pearce for the month of August

Ref: C9

(Dr)	*Receipts*	*Discount allowed* £	*Cash* £	*Bank* £		*Payments*	*Discount received* £	*Cash* £	*Bank* £ (Cr)
1/8	Balances b/f		200	1 925	5/8	General expenses			50
6/8	Sales		420		6/8	Drawings		120	
7/8	D Smith	10.0		200	10/8	SEB			43
13/8	Sales		345		12/8	General expenses			50
19/8	B Kings	21.5		420	13/8	Drawings		120	
20/8	Sales		410		15/8	SG (gas)			85
21/8	Contra (cash)			800	20/8	Drawings		120	
27/8	Sales		450		21/8	Contra (bank)		800	
					23/8	Stationery		25	
					26/8	General expenses			50
					27/8	Drawings		120	
					28/8	BT (telephone)			67
					30/8	Slazenger			250
						Metro			1 000
						Auto			500
					31/8	International	15		675
						Drawings		150	
						Balances c/f		370	575
		31.5	1 825	3 345			15	1 825	3 345
1/9	Balances b/f		370	575					

Sales ledger

		Folio £	Debit £	Credit £	Balance £
D Smith account S11					
1/8	Balance				210.0 Dr
7/8	Bank	C9		200	
	Discount allowed			10	—
B Kings account S09					
1/8	Balance				441.5 Dr
19/8	Bank	C9		420	
	Discount allowed			21.5	—

Bought ledger

		Folio £	Debit £	Credit £	Balance £	
Slazenger Sports account P65						
1/8	Balance				594.1	Cr
30/8	Bank	C9	250		344.1	
Metro Sports account P60						
10/8	Balance				1 909.0	Cr
30/8	Bank	C9	1 000		909.0	
Auto Sports account P55						
27/8	Balance				920.0	Cr
30/8	Bank	C9	500		420.0	
International account P70						
21/8	Balance				690.0	Cr
31/8	Bank	C9	675			
	Discount received		15		—	

Nominal ledger

		Folio £	Debit £	Credit £	Balance £	
Sales account N42						
1/8	Balance				2 480	Cr
6/8	Cash	C9		420	2 900	
13/8	Cash	C9		345	3 245	
20/8	Cash	C9		410	3 655	
27/8	Cash	C9		450	4 105	
General expenses account N36						
1/8	Balance				380	Dr
5/8	Bank	C9	50.0		430	
12/8	Bank	C9	50.0		480	
26/8	Bank		50.0		530	
Drawings account N31						
1/8	Balance				1 020	Dr
6/8	Cash	C9	120.0		1 140	
13/8	Cash	C9	120.0		1 260	
20/8	Cash	C9	120.0		1 380	
27/8	Cash	C9	120.0		1 500	
31/8	Cash	C9	150.0		1 650	

(Continues)

		Folio	Debit	Credit	Balance
Light and heat account N37					
1/8	Balance				280.0 Dr
10/8	Bank	C9	43.0		323.0
15/8	Bank	C9	85.0		408.0
Stationery account N38					
1/8	Balance				20.0 Dr
23/8	Bank	C9	25.0		45.0
Telephone account N39					
1/8	Balance				55.0 Dr
28/8	Bank	C9	67.0		122.0
Discount allowed account N34					
1/8	Balance				70.0 Dr
7/8	Bank	C9	10.0		80.0
19/8	Bank	C9	21.5		101.5
Discount received account N35					
1/8	Balance				60.0 Cr
31/8	Bank	C9		15	75.0

A modified cash book

In practice there are many different types of cash book, each designed and adapted to suit the nature of the business. If R Pearce, for example, wanted to bank his cash sales each day and retain a cash float for his change, he may want a different format to analyse his takings and expenses. He may prefer to:

a) show sales and Vat separately;
b) analyse separate debtors' and creditors' totals to facilitate posting to the control accounts in the nominal ledger;
c) use separate columns for general expenses and his drawings;
d) group all his other expenses under the heading 'overheads'.

R Pearce's modified cash book is shown opposite.

A modified cash book – R Pearce

Date	Details	Discount allowed £	Debtors £	Sales £	Vat £	Total £	Bank £
1/8	Balance b/f						1 925
6/8	Sales			365	55	420	
7/8	D Smith	10.0	200			200	
13/8	Sales			300	45	345	
19/8	B Kings	21.5	420			420	
20/8	Sales			356	54	410	
27/8	Sales			391	59	450	
		31.5	620	1 412	213	2 245	2 245
							4 170
1/9	Balance b/f						745

Date	Details	Discount received £	Cred-itors £	General expenses £	Over-heads £	Drawings £	Total £	Bank £
5/8	General expenses			50			50	
6/8	Drawings					120	120	
10/8	SEB				43		43	
12/8	General expenses			50			50	
13/8	Drawings					120	120	
15/8	SG (gas)				85		85	
20/8	Drawings					120	120	
23/8	Stationery				25		25	
26/8	General expenses			50			50	
27/8	Drawings					120	120	
28/8	BT (telephone)				67		67	
30/8	Slazenger		250				250	
	Metro		1 000				1 000	
	Auto		500				500	
31/8	International	15	675				675	
	Drawings					150	150	
		15	2 425	150	220	630	3 425	3 425
31/8	Balance c/f							745
								4 170

NOTE

The advantage of this cash book format is that:

a) total columns identify group figures;

b) totals facilitate ledger postings.

Nominal ledger

		Folio £	Debit £	Credit £	Balance £
Sales account N42					
1/8	Balance				2 480.0 Cr
31/8	Bank	C9		1 412.0	3 892.0
Vat account N30					
1/8	Balance				147.9 Cr
31/8	Bank	C9		213.0	360.9
General expenses account N36					
1/8	Balance				380.0 Dr
31/8	Bank	C9	150.0		530.0
Overheads account N37					
1/8	Balance				355.0 Dr
31/8	Bank	C9	220.0		575.0
Drawings account N31					
1/8	Balance				1 020.0 Dr
31/8	Bank	C9	630.0		1 650.0
Bought ledger control account N45					
30/8	Balance				4 113.1 Cr
31/8	Bank	C9	2 425.0		
	Discount received		15.0		1 673.1
Sales ledger control account N40					
30/8	Balance				2 755.5 Dr
31/8	Bank	C9		620.0	
	Discount allowed			31.5	2 104.0
Discount allowed account N34					
1/8	Balance				70.0 Dr
31/8	Bank	C9	31.5		101.5
Discount received account N35					
1/8	Balance				60.0 Cr
31/8	Bank	C9		15.0	75.0

Summary

1 The cash book is used to separate all cash and bank transactions from the nominal ledger, thereby allowing more space for other accounts.

2 In practice, cash books are modified and designed to meet the needs of the business, probably having a number of columns for analysis purposes.

3 If a computer program is used for the nominal ledger (in Chapter 10), the bank account would perhaps be coded to analyse different groups of receipts and expenditure.

4 Making entries in a cash book is only half of a transaction. The corresponding other half needs to be recorded in the respective ledger account.

5 Debit entries in the cash book are posted to the credit side of their respective ledger accounts. Credit entries are posted to the debit side. The discount totals remain on the same side when posted to the ledger (to show total balances).

6 By using analysis columns in a modified cash book format, the posting to the nominal ledger is made far easier by simply entering total rather than individual figures. For example, the totals for both debtors' receipts and creditors' payments can be posted to the sales and bought ledger control accounts.

QUESTIONS

1 The following cash/bank transactions occurred during April in the books of G Whitehall:

		£	
1/4	Balances brought forward:		
	Cash	250	Dr
	Bank	1 725	Dr
2/4	Cash sales (week).	440	
3/4	General expenses, cash.	50	
5/4	Drawings (G Whitehall), cash.	125	
9/4	Cash sales.	385	
10/4	Paid Rawlings (creditor) £975 cheque, having been allowed a $2\frac{1}{2}$ per cent discount (on £1000).		
11/4	Assistant's wages, cash.	85	
13/4	Insurance premium by cheque.	122	
16/4	Cash sales into bank.	400	
18/4	General expenses, cash.	50	
20/4	Contra – cash to bank.	500	
23/4	Cash sales.	410	
25/4	Received from Barnes, cheque £390, in settlement of £400 account.		
27/4	General expenses, cash.	50	

(Continues)

		£
28/4	Assistant's wages, cash.	85
30/4	Received from Ewing, cheque £585, in settlement of £600 account.	
30/4	Cash sales into bank.	420
30/4	Paid Long (creditor) cheque £780, in settlement of £800 account.	

REQUIRED:

a) Prepare the cash book of G Whitehall for the month of April and bring down the balances on 1 May.
b) Explain how the personal accounts of G Whitehall would be posted to his sales and bought ledgers.

2 The following balances were brought down from the cash book of B Kings on 1 June:

Cash	£220 Dr	
Bank	£420 Cr	(Overdrawn)

The transactions which occurred during June were as follows:

		£
1/6	Paid general expenses, cheque.	75
5/6	Cash sales into bank.	755
6/6	Paid a cheque to P Williams £290, having been allowed a £10 discount.	
12/6	Cash sales.	635
13/6	Paid general expenses, cheque.	80
14/6	Drawings, cash.	150
15/6	Paid for advertising, cheque.	105
15/6	Transferred to bank (contra).	400
19/6	Cash sales into bank.	785
20/6	Paid cheque to J Grant on account.	600
25/6	Received cheque from P Gibbs, £390 in settlement of £400 account.	
25/6	Received cheque from G Walton in settlement of £500 account, less 5 per cent discount.	
26/6	Cash sales into bank.	625
26/6	Drawings, cheque.	180
28/6	Paid general expenses, cheque.	75
30/6	Paid bills for light and heat, cheque.	115

REQUIRED:

a) Prepare the cash book for B Kings for the month of June and bring down the balances on 1 July.
b) Prepare the nominal ledger accounts for sales and general expenses, commencing balances on 1 June with 'nil'.

3 On 1 May, P Goldney had the following balances in his books:

	£
Cash book:	
Cash	350 Dr
Bank	825 Dr
Sales ledger:	
E Allen	400 Dr
M Doe	360 Dr
Bought ledger:	
R Baker	875 Cr
V Winch	380 Cr

During the month of May, the transactions of P Goldney were as follows:

Cheques paid:
2/5 Withdrew from bank, for personal use, £150 per week (to 30 May).
3/5 To R Baker in settlement of account, £850.
7/5 To Southern Gas, £184.
12/5 To Southern Electricity Board, £95.
18/5 To V Winch, £361 in settlement.

Cheques received:
25/5 From E Allen, £390, in settlement of account.
27/5 From M Doe, in settlement, less 5 per cent discount.
30/5 From Inland Revenue, rebate of £335.

Cash received:
5/5 Cash sales £725, £500 into bank.
12/5 Cash sales £800, all into bank.
19/5 Cash sales £650, £500 into bank.
26/5 Cash sales £735, all into bank.

Cash paid:
5/5 Shop assistant's wages, £80 per week (to 26 May).
7/5 General expenses, £40 per week (to 28 May).
10/5 Petty cash, £100.

REQUIRED:

a) Prepare the cash book for P Goldney for the month of May and bring down the balances on 1 June.
b) Show the personal accounts of P Goldney as they would appear in his ledgers on 31 May.

4 Entrepreneur, I Creese, used a modified cash book in his business. All payments were made by cheque, all shop takings banked each day. He retained an adequate cash float for his 'change'.

On the debit side of his cash book he used columns for:

Discount allowed	*Debtors*	*Sales*	*Bank*
£	£	£	£

On the payments side (credit), he had columns for:

Discount received	*Creditors*	*Drawings*	*Wages*	*Other expenses*	*Bank*
£	£	£	£	£	£

On 1 June, I Creese's bank balance was £485 Dr. During the month, his transactions were:

Money received:

		£
3/6	Cash sales for the week	450
10/6	Cash sales for the week	385
17/6	Cash sales for the week	455
24/6	Cash sales for the week	435

All shop takings are banked on the dates given.

5/6	From Lewis £195, discount £5.
11/6	From Smith £100 on account.
13/6	From Taylor £475, discount £15.
20/6	From Johnson £250 on account.

Cheques issued:

2/6	Drawings, £120 per week (to 30 May).
5/6	Wages, £60 per week (to 26 May).
10/6	To B Woods, £1250 on account.
11/6	General expenses, £170.
15/6	Rates, £345.
21/6	To R Carlton, £570 in settlement of £600 account.
25/6	General expenses, £150.
27/6	Petty cash, £100.

REQUIRED:

Draw up the cash book (modified) for I Creese, for the month of June, balancing at the end of the month and bringing down the balance on 1 July.

5 On 1 January L Dawson, a retailer, has the following balances in his cash book: cash £42; bank (overdrawn) £150. During January his cash transactions were as follows:

Cheques paid:

January 3	To Smith for £195 in settlement of £200 debt.
9	To Harrison £76 in settlement of £80 debt.
17	To Jones £160 on account.
22	Withdrawn from bank to cash £200 (contra).
28	Proprietor took for his own use £80 (drawings).

Cheques received:

16	From Bradshaw £95 in settlement of £100 account.
22	From Green £50 on account.

Cash received:

5	Shop takings for the week £125, £100 in bank.
12	Shop takings for the week £180, £125 in bank.
19	Shop takings for the week £124, £100 in bank.
26	Shop takings for the week £130, £100 in bank.

Cash paid:

5	Assistant's wages, £35 per week for the month, to 26 January.
22	Gas bill, £56.
27	Electricity bill, £27. Telephone, £30.

REQUIRED:

a) Prepare a cash book for Dawson for the month ending 31 January and bring down the balances on the next day.
b) What do you think 'returned to drawer' or 'R/D' means marked on a cheque?

6 A wine shop owned by R Lees kept an analysis cash book using columns for: wine, beer and lager, spirits, other sales, total sales, Vat and bank. The daily takings are banked each day at the local branch. The cash register calculates the Vat separately when a sale goes through the till.

The takings over four days were as follows:

		Wine	*Beer and lager*	*Spirits*	*Other sales*	*Total sales*
		£	£	£	£	£
June 2	Takings	200.0	250.0	80.0	30.0	
	Vat	30.0	37.5	12.0	4.5	
3	Takings	150.0	200.0	50.0	20.0	
	Vat	22.5	30.0	7.5	3.0	

(Continues)

		Wine	*Beer and lager*	*Spirits*	*Other sales*	*Total sales*
		£	£	£	£	£
4	Takings	180.0	240.0	60.0	24.0	
	Vat	27.0	36.0	9.0	3.6	
5	Takings	300.0	340.0	100.0	60.0	
	Vat	45.0	51.0	15.0	9.0	

REQUIRED:

a) Prepare a suitable cash book using the above columns to analyse the different sale categories.
b) Post the sales and Vat to the ledger.
c) Why is it sometimes useful to make analysis columns?

7 At 1 May, Jack, a retailer, has the following balances in his cash book: cash in hand £42; overdraft at bank £138.

During the month of May:

Cheques were issued as follows:

2 To Surrey for £95 in full settlement of a debt of £100.
8 To Hampshire who is owed £80 and who is prepared to allow $2\frac{1}{2}$ per cent cash discount.
19 To Kent RDC £66 in payment of rates.
25 Withdrawn from bank for use as change in the till, £20.
31 Proprietor withdrew for private purposes £100.

Cheques were received as follows:

17 From Mrs Lancashire £26 in payment of a monthly account.
(On 30 May you are advised by the bank that this cheque has been returned marked R/D.)

Cash received during the month:

Shop takings for week ending 5 May £125, of which £100 was paid to the bank.
Shop takings for week ending 12 May £144, of which £120 was paid to the bank.
Shop takings for week ending 19 May £159, of which £150 was paid to the bank.
Shop takings for week ending 26 May £148, of which £105 was paid to the bank.

Cash paid out during month:

Wages 5, 12, 19, 26 of month; £28 on each date.
23 Telephone account £15.
29 Delivery charges £8.

You are required to draw up a cash book for the month of May and enter the above transactions in date order. Balance the book as at 31 May and bring down the balances.

(RSA)

8 J Durham had the following balances in her cash book on 1 July:

	£
Cash	200
Bank	455 Cr (Overdraft)

During the month the transactions were as follows:

Cheques received:		£	Discount allowed:	£
2/7	Jackson and Son	186		14.00
3/7	Chappell Ltd	250		18.75
12/7	Clogg and Co	100		—
28/7	Hughes, K	358		17.90

Cheques issued:		£	Discount received:	£
2/7	Mitre Sports	500.00		12.50
4/7	Arena	160.00		8.00
22/7	Dunlop	80.50		—
28/7	Slazenger Sport	172.50		7.50

Cash received:

Week ending			
6/7	Shop takings	258.75	Paid £200 into Bank
13/7	Shop takings	196.80	Paid £150 into Bank
20/7	Shop takings	220.00	Paid £175 into Bank
27/7	Shop takings	187.75	Paid £150 into Bank

Cash paid out:

6, 13, 20, 27/7	Assistant salaries	£56.75 (each date)
22/7	Advertising	£42.24
23/7	Delivery expenses	£14.75
25/7	Petty expenses	£8.50
29/7	Delivery expenses	£10.50

REQUIRED:

a) Enter the above transactions in *date order* for the month of July.

b) Ledger accounts required – for nominal accounts only. Assume balances are nil on 1 July.

(Institute of Bankers)

CHAPTER

12 The bank reconciliation statement

- *What is the function of a bank reconciliation statement?*
- *Why is it essential to prepare one?*

Introduction

When the bank statement arrives from the bank giving details of the business's transactions, it very rarely agrees with the bank balance as recorded either in the cash book or as a nominal account in the ledger. The major reason for this is that there is a time discrepancy between recording the business's bank transactions in the cash book and the bank's recording of them.

This is particularly the case with 'unpresented cheques'. When payments by cheque are prepared and recorded in the cash book, it may take a number of days for the bank to clear them and, therefore, the bank records these at a later point in the bank statement.

The banks arrange for many items to be paid directly through the banking systems, such as credit transfers, direct debits and standing orders, and the business may record these items on receipt of the bank statement and usually not before.

The banks also may make charges for handling accounts and interest may either be paid or charged depending on whether the bank account is in credit with the bank or is in an overdraft position. A *credit* in the bank statement balance is, in effect, 'money in the bank' because from the bank's point of view, it owes money to the business. In the cash book, the bank will show a debit entry. On the other hand, a *debit* in the bank statement balance will indicate an overdraft, which, in the cash book, will appear as a credit balance.

The procedure for bank reconciliation

When the bank statement is received from the bank, the general practice is to:

a) Check carefully all banking items between the cash book and the bank statement. Those items found in both sets of records may be given a light tick as items agreed. The receipts side of the cash book will be checked with the receipts (credit side) of the bank statement; the payments side of the cash book with the payments side (debit side) of the statement. The opening balance on both records must also be checked.

b) This will leave some items left unticked. Some unticked items may appear both in the cash book and bank statement. Those items left unticked in the bank statement must first be recorded in the cash book, to bring it up-to-date. These may include items such as bank charges, direct debits and standing orders.

c) Once the cash book is brought up-to-date with those unticked items from the bank statement, it is balanced. The reconciliation statement can then be prepared, bringing the adjusted cash book balance into agreement with the bank statement.

d) The reconciliation statement is the verifying check between the bank account in the cash book and the bank statement balance. The procedure in summary is as follows:
1 balance as per bank statement (final balance);
2 add any undeposited cheques (unticked items, debit side of cash book);
3 less any unpresented cheques (unticked items, credit side of cash book);
4 balance as per cash book.

Example
Prepare the bank reconciliation statement of Robert James for the month of May. Find the balance of the cash book first and include any items unticked from the bank statement. The items on both sets of records have already been ticked.

Cash book of R Jones

Date	*Details (bank)*	*£*		*Date*	*Details (bank)*	*£*	
May 1	Balance b/d	93	√	May 2	Motor expenses	52	√
4	Sales to bank	88	√	8	Office costs	24	√
7	Sales to bank	87	√	9	Jack Soames	141	
16	Sales to bank	228	√	10	Light and heat	34	√
18	Tom Smith	74	√	12	Ron James	108	√
21	Sales to bank	255	√	17	Stationery	46	√
28	D Marks	54		21	Wages	84	√
31	Sales to bank	36		30	P Jackson	116	
				31	Balance c/d	310	
		915				915	
	Balance b/d	310					

Bank statement of R Jones for month of May

Date		Details	Debit	Credit	Balance	
			£	£	£	
May	1	Balance b/f			93 ✓	Cr
	4	Deposit		88 ✓	181	
	8	Deposit		87 ✓	268	
	11	100452	52 ✓			
		100453	24 ✓		192	
	12	STO (rates)	55		137	
	14	DDR (insurance)	18		119	
	16	Deposit		228 ✓	347	
	17	100455	34 ✓		313	
	18	100456	108 ✓		205	
	19	Deposit		74 ✓	279	
	21	Deposit		255 ✓	534	
	22	100457	46 ✓		488	
	24	100458	84 ✓		404	
	29	DIV		16	420	

Abbreviations: STO Standing Order, DDR Direct Debit,
BGC Bank Giro Credit, DIV Dividend,
ATM Cash Dispenser, DR Overdrawn

REQUIRED:

a) Check and tick alike items in both the cash book and bank statement.

b) Bring the cash book up-to-date with those unticked items from the bank statement.

c) Prepare the bank reconciliation statement for the month of May.

Unticked items in the cash book:

Debits	£	*Credits*	£
D Marks	54	Jack Soames	141
Sales to bank	36	P Jackson	116

Unticked items in the bank statement:

Debits	£	*Credits*	£
STO	55	DIV	16
DDR	18		

Cash book updated

			May 31	Balance c/d	310
		915			915
June 1	Balance b/d	310	June 1	STO – rates	55
	Dividend	16		DDR – insurance	18
				Balance c/d	253
		326			326
	Balance b/d	253			

Bank reconciliation statement as on 31 May

	£	£
Balance as per bank statement (29/5)		420 Cr
Add		
Deposits not yet credited: Marks	54	
Sales	36	90
		510
Less		
Unpresented cheques: Soames	141	
Jackson	116	257
Balance as per cash book		253

Summary

1 The bank reconciliation statement is a verifying procedure which states that the balance found in the bank statement agrees with the bank balance found in the cash book or nominal ledger.

2 There is a need to reconcile periodically between the balance calculated at the bank and the balance calculated in the bank account. First, there is a double check for accuracy and second, there is an aspect of financial control over a significant asset.

3 If the bank reconciliation statement is the responsibility of a person other than one charged with keeping the cash book records, it may be more difficult to defraud the business against unauthorised disposals through the bank account.

4 The bank statement may often have details of payments which have been arranged through the banking system. It is not until the statement is received by the business that such details may be entered in the cash book to bring it up-to-date.

5 The bank reconciliation statement may therefore be viewed as a form of audit of the banking transactions of the business enterprise.

QUESTIONS

1 The following information represents the cash book and bank statement of B Wood, for the month of June:

Cash book (bank only)

		£			£
1/6	Balance b/f	1 407	5/6	Wages	390
8/6	Sales	1 179	8/6	Purchases	189
16/6	Sales	600	19/6	D Smith	876
26/6	Sales	615	26/6	Rent	234
			30/6	Balance c/f	?
		____			____
		____			____

Bank statement

		Debit (Payments) £	*Credit (Receipts)* £	*Balance* £
1/6	Balance			1 407 Cr
8/6	Credit		1 179	2 586
12/6	712	390		2 196
18/6	713	189		2 007
20/6	Credit		600	2 607
26/6	Credit transfer:			
	D Lewis		300	2 907
28/6	STO Abbey Build Society	258		2 649
29/6	Bank charges	57		2 592

REQUIRED:

a) Balance the cash book of B Wood on 30/6, bring down the balance.
b) Bring the cash book up to date with those unticked items found in the statement. Bring down the new balance on 1/7.
c) Prepare the bank reconciliation statement as on 30/6.

2 The following information relates to the banking transactions of L Jones for the month of July:

Cash book (bank only)

		£			£
1/7	Balance b/f	9 200	2/7	Rent	616
3/7	Sales	1 368	3/7	Brown	672
6/7	Birdwood	512	10/7	Wages	872
9/7	Sales	1 736	16/7	Whitehall	2 068
15/7	Peters	900	20/7	Purchases	104
24/7	Sales	716	30/7	Balance c/f	?

Bank statement

		Dr £	*Cr* £	*Balance* £
1/7	Balance			9 200 Cr
3/7	Credit		1 368	10 568
6/7	558	672		9 896
7/7	Credit transfer J Jack		1 740	11 636
7/7	Credit		512	12 148
11/7	559	872		11 276
12/7	STO WDC	500		10 776
12/7	Credit		1 736	12 512
13/7	DD (SEB)	176		12 336
15/7	Credit		900	13 236

REQUIRED:

a) Adjust the cash book with the appropriate entries and balance as on 30/7.
b) Prepare the bank reconciliation statement as on 30/7.

3 The bank reconciliation of R Pearce

The cash book of R Pearce for the month of August

Ref: C9

(*Dr*)	*Receipts*	*Discount allowed* £	*Cash* £	*Bank* £		*Payments*	*Discount received* £	*Cash* £	*Bank* £ (*Cr*)
1/8	Balances b/f		200	1 925	5/8	General expenses			50
6/8	Sales		420		6/8	Drawings		120	
7/8	D Smith	10.0		200	10/8	SEB			43
13/8	Sales		345		12/8	General expenses			50
19/8	B Kings	21.5		420	13/8	Drawings		120	
20/8	Sales		410		15/8	SG (gas)			85

(Continues)

Ref: C9

(Dr)	Receipts	Discount allowed	Cash	Bank		Payments	Discount received	Cash	Bank (Cr)
		£	£	£			£	£	£
21/8	Contra (cash)			800	20/8	Drawings		120	
27/8	Sales		450		21/8	Contra (bank)		800	
					23/8	Stationery		25	
					26/8	General expenses			50
					27/8	Drawings		120	
					28/8	BT (telephone)			67
					30/8	Slazenger			250
						Metro			1 000
						Auto			500
					31/8	International	15		675
						Drawings		150	
						Balances c/f		370	575
		31.5	1 825	3 345			15	1 825	3 345
1/9	Balances b/f		370	575	1/9	Bank charges			8
	M Johnson			300		WDC – rates			170
						Balance c/f		370	697
			370	875				370	875
	Balances b/f		370	697					

Using the three-column cash book figures for the month of August, *check* R Pearce's bank statement against the bank columns of the cash book.

Details from the bank statement were:

		Payments (Dr)	*Receipts (Cr)*	*Balance*
		£	£	£
1/8	Balance b/f			1 925 Cr
6/8	665	50		1 875
6/8	Credit		200	2 075
13/8	666	43		2 032
15/8	667	50		1 982
18/8	668	85		1 897
19/8	Credit		420	2 317
21/8	Credit		800	3 117
28/8	669	50		3 067
30/8	Charges	8		3 059
	Credit transfer – M Johnson		300	3 359
	WDC – rates	170		3 189

REQUIRED:

a) Tick the alike items on both sets of records.

b) The cash book has been brought up to date, but check the items which have been taken from the bank statement.
c) Prepare the bank reconciliation statement for the month of August.

4 From the following extract from the cash book of D W Lane and the bank statement from his bank, received by him at the beginning of June:

a) Calculate the amount of D W Lane's bank balance on 31 May after making the necessary corrections in the cash book.
b) Prepare a bank reconciliation statement to reconcile the corrected cash book balance with the balance of the bank statement.

Extract from the cash book of D W Lane:

		Discount	*Bank*			*Discount*	*Bank*
		£	£			£	£
1 May	Balance		300	9 May	P Stone	1	28
7 May	Cash		162	14 May	Alpha Properties – Rent		50
16 May	C Brewster	2	80	29 May	E Deakin		10
16 May	A Kennedy		9				
24 May	Cash		60				
31 May	Cash		40				

Bank statement received by D W Lane at the beginning of June:

Date	*Particulars*	*Payments*	*Receipts*	*Balance*
		£	£	£
1 May	Balance			300
4 May	Stone	28		272
7 May	Cash		162	434
10 May	Dividend from investment		63	497
17 May	Insurance premium standing order	5		492
17 May	Cheques		89	581
18 May	Property company	50		531
25 May	Cash		60	591
31 May	Charges	1		590

(RSA)

5 On 31 May 1985 the bank columns of R Barker's cash book showed a balance at bank of £850. A bank statement written up to the same date disclosed that the following items had not been entered in the cash book.

i) The sum of £42 paid to White Rose Insurance Company by standing order on 28 May.

ii) Commission received £120 from M Newall had been paid directly into Barker's account by credit transfer on 25 May.

iii) Bank charges of £90 had been charged directly to Barker's account on 29 May.

A further check revealed the following:

i) Cheques drawn in favour of creditors totalling £642 had not yet been presented.

ii) Cash and cheques £210 deposited at the bank on 30 May had been entered in the cash book but did not appear on the bank statement.

REQUIRED:

Write up Barker's cash book on 31 May 1985 after taking into account the above matters and prepare a bank reconciliation statement showing the balance appearing in the bank statement.

(RSA)

6 The following were from the bank columns of the cash book of V White:

Dr					*Cr*
		£			£
Mar 1	Balance b/f	150	Mar 8	A Roe	30
6	Cash	75	16	T Salmon	15
13	W Wing	17	28	A Bird	29
31	R Nest	39	31	Balance c/f	
		—			—
		—			—

On 31 March she received the following bank statement from her bank:

		Debits	*Credits*	*Balance*
		£	£	£
Mar 1	Balance (Cr)			150
6	Cash		75	225
10	A Roe	30		195
13	W Wing		17	212
15	Credit transfer (M Fish)		16	228
18	T Salmon	15		213
31	Charges	10		203

REQUIRED:

a) Bring the cash book up to date, and state the new balance at 31 March.

b) Prepare a statement, under its proper title, to reconcile the difference between the new up-to-date balance in the cash book and the balance in the bank statement on 31 March.

(GCE O Level)

7 The following represents the cash book and bank statement of George Gershwin for the month of June:

Cash book (bank only)

		£			£
1/6	Balance b/f	180	16/6	Wages	725
14/6	Sales	450	19/6	Purchases	373
18/6	R Hammerstein	375	23/6	D Smith	405
28/6	Sales	528	28/6	Rent	250
30/6	Balance c/f	220			
		1 753			1 753
				Balance b/f	220

Bank statement for June

		Dr £	*Cr* £	*Balance* £
1/6	Balance			380 Cr
2/6	971	200		180
15/6	Credit		450	630
19/6	972	725		95 Dr
19/6	Credit		375	280 Cr
21/6	C/T: R Jones		135	415
23/6	973	405		10
28/6	WDC – Rates	185		175 Dr
29/6	Bank Charges	15		190 Dr

NOTE
C/T = credit transfer.

REQUIRED:

a) Bring the cash book up to date and balance on 30/6, bringing down the balance the next day.
b) Prepare the bank reconciliation statement for the month of June.

Note: The difference between the two opening balances, £180 in the cash book and £380 in the statement. Cheque number 971 on 2/6 links the two together, an unpresented cheque from the previous period.

(GCSE)

8 The following information relates to the cash ledger of A D Robert for the month of June 1989:

		Debit £		*Credit* £
1/6	Balance b/f	2 870	General expenses	2 420
	Debtors	8 755	Creditors	10 455
	Cash sales	6 420	Salaries	2 815
	Other receipts	895	Rental charges	400

The bank statement received by the business on 30 June showed a balance of £1935 (credit).

When the proprietor checked his records with those of the statement, the following facts were revealed:

a) The bank's commission and other charges amounted to a total of £79.
b) A customer's cheque which had been sent to Robert, had been marked 'R/D' and dishonoured by the bank. The cheque was for £1353.
c) A receipt of £300 from a customer of Robert, had wrongly been entered as a payment in his cash ledger.
d) The opening cash ledger balance of £2870 was brought forward in error and should have been £2780.
e) Several cheques signed by Robert and presented for payment, had not yet been cleared by the bank. The cheques were for: £315, £455, £170 and £595.
f) Wages of £200 had been undercast in error and had not been recorded in the cash ledger.
g) A credit transfer of £420 from a Robert customer had been directly paid into the bank.
h) Other entries in the statement included £212 paid to Robert as a dividend from ACY Ltd and a direct debit relating to an insurance premium for £70.
i) The final paying-in-book deposit of £1800 had not yet been credited by the bank.

REQUIRED:

a) Reconstruct the cash ledger for the month of June 1989, bringing down the balance on 30 June. Prepare the bank reconciliation statement for the month ending 30 June 1989.
b) Why is there a need to reconcile banking transactions?

(Institute of Bankers)

CHAPTER

13 The petty cash book

- *What purpose does the petty cash book serve?*
- *Why is a petty cash voucher necessary?*
- *How are petty cash expenses posted to the ledger?*

Introduction

When businesses expand their operations a more formalised system of accounting is needed. In a small business, run by a sole trader, it is likely that the accounting records are minimal and that these will relate to the routine transactions of keeping a check on cash and banking transactions, and invoices (either sales or purchases). Larger organisations need to keep accurate day-to-day records and a formal ledger system.

It may be necessary to keep a distinct record of frequent minor cash payments, separate from the mainstream of the cash book. In this way, a number of small payments need not interfere with the main course of cash transactions.

To initiate a petty cash system, a certain sum of money which can be used for petty cash purposes must be allocated, perhaps once a month, and this must be adequate to cover a specific time period. The business may decide to allocate £100 a month for these payments. This sum will, of course, depend on the nature of the enterprise. For some, £100 per month might be perfectly sufficient, for others, £100 per week may be required.

The double entry to commence and proceed with a petty cash system is:

Debit: the petty cash book (with sum received);
Credit: the cash book (with sum given).

If £100 per month is allocated:

Dr		*Petty cash book*			*Cr*
£					
100	1/8	Cash book			

Dr			*Cash book*		*Cr*
					£
			1/8	Petty cash	100

Once a petty cash system is set up, further reimbursements can be made by crediting the cash book and debiting the petty cash book, when the *float* (in this case £100) needs topping up to the sum required.

Petty cash vouchers

It may be prudent to give the responsibility for handling petty cash to an accounts junior. In this way, a more senior member of staff can be left to concentrate on aspects demanding more attention. The junior member can then learn and be held responsible for all allocations of minor cash payments.

When handling the business's money, whether large or small, the correct and authorised procedure should be followed. For example, before any payment is made, it should be authorised by an appropriate staff member, perhaps of management status. A voucher system will help to formalise the handing out of money. It should have details relating to:

a) what the payment is for;
b) the signature of the person authorising payment;
c) the signature of the person who is to take the money.

In this way, control is maintained. Each cash payment should, therefore, be supported by some documentary evidence such as a voucher. Vouchers can be numbered consecutively and the number entered in the appropriate petty cash column. An example of a voucher is shown below:

PETTY CASH VOUCHER

Number:
Date:

Details	**Amount £**	**Vat £**
Total		

Authorised by:
Received by:

It may be advisable to retain any receipts particularly for those items where Vat is charged because these may be debited and reclaimed against the Vat account.

Random checks should be made on petty cash payments, just to keep the person responsible for payments alert. The balance of money in hand, added to the vouchers used, should always equal the *imprest sum* (the float). For example:

	£
Cash in hand	27.50
Vouchers used	72.50
Float:	100.00

The style used in the petty cash system of having analysis columns for the different type of petty cash expenses will indicate where payments are being made and will also facilitate ledger posting.

Example

Christopher Jones keeps petty cash records and uses analysis columns for: total sum; Vat; postage; stationery; travel; cleaning; and sundries. The agreed impress is £100 per month.

Transactions relating to petty cash payments for the month of August were:

		£	
1/8	Balance of cash on hand	4.50	
	Reimbursement from cash book	95.50	
3/8	Postage, envelopes	5.70	
4/8	Cleaning	7.50	
5/8	Bus fares	2.50	
7/8	General stationery	3.45	(Vat £0.45)
9/8	Stamps	3.60	
11/8	Cleaning	7.50	
13/8	Bus fares	2.25	
14/8	Coffee, tea	5.50	
15/8	Typing paper	13.80	(Vat £1.80)
18/8	Cleaning	7.50	
19/8	Paper clips	1.60	
21/8	Postage	2.90	
24/8	General stationery	9.20	(Vat £1.20)
27/8	Bus fares	2.25	
28/8	Parcel post	5.00	
30/8	Gummed paper	2.50	

REQUIRED:

a) A petty cash book for the month of August.
b) Nominal ledger accounts for the above transactions.

NOTES

a) The 16 vouchers used in August amounted to £82.75, leaving a balance of £17.25 cash in hand. The total of these equals the imprest of £100.
b) The balance is brought forward to the beginning of the following month on 1/9. The cash book reimbursement of £82.75 tops up the imprest back up to £100 for September.

Petty cash book

August | No. 4

£	Date	Details	Voucher no.	Total £	Vat £	Postage £	Stationery £	Travel £	Cleaning £	Sundries £
4 50	1	Balance b/f								
95 50		Cash book								
	3	Postage, envelopes	1	5 70		5 70				
	4	Cleaning	2	7 50					7 50	
	5	Bus fares	3	2 50				2 50		
	7	Stationery	4	3 45	45		3 00			
	9	Stamps	5	3 60		3 60				
	11	Cleaning	6	7 50					7 50	
	13	Bus fares	7	2 25				2 25		
	14	Coffee, tea	8	5 50						5 50
	15	Typing paper	9	13 80	1 80		12 00			
	18	Cleaning	10	7 50					7 50	
	19	Paper clips	11	1 60			1 60			
	21	Postage	12	2 90		2 90				
	24	Stationery	13	9 20	1 20		8 00			
	27	Bus fares	14	2 25				2 25		
	28	Parcel post	15	5 00		5 00				
	30	Gummed paper	16	2 50			2 50			
				82 75	3 45	17 20	27 10	7 00	22 50	5 50
		Balance c/f		17 25						
100				100						
17.25		Balance b/f								
82.75		Cash book								

Posting to the nominal ledger

The totals of the analysis columns may be posted to the nominal ledger. To complete the double entry, either one of two methods may be followed:

a) *Debit:* the petty cash expenses (total in cash book)
Credit: the cash book

or

b) *Debit:* each analysis total (from the petty cash book)
Credit: the cash book.

Method b)

Nominal ledger

		Folio	*Debit*	*Credit*	*Balance*
Vat account					
30/8	Petty cash	PC4	3.45		3.45 Dr
Postage account					
30/8	Petty cash	PC4	17.20		17.20 Dr
Stationery account					
30/8	Petty cash	PC4	27.10		27.10 Dr
Travel expenses account					
30/8	Petty cash	PC4	7.00		7.00 Dr
Cleaning expenses account					
30/8	Petty cash	PC4	22.50		22.50 Dr
Sundry expenses account					
30/8	Petty cash	PC4	5.50		5.50 Dr

Summary

1 The petty cash book is a subsidiary book of the cash book and deals with the small payments of cash.

2 It is based on the imprest system where a float of money is used to meet the day-to-day requirements of small sums of cash.

3 The petty cash book may have columns for the purpose of analysing cash payments. This can facilitate the posting of totals to the nominal ledger.

4 The use of petty cash vouchers helps to control cash payments. Vouchers need to be properly authorised and signed for by the recipient of the cash.

5 The double entry for cash reimbursements is:
Debit (*Dr*) the petty cash book
Credit (*Cr*) the cash book.

When posting to the nominal ledger, the payments may either be posted (as debit entries):

a) in total from the cash book, or
b) in individual analysis totals from the petty cash book.

QUESTIONS

1 G Walton uses a petty cash book in her business. She uses the following analysis column headings: cleaning; office refreshments; travel; postage and telegrams; Vat; and Sundries.

Her petty cash float is £150 per month. The balance brought forward on 30/6 was £2.75. The transactions for the month of July were:

			Voucher no.	*Total sum* £	*Vat (inclusive)* £
July	1	Balance b/f		2.75	
		Cash book (reimbursement)		147.25	
	3	Office coffee, tea, etc.	1	7.50	
	5	Fares – taxi	2	15.00	
	7	Cleaning	3	9.20	(1.20)
	8	Bus tickets	4	2.45	
	11	Stamps	5	7.50	
	12	Crockery (sundries)	6	17.25	(2.25)
	15	Telegrams, parcel post	7	5.25	
	17	Journals and newspapers	8	8.55	
	22	Cleaning	9	9.20	(1.20)
	23	Bus tickets	10	3.30	
	24	Office refreshments	11	6.20	
	27	Replacement glass	12	24.15	(3.15)
	28	Fares – taxi	13	14.00	
	30	Postage	14	8.40	

REQUIRED:

a) Prepare the petty cash book for G Walton for the month of July.
b) Indicate briefly how the analysis columns may be posted to the ledger.

2 D Lewis uses an imprest system for the payment of minor expenses. The imprest is £150. Analysis columns are used for: stationery; Vat; travel; office refreshments; and sundries.

On 1/7 his balance brought forward was £9.50. He was reimbursed with the imprest balance on the same day. You are to prepare the petty cash book for D Lewis for July. Transactions for July were as follows:

			Voucher no.	Total sum £	Vat (if applicable) £
July	3	General stationery	1	12.65	(1.65)
	4	Taxi fares	2	5.85	
	5	Stamps	3	7.20	
	7	Typing paper	4	16.10	(2.10)
	8	Bus fares	5	3.50	
	10	General stationery	6	13.80	(1.80)
	12	Cleaning materials	7	11.50	(1.50)
	15	Refreshments	8	6.25	
	18	Bus fares	9	3.20	
	19	Writing materials	10	18.40	(2.40)
	22	Bus fares	11	3.75	
	23	Newspapers, etc.	12	5.15	
	24	Stamps, parcels	13	8.00	
	27	Refreshments	14	6.20	
	28	Tea tray, cups	15	9.20	(1.20)
	30	Taxi fares	16	3.25	

REQUIRED:

a) Balance the petty cash book on 31 July, bringing down the balance the next day.
b) Post the totals of the analysis columns to the ledger.

3 Smith & Jones uses a petty cash book system. On 30 April the cash in hand was £0.25 from an imprest of £100. The business uses a voucher system, all vouchers commencing from number 1 on the first of every month.

Analysis headings are used for: cleaning; travel; newspaper/journals; stationery; post office; refreshments; sundries; and Vat.

Transactions for May were as follows:

			Total sum £	Vat (if applicable) £
May	1	Cash book reimbursement		
	3	Office cleaning	11.50	(1.50)
	4	Stamps, post	8.50	
	7	Pencils, pens, etc.	5.52	(0.72)
	11	Newspapers, magazines	2.20	
	13	Tea, coffee	4.85	
	14	Envelopes, ribbons, etc.	11.50	(1.50)
	15	Postage, telegrams	9.50	
	17	General stationery	23.00	(3.00)
	19	Charity donations	10.00	
	20	Increase of imprest from cash book	25.00	
	23	Taxi fares	8.00	
	24	Office cleaning	11.50	(1.50)
	27	Stamps	3.50	
	28	Floor polish	0.80	
	30	Newspapers	1.30	

REQUIRED:

a) Prepare the petty cash book for Smith & Jones for the month of May. Bring down the balance on 1 June.
b) Post the analysis totals to the nominal ledger as on 31 May. Commence each expense type, including Vat, with a nil balance.
c) Is the use of vouchers a waste of time? The petty cash book can still be prepared without them, so why bother? Briefly explain your view.

4 The following information relates to J Robertson's petty cash. He keeps an imprest of £125 per month. The cash in hand on 1 July was £8.40 and the necessary reimbursement from the cash book was made on the same date.

In the 'total sum' column, some items are inclusive of Vat. To find the Vat charged divide the sum by 1.15 which will give the answer before Vat. Using voucher number 1 as an example:

	£
Motor expenses	$\frac{8.05}{1.15}$
=	7.00
+ Vat (15%)	1.05
	8.05

Transactions for July were as follows:

			Voucher no.	*Total sum* £	
July	1	Cash book reimbursement			
	3	Motor expenses	1	8.05	(Vat inc.)
	5	Stationery	2	4.60	(Vat inc.)
	8	Office cleaning	3	10.00	
	9	Refreshments	4	7.25	
	10	Newspapers	5	1.25	
	11	Postage	6	6.60	
	14	Envelopes, paper	7	16.10	(Vat inc.)
	16	Office cleaning	8	10.00	
	17	Motor expenses	9	12.65	(Vat inc.)
	20	Repair to chair	10	17.25	(Vat inc.)
	23	Coffee, tea	11	8.35	
	26	Parcel post	12	3.65	

REQUIRED:

a) Prepare the petty cash book for J Robertson for the month of July. Use appropriate analysis columns of your choice.
b) Balance as on 31 July, bringing forward the balance on 1 August and showing the appropriate cash book reimbursement.

5 ABC Co uses the bank for all significant receipts and payments of cash. All cash payments under £10 come out of the petty cash. The imprest is £100 and is reimbursed every month by a cheque payment from the cash book.

The headings used by ABC Co are as follows: cleaning; travelling expenses; stationery; post office; refreshments; general; and Vat.

The balance of the petty cash on 30 June was £15.65. The firm uses the voucher system, all vouchers being from number 1 on the first of the month.

The transactions for July were as follows:

			£
July	2	Reimbursement from cash book	
	2	Cleaning materials	1.50
		Vat	0.22
	3	Stamps and parcel post	8.68
	6	Window cleaning	6.00
		Vat	0.90
	8	Pens, pencils, typing paper	10.00
		Vat	1.50
	11	Newspapers	0.85
	12	Tea, coffee and sugar	3.76
	15	Envelopes, ribbons	2.40
		Vat	0.36
	19	Telegrams	4.60
	20	Taxi fares	3.85
	23	Charity donations	1.50
	27	Bus fares	4.50
	28	Window cleaning	6.00
		Vat	0.90
	29	Floor polish and dusters	2.80
		Vat	0.42

REQUIRED:

a) Draw up a petty cash book using the appropriate columns. Bring the imprest balance up to date on 2 July.
b) Enter the above transactions and balance the book on 31 July. Bring down the balance and make the appropriate reimbursement on 1 August.
c) Post the analysis totals to the general ledger on 31 July.

(BTEC National)

CHAPTER

14 Control accounts

- *What function do the sales and purchases ledger control accounts play?*
- *How might control accounts assist management?*
- *How can control accounts help to locate errors?*

Introduction

In Chapters 6 and 7, both sales and bought ledger control accounts were used as a cross-checking device against the total individual balances of debtors and creditors recorded in the personal ledgers.

The two control accounts are recorded in the nominal ledger and should verify the total balances of debtors and creditors in the sales and bought ledgers respectively, at any given time.

If an organisation has numerous customers and suppliers it is advisable to use control accounts to confirm the accuracy of recording personal accounts. If a computer program is used, it will give immediate access to the totals of both debtors and creditors. If records are kept manually, the control accounts will also give this information - perhaps not as expediently as a computer but total debtors and creditors will be confirmed.

Total figures for debtors and creditors may also be required for management purposes. How much is owed by debtors? When can the business expect its cash to come in? How much is owed to creditors? How much cash is due to be paid? These questions reflect the future cash flow of the business and the amount of working capital which will be available for trading. It is therefore important to have up-to-date access to these figures at any time.

Once the control accounts have verified the sales and bought ledger balances, the control balances are listed in the trial balance, not the individual balances for debtors and creditors. This makes the task of balancing the trial balance a little easier because if errors prevent a balance, they can not be associated with either debtors or creditors. The control accounts have already confirmed the accuracy, being arithmetical proofs of individual debtors and creditors.

If either of the control accounts do not agree with the total balances of the sales and bought ledgers (that is, the schedules of debtors and creditors), a detailed check will need to be made to locate the errors. Both individual accounts and control accounts will have to be investigated to locate and correct the errors.

Locating an error

A likely source of error may be due to an incorrect addition or posting from a subsidiary book such as the journals or cash book. In the following case, an error is located in the sales journal:

Sales journal	£	£	£	
D Lewis	200	30	230	Dr
D Smith	420	63	483	Dr
B Kings	500	75	575	Dr
	1 120	168	1 388	
	Cr	Cr	Dr	
	Sales	Vat	S/L control	

Sales ledger posting: Each debtor could be posted correctly to the debit side of their respective accounts.

Nominal ledger posting: Sales and Vat totals are posted correctly to the credit side of their respective accounts.

The sales ledger control account is debited with £1388 (the figure should be £1288), an error of £100, overstated. When cross-checking the sales ledger control account with the sales ledger, there would be a difference of £100. To locate this error, a thorough check of the control account and the sales ledger will need to be carried out.

Preparing control accounts from given data

Prepare the sales ledger control account from the following information:

	£	
Sales ledger control account		
Balance b/f 1 July	21 900	Dr
Credit sales	37 500	
Bank/cash from debtors	34 500	
Returns inward	1 200	
Bad debts written off	800	
Discount allowed to customers	840	
Cheques dishonoured	100	
Cash sales	10 500	
Sales ledger Dr balance from debtors schedule: 31 July	22 160	

NOTES

The control account may be prepared either in the traditional or running balance method of recording. Both methods will be shown.

Cash sales is a 'red herring' because it does not affect debtors.

The sales ledger control account (nominal ledger)

Dr		*Sales ledger control account*			Cr
		£			£
1/7	Balance b/f	21 900	31/7	Bank/cash	34 500
31/7	Sales	37 500		Discount allowed	840
	Dishonoured cheques	100		Returns in	1 200
				Bad debts	800
				Balance c/f	22 160
		59 500			59 500
1/8	Balance b/f (as per S/L)	22 160			

The running balance format

Sales ledger control account		*Dr* £	*Cr* £	*Balance* £
1/7	Balance b/f			21 900 Dr
31/7	Sales	37 500		59 400
	Bank/cash		34 500	24 900
	Discount allowed		840	24 060
	Returns in		1 200	22 860
	Dishonoured cheque	100		22 960
	Bad debts		800	22 160
	Balance (S/L)			22 160 Dr

NOTE

The balance on 31 July agrees with the debtors' schedule in the sales ledger.

Prepare the bought ledger control account from the following information:

Bought ledger control account	£
Balance b/f 1 July	37 500
Credit purchases	59 250
Payments to suppliers	54 600
Discounts received	1 435
Returns outward	1 635
Refund received from suppliers due to overcharge	200
Debit note from supplier because of undercharge on invoice	150
Bought ledger Cr balance from creditors' schedule: 31 July	39 400

The bought ledger control account (nominal ledger)

Dr		*Bought ledger control account*			*Cr*
		£			£
31/7	Bank	54 600	1/7	Balance b/f	37 500
	Discount received	1 435	31/7	Purchases	59 250
	Returns out	1 635		Refund	200
	Balance c/f	39 430		Dr Note	150
		97 100			97 100
			1/8	Balance b/f	39 430
				(B/L balance)	39 400

NOTE

An error has been made and must be located and corrected. This is a difference of £30. Is it a bought ledger error or control account error? It was found that in the bought ledger, Vat of £30 had not been posted to a supplier's account, therefore the B/L balance should have read £39 430.

The running balance format

Bought ledger control account		*Dr* £	*Cr* £	*Balance* £
1/7	Balance b/f			37 500 Cr
31/7	Purchases		59 250	96 750
	Bank	54 600		42 150
	Discount received	1 435		40 715
	Returns out	1 635		39 080
	Dr note		150	39 230
	Refund		200	39 430
	Balance (B/L)			39 430 Cr

An important point to remember is that every transaction that affects an individual debtor or creditor, must correspondingly affect the control account. Control accounts represent the totals for debtors and creditors.

It may occur, from time to time, that a debtor is in credit owing to an over payment, or that a creditor is in debit because he or she is overpaid. This may also be reflected in the control accounts and both debit and credit balances may be shown at both the commencement and ending of the control account period.

Example

	Dr £	*Cr* £
Sales ledger control account		
Balances b/f 1 July:	21 160	520
31 July:	21 000	340
Bought ledger control account		
Balances b/f 1 July:	440	10 500
31 July:	100	7 000
Credit sales		57 000
Credit purchases	38 400	
Returns in	700	
Returns out		3 300
Receipts from debtors	52 560	
Payments to suppliers		36 960
Bad debts	1 520	
[1]Contra entries £300		
Cash sales		13 855
Interest charges to customers due to overdue accounts	100	
[2]Bills payable		1 000
[2]Bills receivable	2 000	

NOTES

1 Contra entries refer to those accounts which are 'set off' against each other, that is, where a customer may also be a supplier. For example, if a customer owes £300 (debtor) and the business owes the same customer £1000 (creditor), the contra entry will be:

Debit: the creditor's account £300 (debt now £700)
Credit: the debtor's account £300 (account cleared).

Therefore, with contra entries:

Debit: bought ledger control account
Credit: sales ledger control account.

2 Bills payable and receivable are like post-dated cheques, payments are made when the dates are due. Bills payable refers to payments to creditors and bills receivable refers to receipts from debtors:

Debit: bills payable to bought ledger control account
Credit: bills receivable to sales ledger control account.

The control accounts in traditional format

Dr		*Sales ledger control account*			Cr
		£			£
1/7	Balance b/f	21 160	1/7	Balance b/f	520
31/7	Sales	57 000	31/7	Bank	52 560
	Interest	100		Returns in	700
	Balance c/f	340		Bad debts	1 520
				Contra	300
				Bills receivable	2 000
				Balance c/f	21 000
		78 600			78 600
1/8	Balance b/f	21 000	1/8	Balance b/f	340

Dr		*Bought ledger control account*			Cr
		£			£
1/7	Balance b/f	440	1/7	Balance b/f	10 500
31/7	Bank	36 960	31/7	Purchases	38 400
	Returns out	3 300		Balance c/f	100
	Contra	300			
	Bills payable	1 000			
	Balance c/f	7 000			
		49 000			49 000
1/8	Balance b/f	100	1/8	Balance b/f	7 000

NOTE

Cash sales amount (£13 855) is not entered in the control account because there is no effect on debtors. The same applies to cash purchases, there is no effect on creditors.

Summary

1 Control accounts are used to verify the accuracy of the sales and bought ledgers. They are recorded in the nominal ledger.

2 Where a business holds numerous accounts for either debtors or creditors, it makes sense to use control accounts as a cross-checking device. Control accounts act as 'mini' trial balances for debtors and creditors.

3 The sales and bought ledger control accounts represent totals for debtors and creditors in the trial balance. It becomes easier to locate errors in a trial balance where control accounts are used.

4 Control accounts are useful for management purposes because figures for total debtors and creditors affect both the cash flow and the working capital of a business.

5 Control accounts are not part of the double entry. They simply represent total balances for debtors and creditors. Any transaction, therefore, which affects either a debtor or creditor must be recorded in the control accounts.

QUESTIONS

1 The following information relates to the accounts of E Gibbs for the month of July:

	£ *Dr*	£ *Cr*
Balance b/f from sales ledger (1/7)	41 220	
Credit sales, July		37 350
Returns inward	500	
Receipts from debtors	27 800	
Bad debts written off	950	
Discounts allowed	675	
Cheques from customers marked R/D – insufficient funds		790
Cash sales		21 500
Interest charged to customers		40
Debit note sent to customer (account undercharged)		300
Contra entry between sales and bought ledgers, £800		
Balance b/f from sales ledger (31/7)	48 975	

REQUIRED:

Prepare the sales ledger control account of E Gibbs for the month of July. The opening balance on 1/7 confirms with the control account.

2 The following information has been taken from the accounts of G Grant for the month of July:

	£ *Dr*	£ *Cr*
Balance b/f from bought ledger (1/7)		6 432
Credit purchases, July	81 360	
Payments made to suppliers		58 200
Discounts received		2 450
Returns outward		11 285
Received from a supplier due to an overpayment	125	
Cash purchases	2 455	
Balance b/f from bought ledger (31/7)		15 982

REQUIRED:

Prepare the bought ledger control account of G Grant for the month of July. The opening balance on 1/7 confirms with the control account.

3 The following details were extracted from the books of a company for the month ended 28 February 1987.

		£	
February 1	Purchase ledger	9 000	Cr
	Sales ledger	5 000	Dr
February 28	Credit purchases for the month	72 000	
	Credit sales for the month	103 000	
	Cash paid to creditors	74 000	
	Cash received from debtors	81 000	
	Discounts received	1 200	
	Discounts allowed	1 500	
	Returns outwards	600	
	Returns inwards	400	
	Bad debts written off in month	200	
	Dishonoured cheque from debtor	300	

On 28 February 1987 the balances extracted from the ledgers were:

Purchase ledger	£5 200
Sales ledger	£25 110

REQUIRED:

a) Prepare the sales ledger control account.
b) Prepare the purchase ledger control account.
c) Briefly comment on the control accounts prepared in a) and b) above.

(The Institute of Commercial Management)

4 The following details were extracted from the books of a company for the month ended 31 March 1986.

		£	£	
Mar 1	Purchase ledger (debit balance)	200		
	(credit balance)	12 000		
	Sales ledger (debit balance)	35 000		
	(credit balance)	400		
Mar 31	Purchase ledger (debit balance)	100	23 420	(credit balance)
	Sales ledger (credit balance)	200	39 050	(debit balance)
	Purchases (credit)	24 000		
	Sales (credit)	36 000		
	Discount received	600		
	Discount allowed	500		
	Returns inwards	200		
	Returns outwards	100		
	Cheques received from debtors	30 400		

(Continues)

	£	£
Cheques paid to creditors	11 400	
Contras	400	
Bills receivable (debtors)	1 000	
Bills dishonoured (debtors)	200	
Cheques dishonoured	100	
Cheques received from creditors	20	
Cheques paid to debtors	50	

REQUIRED:

a) Prepare the purchase ledger control account.
b) Prepare the sales ledger control account.
c) Give three reasons why control accounts are used.

(The Institute of Commercial Management)

5 The financial year of Handile plc ended on 31 March 1986. A trial balance extracted as at that date reveals a difference of £100 in the books. It is decided to draw up a sales ledger control account and a purchases ledger control account to help locate any errors. The trial balance figures for debtors and creditors were £16 940 and £23 188 respectively. These represent the totals of the balances on the individual debtors' and creditors' accounts in the sales and purchases ledgers.

The following information is obtained from the books of original entry

Cash book:	£
Discounts allowed	3 112
Cash and cheques from customers	125 050
Discounts received	2 097
Cash and cheques paid to suppliers	139 830
Refunds given to customers	231
Customers' cheques dishonoured	55

Journal:	£
Balances in the purchases ledger set off against balances in the sales ledger	460
Bad debts written off	661
Decrease in the provision for bad debts	51
Sales book	130 411
Purchases book	155 603
Returns in book	3 150
Returns out book	3 227

According to the audited accounts for the previous year debtors and creditors as at 1 April 1985 were £18 776 and £13 199 respectively

REQUIRED:

a) Draw up the relevant control accounts.
b) Suggest where an error might have been made.

(The Association of Accounting Technicians)

6 L Ashurst's sales ledger contains the accounts of many debtors. The information given below relates to the accounts of A Durban and W Elliott, which had been mislaid at the time of preparation of the remaining debtors' accounts.

1986		£
March 1	A Durban	400 debit
	W Elliott	240 debit

During March the following transactions took place.

1986		
March	3	Sold goods to A Durban £925 on credit.
	5	Sales on credit to W Elliott £1200.
	8	Sent a credit note to A Durban for £23 relating to damaged goods.
	16	Received a cheque from A Durban in settlement of his account at 1 March, less 5 per cent cash discount.
	17	Sold goods to W Elliott, on credit, list price £1000 less 15 per cent trade discount.
	20	A Durban complained that the credit note issued on 8 March should have been £32. Correct this error.
	31	L Ashurst also bought some goods from W Elliott. The credit balance of £168 on Elliott's account in the bought ledger was transferred to his account in the sales ledger.

REQUIRED:

a) i) The accounts of A Durban and W Elliott, as they would appear in Ashurst's sales ledger for the month of March 1986.

ii) Ashurst's sales and returns inwards accounts for the month ended 31 March 1986.

The following total figures relate to the debtors' accounts in C Nelson's sales ledger for the month ended 31 January 1986.

	£
Opening debit balances (at 1 January 1986)	42 606
Sales	160 000
Cheques received	142 220
Discounts allowed	7 321
Bad debts	1 306
Returns inward	621

REQUIRED:

b) Preparation of the sales ledger control account of C Nelson for the month of January 1986.

c) A comment on the main purpose of control accounts.

d) Where, and under what headings does the balance of the sales ledger control account appear in the final accounts?

(Associated Examining Board, June 1986)

7 *Situation:* As a member of the accounting team of ABC Co Ltd you are asked to prepare the control accounts of both the sales ledger and bought ledger for the month ended 31 March 1986.

Information: The following were balances taken from the books of ABC Co Ltd for the month March 1986:

		£
1 March 1986		
Bought ledger	Cr balance	12 860
Bought ledger	Dr balance	225
Sales ledger	Dr balance	34 755
Sales ledger	Cr balance	372
31 March 1986		
Purchases journal		23 805
Sales journal		37 215
Discount received		621
Discount allowed		558
Cheques received from customers		29 950
Cash/cheques to suppliers		22 140
Contra entries between debtors and creditors		420
Cash purchases		1 285
Bad debts written off		470
Returns outward journal		950
Dishonoured cheques from customers		155
Interest charged to customers on overdue accounts		85
Returns inward journal		1 472
Received from creditor in respect of over payment		25
Bills receivable		1 150
Cash refund to customer		50
Provision for bad debts		750

The balances extracted from the personal ledgers of ABC Co Ltd on 31 March 1986 were:

		£
Bought ledger	Cr balance	12 484
Bought ledger	Dr balance	150
Sales ledger	Dr balance	38 124
Sales ledger	Cr balance	456

TASKS:

a) Prepare the bought ledger control account and the sales ledger control account for the month ended 31 March 1986.
b) From the figures you have prepared for task a) what conclusions can you draw?
c) Briefly explain, by means of memorandum to the junior accounts clerk, why in some business enterprises, there is a need to keep control accounts.

(Institute of Bankers)

CHAPTER

15 A model exercise: subsidiary books to trial balance

- *Can you follow the various stages of this exercise from its initial balance sheet to the trial balance?*

The books of R Pearce

This extended example will illustrate the following:

a) Preparing the initial balance sheet.
b) Setting up the ledgers.
c) Preparing the sales journal.
d) Preparing the purchases journal.
e) Preparing the modified cash book.
f) Preparing the bank reconciliation statement.
g) Extracting a trial balance.

You are to place yourself in the position of R Pearce's accounts assistant responsible for preparing all the necessary entries for the month of January 1990.

Opening financial position

The following information represents the accounts of R Pearce on 1 January 1990.

	£
Premises (cost)	100 000
Equipment, machinery (cost)	13 500
Motor vehicle (cost)	5 000
Bank (Dr)	455
Petty cash float	150
Sales ledger control (debtors)	2 575
Bought ledger control (creditors)	5 640
Stocks	3 680
R Pearce: Capital	50 000
Mortgage on premises	69 720

a) Prepare the balance sheet of R Pearce as on 1 January to show the company's financial position as on that date. Show working capital.

Personal ledger accounts as on 1 January

Sales ledger

	£	
D Lewis	1 025	Dr
D Smith	200	Dr
B Kings	600	Dr
C Taylor	285	Dr
M Johnson	465	Dr
	2 575	

Bought ledger

	£	
Slazenger Sports	1 975	Cr
Metro Sports	300	Cr
Auto	1 215	Cr
International	2 150	Cr
	5 640	

b) Set up the ledger system of R Pearce using sales, bought and nominal ledgers, from personal ledger accounts and the opening financial position as above. The bank balance of £455 will be recorded in the cash book.

Credit sales and credit purchases

The credit sales for January were as follows:

Date	*Customer account*	*Invoice no.*	*Net sales*	*Vat*	*Total*
			£	£	£
Jan 5	D Lewis	4219	500		
8	D Smith	4220	240		
12	D Lewis	4221	168		
17	C Taylor	4222	350		
18	B Kings	4223	450		
24	D Smith	4224	180		
25	D Lewis	4225	290		
27	B Kings	4226	650		
30	M Johnson	4227	300		

c) Use the above table to record your figures. Calculate Vat at 15 per cent and total the columns. Post the transactions to the ledgers.

The credit purchases of stock for January were as follows:

Date	*Supplier account*	*Invoice no. received*	*Gross purchases* £	*Net purchases* £	*Vat* £	*Total* £
Jan 5	International	3046	1 000	800	114.00	
7	Slazenger Sports	29851	1 200	960	136.80	
10	Metro Sports	4367	500	425	60.56	
15	International	4768	380	304	43.32	
20	Slazenger Sports	34420	530	424	60.42	
25	Auto	2321	240	204	29.07	

d) Use the above table to record your findings. Check the accuracy of the invoices before totalling the columns. International and Slazenger Sports give 20 per cent trade and 5 per cent cash discounts. Metro Sports and Auto give 15 per cent trade and 5 per cent cash discounts. Post to the ledgers.

Cash book entries

All cash receipts and payments of money are to be made through the bank. For receipts use separate columns to identify totals for: debtors; cash sales; Vat; and bank. No discount is given to debtors.

Receipts

		£
Jan 8	B Kings	300
10	C Taylor	200
12	Cash sales	185 + Vat
15	B Kings	300
17	D Lewis	500
18	Cash sales	162 + Vat
20	D Smith	200
26	Cash sales	425 + Vat
29	M Johnson	465

Use separate columns to identify totals for: discount received; creditors; overheads; general expenses; and bank.

Payments

Jan 1	Overheads	250.0	
5	Slazenger Sports	1 000.0	discount taken £50.00
8	Auto	500.0	discount taken £12.50
13	Overheads	250.0	
13	International	1 500.0	
16	Metro Sports	292.5	discount taken £7.50
20	Overheads	350.0	
21	Southern Gas	56.0	
24	British Telecom	122.0	
28	Wages	6 025.0	
28	Tax and insurance	215.5	
30	Overheads	250.0	
31	Miscellaneous expenses	121.0	

e) Prepare the company's cash book for January, balancing at the end of the month (31 January). Bring down the bank balance on 1 February.

Post all relevant transactions from the above information to the appropriate ledgers. Ensure that control accounts in the nominal ledgers cross-check with the personal ledgers. Prepare schedules for debtors and creditors to confirm totals with the control accounts.

f) Bank reconciliation statement – from the information given in the bank statement, cross-check entries made in the cash book. Bring the cash book up-to-date, post any new entries to the ledger and then prepare the bank reconciliation statement on 31 January.

Extract a trial balance for the company as on 31 January.

Statement of account

R Pearce
77 Penhill Avenue
Penhill
Poole
Dorset

Cheque account
104236876

31 January 1990

Details	*Payments* £	*Receipts* £	*Date*	*Balance* £
Balance forward			1/1	455.00 Cr
100197	250.0		1/1	205.00
CC		300.00	8/1	505.00
CC		200.00	10/1	705.00
CC		212.75	12/1	917.75
100198	1 000.0		13/1	82.25 O/D
100200	250.0		15/1	332.25
CC		300.00	15/1	32.25

(Continues)

Details	Payments £	Receipts £	Date	Balance £
100199	500.0		16/1	532.25
CC		500.00	18/1	32.25
100201	1 500.0		19/1	1 532.25
CC		186.30	19/1	1 345.95
CC		200.00	20/1	1 145.95
100202	292.5		20/1	1 438.45
100203	350.0		20/1	1 788.45
CC		488.75	26/1	1 299.70
100204	56.0		27/1	1 355.70
100206	6 025.0		30/1	7 380.70
DDR WDC rates	49.5		30/1	7 430.20
Commission 2 Oct – 2 Jan	12.0		30/1	7 442.20 O/D

NOTES

Commission – charges by the bank
DDR – direct debit
STO – standing order
O/D – overdrawn balances
CC – deposits to bank

Answers

R Pearce –
Balance sheet as at 1 January 1990

	£	£	£
FIXED ASSETS			
Premises (cost)	100 000		
Equipment, machinery (cost)	13 500		
Motor vehicle	5 000		118 500
CURRENT ASSETS			
Stocks	3 680		
Debtors	2 575		
Bank	455		
Petty cash (float)	150	6 860	
CURRENT LIABILITIES			
Creditors		5 640	
WORKING CAPITAL			1 220

(Continues)

	£	£	£
CAPITAL EMPLOYED			119 720
LONG-TERM LIABILITIES			
Mortgage on premises			69 720
			50 000
FINANCED BY:			
R Pearce: Capital			50 000

Sales journal

Page 1

Date	*Customer account*	*Invoice no.*	*Net sales £*	*Vat £*	*Total £*
Jan 5	D Lewis	4219	500	75.00	575.00
8	D Smith	4220	240	36.00	276.00
12	D Lewis	4221	168	25.20	193.20
17	C Taylor	4222	350	52.50	402.50
18	B Kings	4223	450	67.50	517.50
24	D Smith	4224	180	27.00	207.00
25	D Lewis	4225	290	43.50	333.50
27	B Kings	4226	650	97.50	747.50
30	M Johnson	4227	300	45.00	345.00
			3 128	469.20	3 597.20

Purchases journal

Page 3

Date	*Supplier account*	*Invoice no.*	*Net purchases*	*Vat*	*Total*
Jan 5	International	3046	800	114.00	914.00
7	Slazenger Sports	29851	960	136.80	1 096.80
10	Metro	4367	425	60.56	485.56
15	International	4768	304	43.32	347.32
20	Slazenger Sports	34420	424	60.42	484.42
25	Auto	2321	204	29.07	233.07
			3 117	444.17	3 561.17

Sales ledger

D Lewis account		*Folio*	*Dr*	*Cr*	*Balance*
Jan 1	Balance				1 025.00 Dr
5	Sales	SJ1	500.00		
	Vat	SJ1	75.00		1 600.00 Dr
12	Sales	SJ1	168.00		
	Vat	SJ1	25.20		1 793.20 Dr
17	Bank	CB9		500	1 293.20 Dr
25	Sales	SJ1	290.00		
	Vat	SJ1	43.50		1 626.70 Dr

D Smith account		*Folio*	*Dr*	*Cr*	*Balance*
Jan 1	Balance				200 Dr
8	Sales	SJ1	240		
	Vat	SJ1	36		476 Dr
20	Bank	CB9		200	276 Dr
24	Sales	SJ1	180		
	Vat	SJ1	27		483 Dr

B Kings account		*Folio*	*Dr*	*Cr*	*Balance*
Jan 1	Balance				600.00 Dr
8	Bank	CB9		300	300.00 Dr
15	Bank	CB9		300	—
18	Sales	SJ1	450.00		
	Vat	SJ1	67.50		517.50 Dr
27	Sales	SJ1	650.00		
	Vat	SJ1	97.50		1 265.00 Dr

C Taylor account		*Folio*	*Dr*	*Cr*	*Balance*
Jan 1	Balance				285.00 Dr
10	Bank	CB9		200	85.00 Dr
17	Sales	SJ1	350.00		
	Vat	SJ1	52.50		487.50 Dr

M Johnson account		*Folio*	*Dr*	*Cr*	*Balance*
Jan 1	Balance				465 Dr
29	Bank	CB9		465	—
30	Sales	SJ1	300		
	Vat	SJ1	45		345 Dr

Sales ledger

Schedule of debtors as at 31 January 1990

	£
D Lewis	1 626.70
D Smith	483.00
B Kings	1 265.00
C Taylor	487.50
M Johnson	345.00
	4 207.20

Bought ledger

Slazenger sports account		*Folio*	*Dr*	*Cr*	*Balance*
Jan 1	Balance				1 975.00 Cr
5	Bank	CB9	1 000		
	Discount received	CB9	50		925.00 Cr
7	Purchases	PJ3		960.00	
	Vat	PJ3		136.80	2 021.80 Cr
20	Purchases	PJ3		424.00	
	Vat	PJ3		60.42	2 506.22 Cr

Metro sports account		*Folio*	*Dr*	*Cr*	*Balance*
Jan 1	Balance				300.00 Cr
10	Purchases	PJ3		425.00	
	Vat	PJ3		60.56	785.56 Cr
16	Bank	CB9	292.50		
	Discount received	CB9	7.50		485.56 Cr

Auto account		*Folio*	*Dr*	*Cr*	*Balance*
Jan 1	Balance				1 215.00 Cr
8	Bank	CB9	500.00		
	Discount received	CB9	12.50		702.50 Cr
25	Purchases	PJ3		204.00	
	Vat	PJ3		29.07	935.57 Cr

International account		*Folio*	*Dr*	*Cr*	*Balance*
Jan 1	Balance				2 150.00 Cr
5	Purchases	PJ3		800.00	
	Vat	PJ3		114.00	3 064.00 Cr
13	Bank	CB9	1 500		1 564.00 Cr
15	Purchases	PJ3		304.00	
	Vat	PJ3		43.32	1 911.32 Cr

Bought ledger

Schedule of creditors as at 31 January 1990

	£
Slazenger Sports	2 506.22
Metro Sports	485.56
Auto	935.57
International	1 911.32
	5 838.67

Nominal ledger

R Pearce: Capital account		*Folio*	*Dr*	*Cr*	*Balance*	
Jan 1	Balance				50 000	Cr

Mortage on premises account		*Folio*	*Dr*	*Cr*	*Balance*	
Jan 1	Balance				69 720	Cr

Sales account		*Folio*	*Dr*	*Cr*	*Balance*	
Jan 1	Balance				—	
31	Debtors	SJ1		3 128	3 128	Cr
31	Sundry cash sales	CB9		772	3 900	Cr

Vat account		*Folio*	*Dr*	*Cr*	*Balance*	
Jan 1	Balance				—	
31	Debtors	SJ1		469.20	469.20	Cr
31	Creditors	PJ3	444.17		25.03	Cr
31	Cash sales	CB9		115.80	140.83	Cr

Purchases account		*Folio*	*Dr*	*Cr*	*Balance*	
Jan 1	Balance				—	
31	Creditors	PJ3	3 117		3 117	Dr

Discount received account		*Folio*	*Dr*	*Cr*	*Balance*	
Jan 1	Balance				—	
31	Sundries	CB9		70	70	Cr

Expenses account		*Folio*	*Dr*	*Cr*	*Balance*	
Jan 1	Balance				—	
31	Sundries	CB9	576		576	Dr

Premises account		*Folio*	*Dr*	*Cr*	*Balance*	
Jan 1	Balance				100 000	Dr

Equipment, machinery account		*Folio*	*Dr*	*Cr*	*Balance*	
Jan 1	Balance				13 500	Dr

Nominal ledger

Motor vehicle account		*Folio*	*Dr*	*Cr*	*Balance*	
Jan 1	Balance				5 000	Dr

Petty cash float account		*Folio*	*Dr*	*Cr*	*Balance*	
Jan 1	Balance				150	Dr

Sales ledger control account		*Folio*	*Dr*	*Cr*	*Balance*	
Jan 1	Balance				2 575.00	Dr
31	Sales (inc. VAT)	SJ1	3 597.20		6 172.20	Dr
31	Bank	CB9		1 965	4 207.20	Dr

Bought ledger control account		*Folio*	*Dr*	*Cr*	*Balance*	
Jan 1	Balance				5 640.00	Cr
31	Bank	PJ3		3 561.17	9 201.17	Cr
31	Bank	CB9	3 292.50		5 908.67	Cr
31	Discounts received	CB9	70.00		5 838.67	Cr

Stock account		*Folio*	*Dr*	*Cr*	*Balance*	
Jan 1	Balance				3 680	Dr

Wages account		*Folio*	*Dr*	*Cr*	*Balance*	
Jan 1	Balance				—	
31	Sundry	CB9	6 025		6 025	Dr

Overheads account		*Folio*	*Dr*	*Cr*	*Balance*	
Jan 1	Balance				—	
31	Sundries	CB9	1 100		1 100	Dr

Dr **Cash book – receipts** Page 9

Date	*Particulars*	*Debtors*	*Cash sales*	*Vat*	*Bank*
Jan 1	Balance				455.00
8	B Kings	300			300.00
10	C Taylor	200			200.00
12	Cash sales		185	27.75	212.75
15	B Kings	300			300.00
17	D Lewis	500			500.00
18	Cash sales		162	24.30	186.30
20	D Smith	200			200.00
26	Cash sales		425	63.75	488.75
29	M Johnson	465			465.00
31	Balance c/d				7 685.70
		1 965	772	115.80	10 993.50

Cash book – payments

Cr								Page 9
Date		*Particulars*	*Discount received*	*Creditors*	*Overheads*	*Wages*	*Expenses*	*Bank*
Jan	1	Overheads			250			250.00
	5	Slazenger Sports	50.00	1 000.00				1 000.00
	8	Auto	12.50	500.00				500.00
	13	Overheads			250			250.00
	13	International		1 500.00				1 500.00
	16	Metro Sports	7.50	292.50				292.50
	20	Overheads			350			350.00
	21	Southern Gas					56.00	56.00
	24	British Telecom					122.00	122.00
	28	Wages				6 025		6 025.00
	28	Tax and insurance					215.50	215.50
	30	Overheads			250			250.00
	30	WDC rates					49.50	49.50
	30	Commission					12.00	12.00
	31	Miscellaneous					121.00	121.00
			70	3 292.50	1 100	6 025	576.00	10 993.50
Feb	1	Balance b/d						7 685.70

Bank reconciliation as at 31 January 1990

	£	£	
Balance per bank statement		7 442.20	O/D
Add Unpresented cheques:			
British Telecom	122.00		
Tax and insurance	212.50		
Overheads	250.00		
Miscellaneous	121.00	708.50	
		8 150.70	
Less Undeposited cheques:			
M Johnson		465.00	
Balance as per cash book		7 685.70	O/D

R Pearce –
Trial balance as at 31 January 1990

	Dr	*Cr*
	£	£
Premises	100 000.00	
Equipment, machinery	13 500.00	
Motor vehicle	5 000.00	
Petty cash float	150.00	
Sales ledger control (debtors)	4 207.20	
Bought ledger control (creditors)		5 838.67
Stock	3 680.00	
R Pearce: Capital		50 000.00
Mortgage on premises		69 720.00
Sales		3 900.00
Vat		140.83
Purchases	3 117.00	
Discount received		70.00
Expenses	576.00	
Wages	6 025.00	
Overheads	1 100.00	
Bank		7 685.70
	137 355.20	137 355.20

NOTE

If the value of closing stock on 31 January 1990 was £4800, you could prepare the financial statements for the month ending 31 January 1990. You may need Chapter 16 to help you.

PART III, CHAPTER

16 The final accounts of sole traders

- *How are the final accounts of a sole trader prepared?*
- *Which groups of accounts are 'zeroed' at the end of a financial period?*

Introduction

Financial statements were first introduced in Chapter 3. The two basic financial reports refer to the trading and profit and loss account and the balance sheet. These statements (or reports) are commonly referred to as the *final accounts* because, at the end of a financial period, the final balances listed in the trial balance are used to prepare the accounting reports. These reports help to determine the performance of a business in terms of profit or loss and its financial position.

The purpose of the trading and profit and loss account is to determine the business's profit or loss in the accounting period under review. This accounting period is at the end of the financial year for most sole traders. For larger business organisations, the determination of profit or loss may be required more frequently for management purposes.

The preparation of the balance sheet represents the business's financial position in terms of its assets, liabilities and capital, listing its resources (assets) and the financing of these resources (capital and liabilities).

When preparing the final accounts of sole traders (people who own and control businesses by themselves) the accountant is likely to prepare these at the end of the financial year, giving the trader a picture of his or her business performance and also to prepare the necessary figures for the Inland Revenue for the purpose of assessing the trader's personal tax liability.

Profit or loss is basically the difference between revenue and expenses. If revenue is greater, a profit is made. The reverse is true if expenses exceed revenue. Therefore, from the five accounting groups:

revenue
expenses } trading and profit and loss account

assets
liabilities
capital } balance sheet.

The link between the two statements is that, in the event of a profit or loss, capital is either increased or decreased respectively, because profit or loss is transferred to the owner. If capital is affected, by the same token, net assets (assets less liabilities), must be affected equally by the same sum.

Example

Capital	=	Assets	−	Liabilities
£10 000	=	£60 000	−	£50 000

Profit for year: £2000, the accounting equation after adding profit:

Capital	=	Assets	−	Liabilities
£12 000	=	£62 000	−	£50 000

If a loss of £2000 was made in the year, capital would be reduced to £8000, the net assets equalling £8000.

It is the usual practice to prepare the financial statements from a set of accounts listed in the business's trial balance. At the end of a financial period, all revenue and expense accounts are transferred to the trading and profit and loss account and in so doing, their balances are *zeroed*. In the new financial period, revenue and expense accounts will commence with a nil balance. Assets, liabilities and capital accounts are not affected in this way and their balances are carried forward from one accounting period to the next.

The accounts of R Pearce

The last chapter ended with the trial balance of R Pearce as on 31 January. We can use these figures to calculate his profit or loss for the month although we need to know the value of any unsold stock as on 31 January because this will influence how much gross profit he has made. For this example, the unsold value of stock will be £5200.

R Pearce –
Trial balance as on 31 January

	Dr	*Cr*
	£	£
Premises	100 000.0	
Equipment, machinery	13 500.0	
Motor vehicle	5 000.0	
Petty cash (float)	150.0	
S/L control (debtors)	4 207.2	
B/L control (creditors)		5 838.67
Stock (1/1)	3 680.0	

(Continues)

	Dr £	*Cr* £
Capital: R Pearce		50 000.00
Mortgage on premises		69 720.00
Bank (overdraft)		2 185.70
Vat		140.83
Sales		3 900.00
Purchases	3 117.0	
Discount received		70.00
Expenses	576.0	
Wages	525.0	
Overheads	1 100.0	
	131 855.2	131 855.20

NOTE
At 31 January unsold stock was valued at £5 200.

R Pearce –
Trading and profit and loss account, month ended 31 January . . .

	£	£	£
Sales			3 900
*Less cost of sales:			
Stock (1/1)		3 680	
+ Purchases		3 117	
		6 797	
− Stock (31/1)		5 200	1 597
Gross profit			2 303
Less expenses:			
General expenses		576	
Wages		525	
Overheads		1 100	2 201
			102
Add other revenue:			
Discount received			70
Net profit			172

NOTE
*Cost of sales – the cost of selling the goods is an expense, representing the buying price. It is usually made up from:

	£
Opening stock (1/1)	3 680
+ Purchases	3 117
	6 797
− Returns outward	—
	6 797
+ Carriage inwards	—
	6 797
− Closing stock (31/1)	5 200
Cost of sales =	1 597

R Pearce –
Balance sheet as at 31 January

	£	£	£
Fixed assets (at cost)			
Premises	100 000.00		
Equipment, machinery	13 500.00		
Motor vehicle	5 000.00		118 500
Current assets			
Stock (31/1)	5 200.00		
Debtors	4 207.20		
Bank	—		
Petty cash	150.00	9 557.2	
less			
Current liabilities			
Creditors	5 838.67		
Vat	140.83		
Bank (overdraft)	2 185.70	8 165.2	
Net current assets:			1 392
Capital employed:			119 892
less			
Long-term liabilities			
Mortgage on premises			69 720
			50 172
Financed by:			
Capital: R Pearce		50 000.0	
+ Profit		172.0	
− Drawings		50 172.0	
			50 172

NOTES

1 The net profit of £170 is transferred from the profit and loss account to the owner's capital, increasing his net worth in the business.

2 Net current assets (£1390) is an alternative name for working capital (working capital ratio, 1.17 : 1).

3 Capital employed refers to the fixed assets added to the net current assets of the business and indicates the employable assets less current liabilities.

4 Drawings refer to the personal expenses of the owner. In this case, for the month of January, R Pearce had made no drawings.

The transfer of revenue and expense accounts

At the end of a financial period, when revenue and expense accounts are extracted from the trial balance to prepare the trading and profit and loss account, the ledger account balances for these are transferred from the nominal ledger to the trading and profit and loss account. This procedure, in effect, allows the double entry to be completed and effectively zeroes the balances. In the following accounting period, revenue and expense accounts will therefore normally commence with nil balances. The stock account is also adjusted to record the value of the unsold stock at the period end.

For the following example, we will assume that the period end of R Pearce is 31 January.

Nominal ledger

		Dr £	*Cr* £	*Balance* £
Sales account				
31/1	Balance			3 900 Cr
31/1	Trading account	3 900		—
Purchases account				
31/1	Balance			3 117 Dr
31/1	Trading account		3 117	—
Stock account				
31/1	Balance			3 680 Dr
31/1	Trading account		3 680	—
31/1	Trading account	5 200		5 200 Dr
*1/2	Balance			5 200 Dr

(Continues)

		Dr £	Cr £	Balance £
General expenses account				
31/1	Balance			376 Dr
31/1	Profit and loss account		376	—
Wages account				
31/1	Balance			525 Dr
31/1	Profit and loss account		525	—
Overheads account				
31/1	Balance			1 100 Dr
31/1	Profit and loss account		1 100	—

NOTE

*The value of unsold stock on 31 January (£5200) is brought into the account and therefore, the stock end of one period becomes the stock beginning of the next period on 1 February.

Example

The following accounts represent the business of R Pearce at the end of the financial year, 31 December 1990:

	Dr £	Cr £
Capital: R Pearce		50 000
Drawings: R Pearce	5 600	
Premises	100 000	
Equipment, machinery	17 150	
Motor vehicle	4 000	
Mortgage on premises		69 200
Stock (1/1/90)	3 680	
Petty cash	200	
Debtors, creditors	4 650	5 950
Sales		62 900
Returns inward	850	
Purchases	35 800	
Returns outward		1 350
Wages	7 480	
Light and heat	970	
Telephone	480	
Printing and stationery	385	
Carriage inwards	220	

(Continues)

	Dr £	Cr £
Carriage outwards	300	
Advertising	675	
Overheads	12 640	
Discount allowed	100	
Motoring expenses	1 370	
Interest payable	210	
Commission received		300
Discount received		850
Vat (owing)		1 320
Bank (O/D)		4 890
	196 760	196 760

NOTE

The value of unsold stock on 31 December was £5500.

REQUIRED:

a) Prepare the trading and profit and loss account of R Pearce for the year ended 31 December 1990.
b) Prepare the balance sheet of R Pearce as on 31 December 1990 in vertical format, showing clearly his net current assets and the working capital ratio.
c) Comment briefly on R Pearce's working capital.

R Pearce –
Trading and profit and loss account for year ended 31 December 1990

	£	£	£
Sales		62 900	
– Returns inward		850	62 050
Cost of sales:			
Stock (1/1)		3 680	
+ Purchases	35 800		
– Returns outward	1 350	34 450	
+ Carriage inwards		220	
		38 350	
– Stock (31/12)		5 500	32 850
Gross profit			29 200
Less expenses:			
Wages	7 480		
Light and heat	970		

(Continues)

	£	£	£
Printing and stationery	385		
Telephone	480		
Carriage outwards	300		
Advertising	675		
Overheads	12 640		
Discount allowed	100		
Motoring expenses	1 370		
Interest payable	210		24 610
			4 590
Add other income:			
Commission received	300		
Discount received	850		1 150
Net profit			5 740

NOTE

Carriage inwards refers to the cost of delivery for purchases and is therefore a trading expense. Carriage outwards refers to the cost of delivery to customers and is regarded as a profit and loss expense.

R Pearce –
Balance sheet as on 31 December 1990

	£	£	£
FIXED ASSETS			
Premises	100 000		
Equipment, machinery	17 150		
Motor vehicle	4 000		121 150
CURRENT ASSETS			
Stock (31/12)	5 500		
Debtors	4 650		
Bank	—		
Petty cash	200	10 350	
less			
CURRENT LIABILITIES			
Creditors	5 950		
Vat	1 320		
Bank (O/D)	4 890	12 160	
Net current liabilities (0.85 : 1)			(1 810)
Capital employed			119 340

(Continues)

	£	£	£
LONG-TERM LIABILITIES			
Mortgage on premises			69 200
			50 140
FINANCED BY			
Capital: R Pearce	50 000		
+ Net profit	5 740		
	55 740		
− Drawings	5 600		50 140

NOTES

1 The value of unsold stock on 31 December is included in the balance sheet as a current asset.

2 Net profit is added to capital, increasing the owner's net worth. Personal drawings reduces net worth.

3 R Pearce has insufficient working capital because his current assets are less than his current liabilities, a working capital ratio (current ratio) of less than 1. This is known as an 'insolvent position' and R Pearce will need to be aware that his creditors can press for payments and demand their debts to be honoured. He may need to reduce his expenses or increase his sales to be in a better liquidity position.

Summary

1 The two basic financial statements of a business refer to the trading and profit and loss account and the balance sheet. They are also referred to as the final accounts.

2 From the five accounting groups listed in a trial balance, revenue and expenses are matched together to determine the profit or loss of the business. This leaves assets, liabilities and capital to be used in the preparation of the balance sheet.

3 Profit is added to the owner's capital and losses reduce the owner's capital. In this way, the two financial statements are linked, profits increasing net worth and therefore net assets, losses have the effect of doing the reverse.

4 Personal drawings by the owner of a business are a deduction from net worth. Drawings may be in cash, stock or anything else taken from the business by the owner, for his or her own personal use.

5 At the end of the financial period, all revenue and expense accounts are transferred to either the trading or profit and loss account, thereby 'zeroising' these accounts. The next accounting period for all revenue and expense accounts should commence with nil balances. The stock account will also be adjusted to bring in the value of closing stock.

QUESTIONS

1 The following accounts relate to the business of P Jackson as at the month ended 31 January 1990:

P Jackson –
Trial balance as on 31 January 1990

	Dr £	*Cr* £
Bank	2 855	
Premises (cost)	12 000	
Fixtures and fittings (cost)	2 000	
Equipment (cost)	3 000	
Mortgage on premises		8 000
Bank loan (long-term)		2 000
Capital: P Jackson		10 000
Drawings: P Jackson	100	
Wages	375	
Light and heat	220	
General expenses	20	
Purchases	2 370	
Sales		3 085
Commission received		30
Debtors	875	
Creditors		1 435
Stock (1 January)	735	
	24 550	24 550

NOTE

The value of unsold stock on 31 January is £805.

REQUIRED:

a) Prepare the trading and profit and loss account of P Jackson for the month of January 1990.
b) Prepare a balance sheet as on 31 January 1990 and show working capital as part of the format. Calculate the working capital ratio.

2 The following represents the trial balance of D Smith for the month ended 30 June 1990:

	Dr	*Cr*
	£	£
Capital: D Smith		20 000
Drawings: D Smith	540	
Fixtures, fittings	2 100	
Motor vehicle	4 450	
Bank/cash	155	
Debtors	2 440	
Creditors		1 180
Premises	56 600	
General expenses	390	
Wages	665	
Purchases	2 000	
Stock (1 June)	1 900	
Sales		8 070
Mortgage on premises		40 000
Returns inward	60	
Returns outward		50
Loan from bank (4 years)		2 000
	71 300	71 300

NOTE

The value of stock on 30 June was £2 125.

REQUIRED:

a) Prepare the trading and profit and loss account of D Smith for the month ended 30 June 1990.
b) Prepare the balance sheet of D Smith as at 30 June 1990. Show the net current assets and capital employed as part of your answer. Calculate the current ratio (working capital ratio).

3 The following information relates to the accounts of D Balfour as on 31 December 1990:

D Balfour –
Trading and profit and loss account as on 31 December 1990

	Dr £	*Cr* £
Capital: D Balfour		16 600
Drawings: D Balfour	10 200	
Sales		209 200
Returns inward	200	
Purchases	104 350	
Returns outward		50
Stock (1 January)	38 500	
Wages	28 000	
Rent, rates	5 600	
General expenses	2 150	
Insurance	1 850	
Advertising	980	
Postage and stationery	2 150	
Debtors	11 800	
Creditors		4 230
Plant and equipment	42 600	
Fixtures, fittings	6 000	
Motor vehicle	7 900	
Bank loan (1994)		38 000
Bank	5 300	
Cash	500	
	268 080	268 080

NOTE

The value of unsold stock on 31 December was £42 100.

REQUIRED:

a) Prepare the trading and profit and loss account of D Balfour for the year ending 31 December 1990.

b) Prepare the balance sheet of D Balfour as on 31 December 1990, clearly showing working capital. Calculate the current ratio.

4 The following information relates to the accounts of E Mitton for the year ended 31 March 1990:

E Mitton –
Trial balance as on 31 March 1990

	Dr	*Cr*
	£	£
Bank	1 532	
Petty cash	150	
Fixtures and fittings (cost)	2 200	
Motor vehicle	4 025	
Stock (1/4/89)	3 700	
Debtors, creditors	1 943	3 580
Vat	127	
HP loan (3 years)		4 050
Capital: E Mitton		11 000
Drawings: E Mitton	4 100	
Sales		21 360
Returns	400	350
Purchases	13 500	
Carriage inwards	75	
Carriage outwards	250	
Rent	2 500	
Wages	4 150	
General overheads	1 546	
Discount	142	
	40 340	40 340

NOTE

The value of unsold stock on 31 March was £3500.

REQUIRED:

a) Prepare the trading and profit and loss account of E Mitton for the year ended 31 March 1990.
b) Prepare the balance sheet of E Mitton as on 31 March 1990.
c) Make a brief comment relating to the working capital of the owner.

5 Prepare from the following accounts, a trial balance for B Jackson, as on 1 January 1990:

	£		£
Bank overdraft	300	Sales	48 475
Cash	200	Purchases	35 450
Motor van	2 420	General expenses	2 485
Debtors	515	Motor expenses	850
Creditors	1 225	Rent received	840
Capital	10 500		
Bank loan	3 400		
Premises	25 300		
Mortgage	8 950		
Equipment	6 570		

Trial balance of
B Jackson as on 1 January 1990

	Dr	*Cr*
	£	£
Bank overdraft		300
Cash	200	
Motor van	2 420	
Debtors	515	
Creditors		1 225
Capital: P Jackson		10 500
Bank loan		3 400
Premises	25 300	
Sales		48 575
Purchases	35 450	
General expenses	2 485	
Motor expenses	850	
Rent received		840
Mortgage		8 950
Equipment	6 570	
	73 790	73 790

REQUIRED:

a) Check that the list of accounts are entered correctly in the trial balance.
b) There are no opening/closing stocks.
Estimate *your own* value of closing stock on 31 January, say *under* £1000, and proceed to the preparation of the final accounts for the period ending to 31 January 1990.

6 **Trial balance of Jenkins Jeans Co Ltd 31 March 1990**

	Dr	*Cr*
	£	£
Premises	53 150	
Equipment and machines	4 000	
Motor vehicle	4 750	
Stocks	3 680	
Bank		8 022
Petty cash	200	
Debtors, creditors	4 050	4 785
Mortgage on premises		32 450
Bank loan (5 years)		4 725
Sales		11 850
Purchases	5 600	
Vat		248
Gross wages	5 025	
Light and heat	72	
Telephone, insurance	105	
Petty cash expenses	148	
General overheads	800	
Directors' fees	500	
Share capital		20 000
	82 080	82 080

NOTE

On 31 March 1990 stocks were valued at £4580.

REQUIRED:

a) Prepare the trading and profit and loss account of the company for the month ending 31 March 1990.
   Prepare a balance sheet as on that date. Show working capital as part of the presentation.
c) Calculate the appropriate accounting ratio to measure working capital.

(BTEC National)

CHAPTER

17 Adjustments to final accounts

- *What is the accounting period?*
- *How do adjustments affect the preparation of final accounts?*
- *Why is it important to distinguish between capital and revenue expenditure?*

Introduction

The accounting period of R Pearce runs from 1 January to 31 December and, therefore, quite naturally, the next period will recommence on 1 January. Thus accounting is broken down into annual periods by which the performance of the business can be recorded in the preparation of the financial statements in the form of the trading and profit and loss account and the balance sheet. The taxation authorities can then assess the appropriate charge for tax on an annual basis.

The accounting period can commence at any point in time, for example, 1 April to 31 March or 1 June to 31 May, and once established, that period will consistently be used for the preparation of the final accounts of the business. This follows a major concept of accounting called *consistency* which is discussed in Chapter 22. A further important concept in this chapter is the *accruals* concept which indicates that any transaction, in part or whole, which relates to a specific accounting period, *must* be included in that period.

In this way, any distortion to the accounts can be avoided and a more 'true and fair' position of the accounts for the year can be assessed.

Adjustments to the final accounts are usually made as footnotes at the bottom of a trial balance and these are the transactions which need to be included in order to give a more accurate and true record of the final accounts. These adjustments may include items such as accruals, prepayments and provisions for bad debts and depreciation.

It is also important to make the distinction between capital and revenue expenditure because payments for these also affect the outcome of the final accounts. Capital expenditure relates to spending on fixed assets or on items likely to last longer than one accounting period. Revenue expenditure relates to spending where items are expected to be used up within the financial period.

Adjustments to the final accounts

Accrued expenses

These relate to any unpaid expenses at the end of a financial period which must still be included in the financial statements. When preparing the trading and profit and loss account all items of expense, paid or incurred, must be brought into account. The accruals concept recognises that an expense, even though still outstanding, must be included in the accounting period in which it has been used. In this way, any distortion to profit or loss can be avoided.

Example

Using the trial balance figures of R Pearce from the previous chapter, assume that on 31 December, footnotes included:

a) Wages due to an employee, £150.
b) A gas bill of £85 was still unpaid.
c) Interest charges from the bank £35, had to be included under interest payable.

The effect on trading and profit and loss account as on 31 December:

	£	£
Wages	7 480	
Accrued	150	7 630
Light and heat	970	
Accrued	85	1 055
Interest payable	210	
Accrued	35	245

The effect on the balance sheet as on 31 December:

	£
CURRENT LIABILITIES	
Accrued expenses (150 + 85 + 35)	270

NOTES

1 An accrued expense is *added* to the appropriate expense paid.
2 An accrued expense is included under *current liabilities* because they represent short-term debts still unpaid.

Recording in the nominal ledger

		Debit £	Credit £	Balance £
Wages account				
31/12	Balance			7 480 Dr
31/12	Accrual	150		7 630
31/12	P&L account		7 630	—
1/1	Accrual		150	150 Cr
5/1	Bank	150		—

NOTES

1 The accrual is brought down in the new accounting period, 1 January, because the wages are still to be paid.
2 When they are paid by cheque on 5 January, the account is cleared.

Prepayments (prepaid expenses)

These relate to expenses which are prepaid (paid in advance) and therefore should be apportioned to the *next* accounting period, not the period under review.

Example

Using the trial balance figures of R Pearce as on 31 December, the following prepayments were included as footnotes:

a) There was £150 for advertising, already paid, which was for press releases in January.
b) There was still £100 of stationery still in stock, to be used in the next financial period.

The effect on trading and profit and loss account as on 31 December:

	£	£
Advertising	675	
Prepaid expense	(150)	525
Printing and stationery	385	
Prepaid expense	(100)	285

The effect on the balance sheet as on 31 December:

	£
CURRENT ASSETS	
Prepayments (150 + 100)	250

NOTES

1 A prepaid expense has the effect of *reducing* the expense because that portion is part of the next period.
2 The prepayment is regarded as a *current asset* because some value of the expense is still to be used in the next period.

Recording in the nominal ledger

		Debit £	Credit £	Balance £
Advertising account				
31/12	Balance			675 Dr
31/12	Prepayment		150	525
31/12	P&L account		525	—
1/1	Prepayment	150		150 Dr

NOTE

The prepaid expense is brought down as a debit in the new accounting period to indicate that £150 has already been spent on advertising in the new period, 1 January.

Bad debts and the provision for bad and doubtful debts

Accounting tends to be a very cautious profession and will always provide for any possible losses which may occur. This is referred to as the concept of *conservatism* or prudence. On the other hand, accounting will rarely be optimistic and make a provision for a future gain.

A possible loss is likely to be associated with debtors, particularly if the control of credit sales is poor. An accountant is likely to set a sum aside and charge it against profits if it is considered that a proportion of debtors may fail to honour their debts. It may be that some debts will never be paid and these will have to be written off as bad.

Writing off a bad debt

One of R Pearce's customers, D Lewis, has fallen on hard times and gone bankrupt and has had to be written off. The appropriate ledger entries are:

Sales ledger

		Debit £	Credit £	Balance £
D Lewis account				
31/12	Balance			260 Dr
31/12	Bad debts		260	—

Nominal ledger

		Debit £	Credit £	Balance £
Bad debts account				
31/12	D Lewis	260		260 Dr
31/12	P&L account		260	—

NOTE

The double entry:

1. Debit – bad debts account (expense), transferred to profit and loss account.
2. Credit – D Lewis account (debtor written off).

Provision for bad and doubtful debts

The accountant has decided to make a provision of 10 per cent of the debtors taken from R Pearce's sales ledger:

	£	
Balance of debtors (31/12)	4 650	
Less bad debt	260	
10% provision:	4 390	× 10%
	= 439	

The effect on trading and profit and loss account at 31 December:

	£	£
Bad debts	260	
Provision for bad debts	439	699

The effect on the balance sheet as on 31 December:

	£	£
CURRENT ASSETS		
Debtors	4 390	
– Provision for bad debts	439	3 951

NOTES

1 A sum of £699 is charged against profits for the year (£260 writing off a bad debt and £439 set aside as a provision against possible future bad debts).

2 The debtors in the balance sheet, net £3951, is what is considered a realistic sum customers will pay.

Recording in the nominal ledger

		Debit	Credit	Balance
		£	£	£
Provision for bad debts account				
31/12	P&L account		439	439 Cr
1/1	Balance			439 Cr

In his new accounting period, 1991, R Pearce has set aside £439 to catch any future possible bad debts. Any further debtors who go bad will be written off and may either be debited to the bad debts account (as previously with D Lewis), or directly be debited to the provision for bad debts account.

Let us assume that R Pearce writes off debtors worth £325 as bad. These are recorded in the provision for bad debts account. The debtors final balance as on 31 December is £5780 and the accountant wishes to make a further 10 per cent provision against bad debts:

Nominal ledger

		Debit	*Credit*	*Balance*
		£	£	£
Provision for bad debts account				
1/1	Balance			439 Cr
31/12	Bad debts	325		114
31/12	P&L account		464	578
1/1	Balance			578 Cr

The effect on trading and profit and loss account as on 31 December:

	£
Provision for bad debts (expense)	464

The effect on the balance sheet as on 31 December:

	£	£
CURRENT ASSETS		
Debtors	5 780	
– Provision for bad debts	578	5 202

NOTES

1 £464 is charged against profits in the profit and loss account to make the provision up to equal 10 per cent of debtors, £578.

If a provision for bad debts was reduced instead of increased, the effect would be to debit the provision account and credit 'other revenue' in the profit and loss account.

2 The balance sheet shows the 10 per cent provision against the current debtors balance.

Example

How would these adjustments for accruals, prepayments, bad debts and the provision for bad debts all affect the final accounts of R Pearce as on 31 December 1990? At the foot of the trial balance, the adjustments would be listed as on 31 December 1990.

Trial balance – R Pearce
as on 31 December 1990

	Dr	*Cr*
	£	£
Capital: R Pearce		50 000
Drawings: R Pearce	5 600	
Premises	100 000	
Equipment, machinery	17 150	
Motor vehicle	4 000	
Mortgage on premises		69 200
Stock (1/1/90)	3 680	
Petty cash	200	
Debtors, creditors	4 650	5 950
Sales		62 900
Returns inward	850	
Purchases	35 800	
Returns outward		1 350
Wages	7 480	
Light and heat	970	
Telephone	480	
Printing and stationery	385	
Carriage inwards	220	
Carriage outwards	300	
Advertising	675	
Overheads	12 640	
Discount allowed	100	
Motoring expenses	1 370	
Interest payable	210	
Commission received		300
Discount received		850
Vat		1 320
Bank (O/D)		4 890
	196 760	196 760

NOTE

On 31 December, the following were to be taken into account:

a) The value of unsold stock was £5500.
b) Wages due to employee, £150.
c) Gas bill £85 still unpaid.
d) Interest charges owing £35.
e) Advertising prepaid, £150.
f) Unused stationery, still in stock, £100.
g) A bad debt to be written off, £260.
h) A provision to be made to equal 10 per cent of debtors.
i) Stock drawings by R Pearce, £500.

REQUIRED:

Prepare the trading and profit and loss account of R Pearce for the year ended 31 December 1990 and a balance sheet as on that date.

R Pearce –
Trading and profit and loss account for
year ended 31 December 1990

	£	£	£
Sales		62 900	
− Returns inward		850	62 050
Cost of sales:			
Stock (1/1)		3 680	
Purchases	35 800		
− Returns outward	1 350	34 450	
+ Carriage inwards		220	
		38 350	
− Stock drawings (Pearce)		500	
		37 850	
− Stock (31/12)		5 500	32 350
Gross profit			29 700
Less expenses:			
Wages	7 480		
+ Accrued	150	7 630	
Light and heat	970		
+ Accrued	85	1 055	
Printing and stationery	385		
− Prepaid	100	285	
Telephone		480	
Carriage outwards		300	
Advertising	675		
− Prepaid	150	525	
Overheads		12 640	
Discount allowed		100	
Motoring expenses		1 370	
Interest payable	210		
+ Accrued	35	245	
Bad debts	260		
Provision for bad debts	439	699	25 329
			4 371

(Continues)

	£	£	£
Add other revenue:			
Commission received	300		
Discount received	850		1 150
Net profit			5 521

NOTE

The stock drawings made by Pearce are a personal expense, not a business expense, therefore they are a deduction from the cost of sales (business expense).

Stock drawings will also appear under the 'financed by' section of the balance sheet, along with any other drawings made by the owner of the business.

R Pearce –
Balance sheet as on 31 December 1990

	£	£	£	£
FIXED ASSETS				
Premises		100 000		
Equipment, machinery		17 150		
Motor vehicle		4 000		121 150
CURRENT ASSETS				
Stock (31/12)		5 500		
Debtors	4 390			
– Provision for bad debts	439	3 951		
Bank		—		
Cash		200		
Prepayments		250	9 901	
less				
CURRENT LIABILITIES				
Creditors		5 950		
Vat		1 320		
Bank (O/D)		4 890		
Accruals		270	12 430	
Net current liabilities (0.8:1)				(2 529)
Capital employed				118 621
less				
LONG-TERM LIABILITIES				
Mortgage on premises				69 200
				49 421

(Continues)

	£	£	£	£
FINANCED BY				
Capital: R Pearce		50 000		
+ Net profit		5 521		
		55 521		
– Drawings (cash)	5 600			
Stock (stock)	500	6 100		49 421

NOTE

R Pearce's working capital ratio is below 1 : 1 and he is therefore said to be insolvent, that is, he is not in a position to be able to repay current debts. He should try to improve his liquidity by increasing his sales or acquiring more capital, either from his personal finances or from a bank, (long-term loan).

A summary of major adjustments used in final accounts

Type of adjustment	**Effect on final accounts**	
	Trading and profit and loss	**Balance sheet**
1 Accrued expense	Increase expense	Current liability
2 Prepayment	Reduce expense	Current asset
3 Accrued revenue	Increase revenue	Current asset
4 Provision for bad debts (increase)	Increase expense	Reduce debtors
5 Personal stock drawings	Reduce cost of sales	Reduce capital
6 Provision for depreciation (see Chapter 18)	Increase expense	Reduce fixed asset

The distinction between capital and revenue expenditure

It is important to make this distinction in expenditure because if one was confused with the other, it would distort the calculation of profit or loss and therefore affect the preparation of the final accounts.

Capital expenditure

The type of expenditure is associated with the purchase of assets as listed in the balance sheet. For example, the purchase of plant, machinery, equipment, premises, furniture and fittings. These assets are expected to have some permanency and be used over several accounting periods.

Revenue expenditure

This is expenditure which relates to the running expenses charged against the profit and loss account and are expected to be used up within the accounting period. For example, light and heat, insurance, rates, water, telephone, wages, salaries, purchase of goods for resale and so forth. Note that a prepayment of an expense is deducted from revenue expenditure because there is still some portion to be used up in the next financial period.

If capital expenditure, in error, was treated as revenue expenditure, the value of assets and expenses charged to the profit and loss account would be miscalculated. For example:

> The purchase of a typewriter and word processor costing £750 was treated as revenue expenditure and recorded in the purchases account.
> This would have the effect of understating the value of fixed assets by £750 and overstating chargeable expenses by the same sum.
> This would result in reducing the year's profit in the profit and loss account by £750 and understating the value of fixed assets in the balance sheet by £750.

Some items of expenditure could fall into both categories of either capital or revenue expenditure. For example, the painting of premises costing £2000 and expected to last four years. Is this treated as:

a) capital expenditure, because the expense is to be used over a number of accounting periods?
b) revenue expenditure, because it is regarded as maintenance and to be charged against profits irrespective of how long the effect will last before repainting is necessary?
c) revenue expenditure for £500 each year, the balance as capital expenditure?

Whichever method is adopted, it should be used *consistently*. If b) is the adopted method, then it should be consistently applied. All painting and decorating should be charged to maintenance and recorded as revenue expenditure against the profit and loss account.

Example

Check the following:

	Transaction	*Capital expenditure* £	*Revenue expenditure* £
1	Purchase of computer equipment costing £5000.	5 000	
2	Payments of gas and electricity, £344.		344
3	Paid for goods for resale £500.		500
4	Salaries and wages £3550.		3 550
5	New cash till from CRS Ltd £400.	400	
6	Extension to premises £4500.	4 500	
7	Warehouse additional storage facilities costing £800.	800	
8	Discounts allowed, £200.		200
9	Repairs to motor vehicle £500.		500
10	Painting of offices £1500.		1 500
11	Paid rates £1200, £200 in advance.	200	1 000
12	Paid stationery £2475 of which £500 still in stock at period end.	500	1 975

Summary

1 Adjustments to final accounts are those items which, at the financial period end, require inclusion in the trading and profit and loss account and the balance sheet, for the purpose of giving a 'true and fair' financial position of the business.

2 Accruals are referred to as expenses still outstanding and although unpaid, are still incurred and need to be added to the current expenses for the period. They are charged against profits and are also recorded as current liabilities in the balance sheet.

3 Prepayments are referred to as expenses paid in advance of the current period and belong to the next. An advanced payment is therefore excluded from current charges in the profit and loss account and are also recorded as current assets in the balance sheet because there is a sum still to be used up in the next financial period.

4 A provision for bad and doubtful debts is a sum set aside, usually a percentage against debtors, and charged against profits in the profit and loss account and also deducted from debtors in the balance sheet. The provision for bad and doubtful debts account can be amended from year to year as a percentage of the debtors.

5 A bad debt is referred to as a part or whole of a debt from a customer which has been written off as bad. An asset becomes an expense and is charged against profits in the profit and loss account.

6 It is important to make the distinction between capital and revenue expenditure. Capital payments relate to assets and revenue payments to running expenses. The former is seen as a balance sheet item where the payment is expected to be used up over more than one financial period. The latter is seen as a profit and loss expense which is used up within a financial period. If the purchase of an asset is treated as a revenue expense, it has the effect of reducing or understating the value of assets and overstating the expenses charged in the profit and loss account. In this way, the profits are distorted and the balance sheet's assets under-valued.

QUESTIONS

1 The following information represents the accounts of A Land on 31 December 1990:

Trial balance as on 31 December 1990

	Dr	Cr
	£	£
Capital: A Land		18 000
Drawings	5 500	
Bank	4 250	
Cash	200	
Office equipment	5 800	
Motor van	2 575	
Stock (1/1/90)	4 250	
Debtors	3 930	
Creditors		2 185
Sales		37 800
Purchases	22 400	
Returns inward	945	
Returns outward		350
Rent	800	
Discount		225
Stationery	580	
Assistant's wages	4 855	
General overheads	2 800	
Rates, water	115	
Vat (Customs & Excise)		440
	59 000	59 000

NOTES

As on 31 December 1990:

a) Unsold stock valued £4875.
b) Rates paid in advance, £30.
c) Assistant's wages unpaid, £85.
d) Unused stationery, £140.
e) A provision for bad debts is to be made, equal to 10 per cent of debtors.

REQUIRED:

a) A trading and profit and loss account for the period ending 31 December 1990.
b) A balance sheet as at that date.

2 The following accounts were taken from the books of H Smith at the financial year ended 31 December 1990:

	Dr	*Cr*
	£	£
Capital: H Smith		16 000
Drawings	4 200	
Stock (1/1/90)	12 890	
Purchases	22 430	
Sales		32 300
Premises	12 000	
Equipment	760	
Motor van	2 250	
Debtors	23 220	
Creditors		33 600
Returns inward	250	
Returns outward		540
Rates and water	850	
Wages	4 480	
Advertising	250	
Office expenses	280	
Discount received		350
General expenses	820	
Bank overdraft		1 890
	84 680	84 680

NOTE

At 31 December 1990:

a) The value of stock £10 500.
b) Wages owing £42.
c) Rates prepaid £30.
d) An invoice for office stationery still unpaid £55.

REQUIRED:

Prepare the trading and profit and loss account of H Smith for the year ended 31 December 1990 and a balance sheet as at that date.

(BTEC National)

3 The following balances remain in John Wild's books after compilation of his trading account for the year ended 30 June 1981:

	£	£
Capital		80 000
Gross profit		10 000
Shop premises	73 000	
Stock (30/6/81)	9 000	
Trade creditors		2 500
Rates	700	
Insurance	350	
Postage and stationery	270	
Proprietor's drawings	6 000	
Cash in hand and bank	2 380	
Heating and lighting	800	
	92 500	92 500

NOTE

The following additional information is available as at 30 June 1981:

a) Rates paid in advance, £140.
b) Insurance paid in advance, £150.
c) Heating and lighting account due but unpaid, £170.

REQUIRED:

Prepare John Wild's profit and loss account for the year ended 30 June 1981 and a balance sheet as on that date.

(RSA)

4 George Price is the proprietor of a small business. He keeps his financial records on double-entry principles and extracted the following trial balance on 31 May 1983:

	£		£
Stock 1 June 1982	7 000	Capital 1 June 1982	85 000
Cash at bank	8 000	Creditors	3 700
Furniture and fittings	7 500	Sales	40 000
Premises	65 000		
Rates	1 600		
Purchases	30 000		
Heating and lighting	1 500		
Cleaning	1 700		
Packing materials	1 400		
Drawings	5 000		
	128 700		128 700

You are required to take the following into consideration on 31 May 1983:

	£
i) Stock on hand	9 500
ii) Rates paid in advance	400
iii) Stock of packing material	300

and prepare a trading and profit and loss account for the year ended 31 May 1983 and a balance sheet at that date.

(RSA)

5 On 31 December 1990 D Lewis decided to set aside a provision for bad debts to equal 5 per cent of his total debtors.

Debtors, as on 31/12/90: £12 000.

During the following year, 1991, D Lewis had written off £550 of customers as bad debts. These bad debts were transferred to the provision for bad debts account.

On 31 December 1991, D Lewis had debtors owing a total of £14 200 and he decided to maintain his 5 per cent provision.

REQUIRED:

a) Prepare the provision for bad debts account as would be found in Lewis's ledger for the period to 31 December 1991.
b) Show the effect of the above entries on the final accounts for the periods to 31 December 1990 and 1991.

6 The following balances remain on the books of S Davis after completion of his trading account for the year ended 30 October 1985:

	£	£
Gross profit		29 500
Debtors and creditors	2 400	3 600
Premises	50 000	
Bank loan to be repaid over 10 years		21 000
Stock of goods for resale	2 400	
Stationery	1 560	
Rates	350	
Loan interest	300	
Insurance	290	
Cash in hand and cash at bank	1 700	
Proprietor's drawings	5 450	
Wages and salaries	10 500	
Capital		20 850
	74 950	74 950

The following information is available as at 31 October 1985:

i) There is a stock of unused stationery valued at £150.

ii) £50 of the insurance refers to the period 1 November 1985 to 31 January 1986.
iii) There is £300 loan interest outstanding.

PREPARE:

The profit and loss account for S Davis for the year ended 31 October 1985 and a balance sheet as at that date clearly showing fixed and current assets, long-term and current liabilities and capital.

(RSA)

7 The following trial balance was extracted from the books of R Colebrook on 31 May 1986. You are required to prepare the trading and profit and loss account for the year ended 31 May 1986 and the balance sheet as at that date. Your trading account should clearly show the cost of sales.

Trial balance as at 31 May 1986

	Dr	*Cr*
	£	£
Capital		29 250
Drawings	4 600	
Bank and cash	9 200	
Salaries and wages	23 000	
Purchases and sales	35 000	68 000
Debtors and creditors	12 350	18 000
Office expenses	2 500	
Light and heat	1 700	
Rates	1 400	
Premises	15 000	
Fixtures and fittings	2 300	
Vehicles	4 200	
Stock (1/6/85)	4 100	
Sales and purchase returns	400	500
	115 750	115 750

The following information as at 31 May 1986 is also available:

i) Stock on 31 May 1986 was £3900.
ii) Wages owing but not yet paid £100.
iii) Light, heat and rates are to be apportioned –
$\frac{1}{4}$ to trading account
$\frac{3}{4}$ to profit and loss account.
iv) Included in the office expenses is an insurance prepayment of £50.

(RSA)

8 An accounting clerk has produced two lists of expenditure which she has categorised into capital and revenue. Unfortunately, they are not all correct:

Group A	**Group B**
Revenue expenditure:	Capital expenditure:
Carriage inwards	Carriage outwards
Rent and rates	Equipment
Filing cabinet	New tools
Insurance	Unsold stock of goods
Pocket calculators	Advertising
Salaries and wages	Word processor
Postage and telegrams	New staples and gun
Purchases of goods	Painting of office building
Petty cash	Payment of dividends
Office desk and chair	Transfer to reserves
Packing materials	Second-hand motor van
Drawings	New light bulbs

REQUIRED:

a) List the errors you believe are listed in the wrong group or should not be in either group. Which of the above do you think could belong to either group?

b) What affect would it have in the final accounts if these groups were not amended?

9 R Smith bought a motor van for use in his business. Classify the following under either capital or revenue expenditure:

	£
Cost of vehicle	1 800
Additional fittings	450
Motor tax	100
Insurance premium	95
Petrol and oil	400
Service and maintenance	80
New car seats and covers	225
New front tyre	30
Exhaust replacement	100

Those items you have considered as capital expenditure, record them in the nominal ledger under 'Motor vehicle account'. Are there any items which could be recorded as either capital or revenue expenditure? Briefly comment.

10 Why is it important to distinguish clearly between capital and revenue expenditure? Illustrate your answer by using examples and show their effect in the final accounts.

CHAPTER

18 The depreciation of fixed assets

- *What is depreciation?*
- *How does depreciation affect the value of fixed assets?*
- *What are the different methods of depreciation?*
- *How is the disposal of a fixed asset recorded?*

Introduction

Assets lose their value over time. Continuous use of them from one accounting period to the next usually means that some of their value is lost because of wear and tear, damage, obsolescence or any other factor which may diminish their worth. For example, if a motor vehicle was purchased at the beginning of the year for £5000, it may only be worth £4000 at the end of the year, losing its value through depreciation by £1000.

The loss of value (£1000), would be charged against profits for the year in the profit and loss account, and the balance sheet would indicate the vehicle to have a book (or net value) of £4000.

The fixed assets in the books of R Pearce on 31 December were:

	£	£
Premises	100 000	
Equipment	17 150	
Motor vehicle	4 000	121 150

The value of premises may well appreciate rather than depreciate over the years. An increase in value may be recorded under fixed assets and the increase also reflected in the 'financed by' section, usually under the heading 'revaluation account'.

The equipment and motor vehicle would depreciate in value. In each financial period, their estimated loss in value would be charged against profits and the balance sheet would record their book value. Depreciation is therefore regarded as an expense to the business and the purchase of fixed assets is like buying an expense charged against profits over periods of time, until the asset is disposed of.

The three principal methods of depreciation are:

a) The fixed instalment method (or straight-line).
b) The reducing balance method (or diminishing balance).
c) The revaluation method.

The fixed instalment method

This method charges the same depreciation sum each year against profits. Many organisations use this type of depreciation on fixed assets such as furniture, fittings, plant, machinery and equipment. The cost of these assets is simply divided by the estimated time the assets are expected to last, less any residual value.

For example, the equipment of R Pearce may be expected to last an estimated five years and have a scrap or residual value of say £500. How much should be charged against profits in the profit and loss account? The formula is as follows:

$$\frac{\textit{Cost} - \textit{Residual value}}{\textit{Estimate life (years)}}$$

So $$\frac{£17\,150 - £500}{5 \text{ years}} = £3330 \text{ per year.}$$

The profit and loss account will be charged with £3330 depreciation each year for five years as an expense.

The balance sheet will show the cumulative sum of depreciation over the life of the asset, thereby reducing its value over the five years. In its fifth year, the book or net value of the asset should show it is only worth £500, its residual value.

Fixed assets		*Cost*	*Depreciation*	*Net value*
		£	£	£
Year 1	Equipment	17 150	3 330	13 820
Year 2	Equipment	17 150	6 660	10 490
Year 3	Equipment	17 150	9 990	7 160
Year 4	Equipment	17 150	13 320	3 830
Year 5	Equipment	17 150	16 650	500

Recording depreciation in the nominal ledger

The double entry for the recording of depreciation is:

Debit: the profit and loss account with the expense (£3330).
Credit: the provision for depreciation of fixed asset account (the cumulative depreciation).

The fixed asset account is recorded at its cost value and although the depreciation charge each year could be credited against its cost, a separate provision for depreciation is preferred to indicate the cumulative (or total) depreciation charged against the asset over its estimated life.

Nominal ledger

			Debit £	*Credit* £	*Balance* £
Equipment account					
Year 1	1/1	Bank	17 150		17 150 Dr
Provision for depreciation of equipment account					
Year 1	31/12	P&L account		3 330	3 330 Cr
Year 2	31/12	P&L account		3 330	6 660
Year 3	31/12	P&L account		3 330	9 990
Year 4	31/12	P&L account		3 330	13 320
Year 5	31/12	P&L account		3 330	16 650

Each year, using the fixed instalment method, £3330 would be charged as an expense in the profit and loss account. The balance sheet would indicate the *cumulative* depreciation each year and show the asset's book value at the time. For example, in year 5:

Balance sheet

	Cost £	*Depreciation* £	*Net value* £
FIXED ASSETS			
Equipment	17 150	16 650	500

After five years the asset's net value of £500 is in line with its estimated residual value.

The reducing balance method

An alternative method of depreciation of fixed assets is to ensure that the depreciation charge each year diminishes as the asset gets older and is of less value. The argument for using this method assumes that the newer the asset, the more should be charged against profits because presumably more value is lost in the earlier years rather than in the later.

Irrespective of the method of depreciation that is adopted, one of the major concepts in accounting is that of consistency and therefore once a certain method is used, it should be consistently applied throughout the expected life of the asset.

The reducing balance method may be applied by using a fixed percentage rate on the asset's net value each year, thereby effecting a lower depreciation charge each year. For example, using this method to depreciate equipment:

Cost:	£17 150
Fixed percentage rate:	50 per cent
Estimated life:	five years

Formula for rate percentage: $= \left(1 - n\sqrt{\dfrac{\textit{Residual value}}{\textit{Cost of fixed asset}}}\right) \times 100$
(n = number of years)

$$\left(1 - 5\sqrt{\frac{\pounds 500}{\pounds 17\,150}}\right) \times 100$$

= approximately 50 per cent depreciation each year on the net value of the asset.

To check the percentage rate

Year	Reduced balance	*Profit and loss account* Depreciation @ 50 per cent	*Balance sheet* Net value
	£	£	£
1	17 150	8 575	8 575
2	8 575	4 288	4 287
3	4 287	2 143	2 144
4	2 144	1 072	1 072
5	1 072	536	536 (residual value)

Note that with the fixed instalment method, £3330 was charged each year as an expense in the profit and loss account (the same charge for each financial year). After two years, the charge would be £6660 using this method and £12 863 using the reduced balance. A large difference in the first two years. However, after five years, the total depreciation charge is virtually the same for either method, only a small variance in the residual value being the result.

The revaluation method

This method of depreciation may be adopted where an annual valuation of certain fixed assets may be assessed on inspection or by recourse to some guideline from a trade handbook. For example, R Pearce's motor vehicle cost £4000. How much has it lost in value over the financial period? The Automobile Association handbook may indicate the vehicle's market value according to its registration and mileage to be £3500. If this was the case, £500 could be used as the depreciation charge for the year.

The hotel and catering trades tend to use the revaluation method against items such as crockery, cutlery, bedding, kitchen utensils, etc. By appraising their worth annually, any loss of value is treated as the depreciation charge for the year.

The effect on final accounts

By using the fixed instalment method on equipment and the revaluation method on the motor vehicle, the effect on R Pearce's final accounts would be:

Profit and loss account 31 December

	£	£
Depreciation:		
Equipment	3 330	
Motor vehicle	500	3 830

Balance sheet as on 31 December

	Cost £	*Depreciation* £	*Net value* £
FIXED ASSETS			
Premises	100 000	—	100 000
Equipment	17 150	3 330	13 820
Motor vehicle	4 000	500	3 500
	121 150	3 830	117 320

The disposal of a fixed asset

When a fixed asset is finally disposed of, either sold or scrapped, it may be transferred to a disposal of asset account. Any provision for depreciation of the asset is also transferred to the disposal account thereby removing it from the accounts of the business.

If an asset is sold for more than its net book value, the gain may be transferred to the profit and loss account as 'other revenue'. If it is disposed of at less than its net value, the loss may be charged against profits as a further expense to the business.

If, for example, R Pearce decided to sell his equipment in year 4 for £3000, the accounts would show:

Nominal ledger

			Debit £	*Credit* £	*Balance* £
Equipment account					
Year 1	1/1	Bank	17 150		17 150 Dr
Year 4	31/12	Disposal account		17 150	—
Provision for depreciation of equipment account					
Year 4	31/12	Balance			13 320 Cr
		Disposal account	13 320		—
Disposal of fixed asset account					
Year 4	31/12	Equipment	17 150		17 150 Dr
		Provision for depreciation		13 320	3 830
		Bank		3 000	830
		P&L account		830	—

NOTE

The asset was sold for £3000 in year 4, having a net value of £3830 at the time. This would represent a loss on the book value of £830 which would be a charge against profits in the profit and loss account. If £4000 had been the selling price of the asset, a book profit of £170 would have been credited as a gain in the profit and loss account, as other revenue.

Example (from the Institute of Bankers)

The following accounts relate to M Upton, the proprietor of a business as at year ended 31 December 1990:

Trial balance as on 31 December

	Dr £	*Cr* £
Capital		71 000
Premises	57 500	
Equipment	23 000	
Provision for depreciation of equipment		6 000
Motor van	8 000	
Provision for depreciation of motor van		2 000
Stock (1/1/91)	8 300	
Purchases and sales	30 800	66 600
Returns inward	700	
Returns outward		900
Wages	16 500	
Carriage inwards	500	
Carriage outwards	400	
Commission received		500
Bank interest	350	
Lighting and heating	1 650	
Postage and stationery	600	
Insurance	1 200	
Telephone	500	
Provision for bad debts		550
Debtors, creditors	7 000	11 950
Bank	1 950	
Discount	100	
Bad debts	450	
	159 500	159 500

Adjustments to be taken into account at 31 December:

a) Unsold stock valued at cost £9500.
b) Wages due to be paid £550.
c) Upton, the proprietor, takes goods for own use valued at cost £800.
d) Prepaid stationery – unused stock valued £95.
e) Commission still oustanding £180.
f) Depreciation: motor van revalued at £4500; equipment depreciated 20 per cent on net value.
g) Provision for bad and doubtful debts to equal 10 per cent of debtors.

REQUIRED:

a) A trading and profit and loss account for the year ended 31 December 1990.
b) A balance sheet as at this date.

M Upton –
Trading and profit and loss account for
the year ended 31 December 1990

	£	£	£
Sales		66 600	
– Returns inward		700	65 900
Cost of sales			
Stock (1/1)		8 300	
Purchases	30 800		
+ Carriage inwards	500		
	31 300		
– Returns outward	900	30 400	
		38 700	
– Stock drawings		800	
		37 900	
– Stock (31/12)		9 500	28 400
Gross profit			37 500
Less expenses			
Wages	16 500		
+ Accrued	550	17 050	
Carriage outwards		400	
Bank interest		350	
Light and heat		1 650	
Postage and stationery	600		
– Prepaid	95	505	
Insurance		1 200	
Telephone		500	
Discount allowed		100	
Depreciation			
Motor vehicle	1 500	4 900	
Equipment	3 400		
Bad debts		450	
Provision for bad debts		150	27 255
			10 245

(Continues)

	£	£	£
Add other revenue:			
Commission received	500		
+ Accrued revenue	180		680
Net profit			10 925

M Upton –
Balance sheet as on 31 December 1990

		Cost £	*Depreciation* £	*Net value* £
FIXED ASSETS				
Premises		57 500	—	57 500
Equipment		23 000	9 400	13 600
Motor vehicle		8 000	3 500	4 500
		88 500	12 900	75 600
CURRENT ASSETS				
Stock (31/12)		9 500		
Debtors	7 000			
– Provision for bad debts	700	6 300		
Bank		1 950		
Prepayment	95			
Accrued revenue	180	275	18 025	
less				
CURRENT LIABILITIES				
Creditors		11 950		
Accruals		550	12 500	
Net current assets (1.4 : 1)				5 525
Capital employed				81 125
FINANCED BY:				
Capital		71 000		
+ Net profit		10 925	81 925	
– Drawings (stock)			800	81 125

NOTE

The working capital ratio of 1.4 : 1 is an improvement compared to R Pearce's insolvent financial position in Chapter 16. Ideally, the ratio should be about £2 of current assets to £1 of current debt.

Summary

1 Depreciation refers to the loss in value of fixed assets. This may be due to several reasons, but most commonly, it is through old age or wear and tear.

2 Some assets like premises, may increase in value and therefore appreciate. The value of property may be increased under fixed assets and an equivalent increase shown in the 'financed by' section, usually under a capital revaluation account.

3 Depreciation is an expense and is a charge against the profits of the business in the profit and loss account.

4 The provision for depreciation account is a record in the nominal ledger of cumulative depreciation. It may be referred to as a *negative asset* in that it is a deduction from the cost of fixed assets in the balance sheet.

5 There are three major methods of depreciation:
a) fixed instalment
b) reduced balance
c) revaluation.

Once a method is adopted for a particular asset or group of assets, then it is regarded as standard accounting practice to consistently apply the same method of depreciation until the asset or assets are disposed of.

QUESTIONS

1 The following is a trial balance of John Smith Sports Shop proprietor, as at year ended 31 December 1990.

	Dr £	*Cr* £
Capital (1/1/91)		170 350
Drawings	14 240	
Stock (1/1/91)	12 890	
Purchases and sales	122 430	132 370
Returns	5 210	2 470
Premises	110 000	
Fixtures and fittings (at cost)	12 760	
Van (at cost)	7 200	
Trade debtors and creditors	23 270	33 690
Rent	7 850	

(Continues)

	Dr	Cr
	£	£
Wages and salaries	24 480	
Advertising	1 350	
Discount	450	1 260
Office expenses	1 160	
Cash	1 020	
Bank overdraft		4 170
	344 310	344 310

You are required to prepare a trading and profit and loss account for the year 31 December and a balance sheet as at that date, taking the following items into consideration:

i) Stock at 31 December was valued at £15 477.
ii) Depreciation at 31 December: fixtures and fittings 25 per cent of cost; vans have a market value of £5750.

(BTEC National)

2 The following figures have been extracted from the ledgers of Frances Mitchell:

Trial balance as at 30 June 1987

	Dr	Cr
	£	£
Sales		276 156
Purchases	164 700	
Carriage inwards	4 422	
Carriage outwards	5 866	
Drawings	15 600	
Rent and rates	9 933	
Insurance	3 311	
Postage and stationery	3 001	
Advertising	5 661	
Salaries and wages	52 840	
Bad debts	1 754	
Debtors	24 240	
Creditors		25 600
Returns outwards		131
Cash	354	
Bank	2 004	
Stock (1/7/86)	23 854	
Equipment (cost)	116 000	
Capital, F Mitchell		131 653
	433 540	433 540

The following additional information was available on 30 June 1987:

a) Wages are accrued by £420.
b) Rates have been prepaid by £1400.
c) Stock of unused stationery valued £250.
d) A provision for bad debts is to be created to equal 5 per cent of debtors.
e) Unsold stock at the close of business valued at £27 304.
f) Depreciate equipment at 10 per cent of cost.

REQUIRED:

a) Prepare the trading and profit and loss account for the year ended 30 June 1987 and a balance sheet as at that date.
b) Advise F Mitchell on the position of the working capital of the business.

(Institute of Bankers)

3 The following trial balance has been extracted from the ledger of M Yousef, a sole trader:

Trial balance as at 31 May 1986

	Dr £	*Cr* £
Sales		138 078
Purchases	82 350	
Carriage	5 144	
Drawings	7 800	
Rent, rates and insurance	6 622	
Postage and stationery	3 001	
Advertising	1 330	
Salaries and wages	26 420	
Bad debts	877	
Provision for bad debts		130
Debtors	12 120	
Creditors		6 471
Cash on hand	177	
Cash at bank	1 002	
Stock (1/6/85)	11 927	
Equipment		
at cost	58 000	
accumulated depreciation		19 000
Capital (1/6/85)		53 091
	216 770	216 770

The following additional information as at 31 May 1986 is available:

a) Rent is accrued by £210.
b) Rates have been prepaid by £880.
c) £2211 of carriage represents carriage inwards on purchases.

d) Equipment is to be depreciated at 15 per cent per annum using the straight line method.
e) The provision for bad debts to be increased by £40.
f) Stock at the close of business has been valued at £13 551.

REQUIRED:

Prepare the trading and profit and loss account for the year ended 31 May 1986 and a balance sheet as at that date.

(AAT)

4 The following information is taken from the accounts of Mary Walker, a business-woman selling science equipment to colleges:

Trial balance of M Walker as on 30 June 1990

	£	£
Stock (1/7/89)	6 855	
Motor vehicle (cost)	8 750	
Premises (cost)	36 900	
Accumulated depreciation of vehicle		1 750
Purchases	55 725	
Sales		120 344
Discounts	855	1 044
Returns	548	738
Salaries (assistants)	18 346	
Overheads	14 385	
Creditors		6 755
Debtors	7 400	
Bank		2 045
Cash	400	
Drawings	10 420	
Capital		?

On 30 June, the following additional information was also available:

a) Stock in hand valued at £7455.
b) The motor vehicle is depreciated on the straight line principle and is now three years old.
c) Of the overheads, £240 is prepaid and £600 is accrued.

REQUIRED:

Prepare M Walker's trading and profit and loss account for the year ended 30 June 1990 and a balance sheet as on that date.

5 Davy Jones owns a small business. At the close of trading on 31 May 1985 the following balances were extracted from his books:

	£
Stock (1/6/84)	11 000
Purchases	52 000
Sales	84 000
Carriage inwards	150
Sales returns	650
Purchase returns	400
Insurance	250
Heating and lighting	2 500
Stationery	1 500
Rates	1 200
Motor expenses	1 600
Carriage outwards	100
Discounts allowed	140
Discounts received	110
Wages	4 200
Telephone	180

You are required to take the following into consideration on 31 May 1985:

i) Stock in hand £12 000
ii) Insurance paid in advance £50
iii) Stock of stationery £100
iv) Heat and lighting accrued £150
v) Rates prepaid £300
vi) Depreciation – the motor vehicle valued at £4000 cost was depreciated by 20 per cent on reducing balance. It is now three years old.

and prepare a trading and profit and loss account for the year ended 31 May 1985 showing clearly in your trading account the cost of sales.
Note: a balance sheet is not required.

(RSA)

6 The following trial balance was extracted from the books of Gina Chappell a retailer, at 30 June 1990. You work as her assistant and are to prepare the final accounts.

	£	£
Capital (1/7/89)		127 500
Drawings	25 000	
Fixtures and fittings (cost)	100 000	
Delivery van (cost)	25 000	
Sales		500 000
Purchases	400 000	

(Continues)

	£	£
Discount received		2 500
Wages	25 000	
Rent and rates	12 000	
Carriage inwards	1 000	
Insurance	1 500	
Stock (1/7/89)	101 000	
Provision for depreciation: fixtures and fittings		25 000
Provision for depreciation: vehicles		5 000
Creditors		81 500
Debtors	34 000	
Balance at bank	15 000	
Cash in hand	2 500	
Provision for bad debts		500
	742 000	742 000

NOTES (30/6/90)

Stock £132 000
Wages owing £3000
Accrued rent £2000
Prepaid insurance £100
Depreciation is provided at 20 per cent per annum for the van and 25 per cent per annum for fixtures and fittings both on a straight-line basis.
The provision for bad debts is to be increased to £2500.

REQUIRED:

a) Prepare the trading and profit and loss account for the year ended 30 June 1990.
b) Prepare the balance sheet as at 30 June 1990.

7 The following information relates to the fixed assets of Rockbourne Company Limited on 1 January 1987:

	Cost	*Depreciation to 31/12/86*
	£	£
Premises	1 200 000	—
Plant and machinery	950 000	413 500
	2 150 000	413 500

The company depreciates plant and machinery at the rate of 10 per cent per annum on a straight-line basis. A full year's depreciation being provided in the year of purchase, but none in the year of sale.

During the year ending 31 December 1987 the following took place:

i) The directors decided to revalue the premises to £1 500 000.
ii) Plant and machinery purchased in 1983 for £200 000 was sold in October 1987 for £130 000.
iii) New plant was purchased in July 1987 for £150 000.

REQUIRED:

a) Provide relevant ledger accounts including an asset disposal account as they would appear on 31 December 1987.
b) Prepare a schedule of fixed assets for inclusion in the accounts to be published for the year ended 31 December 1987.
c) Provide any details you think are relevant to accompany the accounts to be published for the year ended 31 December 1987.
(Please note that zero scrap value is assumed for plant.)

(Institute of Bankers)

8 A company depreciates its plant at the rate of 20 per cent per annum on the straight-line method for each month of ownership. The following details relate to the purchase and sale of plant for the years 1984, 1985, 1986 and 1987 – the company draws up its final accounts on 31 December of each year.

1984 Bought plant costing £1000 on 1 January
Bought plant costing £500 on 1 July
1986 Bought plant costing £4000 on 1 October
1987 Sold plant which had been bought on 1 January 1984 for the sum of £300 on 1 January 1987.

REQUIRED:

a) Draw up the plant account for the above transactions.
b) Draw up the plant depreciation account for the above transactions.
c) Draw up a plant disposal account.
d) Show the extract from the balance sheet as at 31 December 1987.
e) State two *other* methods of depreciation.

9 Three of the accounts in the ledger of B Clough have the following balances at 31 December 1982: stationery debit £110; rent credit £96 and provision for bad debts credit £249.

During 1983 Clough paid for stationery £406 and rent £768 by cheque (rent is payable at £48 per month). At 31 December 1983 there was a stock of stationery valued at £125. On the same day debtors amounted to £4000 and the provision was adjusted to 5 per cent of that figure.

REQUIRED:

a) Preparation of the stationery, rent and provision for bad debts accounts for the year ended 31 December 1983 showing year-end transfers.

b) Preparation of a profit and loss account extract showing clearly the amounts transferred from each of the above accounts for the year ended 31 December 1983.

An explanation of the effect (if any) on the calculation of the net profit of each of the year-end transfers.

c) An explanation of the effect on, and significance to, final accounts of accounting for accruals and prepayments at year-end.

(AEB Nov '84)

CHAPTER

19 Accounting for partnerships

- *Why is it important for partners to draw up a partnership agreement?*
- *How are the final accounts of a partnership recorded?*
- *How are current accounts prepared?*
- *What is the significance of goodwill?*

Introduction

A partnership may be described as a business having at least two owners, with a view to making a profit. The maximum number allowed in this type of organisation is normally 20 partners, although in professional partnerships, such as solicitors, accountants, estate agents and members of the Stock Exchange, this number may be exceeded on request to the Registrar of Companies.

Although many partnerships convert their businesses to limited companies, in the case of professional partnerships this is against their standard practice and therefore it is exceedingly unlikely to find a group of solicitors bearing the word 'limited' after the title of their business.

As far as legal requirements are concerned, there is little constraint in setting up a partnership and there is no need for complicated documentation. For partnerships, the 1890 and 1907 Partnership Acts apply, the first to all partners and the second to limited partners. A limited partner is one who has relinquished any ideas concerning control or decision making in the business. Only the general partners have the right to control. Limited partners may have once been general partners who have retired from the business, but may still wish to be associated with it by virtue of leaving their capital in the enterprise. However, by applying to the Registrar for limited status, they then become protected against unlimited liability and are only liable to the amount of capital they have in the business. General partners are all unlimited and therefore liable to the debts of the business, even to the extent of their personal wealth.

It is advised that all partners have some form of written agreement between them – a contract which binds them together in law. In the event of any disagreements, the contract can be referred to and upheld in a court of law. A Deeds of Partnership is such an agreement, where the partners draw up a contract which outlines the conditions they have consented to. Agreements usually include items such as:

a) The venue of the business premises and the name of the accountant, solicitors and bank, acting on behalf of the business.
b) How the profits and losses of the business are to be shared by the partners.
c) How salaries or drawings are to be arranged.
d) Whether interest is to be paid on capital accounts.
e) Whether interest is to be charged on any drawings.
f) The rate of interest to be paid on any loans provided by partners.
g) Any aspects concerning control and responsibilities by partners.
h) The procedure in the event of admittance of a new partner or the departure of an existing partner.
i) The procedure in the event of *dissolution* (the partnership being wound up).

In the event of disagreement between partners and where a Deeds of Partnership does not exist, the 1890 Partnership Act applies. In particular, Section 24 of the Act states:

a) Any profit or loss is to be borne *equally* between partners.
b) No interest is to be paid on partners' capital accounts.
c) No interest is to be charged on drawings by partners.
d) No partnership salaries are to be paid from profits.
e) Loans by partners will be entitled to interest at 5 per cent per annum.

Dissolution of a partnership

The decision concerning how the partnership may be dissolved (terminated) may be laid down in the Deeds of Partnership. However, many partnerships may be dissolved in a number of different ways:

a) It may be for a fixed length of time and therefore by the expiration of that time.
b) If the partnership is for an unspecified term, *any of the partners* can give notice to terminate their agreement and therefore dissolve the partnership. A new partnership can be reformed by the existing partners.
c) By the death or bankruptcy of any partner.
d) By an unlawful act which forces the partnership to dissolve.
e) At the conclusion of a venture if the partnership was formed for such a venture.

Once the partnership is dissolved, partners must ensure that all unfinished transactions are wound up and the payments for all outstanding debts are made. Any surplus assets will be due to the partners in proportion to their share of capital and current accounts.

Partners' current accounts

A current account is a record of a partner's personal finances in the partnership. Items recorded in this account will include profit share, interest paid on capital or loans, salary awarded from profits, interest charged on drawings and the total drawings for the period, either in cash, stock or any other items.

The partners' appropriation account which shows how profits (or losses) are to be divided, acts as the double entry between each partner's current account and the appropriation account.

Partners' loans

Any partner may make a loan to the business at an agreed interest rate per cent. The loan is recorded under long-term liabilities and the interest paid will be credited to the partner's current account.

An example of partnership accounts

The preparation of the final accounts of a partnership are almost identical to those of other business organisations. Partnerships do have, however, the appropriation account to show the division of profits or losses between partners.

In the 'financed by' section of the balance sheet, each of the partner's capital accounts will be listed as well as each of their current accounts. The total sum of the partners' capital and current accounts will equal the partners' net worth in the business (that is, the same as the net assets).

The following information relates to the partnership between Graham and Rod who, in their Deeds of Partnership, have stated that profits or losses are to be borne equally. Figures relate to 31 May 1990:

	Graham	*Rod*
	£	£
Capital accounts	10 000	12 000
Current accounts	800 Cr	400 Dr
Drawings for the year	14 500	13 500
Salaries to be credited	8 000	6 000
Rod's loan account (10% p.a.)		3 000
Interest charged on drawings	350	250

Interest to be paid on capital accounts at 8 per cent per annum. The net profit for the period ended 31 May was £28 500.

REQUIRED:

a) Prepare the partnership appropriation account for the year ended 31 May 1990.
b) Prepare each of the partner's current accounts for the same period.
c) Prepare a balance sheet extract which will indicate the partner's 'financed by' section.

Profit and loss appropriation account
Graham and Rod, year ended 31 May 1990

	£	£	£
Net profit b/f			28 500
Deduct:			
Salaries: Graham	8 000		
Rod	6 000	14 000	
Interest on capital: Graham	800		
Rod	960	1 760	
Interest on loan: Rod		300	16 060
			12 440
Add:			
Interest on drawings: Graham	350		
Rod	250		600
			13 040
Share of profit:			
(Residue) Graham	6 520		
Rod	6 520		13 040

NOTE

The residue of profit (£13 040) is the sum *after* items such as partners' salaries, interest on capital, loans and drawings have been taken into consideration. The residue is then divided as per the partnership agreement. In this case, equally.

Partners' current accounts

These are the personal finances of the partners and recorded in the nominal ledger.

Nominal ledger

Current accounts		*Debit* £	*Credit* £	*Balance* £
Graham's account				
31/12	Balance			800 Cr
	Salary		8 000	8 800
	Interest on capital		800	9 600
	Interest charged	350		9 250
	Profit share		6 520	15 770
	Drawings	14 500		1 270

(Continues)

		Debit £	Credit £	Balance £
Rod's account				
31/12	Balance			400 Dr
	Salary		6 000	5 600 Cr
	Interest on capital		960	6 560
	Interest charged	250		6 310
	Profit share		6 520	12 830
	Interest, loan		300	13 130
	Drawings	13 500		370 Dr

NOTE

A debit balance in the partner's current account indicates that the partner has overdrawn on his account.

Balance sheet extract

In the 'financed by' section, the partners' capital and current accounts are both recorded to represent the partners' net worth in the business:

	£	£	£
FINANCED BY			
Capital accounts:			
Graham	10 000		
Rod	12 000	22 000	
Current accounts:			
Graham	1 270		
Rod (Dr)	(370)	900	22 900

Although Rod's loan to the business could be entered in this section of the accounts, it is a long-term liability and should be listed after net current assets, *before* the 'financed by' section.

Goodwill

The term *goodwill* may arise in a business for several reasons. Its meaning is concerned with the good name or reputation of an enterprise, built up over a certain period of time. Its assessment and calculation may be based on a proportion or percentage of average sales or profits over a number of years. For example, if the average sales over five years is £70 000, the figure for goodwill may be arrived at say 15 or 20 per cent of this sum.

When a partner leaves the business, or a new partner is admitted, an assessment of goodwill may become necessary. In the former case, a partner retiring from the business will want his proper share of the business's value. In the latter case, a new partner may be expected to pay some portion or premium to come into an already established business.

When a business is sold or taken over, or two businesses amalgamate, the value of goodwill often needs to be assessed. A business may not simply be worth its net asset value alone, some consideration needs to be given to its *reputation* in terms of its customers and turnover, and its potential profits. It is finally up to the buyer and seller to come to some agreement about the value of goodwill.

If a new partner is admitted to an existing business, he is likely to contribute his share of capital and to pay an agreed sum for goodwill. If the goodwill is assessed to be valued at £4000 and the new partner is able to pay in cash, the double entry is:

Debit: Bank account £4000

Credit: Existing partners' capital accounts, £4000 (shared as per the *profit sharing ratio*).

Alternatively, if the new partner has insufficient resources to pay goodwill in cash or other assets, a goodwill account is debited:

Debit: Goodwill account £4000

Credit: Existing partners' capital accounts, £4000.

It is usually prudent of the partners to write off the amount of goodwill as soon as is practicable because it is only an intangible asset (not a physical thing) and its value is only realistic in terms of changes in the business's circumstances, such as admitting a new partner or the selling of the business. Writing off goodwill is usually based on the partner's profit sharing ratios.

Accounting for goodwill has always been rather a contentious aspect, the main problem being that it is an intangible asset and incapable of being separated from the business as a whole. The basis for its calculation is also very subjective and is likely to change over financial periods.

Example

Diane and Bert are in partnership and have agreed to share profits and losses on the basis of their capital input. At the financial year end 30 June 1990, the following information relating to their accounts revealed:

	Debit	*Credit*
	£	*£*
Capital accounts: Diane		10 000
Bert		20 000
Current accounts: Diane	500	
Bert	350	
Drawings for the year: Diane	7 500	
Bert	12 750	
Fixed assets (net)	48 000	
Stock	3 000	
Debtors	5 500	
Creditors		6 000
Bank overdraft		2 600
Bank loan (five years)		15 000
Net profit for year:		24 000
	77 600	77 600

Jane is to join the partnership at the start of the new financial period, 1 July 1990. She will bring £7000 in cash as her contribution to capital.

Goodwill is considered at a value of 50 per cent of the net profit for the year ended 31 May 1990 and a goodwill account is to be opened. Profits and losses are to be shared in proportion to the members' capital in the new partnership agreement.

Other information is as follows:

a) Interest charged on drawings is at 10 per cent per annum based on the average drawings for the year:
   Diane £5000
   Bert £6400
b) Interest is to be paid on capital at 6 per cent per annum.
c) No partners' salaries are awarded.

REQUIRED:

a) Prepare the partnership profit and loss appropriation account for the year ended 30 June 1990.
b) The partners' current accounts for the period to 30 June 1990.
c) The partnership balance sheet as at 30 June 1990.
d) The balance sheet of the new partnership as it would appear in the new financial period, 1 July 1990.

Profit and loss appropriation account for Diane and Bert, year ended 30 June 1990

	£	£	£
Net profit b/f			24 000
Deduct:			
Interest on capital (6%):			
Diane	600		
Bert	1 200		1 800
			22 200
Add:			
Interest on drawings (10%):			
Diane	500		
Bert	640		1 140
			23 340
Share of profit (1 : 2):			
Diane	7 780		
Bert	15 560		
			23 340

Current accounts of Diane and Bert – Nominal ledger

Current accounts		*Debit* £	*Credit* £	*Balance* £
Diane's account				
30/6	Balance			500 Dr
	Interest on capital		600	100 Cr
	Interest charged	500		400 Dr
	Profit share		7 780	7 380 Cr
	Drawings	7 500		120 Dr
Bert's account				
30/6	Balance			350 Dr
	Interest on capital		1 200	850 Cr
	Interest charged	640		210
	Profit share		15 560	15 770
	Drawings	12 750		3 020

Balance sheet of Diane and Bert as on 30 June 1990

	£	£	£
FIXED ASSETS (net)			48 000
CURRENT ASSETS			
Stock	3 000		
Debtors	5 500		
Bank/cash	—	8 500	
CURRENT LIABILITIES			
Creditors	6 000		
Bank overdraft	2 600	8 600	
Net current liabilities:			(100)
Capital employed:			47 900
LONG-TERM LIABILITIES			
Bank loan			15 000
			32 900
FINANCED BY:			
Capital accounts: Diane	10 000		
Bert	20 000	30 000	
Current accounts: Diane	(120)		
Bert	3 020	2 900	
			32 900

The calculation of goodwill:
This is agreed by the partners to be 50 per cent of net profit:

$$\text{Net profit} \quad \frac{£24\,000}{2} = £12\,000$$

Shared as per profit ratio:

Diane 1
Bert 2

$$\frac{£12\,000}{3} = £4\,000$$

= Diane £4000, Bert £8000

Double entry: Debit – goodwill account £12 000
Credit – capital accounts £4000 (Diane)
£8000 (Bert)

Balance sheet of Diane, Bert and Jane as on 1 June 1990

	£	£	£
FIXED ASSETS (net)			48 000
Intangibles			
Goodwill			12 000
			60 000
CURRENT ASSETS			
Stock	3 000		
Debtors	5 500		
Bank (+ £7000)	4 400	12 900	
CURRENT LIABILITIES			
Creditors		6 000	
Net current assets:			6 900
Capital employed:			66 900
LONG-TERM LIABILITIES			
Bank loan			15 000
			51 900

(Continues)

	£	£	£
FINANCED BY:			
Capital accounts:			
Diane	14 000		
Bert	28 000		
Jane	7 000	49 000	
Current accounts:			
Diane	(120)		
Bert	3 020		
Jane	—	2 900	
			51 900

NOTE

If the partners agree to share profits as a proportion of their capital, the profit share ratio will be:

Diane	£14 000	(2)
Bert	£28 000	(4)
Jane	£7 000	(1)

It is prudent, and also standard accounting practice, to write off goodwill as soon as is practicable. It is usual to write it off in proportion to the profit sharing ratio.

If, at the end of the financial year, 30 June 1991, the partners decided to write off goodwill, and the profit sharing ratio is say, 2 : 3 : 1

Diane 2
Bert 3 $= \dfrac{£12\,000}{6} = £2000$
Jane 1

The double entry would be:

Debit:	Capital accounts	Diane	£4000
		Bert	£6000
		Jane	£2000
Credit:	Goodwill account		£12 000

The new capital accounts would be:

Diane	£10 000	(£14 000 − £4 000)
Bert	£22 000	(£28 000 − £6 000)
Jane	£5 000	(£7 000 − £2 000)

Share of losses

Losses are shared in the same way as profits, that is, according to the partnership agreement. This may be equally, or in the proportion to capital, or in any other way as mutually agreed.

In the event of bankruptcy, where the partnership is to be wound up, any surplus in net assets will be divided in the proportion to the partners' capital and current accounts.

Note that general partners are liable up to their own personal wealth. In the event of a partner having a debit balance in his capital account and who is also insolvent (not in a position to pay off debts), the remaining partners are unfortunately liable for their partner's insolvency.

At the turn of this century, the partnership of Garner, Murray and Wilkins was dissolved, Wilkins ending up with a debit capital account balance and also insolvent. In the 1903 case Garner *v* Murray, it was the opinion of the court that the indebtedness of Wilkins should be borne by Garner and Murray *in proportion to their last capital account balances* and not their profit sharing ratio.

It is therefore held, that in the absence of any written partnership agreement, the case of Garner *v* Murray applies, and any debt by an insolvent partner is to be borne by the other partners as per their last capital ratios. Any losses prior to bankruptcy are to be shared as per the partners agreed profit sharing ratio.

Summary

1 Partnerships are business enterprises having two or more partners, with a view to profit, usually with a maximum of 20 partners.

2 General partners are in control of the business and are responsible for making all major decisions. They have unlimited liability which means that they are liable for all the debts of the business, including up to their own personal wealth. Only limited partners have the advantage of limited liability and are therefore only liable to their capital invested in the business.

3 It is advised that a written agreement exists between partners. A Deeds of Partnership is a written contract between the partners, outlining their mutual agreements and is recognised as a binding and legal document.

4 In the event of any disagreement, where a written contract is absent, Section 24 of the Partnership Act may be applied in relation to the sharing of profits or losses.

5 The preparation of the final accounts are the same as for other organisations. The partners' appropriation account indicates how the profit or loss is to be shared between partners.

6 Dissolution refers to the winding up of a partnership. This may be due to several reasons including the notice given by any of the partners to quit, or by death or bankruptcy of any partner. In the event of bankruptcy of the business, the partnership will be dissolved.

7 Goodwill is seen as an intangible asset arising from circumstances such as the admittance of a new partner or the sale of a business. Its value is a subjective assessment based on the business's good name or reputation. It is regarded as standard accounting practice to write off goodwill in the balance sheet as soon as it is prudent to do so.

QUESTIONS

1 The following information relates to the accounts of Trevalyn & Curtis in partnership and who, in their contract, have agreed to share profits and losses equally:

	Trevalyn	*Curtis*
	£	£
Capital account balances 31/12/90	20 000	25 000
Current account balances 31/12/90	720 (Cr)	180 (Dr)
Drawings for the year:	9 725	10 800
Salaries to be credited	2 500	2 000
Interest to be charged on drawings	360	420

Interest paid on capital accounts is at 5 per cent per annum. The net profit for the year ended 31 December 1990 was £26 800.

REQUIRED:

1a) Prepare the partnership appropriation account for the year ended 31 December 1990.

b) Prepare the partners' current accounts for the year ended 31 December 1990.

c) Prepare a balance sheet extract to show the partners' 'financed by' section as on 31 December 1990.

2 Explain briefly the difference between a general and limited partner. What advantage will the latter have in the event of bankruptcy of the business?

2 Robert, Susan and Thomas are in partnership. The capitals they have invested in the partnership are £50 000, £40 000, and £20 000 respectively. During the financial year ended 30 September 1986 the partnership earned a net profit of £42 000. The partners have agreed the following appropriation scheme:

i) interest to be allowed on capital at 12 per cent per annum,
ii) Susan and Thomas are to receive salaries of £4000 and £5000 respectively, and
iii) profits are to be shared in the ratio 4 : 3 : 1 respectively.

The partners had the following balances on their current accounts as at 1 October 1985

	£	
Robert	121	(credit)
Susan	105	(debit)
Thomas	197	(credit)
	213	

During the year ended 30 September 1986 the partners withdrew the following amounts from the partnership:

	£
Robert	15 940
Susan	16 020
Thomas	10 400
	42 360

REQUIRED:

a) Show the appropriation account for the partnership for the year ended 30 September 1986 under the scheme.

b) Prepare the partners' current accounts for the year ended 30 September 1986.

(AAT)

3 Alan, Bill and Charles are in partnership in a very successful firm. The partners have agreed to share profits and losses in the ratio of Alan 3, Bill 2 and Charles 1. At the year end, on 30 June 1985, the following trial balance was extracted from the books of the firm:

	£	£
Capital accounts:		
Alan		60 000
Bill		40 000
Charles		20 000
Current accounts:		
Alan		5 000
Bill		3 000
Charles		4 000
Drawings:		
Alan	10 000	
Bill	10 000	
Charles	10 000	
Commission		150 000
Property (at cost)	100 000	
Vehicles (at book value)	10 000	
Fixtures (at book value)	2 000	

(Continues)

	£	£
Bad debts	3 000	
Provision for bad debts		3 500
Bank	27 000	
Debtors and creditors	20 000	20 500
Cash in hand	700	
Sundry expenses (including rent, insurance and depreciation for the year to 30 June 1985)	113 300	
	306 000	306 000

REQUIRED:

The partnership profit and loss account (including the appropriation account) for the year ending 30 June 1985, and a balance sheet, in net asset form, as at that date, after taking the following into account:

i) The provision for bad debts is to be reduced to £1000.
ii) At the year end £700 insurance has been paid in advance and rent – £900 – is still owing.

(Institute of Commercial Management)

4 Fairway and Rough, partners in a consultancy business have the following balances in their books at 31 December 1984 (after extraction of the trading and profit and loss accounts):

	£	
Capital accounts (1 January 1984)		
Fairway	20 000	
Rough	25 000	
Current accounts (1 January 1984)		
Fairway	4 200	Cr
Rough	2 060	Dr
Drawings (for the year ended 31 December 1984)		
Fairway	12 000	
Rough	15 000	
Motor van at cost	6 000	
Provision for depreciation on motor van	4 500	
Premises	50 000	
Cash at bank	3 298	
Wages accrued	1 968	

(Continues)

	£
Debtors	3 210
Bank loan (repayable in 1986)	15 000
Interest on bank loan owing	600
Net trading profit	20 300
Interest on drawings:	
Fairway	200
Rough	900

The partners had agreed to allow 8 per cent interest on capital and to share remaining profits equally.

REQUIRED:

a) For the year ended 31 December 1984:
   i) the profit and loss appropriation account of the partnership;
   ii) each partner's current account.

b) The balance sheet of the partnership as at 31 December 1984.

(AEB June '85)

5 Smith and Jones are in partnership, sharing profits and losses in a ratio to their capital accounts. The trial balance as on 31 December was as follows:

	Dr £	*Cr* £
Premises	23 500	
Furniture and fittings	2 750	
Motor van	2 000	
Provision for bad debts		115
Carriage in	142	
Returns	288	343
Purchases	11 665	
Sales		21 429
Discounts	199	146
Stock (1/1)	3 865	
Debtors, creditors	2 355	3 569
Salaries	5 055	
Rates and insurance	645	
Light and heat	162	
Bank	522	

(Continues)

		Dr	Cr
		£	£
Capital:	Smith		18 000
	Jones		12 000
Current accounts:	Smith	625	
	Jones	540	
Drawings accounts:	Smith	2 303	
	Jones	1 500	
Rent received			2 514
		58 116	58 116

NOTES

31 December . . .

1 The value of unsold stock £4200.
2 Gas bill due for payment £66.
3 Rates paid in advance £30.
4 Provision for bad debts to be increased to £250.
5 Depreciation: furniture and fittings by 20 per cent
motor van revalued £1800.
6 Jones is paid a salary of £1000 for extra responsibilities.
7 Interest charged on drawings: Smith £210
Jones £160.

REQUIRED:

a) Prepare the trading, profit and loss appropriation accounts for the year ended 31 December . . . and balance sheet as at that date.
b) Show the current accounts as they would appear in the ledger.

(Institute of Bankers)

6 J Stevenson and S Little, partners in a consultancy business, had the following balances in their books at 31 December 1986 (after the extraction of the profit and loss account):

	£
Capital accounts (1 January 1986):	
Stevenson	35 000
Little	25 000
Current accounts (1 January 1986):	
Stevenson (credit)	6 200
Little (debit)	4 060
Drawings (for year ended 31 December 1986):	
Stevenson	12 000
Little	15 000
Motor van	2 500

(Continues)

	£
Premises	61 290
Cash at bank	3 498
Light and heat accrued	964
Debtors	3 510
Net profit	34 694
Interest on drawings:	
Stevenson	350
Little	940

The partners had agreed to allow 8 per cent per annum on capital, and to pay salaries to Stevenson of £12 500 per annum and to Little of £14 200 per annum. Remaining profits to be shared equally.

REQUIRED:

a) For the year ended 31 December 1986:
   i) the profit and loss appropriation account of the partnership;
   ii) each partner's current account.
b) The balance sheet of the partnership as at 31 December 1986.
c) An explanation of the treatment of employees' salaries in a partnership's final accounts. Why is this treatment different from the treatment of partners' salaries?

(AEB June '87)

7 *Situation*

You work as accountant for Wooldridge & James, a partnership, and have to prepare their final accounts for the year ended 31/5/87.

Data

	£ *Dr*	£ *Cr*
Capital account balances: 1/6/86		
Wooldridge		50 000
James		30 000
Current account balances: 1/6/86		
Wooldridge		1 000
James		2 000
Drawings on 30/11/86		
Wooldridge	5 000	
James	8 000	
Drawings on 31/5/87		
Wooldridge	8 000	
James	10 000	

(Continues)

	Dr	*Cr*
	£	£
Fixed assets (net) 31/5/87	114 000	
Current assets 31/5/87	80 650	
Deferred liabilities 31/5/87		29 000
Current liabilities 31/5/87		75 000
Profit for the year		38 650
	225 650	225 650

The partnership agreement between Wooldridge & James stipulates:

i) Profits and losses to be shared 60 per cent Wooldridge and 40 per cent James.
ii) Salaries to be received Wooldridge £9000, James £12 000.
iii) Interest to be paid on capital and current account balances as on 1/6/86 at 10 per cent per annum.
iv) Drawings also to be subject to interest at a rate of 10 per cent per annum.

TASKS:

a) Prepare the partnership profit and loss appropriation account for the year ending 31/5/87.
   Prepare the partners' current accounts after completion of the profit and loss & appropriation account.
b) Prepare the partnership balance sheet in its abbreviated form as on 31/5/87.
c) Write a memorandum to the partners explaining the situation under Section 24 of the Partnership Act 1890 if no partnership agreement existed.
d) Prepare a statement, to be sent with the above memorandum, showing how the profits would be divided if Section 24 of the Partnership Act 1890 applied.

(BTEC National)

8 The following is the trial balance of Dick and Tom who trade in partnership, at 31 March 1985:

	£	£
Capital account balances 1 April 1984		
Dick		15 000
Tom		15 000
Current account balances 1 April 1984		
Dick		1 500
Tom		2 500
Sales		75 000
Stock (1 April 1984)	15 000	
Wages	7 250	
Rent	2 500	
Expenses	1 500	
Heat and light	600	

(Continues)

	£	£
Debtors/creditors	7 000	5 750
Delivery costs	2 650	
Drawings:		
Dick	3 500	
Tom	4 500	
Cash	2 250	
Fixed assets	13 000	
Purchases	55 000	
	114 750	114 750

NOTES

1 Stock at 31 March 1985 was valued at £19 480.
2 Depreciation of £1750 is to be written off the fixed assets for the year to 31 March 1985.
3 At 31 March 1985 wages accrued amounted to £250, and rent of £500 was prepaid.
4 On 1 February 1985 the partnership ordered and paid for goods costing £350. These were recorded as purchases but were never received as they were lost by the carrier responsible for their delivery. The carrier accepted liability for the loss during March 1985 and paid full compensation of £350 in April 1985. No entries had been made in the books in respect of the loss or claim.
5 Dick took goods which had cost the firm £170 for his own use during the year. No entry has been made in the books to record this.
6 The partnership agreement provided that profits and losses should be shared equally between the partners after:
   a) allowing annual salaries of £1000 to Dick and £2000 to Tom.
   b) allowing interest of 5 per cent per annum on the balance of each partner's capital account; and
   c) charging Dick £210 and Tom £290 interest on drawings.
7 The balances on the capital accounts shall remain unchanged, all adjustments being recorded in the current accounts.

REQUIRED:

a) Prepare the trading, profit and loss and appropriation accounts for the Dick and Tom partnership for the year to 31 March 1985.
b) Prepare the balance sheet at 31 March 1985 showing working capital.
c) Write a brief statement to the owners of the enterprise outlining the profit return for the year.

(RSA)

9 The following information refers to the accounts of Smith, Jones & Rogers who are in partnership and according to their deeds, share profits and losses in the ratio of 2 : 2 : 1 respectively.

During the financial period ended 31 May 1987, the net profit of the business was £7300 and the partners' drawings for the year were:

	£
Smith	2 000
Jones	1 900
Rogers	1 500

Interest on partners' drawings has been calculated as follows:

	£
Smith	65
Jones	55
Rogers	45

As far as the partners' capital accounts are concerned, the agreement states that 6 per cent will be allowed as interest payment. The partners had agreed that Smith should withdraw £1000 from his capital account on 1 December 1986 and that Rogers should contribute the same amount on that date. Jones is awarded a salary of £900 for extra responsibilities.

The balances on the partners' accounts on 1 June 1986 were:

	Capital accounts	*Current accounts*
	£	£
Smith	9 000	600 Cr
Jones	8 000	400 Dr
Rogers	7 000	300 Dr

Other balances on 31 May 1987 were as follows:

	£
Fixed assets (net)	30 700
Stocks	12 750
Debtors	4 655
Cash	500
Bank (Cr)	2 995
Creditors	14 560
Accruals	300
Bank loan (5 years)	4 950

REQUIRED:

a) Prepare the partnership profit and loss appropriation account and the partners' current accounts for the year ended 31 May 1987.
b) Prepare the partners' balance sheet as at 31 May 1987 and show net current assets as part of its construction.
c) Make a brief comment on the partners' financial position as at 31 May 1987.

(Institute of Bankers)

10 *Situation*

French & Saunders run a business consultancy and have the following account balances in their books on 31 March, 1990:

	£	
Capital accounts:		
French	20 000	
Saunders	25 000	
Current accounts:		
French	4 200	Cr
Saunders	2 060	Dr
Drawings for the year:		
French	12 000	
Saunders	15 000	
Premises	60 000	
Vehicles	6 000	
Depreciation of vehicles	5 000	
Bank	3 800	
Debtors	3 210	
Creditors	6 970	
Bank loan 11% 1995	20 000	
Net trading profit for year	19 800	
Interest accrued on loan (6 months)		

NOTES

1 The partners have agreed on equal sharing of profits/losses.
2 The partners have agreed 8 per cent interest on capital accounts.
3 Interest charges on drawings amount to: French £200, Saunders £600.

As an assistant to a group of accountants who have French & Saunders as one of their clients, you have been asked to prepare in draft form:

TASK A:

The profit and loss appropriation account of French & Saunders for the year ended, 31 March 1990 and the current accounts of each partner.

TASK B:

The balance sheet of the partnership as on 31 March 1990.

TASK C:

A brief memorandum, addressed to the partners, commenting on the partnership liquidity and suggesting how it could be improved.

TASK D:

French has used her own premises for the business partnership and £500 has been agreed for running costs. No entries have been made. What effect would this have on the preparation of the above accounts?

(BTEC National)

CHAPTER

20 Accounting for limited companies

- *How are limited companies formed?*
- *What is the difference between ownership and control?*
- *What information does the 1985 and the 1989 Companies Acts provide?*
- *How are company accounts prepared?*
- *What information is found in a company's corporate report?*

Introduction

There are basically two types of limited company – private limited or public limited. Both belong to the private sector of business as distinct from public ownership, which refer to the Government's business enterprises, such as British Rail or British Coal.

There is no restriction as to the number of shareholders who may contribute capital to a company. However, the private company can only sell its shares privately as its title suggests, and cannot resort to publishing a prospectus, inviting the public to buy its shares. A public limited company (plc) may do this, having no such binding restriction as that of the private company. A public company may offer its shares to the public by issuing a prospectus, thereby advertising its share issue to the public, inviting it to purchase its shares. Merchant banks like Hambros, Rothschilds or Barings are part of the 60 issuing houses in the UK, whose interest is to organise and arrange for the public issue of shares. The success of the new share issue will, to a large degree, depend upon the reputation and good name of the issuing house.

By the issue of shares to the public, very large sums of capital can be raised and public companies can take credit for stimulating the growth of share capital investment over the last 100 years or so.

For a public company, at least £50 000 of share capital must be registered with the company, of which a minimum of 25 per cent must be issued and paid for before it can commence business operations.

Shareholders of both private or public companies are part owners of their companies. They are not creditors. They actually own a proportion of the company in relation to the number of shares they have. The reward for owning shares comes from either dividends (a share of the company profits), or from an increase in the value of their shares (capital gain). Dividends are paid on the basis of the nominal value of shares, that is, their face value, not their market value. Dividends are usually expressed in terms of so many pence per share. For example, 10p per share. They may also be determined as so much in the pound, so that 10p per £ would gain £10 per 100 shares.

Limited companies have the advantage of having *limited liability*, a warning to potential creditors that shareholders are only liable up to the value of their nominal capital. They are protected against the debts of the company up to the value of issued and paid-up capital.

Most private companies are relatively small business ventures having a limited number of members as shareholders and being restricted to selling its shares to family and friends or business acquaintances. Public limited companies can often be very large business concerns like ICI plc, Barclays Bank plc and Fords plc, which have thousands of shareholders and employees.

The shares of the plcs may be listed on the Stock Exchange once they have been vetted by the Stock Exchange Council and been given an official market quotation. When this has been granted, the shares (or securities) may be included in the Exchange's Official List and therefore be quoted on the Stock Market. To become a listed company, the Exchange can ensure that the company is providing all the relevant information which is necessary to enable investors to assess their securities fairly and squarely and that they comply with all the necessary standard practice of companies. Private limited company shares are not listed.

Formation of limited companies

A limited company must prepare two important documents which are sent to the Registrar at Companies House, in order to become a registered limited company. All companies are regulated by the 1985 Companies Act which consolidates all previous Acts, 1948 to 1981.

The principal document is the Memorandum of Association which attempts to give the *external* view of the company to the public, including such details as the company's name, address, registered office, share capital and, most significantly, its objectives which set out what it proposes to do. In the final part of the Memorandum comes the *association clause* which is a declaration signed by the founder members of the company, stating that they desire to form themselves into a company (a corporated body).

The second document is the Articles of Association which gives the *internal* view of the company in the form of a list of regulations which will serve as a guideline to the general conduct of running the company. This includes its organisation and control, voting rights, conduct at directors' meetings, power of directors, the rights attached to the different classes of shares and also meetings between shareholders and directors such as the annual general meeting. The Articles must be signed by the founder members. A model form of Articles are to be found in Schedule A of the Companies Act.

Once approval is confirmed by the Registrar, a company is issued with its Certificate of Incorporation, which gives it the status of an incorporated body having a separate legal entity from the owners of the company (its shareholders). The company attains the right of its own identity and can proceed and act under its own name. It has its own existence.

A company is under the control of its board of directors who *direct* the company on behalf of its shareholders – directors control, the shareholders own.

On receipt of a Certificate of Incorporation, a private company may commence trading operations. However, a plc must first issue its prospectus to sell its shares and acquire the minimum share capital it needs to commence operations, as stated in its prospectus. The prospectus must also give details concerning the underwriting of the issue which will ensure that the minimum capital is raised. Once the minimum capital is raised, the Registrar will issue the new company its Certificate of Trading. The plc can then commence trading.

Classes of shares

There are two distinct classes of shares:

a) *Ordinary shares*. These are also referred to as *equities*. They represent the most common type of share and are considered the true shares of a company, taking the greater risk compared to preference shares. The rate of dividend will depend on the profits of the company, and how much the board is willing to distribute and how much it would like to retain. These shares have voting rights, one share, one vote. In the event of the company being liquidated (wound up), these shares are paid last from any surplus of net assets.
b) *Preference shares*. These shares are considered a little less of a risk than equities. They are paid at a *fixed rate of dividend* and are entitled to be paid before any dividend to ordinary shares. They do not however, have any voting rights. Some preference shares are *cumulative* in that any dividend which is not paid in one year, can be claimed in other years. These shares are suitable for those investors who want an assurance of a certain fixed dividend rate from one financial period to the next.

Loan stock

A company may issue *debentures* as well as shares if it wishes to raise finance. This stock is not part of the share capital but represents loan capital and is recorded under long-term liabilities rather than the 'financed by' section.

Debenture holders, who are creditors of the company, are paid at a *fixed rate of interest* over the specified period of the loan. The interest is an expense to be paid and recorded in the profit and loss account. *Redeemable debentures* are those which are redeemed (or paid back) when the stock matures. For example, 9 per cent debentures, 1992, 1995 refers to the earliest and latest dates the stock may be redeemed.

The share and loan capital are both marketable securities and may be bought and sold on the Stock Exchange, if they are officially listed.

Example of distribution of dividends and interest

Allied Components plc have made a profit before interest payments and tax provision of £80 000. It has a registered capital of:

200 000 @ £1 ordinary shares
100 000 @ £1 8 per cent preference shares and
50 000 @ £1 debenture stock at 11 per cent.

Taxation is to be provided for £25 000 and the board has recommended an ordinary share dividend of 10 per cent. Show how the profit is to be distributed.

Allied Components plc

	£	£
Profit (before interest and taxation)		80 000
Interest payable:		
11% debenture stock		5 500
Profit (before tax)		74 500
Provision for tax		25 000
Profit (after tax)		49 500
Provision for dividends:		
8% preference shares	8 000	
Ordinary shares (10%)	20 000	28 000
Retained profits (P&L balance)		21 500

NOTES

1 The interest payable of £5500 is an expense which must be paid irrespective of profits and is part of the company's profit and loss account.

2 The provision for taxation and dividends is part of the company appropriation account, that is, how the company distributes its profits *after* taxation.

3 The retained profits are either transferred to what are known as *revenue reserves* which are merely profits retained over the years, or simply retained in the profit and loss balance.

The divorce between ownership and control

Limited companies are owned by their shareholders. The more shares owned by a shareholder, the greater the ownership in the company. If a shareholder owns the majority of shares, that is over 50 per cent, he or she can take control because the combined number of remaining shares cannot upset the balance of power. In effect, in some circumstances, power can be held by a small number of shareholders owning less than 50 per cent.

The shareholders have the responsibility of electing a board of directors to manage the company on their behalf. In this way the shareholders own a company, the board take control of it. The shareholders can hire or fire their directors at annual general meetings although this rarely occurs in practice.

The board of directors may include both executive and non-executive directors. An executive director takes responsibility for the day-to-day running of his particular department, for example the sales or managing director. Non-executive directors may be invited to join the board for various reasons, for example to give specialist consultation.

The board of directors are responsible for appointing managers to run various departments and to delegate authority and responsibility to them in order that they can carry out the decisions made by the board.

Authorised and issued capital

Authorised capital is also known as the *nominal* capital and is the company's registered capital. The *issued* capital is that capital issued to shareholders. If all the authorised capital is issued, then the authorised and issued capital will be the same figure. *Unissued* capital is that capital still left to be issued. *Paid-up* capital refers to the issued capital which has been paid by shareholders.

Example

	£
Authorised capital	
100 000 @ £1 ordinary shares	100 000
Issued and paid-up capital	
80 000 @ £1 ordinary shares	80 000
Unissued capital	
20 000 @ £1 ordinary shares	20 000

Revenue reserves

Revenue reserves are amounts which are retained from the profits of a company and may be available for distribution as dividends to shareholders. The reserves will increase as more profits are retained from year to year. Reserves will help a company to expand and grow, and transfers to reserve may be used for specific purposes like building up fixed assets or held for general financing. Retained profits are an important source of capital for company growth.

Capital reserves

Capital reserves are retained profits which have not been created from what has been considered normal trading. The share premium account is such a reserve where a company has sold its shares above the par value (face value) and retained the extra money it has received. The revaluation of fixed assets is another example. If land and buildings have increased in value fairly substantially, the amount of the increase could be debited to the asset and the same amount credited to the capital reserve account. These capital reserves are not available for shareholders' dividends and they are shown with other general reserves as part of the shareholders' funds in the balance sheet of the company.

Example
On issuing its prospectus, a company sold all its shares: 500 000 @ £1 ordinary shares at £1.25 each.

Balance sheet (extract)

	£
Shareholders' funds:	
Issued and paid-up capital	
500 000 @ £1 ordinary shares	500 000
Share premium account	125 000
	625 000

Example
A company decided to revalue its property to bring it into line with current prices. Premises were recorded at a cost of £80 000 and were now to be revalued to £150 000.

Balance sheet (extract)

	£	£
Fixed assets:		
Premises	80 000	
+ Revaluation	70 000	150 000
Shareholders' funds:		
Revaluation reserve account		70 000

Accounting requirements of the 1985 Act

Under Part VII of the 1985 Companies Act and particularly, sections 221 and 222, the main points state:

1 Every limited company must keep accounting records, with reasonable accuracy, to disclose the financial position of the company.
2 Financial records must be kept daily including receipts and payments of money, the assets and liabilities of the company, including stock-taking at the year-end. These records must be kept for a period of three years for a private company and six years for a public company.
3 The final accounts of the company must be kept in accordance with the formats laid down in *Schedule 4 of the Act*. This must include:
a profit and loss account
a balance sheet, as at the same period
an auditors' report
a directors' report.

Public companies must have at least two directors and a private company, one. Every company must have a secretary. The directors of a company must make a report as part of the annual accounts and must present a fair view of the business's development in its financial year. The directors must also indicate the dividend they wish to recommend and also the amount they propose to withold as reserves.

Annual reports must be filed with the Registrar at Companies House. For companies registered in England and Wales, there is an address in London and Cardiff. For companies registered in Scotland, there is an address in Edinburgh.

A company must show its accounts to its members for each accounting period at its annual general meeting. It must ensure that a copy of its accounts is sent to the Registrar within a period of ten months following the end of the financial period for a private company and seven months for a public company.

The Companies Act 1989

The new Companies Act, 1989, is a supplementary Act and does not replace the 1985 Companies Act, which in effect, consolidated all previous Acts from 1948–81. The 1989 Act amends and adds to the existing legislation of the 1985 Act. It is expected that the accounting provisions relating to Part I are likely to be effective in respect to accounting periods beginning on or after 1 January 1990.

The new Act came about as a result of the UK's obligation to implement the European Community's Seventh Directive on consolidated accounts and its Eighth Directive on the regulation of company auditors. At the same time, the Government had an opportunity to take stock of its company law and to bring in desired amendments such as the power to investigate and obtain information, to make provision for the safeguarding of certain financial markets and to amend the Financial Services Act 1986 and the Company Securities Act 1985 (Insider Dealing).

As far as company accounts go, the provisions of the Act under sections 221 and 222 (Part VII), emphasise the duty of all companies to keep accounting records.
Some of the 1989 Act's interesting sections are outlined below:

221:(1) Every company shall keep accounting records, sufficient to show and explain the company's transactions with reasonable accuracy at any time, the financial position of the company and to enable the directors to ensure that the balance sheet and profit and loss account complies with the requirements of the Companies Act.

A company's accounts shall be kept at its registered office or such other place where the directors think fit and shall at all times be open to inspection by the company's officers.

221:(2) Accounting entries shall contain day-to-day records of all sums of money received and spent as well as a record of its assets and liabilities.

221:(3) If a company deals with goods for resale, the accounts must contain statements of the value of stock held at end of the financial year and to show sufficient details of buyers and sellers, except by way of ordinary retail trade.

226: It is the duty of the directors to have individual, as well as group company accounts prepared for each financial period, a balance sheet as at the last day of that period and a profit and loss account for that period. Both these financial reports must give a 'true and fair' view of the state of affairs of the company for the financial period under review.

227: Where a company acts as a parent company and has subsidiary companies, the directors must prepare individual accounts for each company and also consolidated accounts for the group, as a whole.

238: The persons entitled to receive copies of the annual accounts and directors' and auditors' reports are:
a) every member of the company,
b) every holder of the company's debentures,
c) every person entitled to receive notice of general meetings (not less than 21 days before the meeting is held).

242: Directors must send to the Registrar at Companies House, a copy of the company's annual accounts and also a copy of the directors' and auditors' reports. Penalties for not complying within the stated specified time (within ten months of the financial period end for a private company and seven months for a public company) will be fined according to the length of time the accounts are delayed. For a public company, the fine will range between £500 and £5000 and for a private company, the fine will range between £100 and £1000.

Other sections of the 1989 Companies Act deal with aspects outside the scope of this publication. These include matters relating to the following:
a) investigations and power to obtain information,
b) the eligibility for the appointment of company auditors,
c) various amendments to company law,
d) mergers and related matters,
e) financial markets and insolvency,
f) the Financial Services Act 1986 – amendments,
g) the transfer of securities.

The preparation of company accounts

The 1985 (Consolidated) Companies Act gives guidance as to the preparation of final accounts of companies, that is, the trading and profit and loss account and the balance sheet. The trading and profit and loss account is sometimes referred to as the profit and loss statement, or the revenue statement.

The 1985 Act outlines a choice of four different formats of presentation for the profit and loss statement. The first format will be adopted because it is already in the same style as is used in this text. The expenses are sub-divided into two major categories, that is, sales and distribution costs and administration expenses. There is also a separate category for listing interest payable. Net profit is shown before and after tax.

The company appropriation account is part of the profit and loss statement and shows how the profits are divided. Some profits may be retained and will not be available for distribution. Retained profits may be held in the profit and loss account or in revenue reserves, or in both.

In a company balance sheet, the Companies Act outlines a choice of just two formats. The first format of presentation will be used because it is in the vertical form as already followed in this text. The alternative method is often adopted by banks and is represented in horizontal format.

Company accounts may be prepared either for internal use or for publication. Accounts for internal use represent a full version of the accounts as is generally prepared for sole traders or partnerships, that is, full details of revenue and expenses may be indicated. Accounts for external use only need indicate the sub-totals for each of the major headings. When preparing the profit and loss statement, only the external version needs to be sent to the Registrar to be filed. A full version of the balance sheet is normally prepared, either for internal or external use, the Registrar requiring the full version to be filed.

The following information illustrates the final accounts for internal use of Allied Components plc, for the year ended 31 December 1990:

Allied Components plc –
Trial balance
as at year ended, 31 December 1990

	£000	£000
Land, buildings	1 800	
Equipment, machinery	650	
Motor vehicles	450	
Investments	600	
Provision for depreciation:		
Land, buildings		20
Equipment, machinery		140
Motor vehicles		110
Debtors, creditors	280	50
Bank/cash	330	
Prepayments, accruals	5	10
Bank loan (10 years)		123
Issued and paid-up capital:		
Ordinary shares		1 000
8% preference shares		1 000
Share premium account		100
Profit and loss balance (1/1)		5
Purchases, sales	1 200	3 500
Stock (1/1)	85	
Sales and distribution costs:		
Sales salaries	85	
Warehouse costs	150	
Advertising, publicity	250	
Motor expenses	150	

(Continues)

	£000	£000
Administration expenses:		
Office salaries	80	
General overheads	255	
Rates, insurances	15	
Light, heat	11	
Telephone	12	
Interest paid	60	
Dividends received		10
Reserves		400
	6 468	6 468

Other information as on 31 December:

a) Stock valued at £65 000.
b) Depreciation charges for the year:
   Equipment, machinery £230 000
   Motor vehicles £300 000.
c) The board of directors recommend that the preference shareholders be paid their dividend and that 10 per cent should be provided for ordinary shares.
d) A sum of £200 000 is to be set aside for corporation tax and £300 000 is to be transferred to reserves.

REQUIRED:

a) For internal use: a trading, profit and loss account for Allied Components plc, for the year ending, 31 December 1990.
b) A balance sheet for Allied Components plc as on 31 December 1990.

Note: The final accounts are to follow Format 1 of the 1985 Companies Act. There is £2 million of authorised ordinary shares. All preference shares have been issued.

Allied Components plc –
trading and profit and loss account,
year ending 31 December, 1990

	£000	£000	£000
Turnover (net sales)			3 500
less			
Cost of sales			
Stock (1/1)	85		
Purchases	1 200		
	1 285		
Stock (31/12)	65		1 220
Gross profit			2 280

(Continues)

	£000	£000	£000
less			
Sales and distribution costs:			
Sales salaries	85		
Warehouse costs	150		
Advertising, publicity	250		
Motor expenses	150		
Depreciation, motor vehicles	300	935	
Administration expenses:			
Office salaries	80		
General overheads	255		
Rates, insurances	15		
Light, heat	11		
Depreciation, equipment	230		
Telephone	12	603	1 538
			742
add			
Other income			
Dividends from other companies			10
			752
less			
Interest payable			60
Net profit (before tax)			692
Corporation tax (provided)			200
Net profit (after tax)			492
add			
Profit and loss balance (1/1)			5
			497
Provision for dividends:			
8% preference shares	80		
Ordinary shares	100		180
			317
Reserves			300
Profit and loss balance (31/12)			17

NOTES

1 The profit and loss balance is the residue of profit after the appropriations to dividends and reserves. The balance at the end of one financial period becomes the opening balance in the next.

2 The provision for dividends were based on:
 1 000 000 8% preference (£80 000)
 1 000 000 ordinary, 10% recommended, (£100 000).
3 The provision for both taxation and dividends will also be listed as current liabilities in the balance sheet, funds not to be distributed from calculated profits.
4 The retained profits will be listed under shareholders' funds, in the 'financed by' section of the balance sheet.

Allied Components plc –
Balance sheet as at
year ending 31 December 1990

	Cost *£000*	*Depreciation* *£000*	*Net value* *£000*
FIXED ASSETS			
Intangibles			—
Tangibles			
Land, buildings	1 800	20	1 780
Equipment, machinery	6 050	370	280
Motor vehicles	450	410	40
Investments	600		600
	8 900	800	2 700
CURRENT ASSETS			
Stock (31/12)	65		
Debtors	280		
Bank/cash	330		
Prepayments	5	680	
less			
CREDITORS FALLING WITHIN 12 MONTHS			
Creditors	50		
Accruals	10		
Provision for taxation	200		
Provision for dividends	180	440	
Net current assets			240
Total assets less current liabilities			2 940
less			
CREDITORS FALLING AFTER 12 MONTHS			
Bank loan (10 years)			123
			2 817

	Authorised capital £000	*Issued and paid-up capital £000*	
FINANCED BY:			
Shareholders' funds			
Ordinary shares	2 000	1 000	
8% preference shares	1 000	1 000	
	3 000	2 000	
Share premium account		100	
Reserves		700	
Profit and loss balance (31/12)		17	2 817

NOTES

1 Creditors falling within 12 months and after 12 months relate to current and long-term liabilities. Total assets less liabilities refers to the capital employed.

2 The authorised capital is the sum as stated in the company's Memorandum of Association. A public limited company must have at least £50 000 worth of registered (authorised) capital. It is the issued and paid-up capital which are the relevant figures for balancing.

3 The share premium account relates to the company's capital reserves and represents the sum received in excess of the nominal value of the shares issued. In the above case, the ordinary shares sold at £1.10 each, a premium of 10p per share.

An example of financial statements prepared for private limited companies

The Rafael Private Co Ltd

The following information relates to the documents prepared for filing with the Registrar at Companies House, London. Rafael is a small manufacturing company, producing clothing for the home market. Its financial period runs from 1 January to 31 December.

It is a typical, small, private company, held in ownership by the Jones and Smith families who have an equal number of shares between them. Its four directors have 250 shares each, a total of 1000 ordinary shares. It employs fewer than 20 in its workforce.

The financial statements attached are the type of external reports which are sent to the Registrar. The funds flow statement is also included and information concerning this account is found in the following section.

Note that the previous year's financial figures (1988) are always included with the current year as a matter of standard practice. The company made a loss of £14 350 in the current year, having made a profit of £9524 in the previous period. This was largely due to diminishing sales and costs which did not fall in proportion.

Study the figures as to the general presentation and content of the accounts, prepared in accordance with the Companies Act 1985.

The financial statements
for the year ended 31 December 1989

The financial statements for the year ended 31 December 1989 include:

- the directors' report
- the auditors' report
- the profit and loss account
- the balance sheet.

The directors' report

The directors present their report together with financial statements for the year ended 31 December 1989.

1 **Principal activities:** the company is principally engaged in the production of clothing, mainly men's and children's.

2 **Results:** The company's results reflect both the move to the new premises in the year and the recruitment of two sales staff who proved unsuccessful. As a result a small loss was recorded. The directors are confident that the company will shortly revert to profitability. The directors consider the position at the year-end to be satisfactory.

The loss for the year after taxation amounted to £10 850. The directors do not recommend payment of a dividend and the loss has therefore been deducted from reserves.

3 **Directors:** the directors in office at the end of the year are listed below. All served on the board throughout the year.

The interests of the directors in the shares of the company at 1 January 1988 and at 31 December 1989 as recorded in the register maintained by the company in accordance with the provisions of the Companies Act 1985, were as follows:

	1989 and 1988 ordinary shares
T Jones	250
R Jones	250
D Smith	250
L Smith	250

The auditor's report

REPORT OF THE AUDITORS TO THE MEMBERS OF THE RAFAEL PRIVATE CO LTD
We have audited the financial statements of the company on the following pages in accordance with auditing standards.

In our opinion, the financial statements have given a true and fair view of the state of the company's affairs at 31 December 1989 and of its result and sources and application of funds for the year ended. These have been properly prepared in accordance with the Companies Act, 1985.

Rosenthal & Rosenthal
Chartered Accountants

25 February 1990

Rafael Private Co Ltd – Profit and loss account for the year ended 31 December 1989

	1989	*1988*
	£	£
Turnover	458 227	553 586
Cost of sales	(313 377)	(369 800)
Gross profit	144 850	183 786
Distribution costs	38 000	42 094
Administrative expenses	118 400	131 606
	(156 400)	(173 700)
Operating loss/profit	(11 550)	10 086
Interest receivable and similar income	600	638
Interest payable and similar charges	(3 400)	(1 200)
(Loss)/profit (before taxation)	(14 350)	9 524
Tax on (loss)/profit on ordinary activities	3 500	(3 324)
Retained profits (after taxation)	(10 850)	6 200
Statement of retained profits		
At 1 January 1988	36 760	30 560
Transfer to reserves	(10 850)	6 200
At 31 December 1989	25 910	36 760

Rafael Private Co Ltd – Balance sheet at 31 December 1989

	1989 £	*1988* £
FIXED ASSETS		
Tangible assets	45 762	35 270
CURRENT ASSETS		
Stocks	48 810	70 187
Debtors	102 462	88 651
Cash at bank and in hand	133	25 965
	151 405	184 803
CREDITORS: AMOUNTS FALLING DUE WITHIN ONE YEAR	(161 397)	179 701
Net current (liabilities)/assets	(9 992)	5 102
Total assets less current liabilities	35 770	40 372
CREDITORS FALLING DUE AFTER MORE THAN ONE YEAR	7 560	1 286
PROVISIONS FOR LIABILITIES AND CHARGES		
Deferred taxation	1 300	1 326
	(8 860)	(2 612)
	26 910	37 760
CAPITAL AND RESERVES		
Called-up share capital	1 000	1 000
Profit and loss account	25 910	36 760
	26 910	37 760

The financial statements were approved by the board of directors on 25 February 1990.

The corporate report

Why does a business enterprise prepare financial statements? A business should produce information concerning its activities because different groups of people want to know a variety of information, primarily concerning the financial performance of the business. There may well be other areas of information which they may be interested in such as future developments, customer service, staff satisfaction and the relationship of the company with that of its environment, that is, its social responsibility.

The corporate report is basically concerned with the company's financial activities. Shareholders will want to know how well their investment is doing. Is the company maximising profits? Is it financially secure? Will it continue to trade confidently in the future? Should the shareholder hang on to his stock or sell it?

Financial reports do not profess to tell the whole story, but at least, there is an attempt to relate the financial facts to those parties who have an interest in their content. Various groups of people, such as shareholders, management, creditors and other providers of finance, the tax authorities and staff members, all have a right to know of the activities of a business enterprise. Is the business going in the right direction? Is its future looking bright or are there distinct clouds looming over the horizon?

A corporate report, prepared by the company's management, is primarily about the company's financial activities concerning past, current and forecasted figures. Corporate aims and objectives may not always be the same for every type of company, each corporate body chooses its own goals to achieve. However, the general consensus of most organisations is to:

a) Provide goods or services which are marketable and can reliably earn revenue for the enterprise.
b) Be efficient and productive, to eliminate waste in terms of labour, materials and capital. In other words, to maximise the resources of the enterprise as efficiently as possible.
c) As a consequence of a) and b) above, to maximise the profit potential of the business. To achieve greater profits in real terms each financial year (taking into account inflation), increasing the earnings per share of its shareholders and the return of profit on the company's capital employed. In the daily newspapers, when financial results are published by companies, they always emphasise, often by graphs or tables, the details of profit growth and earnings. For example:

   Sales up by 40 per cent
   Pre-tax profits up by 20 per cent
   Earnings per share up by 25 per cent
   Dividends up by 50 per cent.

   Thus a company will advertise its success for the year and hope to keep the confidence of its shareholders and also the market for its products or services.

   A company's profit may be described as *trading* or *operating* profit which refers to profits made from trading operations, excluding taxation and interest payments. *Pre-tax profits* refer to profit before taxation is provided for, but after the payment of interest (if any). *Profit after tax* is profit after taxation has been provided for and is the net income available to the enterprise which is available for distribution – some as dividends to shareholders and some as retained profits in the business.
d) Take care of its staff, that is, to provide opportunities for them to achieve their goals, good rates of pay, job satisfaction, employee participation, training, promotion, and generally motivating them to achieve their best for themselves and for the company.
e) Be aware of its social responsibilities in that an organisation not only has a duty to its shareholders and staff, but to the social community as a whole in terms of enterprise, jobs, careers, welfare, sports and the general well being of the environment.

   Therefore, the corporate aims and objectives are to ensure a good level of profit returns, growth of markets, employee satisfaction and also a degree of social responsibility to the community.

Summary

1 A limited company is an incorporated body which is a separate legal entity from its owners (the shareholders).

2 There are basically two categories of limited company: private limited and public limited. The latter, abbreviated to plc, is generally regarded as the largest form of business organisation found in the private sector of business. It can issue a prospectus, thereby tapping the potential investment from the general public at large. The private company may only offer its shares privately to family or friends.

3 The most common type of share capital comes from ordinary shares (equities). Preference shares are not true shares as ordinary shares are because they do not have voting rights and are paid a fixed percentage rate of dividend.

4 Debentures may be part of a company's loan capital, not share capital. They are paid at a fixed rate of interest which is recorded under the 'interest payable' section of the profit and loss statement.

5 The 1985 Companies Act regulates the activities of companies and consolidates all previous acts. A model form of Articles of Association may be found under Schedule A of the Act. The Act lays down the guidelines for the preparation of a company's final accounts. The 1989 Companies Act does not replace the 1985 Act – it is a supplementary act.

6 The corporate report is a company report which concerns itself primarily with the financial activities of the business but it also outlines the corporation's aims and objectives, including marketing its product, achieving desirable profits, staff welfare and community responsibilities.

QUESTIONS

1 You work for the financial accountant of Compton Ltd, manufacturers of cosmetics, and are working on the annual accounts.

Information
The following balances remain in the ledger of Compton Ltd after the preparation of the profit and loss account for the year ended 31 March 1986.

	£
Stocks and work in progress	98 000
Debtors	87 000
Provision for bad debts	4 000
£1 ordinary shares [authorised £600 000]	400 000
16% preference shares of £1 each [authorised £200 000]	100 000

(Continues)

	£
Creditors	74 000
Balance at bank	4 000
Accruals	3 500
Prepayment	2 500
General reserve account	14 000
Share premium account	20 000
Net profit for the year ended 31/3/86	108 000
Profit and loss account balance 1/4/85	22 000
Premises (at cost)	300 000
Plant and equipment (at cost)	310 000
Vehicles (at cost)	200 000

The directors propose the following:

i) To transfer £20 000 to general reserve.
ii) To propose an ordinary dividend of 12 per cent and to pay the preference dividend.
iii) To provide for corportion tax of £30 000, payable in October 1987.

Depreciation of fixed assets has been calculated as follows:

i) Plant and equipment has a residual value of £30 000 and a 'life' estimated at ten years. It is five years old and depreciation is based on the straight-line method.
ii) The vehicles are valued at current market price of £84 000.
iii) There is no depreciation on premises.

REQUIRED:

A profit and loss appropriation account for the year ended 31 March 1986 and a balance sheet as at that date.

2 The following information relates to an electrical components manufacturing company, Hardcastle Co Ltd. Its cost of production (factory cost) is transferred to the cost of sales in the profit and loss statement. The figures are for the financial year end of 31 December 1989:

	£	£
Turnover		327 000
Stock (1/1/89)	58 750	
Cost of production	201 500	
Sales and distribution	44 800	
Administration expenses	38 700	
Interest charges	5 500	
Fixed assets (net)	135 100	
Debtors and creditors	76 750	89 400

(Continues)

	£	£
Bank overdraft		10 800
Accruals		4 900
Prepayments	500	
Loans (15 years)		52 000
Issued and paid up ordinary shares (£1)		50 000
Share premium account		10 000
Reserves		17 500
	561 600	561 600

NOTES

As on 31 December 1989:

1 Stock value £68 750.
2 A proposed dividend of 5p per share.
3 To provide £14 500 for corporation tax.
4 To transfer £25 000 to reserves.

REQUIRED:

Prepare the profit and loss account of the company for the period ending 31 December 1989 and a balance sheet as on that date. Use Format 1 of the 1985 Act.

(BTEC National)

3 *Situation*

You work as an assistant to the accountant for Jason Ltd which has an authorised capital of £500 000, divided into 800 000 ordinary shares of 50p each and 200 000 8 per cent preference shares of 50p each. The following balances remained in the accounts of the company after the trading and profit and loss accounts had been prepared for the year ended 30 November 1986.

	Debit £	*Credit* £
General reserve		5 000
Ordinary share capital: fully paid		100 000
8% preference shares: fully paid		30 000
Premises at cost	140 000	
Light and heat owing		840
Profit and loss account balance (1/12/85)		19 200
Bank		8 200
Debtors and creditors	5 800	1 120
Net profit (for year ended 30/11/86)		40 600
Machinery and plant at cost	50 000	
Provision for depreciation on machinery and plant		25 000
Stock	33 340	
Insurance prepaid	820	
	229 960	229 960

Information as on 30 November 1986
The directors of Jason Ltd have recommended:
i) A transfer of £10 400 to reserve.
ii) An ordinary dividend of 12 per cent.
iii) To provide payment of the year's preference dividend and also to provide for corporation tax of £10 000.

TASK A:

Prepare the profit and loss appropriation account for the year ended 30 November 1986.

TASK B:

Prepare the balance sheet as at 30 November 1986 showing clearly the shareholders' funds and the working capital.

4 Hurley Ltd had a registered capital of £250 000, divided into 400 000 ordinary shares of 50p each and 100 000 8 per cent preference shares of 50p each. The following balances remained in the accounts of the company after the trading and profit and loss accounts had been prepared for the year ended 31 May 1986.

	Debit	*Credit*
	£	£
Ordinary share capital: fully paid		50 000
8% preference shares: fully paid		15 000
Premises at cost	65 000	
Light and heat		420
Profit and loss account balance (1/6/85)		9 600
Bank		4 100
Debtors and creditors	2 900	560
Net profit (for year ended 31/5/86)		10 300
Machinery and plant at cost	25 000	
Provision for depreciation on machinery and plant		15 000
Stock	11 670	
Insurance	410	
	104 980	104 980

The directors have recommended:

a transfer of £12 000 to general reserve;
an ordinary dividend of 12 per cent; and
to provide for payment of the year's preference dividend.

REQUIRED:

a) The profit and loss appropriation account for the year ended 31 May 1986.
b) The balance sheet as at 31 May 1986, in a form which shows clearly the shareholders' funds and the working capital.
c) An explanation of the term 'interim dividend' and two differences between an ordinary share and a preference share.

(AEB June '86)

5 *Situation/information*

You work in the financial accounts department of the ABC Trading Co Ltd which is registered with an authorised capital of £2 000 000 divided into 800 000 10 per cent preference shares of £1 each and 1 200 000 ordinary shares of £1 each.

After completion of the trading and profit and loss account for the year ended 31 May 1986 the following balances remain in the books:

	£000	*£000*
Preference share capital (fully paid)		500
Ordinary share capital (fully paid)		900
Profit and loss account balance brought forward		10
General reserve		50
Net profit for the year ended 31/5/86		300
Premises (at cost)	1 250	
Delivery vans (at cost)	125	
Provision for depreciation of delivery vans		35
Fixtures and fittings (at cost)	60	
Provision for depreciation of fixtures and fittings		20
Cash in hand and at bank	314	
Trade debtors	27	
Provision for doubtful debts		1
Creditors		12
Stocks	50	
Payments in advance	2	
	1 828	1 828

The directors propose to pay the preference dividend, a dividend of 20 per cent to the ordinary shareholders and transfer £40 000 to general reserve, and to provide for taxation of £10 000.

REQUIRED:

a) Prepare the profit and loss appropriation account for the year ended 31 May 1986.
b) Prepare the balance sheet as at 31 May 1986.
c) State the amount of working capital.
d) State the total equity (or ordinary shareholders') funds.

6 The accounts of Robertson & David Co Ltd were extracted from the books on 30 June 1988:

Trial balance as on 30 June 1988

	Dr £	*Cr* £
Issued and paid-up capital:		
160 000 ordinary shares @ £1		160 000
40 000 8% preference shares @ £2		80 000
P&L account (1/7/87)		7 780
General reserve		25 000
7% debentures		40 000
Premises cost	287 910	
Motor vehicles (cost)	32 000	
Plant, equipment (cost)	16 880	
Provision for depreciation of motor vehicles		4 800
Stock (1/7/87)	49 600	
Bank		11 752
Cash	1 558	
Purchases	535 600	
Sales		696 500
Returns	500	1 600
Wages	65 460	
Rates, water, insurance	3 600	
General expenses	22 536	
Preference dividend paid (31/12/87)	3 200	
Debtors, creditors	63 380	53 944
Bad debts	2 150	
Provision for bad debts		3 120
Discount allowed	122	
	1 084 496	1 084 496

NOTES

Additional details as at 30 June 1988:

a) Stock value £39 400.
b) Rates pre-paid £1000. Wages still outstanding £3360.
c) Invoice unpaid for general expenses £30.
d) Depreciation: motor vehicles 20 per cent on book valuation
plant and equipment 25 per cent on cost.
e) Adjust the provision for bad debts to equal 5 per cent of debtors.
f) The Directors of the company propose a dividend of 10 per cent for ordinary shares. Preference shares to receive their final dividend.
g) No interest has been paid on the debentures.
h) A transfer of £4000 is to be made to general reserve.
i) A provision of £19 200 is to be made for taxation.

REQUIRED:

Prepare the trading, profit and loss appropriation accounts for the year ended 30 June 1988, and a balance sheet as at that date.

(Institute of Bankers)

7 The following balances, at 1 January 1987, were taken from the books of Seaham plc, which had an authorised capital of 250 000 ordinary shares of £1 each and 100 000 9 per cent preference shares of £1 each:

issued share capital £100 000 in ordinary shares of £1 each, fully paid; premises £75 000; fittings and equipment £18 900; debtors £10 600; creditors £5300; stock £7861; balance at bank £8079; profit and loss account, credit balance £7640; proposed ordinary dividend for 1986, £7500.

During the month of January 1987, some of the company's transactions were:

1 sold an item of equipment, book value £4600, for £5600 by cheque;
2 bought goods on credit £5000;
3 sold goods on credit £8000, which had been marked up by $33\frac{1}{3}$ per cent on cost.

REQUIRED:

a) The balance sheet of Seaham plc at 31 January, assuming there were no other transactions in January, in a form which shows clearly the shareholders' funds and the working capital.
   Your balance sheet must include the three transactions occurring in January. Where a balance sheet figure has changed as a result of these transactions, you are advised to indicate the direction and amount of the change in brackets, next to the item concerned, within the balance sheet.
b) The main danger to a firm of:
   i) holding too little working capital;
   ii) holding too much working capital.

(AEB June '87)

8 The following balances appeared in the books of Carlos Ltd at 31 December 1984:

	£
Premises	62 000
Equipment	18 000
Fittings	7 904
Gross profit (for year ended 31/12/84)	25 300
Authorised and issued capital (in ordinary shares of £1 each)	60 000
Directors' fees	4 000
10% debentures	30 000
Stock in trade	6 200
Debenture interest	1 500

(Continues)

	£
Profit and loss account credit balance at 1/1/84	3 200
Cash at bank	18 070
Sundry expenses	5 816
Debtors	1 600
Creditors	5 110
Auditors' remuneration	1 620
Commission received	850
Discount allowed	250
Discount received	700
Profit on sale of motor van	1 800

The following additional information is also available:

equipment and fittings are to be depreciated by a total of £5000;
debenture interest for the final six months of the year remains outstanding;
£2000 is to be transferred to general reserve;
a dividend of 12 per cent has been proposed on the ordinary shares.

REQUIRED:

a) Preparation of a profit and loss account, including the appropriation section, for Carlos Ltd for the year ended 31 December 1984.
b) Preparation of the liabilities section of the balance sheet of Carlos Ltd as at 31 December 1984. This section should be set out to show clearly shareholders' funds, long-term and current liabilities.
c) An explanation of the meaning of the terms:
   i) 'limited liability';
   ii) 'authorised capital';
   iii) 'issued capital';
   iv) 'working capital';
   v) 'current assets'.

(AEB Nov '85)

9 The following information relates to an electrical components manufacturing company, Arrowsmith Co Ltd. Its cost of production (factory cost) is transferred to the cost of sales in the profit and loss statement. The figures are for the financial year end of 31 December 1989:

	£	£
Turnover		356 000
Stock (1/1/89)	62 000	
Cost of production	256 500	
Sales and distribution	28 100	
Administration expenses	44 400	

(Continues)

	£	£
Interest charges	4 000	
Fixed assets (net)	156 500	
Debtors and creditors	84 200	86 500
Bank/cash	4 800	
Accruals		500
Prepayments	—	
Loans (15 years)		40 000
Issued and paid-up ordinary shares (£1)		100 000
Share premium account		20 000
Reserves		37 500
	640 500	640 500

NOTES

As on 31 December 1989:

1 Stock value £84 000.
2 A proposed dividend of 9p per share.
3 To provide £15 500 for corporation tax.
4 To transfer £20 000 to reserves.

REQUIRED:

a) Prepare the profit and loss account of the company for the period ending 31 December 1989 and a balance sheet as on that date. Use Format 1 of the 1985 Act. These accounts are for *external* use.
b) Calculate the company's current ratio and comment briefly on its adequacy.

10 *Situation*

You are an assistant to the accountant at J P Davies plc, which has been in business for several years. The trial balance on 30 June 1990 was as follows:

J P Davies plc –
Trial balance as on 30 June 1990

	Debit £	*Credit* £
£1 preference shares (15%) (authorised £200 000)		100 000
£1 ordinary shares (authorised £500 000)		200 000
Revenue reserves		45 000
Debenture stock (12.5%), 1995		100 000

(Continues)

	Debit £	*Credit* £
Profit for year ending 30/6/90 (before debenture interest)		80 000
Profit and loss balance (1/7/89)		40 000
Stocks	200 000	
Premises	200 000	
Plant and machinery	180 000	
Vehicles	50 000	
Office equipment	90 000	
Provisions for depreciation:		
Premises		10 000
Plant and machinery		70 000
Vehicles		30 000
Office equipment		55 000
Debtors	220 000	
Creditors		190 000
Cash	500	
Provision for bad debts		11 000
Prepayments	9 500	
Accruals		21 000
Bank overdraft		5 500
Interim preference dividend paid	7 500	
	957 500	957 500

NOTES

1 A full year's debenture interest is still to be charged.
2 Corporation tax is to be provided for, payable in March 1991, £20 000.
3 The final dividend on preference shares is to be provided for.
4 To propose an ordinary dividend of 20 per cent.
5 To transfer £25 000 to revenue reserves.

TASK A:

You are to draw up, in draft form, for the accountant of the company, the profit and loss appropriation account for the year ended 30 June 1990 and a balance sheet as at that date. The accounts are for internal use but should follow Format 1 as per Companies Act 1985.

TASK B:

Your accountant has also asked you to prepare a brief memorandum, suitable for trainees in the office, explaining the importance of SSAP No. 2 when preparing accounting statements. You may use any examples from the accounting statements prepared in Task A to illustrate your answer.

(BTEC National)

CHAPTER

21 The statement of sources and application of funds

- *What is a funds flow statement?*
- *Why is it included as part of a company's accounting reports?*

Introduction

Agreement was reached by the accounting profession that the conventional final accounts of businesses should include a funds flow statement. All audited statements (meaning company accounts, by and large), should include the funds flow statement as a supplement to the trading and profit and loss account and the balance sheet to give a 'true and fair' view of the accounts, unless the turnover of the business is under £25 000 per annum.

The objective of the funds flow is to identify the movement of funds (or resources) coming in and going out of a business within the financial period. Basically, the funds flow will emphasise where funds have come from and where they have gone. For example, if £100 000 of share capital has been issued by the company (source of funds), what was it used for, if anything (application of funds)?

The funds flow is a link between the profit and loss account and the balance sheets of two successive periods. The statement makes it easier to identify new sources of finance and how these have been allocated. A new share issue may have financed the purchase of plant, machinery and equipment. Any surplus or deficit resulting from the difference between the sources and application of funds should equal the business's change in working capital, over the financial period.

The guideline to preparing the funds flow is given in the accounting profession's Statement of Standard Accounting Practice (SSAPs) of which Statement No.10 deals with funds flow. SSAPs are dealt with in Chapter 22.

The funds flow statement

The statement is in four sections:

1 *Sources of funds:* Commences with the net profit (or loss) before tax. Any expense items which are provided, such as depreciation or provision for bad debts, are *added back* to the net profit because provisions do not represent cash withdrawn. Any other financing coming from the issue of shares or sources of loan capital, is added to profits.

2 *Application of funds:* There are three major items where resources are allocated. These are the purchases of fixed assets, the payment of dividends and the payment of taxation.

3 *Changes in working capital:* The surplus (or deficit) arising from the difference between the sources and application of funds in *1* and *2* above, must equal the change in working capital for the period. This section basically deals with the changes in value to stock, debtors and creditors during the financial period. Any accruals or prepayments may be added to creditors and debtors respectively.

4 *Movement in net liquid funds:* This represents the change in bank, cash or short-term investments during the financial period, although a part of working capital, bank and cash is headed separately, perhaps to emphasise their importance to the liquidity of a business. The net result of *3* and *4* equals the change in working capital and should equal the difference between source and application of funds, represented in *1* and *2*.

NOTE

The provisions for tax and dividends are not part of creditors in *3*. The payments for these in the year are listed in *2*, application of funds.

Presentation

The funds flow statement of P Land Ltd
year ending 31 December 1990

	£000	£000
1 Sources of funds		
Net profit (before tax)	2 860	
Add depreciation charges	760	
	3 620	
Other sources:		
Issue of ordinary shares	160	
Bank loan	16	
Sale of fixed asset	4	
	180	3 800

(Continues)

	£000	£000
2 Application of funds		
Purchase of fixed assets	900	
Dividends paid during year	800	
Tax paid during year	850	2 550
Surplus during year		1 250
3 Changes in working capital		
Increase in stocks	600	
Increase in debtors and prepayments	340	
Increase in creditors and accruals	(240)	
	700	
4 Movement in net liquid funds		
Increase in bank	500	
Increase in cash	50	
	550	1 250

Example

As the accounting executive of ABC Co Ltd you need to determine the financial trends of the company.

Study the following balance sheets and abbreviated profit and loss accounts of the firm over the previous two years.

ABC Co Ltd –
Balance sheets as at 31 May

	1988		*1989*	
	£	£	£	£
FIXED ASSETS				
Cost	180 000		260 000	
Provision for depreciation	40 000	140 000	60 000	200 000
Investment (cost)		10 000		5 000
		150 000		205 000
CURRENT ASSETS				
Stocks	50 000		60 000	
Debtors	30 000		47 000	
Bank	10 000		18 000	
	90 000		125 000	

(Continues)

	1988 £	1988 £	1989 £	1989 £
LESS CURRENT LIABILITIES				
Creditors	17 000		18 000	
Taxation	16 000		18 000	
Dividends	12 000		14 000	
	45 000	45 000	50 000	75 000
		195 000		280 000
FINANCED BY:				
Ordinary shares	170 000		200 000	
Premium account	17 000		20 000	
P&L balance	8 000	195 000	10 000	230 000
Long-term liability				
9% debenture stock		—		50 000
		195 000		280 000

ABC Co Ltd – Abbreviated profit and loss accounts for years ending 31 May

	1988 £	1988 £	1989 £	1989 £
Sales	200 000		250 000	
Net trading profit	25 000		30 000	
+ Profit on investment	—		4 000	
	25 000		34 000	
Less taxation	16 000	9 000	18 000	16 000
+ Profit and loss account balance b/f		11 000		8 000
		20 000		24 000
– Dividends (Provisional)		12 000		14 000
Profit and loss account balance c/f		8 000		10 000

REQUIRED:

a) Prepare a statement of sources and application of funds for the year ended 31 May 1989.

b) Draft a memorandum to your immediate superior, commenting on the business's liquidity position on both 31 May 1988 and 31 May 1989.

1

ABC Co Ltd –
Funds flow statement, year ended 31 May 1989

	£	£
1 Sources of funds		
Trading profit	30 000	
+ Depreciation charges	20 000	
	50 000	
Other sources:		
Issue of share capital	30 000	
Share premium account	3 000	
Issue of debentures	50 000	
*Sale of investment	9 000	
	92 000	142 000
2 Application of funds		
Purchase of fixed assets	80 000	
Dividends paid	12 000	
Tax paid	16 000	108 000
Surplus		34 000
3 Changes in working capital		
Stocks	10 000	
Debtors	17 000	
Creditors	(1 000)	26 000
4 Movement in net liquid funds		
Bank		8 000
		34 000

NOTES

*Sale of investment: calculated from the difference in cost, 1988 £10 000 and 1989 £5000. If sold at cost, £5000 would have been received from the sale. The profit on the sale was £4000, therefore the actual sale contributed £9000.

An increase in creditors in the year from £17 000 to £18 000 (£1000), has the effect of decreasing working capital, hence the figure is in brackets.

2

Liquidity	*1988*	*1989*
Current ratio	2.1 : 1	2.5 : 1

Sound working capital, an improvement over the year. £2.50 in current assets to cover £1 of current debts.

Calculations of the funds flow statement

	1988 £	*1989* £	*Funds flow* £
Sources			
Profit for year			30 000
Depreciation charges	40 000	60 000	20 000
			50 000
Sale of investment	10 000	5 000	
Add profit £4000			9 000
Share issue	170 000	200 000	30 000
Premium account	17 000	20 000	3 000
9% debentures	—	50 000	50 000
			142 000
Application			
*Purchase of fixed assets	180 000	260 000	80 000
Taxation provision	16 000	18 000	16 000
Dividends provision	12 000	14 000	12 000
			108 000
Surplus			34 000
Change in working capital			
Stocks	50 000	60 000	10 000
Debtors	30 000	47 000	17 000
Creditors	17 000	18 000	(1 000)
			26 000
Movement in net liquid funds			
Bank	10 000	18 000	8 000
			34 000

NOTES

*Purchase of fixed assets: if these were given at a net value (the depreciation already deducted), you will need to add back on the depreciation charges for the year.

The tax and dividends provision for 1988 will not be paid until the following year, 1989, therefore the 1988 figures are listed in the funds flow for that year.

Summary

1 The statement of sources and application of funds statement is abbreviated to the funds flow statement. It is a link between the profit or loss for the year as indicated in the profit and loss account and two successive balance sheets, one at the beginning of the financial year, the other at the year end.

2 The funds flow has a basic purpose to identify where funds have come from (sources) and where they have gone (application), during the financial year.

3 The funds flow gives a further aspect to the final accounts of organisations in that a 'true and fair view' is given to those interested parties such as investors, creditors and financial institutions.

4 The funds flow is presented in four sections: sources, application, working capital change and movement in net liquid funds. The net result of the first two should equal the net result of the last two. A glance at the statement should indicate where a surplus or deficit of funds has occurred during the year and its affect on the business's working capital.

5 The guidelines to preparing the funds flow is given in SSAP No.10 (Statement of Standard Accounting Practice).

QUESTIONS

1 The final accounts of Wexford & Co Ltd for the year ended 31 December 1990 were as follows:

Balance sheet as at 31 December

	1989	*1990*
	£	£
FIXED ASSETS (COST)	16 600	21 000
Depreciation	1 020	1 600
	15 580	19 400
CURRENT ASSETS		
Stock	1 950	3 555
Debtors	2 140	3 000
Bank	1 750	2 170
	5 840	8 725

(Continues)

	1989	1990
	£	£
CURRENT LIABILITIES		
Creditors	400	2 095
Provision for tax	160	400
Provision for dividends	30	50
	590	2 545
Net current assets	5 250	6 180
Capital employed	20 830	25 580
LONG-TERM LIABILITIES		
Bank loan	600	5 000
	20 230	20 580
FINANCED BY		
Issued and paid-up capital	20 000	20 000
P&L balance	230	580
	20 230	20 580

Profit and loss statement, year ended 31 December 1990

	£	£
Net profit		800
(after charging depreciation £580)		
P&L balance (1/1)		230
		1 030
Provisions for: tax	400	
dividends	50	450
P&L balance (31/12)		580

REQUIRED:
A funds flow statement for the year ended 31 December 1990.

2 **Rock Ltd – Funds flow statement year ended 31 December**

	1990	1989
	£	£
Balance sheet		
Fixed assets (cost)	9 000	2 500
Depreciation	1 000	800
	8 000	1 700

(Continues)

	1990	*1989*
	£	£
CURRENT ASSETS:		
Stock	2 500	2 000
Debtors	1 000	800
Bank		500
Cash		50
	3 500	3 350
CURRENT LIABILITIES:		
Creditors	1 000	700
Bank (overdraft)	250	
Tax provision	350	250
Dividends provision		100
	1 600	1 050
Working capital	1 900	2 300
Capital employed	9 900	4 000
– Loan capital	5 450	
	4 450	4 000
FINANCED BY:		
Issued and paid-up capital	3 000	2 800
P&L balance (31/12)	1 450	1 200
	4 450	4 000

Profit and loss account, year ended 31 December 1990

	£
Net trading profit (after £200 depreciation charges)	600
Provision for tax	350
	250
+P&L balance (1/1)	1 200
P&L balance (31/12)	1 450

REQUIRED:

Prepare a funds flow statement for Rock Ltd for the year ended 31 December 1990.

(Institute of Bankers)

3 The following information refers to the accounts of P Jackson & Co Ltd. Prepare a funds flow statement for year ended 31 December 1988.

	31/12/87	*31/12/88*
	£	£
ASSETS		
Premises (cost)	35 000	45 000
Machinery*	20 000	21 500
Stock	15 000	20 580
Debtors	8 450	12 375
Bank/cash	2 255	1 835
	80 705	101 290
LIABILITIES		
Creditors	10 150	12 755
Accruals	1 125	955
Taxation due	5 100	6 530
	16 375	20 240
CAPITAL		
Issued @ £1 ordinary shares	50 000	60 000
P&L account	14 330	21 050
	64 330	81 050

MACHINERY*

	Cost	*Depreciation*	*Net*
	£	£	£
Balance (31/12/87)	25 000	5 000	20 000
Additions 1988	6 000		
	31 000		
Sale of old stock	(3 000)	(2 000)	
Depreciation 1988		3 500	
Balance (31/12/88)	28 000	6 500	21 500

Profit and loss account year ended 31 December 1988

	£
Net trading profit	12 750
+ Gain on sale of machinery	500
	13 250
Corporation tax	6 530
Retained to P&L account	6 720

NOTE

Any gain or loss on the sale of a fixed asset is *not* included in the 'source of funds' as net profit although the actual sum received *is* included.

(Institute of Bankers)

4 *Situation/information*

You work in the accounts department of Maxpax Ltd and are assisting in the preparation of the annual accounts. The summarised balance sheets of Maxpax Ltd at 31 May are as follows:

		1988		*1989*
	£	£	£	£
FIXED ASSETS				
Premises		100 000		100 000
Plant at cost	80 000		120 000	
Less cumulative depreciation	(48 000)	32 000	(60 000)	60 000
		132 000		160 000
CURRENT ASSETS				
Stocks	24 000		50 000	
Debtors	16 000		12 000	
Bank	8 000		14 000	
	48 000		76 000	
CURRENT LIABILITIES				
Creditors	14 000		17 000	
Proposed taxation	14 000		15 000	
Proposed dividends	16 000		8 000	
	44 000	4 000	40 000	36 000
		136 000		196 000
FINANCED BY:				
£1 ordinary shares		100 000		140 000
Shares premium account		24 000		40 000
P&L account		12 000		16 000
		136 000		196 000

NOTES

1 There have been no asset disposals during the year ended 31 May.

2 An interim dividend for the year ended 31 May 1989 of £10 000 has been paid in December 1988.

REQUIRED:

a) Calculate the net profit for the year ending 31 May 1989. Note: you will need to reconstruct the P&L appropriation account.

b) Prepare a sources and application of funds statement for the year ended 31 May 1989.

c) Use any ratios you feel appropriate to compare the profit and liquidity over the two years.

(BTEC National)

5 *Situation/information*

You work for a small limited company and are assisting in the preparation of the annual accounts for the year ending 30/5/88. The details are as follows:

Aspen Ltd balance sheet as at 30 May

		1987			*1988*	
	£	£	£	£	£	£
Fixed assets at cost		173 000			243 400	
Less depreciation		57 800	115 200		78 100	165 300
Current assets						
Stock		74 400			72 080	
Debtors		97 920			100 020	
Bank		10 880			—	
		183 200			172 100	
Current liabilities						
Creditors	41 440			37 080		
Overdraft	—			2 320		
Provision for tax	17 120			12 400		
Proposed dividend	10 000	68 560	114 640	12 000	63 800	108 300
			229 840			273 600
Financed by:						
£1 ordinary shares			200 000			220 000
Reserves			29 840			53 600
			229 840			273 600

Aspen Ltd profit and loss account for year ended 30/5/88

	£
Profit for the year	48 160
Provision for tax	12 400
	35 760
Undistributed profits from last year	29 840
	65 600
Proposed dividend	12 000
Undistributed profits carried to next year	53 600

TASKS:

a) Prepare the sources and application of funds statement of Aspen Ltd for the year ended 30/5/88.
b) Compute the current ratio for both years.
c) Compute the return on capital employed for the year ended 30/5/88.

(Institute of Commercial Management)

6 As an assistant to the financial accountant you have been asked to assist in the preparation of the following company's figures relating to funds flow:

The balance sheets of John Francis Enterprises Ltd on 31/3/88 and 31/3/89

	1988	*1989*
	£	£
*Fixed assets (net)	86 000	94 400
Stocks and work-in-progress	32 800	35 600
Debtors	27 200	32 000
Bank	4 000	—
	150 000	162 000
Creditors	24 000	26 000
Provision for tax	12 000	8 000
Bank	—	2 000
	36 000	36 000
Loan (5 years)	4 000	3 000
	110 000	123 000
Issued and paid-up capital	60 000	70 000
P&L balance	50 000	53 000
	110 000	123 000

NOTE

*Fixed asset movements to 31 March 1989:

	Cost	*Depreciation*	*Net value*
	£	£	£
Balance (31/3/88)	110 000	24 000	86 000
Additions during the year	20 000		
Depreciation provided during the year		8 000	
	130 000	32 000	
Disposals during the year	8 000	4 400	
Balance (31/3/89)	122 000	27 600	94 400

The profit and loss statement summary for 31 March 1989

	£
Operating profit	10 400
+ Gain on fixed asset sale	600
	11 000
Taxation provision	8 000
Retained profits	3 000

TASKS:

a) Draw up a statement of sources and application of funds for the year ended 31 March 1989.
b) Calculate the current ratios for each year.
c) From the figures you have prepared, write a brief report to the client with your assessment of working capital position on 31 March 1988 and 31 March 1989.

(BTEC National)

7 *Situation*

You work in the accounts office of XYZ Ltd and the accountant has provided you with the following information at the end of the financial period, 31 March 1987:

Balance sheets of XYZ Ltd at 31 March 1986 and 31 March 1987

	1986 £	*1987* £		*1986* £	*1987* £
Freehold property			Issued share capital	30 000	30 000
at cost	25 000	25 000	Profit and loss account	27 000	33 000
Equipment (see note)	18 000	22 200	Corporation tax due:		
Stock in trade	16 400	17 800	1 January 1986	6 000	—
Debtors	13 600	14 000	1 January 1987	—	4 000
Bank	2 000	1 000	Creditors	12 000	13 000
	75 000	80 000		75 000	80 000

NOTE

Equipment movements during the year ended 31 March 1987 were:

	Cost £	*Depreciation* £	*Net* £
Balance at 31 March 1986	30 000	12 000	18 000
Additions during year	9 000		
Depreciation provided during year		3 800	
	39 000	15 800	
Disposals during year	4 000	3 000	
Balance at 31 March 1987	35 000	12 800	22 200

The company's summarised profit calculation for the year ended 31 March 1987, revealed:

	1986	*1987*
	£	£
Sales	95 000	100 000
Gain on sale of equipment		2 500
Less		102 500
Cost of sales and other expenses	84 800	92 500
Net profit	10 200	10 000
Corporation tax on profits of the year	6 000	4 000
Retained profit of the year (after tax)	4 200	6 000

TASK A:

From the information given above prepare a funds flow statement for the year ended 31 March 1987.

TASK B:

What is the purpose of preparing such a statement. Give a brief answer only.

8 The balance sheets of F Laker Ltd on 31 December 1987 and 31 December 1988 were as follows:

	1987		*1988*	
	£	£	£	£
TANGIBLE ASSETS				
Land and buildings (at cost)	50 000		130 000	
Plant and machinery (NBV)*	50 000		85 600	
		100 000		215 600
CURRENT ASSETS				
Stock	85 000		50 000	
Debtors	96 300		71 900	
Bank	3 000		3 000	
Cash	8 000		6 100	
	192 300		131 000	
LESS CURRENT LIABILITIES				
Creditors	42 000		65 000	
Proposed dividends	20 000		19 000	
	62 000	130 300	84 000	47 000
		230 300		262 600

(Continues)

		1987		*1988*
	£	£	£	£
Share capital		150 000		200 000
Share premium		10 000		20 000
P&L account balance		70 300		42 600
		230 300		262 600

The profit and loss summary for the year is as follows:

	£	£
Net loss for the year		(6 000)
Interim dividend (paid)	2 700	
Final dividend (proposed)	19 000	
	21 700	

NOTES

A depreciation provision of £25 000 was made during 1988.
*NBV = Net book value.

TASKS:

a) Draw up a statement of sources and applications of funds for the year ended 31 December 1988.
b) Write a brief report based on the figures you have prepared, assessing in particular whether in your opinion the additional capital expenditure was financed in a suitable manner.

(BTEC National)

9 The following information refers to the accounts of Wilkinson & Vines plc for the periods 1 January to 31 December 1990:

	Debit	*Credit*
	£	£
Premises (cost)	220 000	235 000
Investments (cost)	115 000	180 000
Plant (NBV)	114 000	127 000
Motor vans (NBV)	16 000	25 000
Stocks	64 500	113 900
Debtors	114 500	294 600
Bank/cash	123 000	6 800
	767 000	982 300

(Continues)

	Debit	Credit
	£	£
Profit (after tax, dividends and transfer to reserve)	—	95 600
Ordinary shares	300 000	350 000
Reserves	120 000	140 000
P&L balance	70 000	70 000
Debtors	50 000	200 000
Proposed dividends	21 000	17 500
Creditors	174 000	65 200
Taxation	32 000	44 000
	767 000	982 300

NOTES

At 31 December, 1990:

1 During the year, vans having a NBV (net book value) of £7000, were sold for £13 000.

2 Depreciation for the year: plant £16 000; vans £8000.

3 The taxation account showed:

		Dr	*Cr*	*Balance*
		£	£	£
31/12/88	Balance			32 000 Cr
05/07/89	Tax paid	29 000		3 000
31/12/89	P&L account		41 000	44 000

REQUIRED:

a) Prepare a statement of sources and application of funds for the year ended, 31 December 1990.

b) Briefly state why you think the bank balance has declined during the year.

CHAPTER

22 Statements of Standard Accounting Practice (SSAPs)

- *Why has the accounting profession prepared statements of standard practice?*
- *What is their importance in the preparation of final accounts?*

Introduction

Statements of Standard Accounting Practice (SSAPs) represent the profession's accounting standards. These statements are prepared for the purpose of standardising the final accounts of a business. Any accountant preparing accounts is obliged to conform to the standards laid down by the profession, otherwise he may be required to explain why he has not done so to his professional body.

The Accounting Standards Committee of the six major accounting bodies of the UK has been responsible for the publication of the SSAPs and over the years, accountants, by and large, have complied with these standards. It is not the intention here to make a detailed study of these statements. The student should realise that they exist and in particular be familiar with *Statement No.2, Disclosure of Accounting Policies* which outlines the major concepts adopted by the accounting profession.

In all, there are about 20 of these statements in current use. For example, SSAP No.10 is the standard relating to the funds flow statement as outlined in the previous chapter. The statement indicates that all audited financial statements intended to give a true and fair view of the business should include a funds flow aimed to indicate where funds have been generated from and where they have gone.

SSAPs of interest

This is not a full list of the current SSAPs in use but some of the following relate to a number of chapters in this publication.

SSAP No.2 Disclosure of Accounting Policies: This is one of the most significant because it relates to the basic accounting concepts. The policies to be disclosed by a business refers to the use of appropriate accounting bases which it has adopted and which will affect the business's profits and financial position. When the final accounts are prepared, the accounting policies adopted are disclosed in notes to the accounts. For example, the method of depreciation the business uses.

SSAP No.5 Vat: This standard aims to achieve uniformity in the treatment of Vat in published accounts. Vat is currently charged at the rate of 15 per cent on many of our goods and services. Registered traders (those listed with Her Majesty's Customs & Excise), collect Vat on sales which is offset by the payment of Vat to other traders. The net sum is paid as indirect tax to Customs & Excise. The trader who is not registered, does not have to charge Vat but cannot recover any which has been charged to him. Turnover (sales), should *exclude* Vat on taxable items and should also be *excluded* from purchases.

SSAP No.8 Taxation: This provides a standard for the treatment of corporation tax and the payment of tax on dividends, known as advanced corporation tax. The statement seeks to ensure uniformity in the published accounts of companies. There are two rates to be charged as liabilities for tax: one for large companies, the other for small. Corporation tax is charged on the company's profits and is normally due to be paid nine months after the end of the accounting year. However, companies which were in business prior to 1965 will have a period which ranges from over nine months up to 21 months. This means that companies after 1965 will normally have a single tax liability shown under current liabilities and those before 1965 may have two such liabilities, one as current liabilities and one as long-term (deferred) liabilities. By 1991–2 *all* companies will need to submit their tax payments within nine months after the end of their accounting period.

SSAP No.9 Stock and work in progress: This standard seeks to establish a broad band of generally accepted techniques in the valuation of stock because of its bearing on the calculation of profit. It also requires the precise accounting policies adopted in stock value to be stated. Stocks comprise of goods for resale, raw materials and partly finished goods (work in progress). The normal basis for valuation of stock is referred to as:

'the lower of cost and net realisable value (NRV)'.

The NRV usually refers to the selling price less any costs of getting the goods sold. In other words, if any stock is likely to fetch less than its cost, it is reasonably prudent to write them down at their lower value.

SSAP No.10 The funds flow statement: This was discussed in Chapter 21.

SSAP No.12 Depreciation: Defined as the loss in value of fixed assets, over periods of time. The standard is to provide depreciation for all fixed assets which have a finite useful life. There are some exceptions such as investments, goodwill and freehold land. Buildings however, should be depreciated too, even though their market value may increase. It is still prudent to depreciate buildings because they do deteriorate with time. The straight-line method of depreciation is one of the most common but is not always the most appropriate for some type of fixed assets. The standard indicates that a change of method (or base) is only acceptable if it is thought that it will give a better or fairer position of the accounts.

SSAP No.22 Goodwill: The standard recognises that it is difficult to separate goodwill from the business as a whole. Its calculation tends to be subjective and to fluctuate in value over time. It has not been the practice to recognise goodwill in published accounts and therefore it should be written off as soon as is practicable, particularly the goodwill arising from the purchase of a business. It can be depreciated over a period of time if it is seen as more appropriate to the business. The statement does not indicate or fix any limit on the length of time but it must be estimated at the outset, that is, at the time the business was purchased.

SSAP No.2 Disclosure of accounting policies: It has already been stated how significant this standard is and it is assumed that accountants have incorporated at least the four basic concepts, unless otherwise stated. A clear and brief description of the accounting policies used by a business should be provided with the final accounts. The SSAP makes it obligatory to disclose the accounting policies to be adopted. The four basic accounting concepts are:

1 *Going concern concept:* It is assumed that the business will continue its operations from one accounting period to the next, thus the value of its assets are based on the business carrying on trading. For example, the fixed assets are valued at cost less depreciation but if there was some reason to suggest that the business was to be sold or fall into bankruptcy, then the assets would have to be valued differently to reflect the circumstances. The value of stock may also be affected and may have to reflect net realisable values well below cost.

2 *Accruals concept:* This concept matches revenue with expenses and it is firmly assumed that the final accounts will incorporate all expenses paid or incurred as well as all the income earned. If a wages bill of say £10 000 was still due to be paid at the end of the accounting period, it would be taken for granted that this would be charged to the profit and loss account and also listed as a current liability, until paid.

3 *Consistency concept:* It is assumed that similar accounting items are treated on a consistent basis, otherwise distortions to profits may easily occur. For example, inconsistencies relating to the methods adopted for depreciation or stock valuation could have unfair distortions to profit. As indicated previously in SSAP No.12 Depreciation, a change in method may only be permitted if it gives a *fairer* representation to the accounts. Any material effect on the charge for depreciation must be explained clearly in the notes to the accounts.

4 *Prudence (conservatism) concept:* It is the standard to adopt a conservative view in the preparation of final accounts so that revenue must be reasonably certain before it is to be recognised and recorded. At the same time, the accountant is expected to provide for any unexpected losses such as providing for bad debts or writing the value of stock down in the event that demand is likely to fall. Thus the accountant is seen to be rather pessimistic rather than overtly optimistic and is likely to be cautious in the valuation of a business's assets.

Other concepts

In addition to the four basic concepts outlined above, there are a number of other concepts which may be included in a business's accounting policies:

Materiality: This concept relates to the view that small or insignificant items may be excluded from the final accounts. For example, to omit pence from the figures is quite a normal practice. The size of the business organisation will influence what is considered material or not. A large business may consider a valuation of a fixed asset under say £500 as relatively insignificant and treat it as an expense item, charged to profit and loss in the year purchased. A smaller organisation may consider a sum of £500 as significant and treat it as capital expenditure and include it as a fixed asset.

Money measurement This concept recognises that accounts may only reflect the outcome of financial transactions and items are given money values to measure their worth. Intangible items such as the skills of staff cannot be measured although they may be of great value to a business.

Dual aspect This concept recognises the fact that the business is represented by its assets, and that these assets are financed by the owner or owners, and the liabilities. The accounting equation reflects the dual aspect:

Assets	= Capital + Liabilities
(the business)	(claims on the business)

Realisation This concept recognises the importance of both prudence and the matching between income and expenditure. Only when a definite sale has been transacted can it be recorded and therefore realised. A sale should not be recorded on the basis of an order, rather on the issue of the sales invoice or the signing of a contract.

Cost This concept is based on the view that most recording of transactions should be on the basis of the cost price. For example, the purchase of fixed assets is recorded at cost and charges for depreciation will be calculated on this figure. It is most convenient and straightforward to record transactions on a *historic* cost basis, that is, until periods of high inflation tends to distort profits and the value of assets. Inflation accounting only comes into vogue when the nation is struggling to keep abreast of inflation and the increase in prices tends to upset the accounting system.

Accounting bases

These bases refer to the methods adopted by businesses when they apply the basic concepts in accounting in the preparation of their final accounts. As there are alternative methods available, for example, in the valuation of stock or the depreciation of assets, the accounting policies must disclose which bases are being used and that such bases are consistently applied. Accounting policies help those interested parties to know how certain fundamental items are being dealt with.

An example of an accounting policy

'The company adopts the accrual concept in the preparation of its accounts with the exception of items where, in the opinion of the directors, the inclusion would have no material effect on the profits of the organisation.

The company has a policy where it capitalises the cost of additions and major works to premises at the cost price.

The company adopts a straight-line basis when providing for depreciation of machinery and equipment. Revaluation is adopted for the depreciation of the company's motor vehicles. These policies will continue until the assets are disposed of.

Stocks are valued at the "lower of cost or net realisable value" computed on the basis of selling price after the deduction of all relevant overheads.

Land and buildings are recorded at cost and a 5 per cent depreciation will be charged annually on the straight-line basis.'

The concepts to be identified

It is important to realise that an organisation would naturally accept that the four basic concepts would be adopted in the preparation of their final accounts:

a) Going concern: the accounts are valued on the basis that the company will continue trading.
b) Accruals: line 1, revenue is matched against expenses relating to the financial period.
c) Consistency: charges for depreciation and stock are using the same method (or base) from one period to the next.
d) Prudence: stock valuation at the lower of cost.
e) Other concepts: materiality and cost.

Summary

1 SSAPs are the accounting standards provided by the Accounting Standards Committee for the purpose of achieving uniformity amongst accountants in the way accounts are prepared and presented.

2 There are some 20 SSAPs in all. *No.2 Disclosure of accounting policies* is very significant because it relates to the basic concepts used by the profession and provides an obligation by all accountants to adopt them when preparing their final accounts.

3 The four basic concepts relating to SSAP No.2 are going concern, accruals, consistency and prudence.

4 Accounting bases refer to the methods which have been adopted in the preparation of accounts, for example, using a straight-line method for depreciation charges or cost for the valuation of assets. Once a method has been adopted, it should be used on a consistent basis.

5 Accounting policies are usually provided as notes immediately after the presentation of final accounts. This is particularly the case for the accounts of companies.

QUESTIONS

1 If the accounting profession had not drawn up a set of SSAPs, what could have been the effect on the preparation and presentation of final accounts of different business organisations?

2 SSAP No.2 is seen to be of fundamental importance to the accounting profession. Why do you think this is the case?

3 If accounting bases were not used in a consistent manner by accountants, what effect could this have on the final accounts?

4 Accounting policies: Renton Industries plc, year ended 30 April:

'The accounts are prepared under the historical cost convention (concept), modified to include the revaluation of investment properties which are included at their market value.

Other fixed assets are stated at cost, less accumulated depreciation in equal annual instalments over their estimated useful lives – plant and equipment and motor vehicles all over a period of five years.

Stock is valued at the lower of cost and net realisable value, which is based on the estimated selling price less any further cost of disposal.

Sales will only be accounted for from the actual date of a contract exchange.

Interest payments and other accruals are to be written off to the profit and loss account as incurred.

Where any contracts are expected to be unprofitable, full provision is made for the anticipated loss.'

REQUIRED:

Identify and briefly discuss the underlying concepts of the above accounting policy adopted by the company.

PART IV, CHAPTER

23 Accounting ratios

- *What are accounting ratios?*
- *How are they calculated?*
- *Can they be useful to management?*
- *How do they help to evaluate business performance?*

Introduction

The final accounts of a business are prepared to show the profit and loss account for the year as well as the overall financial position as indicated in the balance sheet. Do these accounts tell us anything else about the business which could be useful?

Accounting ratios can assist both owners and management to make better decisions concerning their businesses. The calculation of ratios helps to provide a means of measurement to enable comparisons to be made. Ratios help to relate figures over periods of time and trends may be identified more clearly than just the absolute figures taken from the accounts. Management will want to know how current performances compare with previous years and with their competitors, or with industries similar to themselves.

From a study of accounting ratios, key questions may be analysed concerning aspects such as profits, efficiency and liquidity. Is a business becoming more or less successful? What factors might be identified to help management decide what to do to improve a given situation? If profits are down, what are the resons and what can be done about it? What will be the best plan of action to correct a given situation?

Accounting ratios

Accounting ratios may be classified in a variety of different ways. The important thing is to be *consistent* and *use a standard guideline* which can bear comparison from one financial period to the next, without any degree of distortion that may give an unfair view of performance. Such guidelines, which may be used as a yardstick for the calculation of ratios, are given below.

1 *Profit ratios*
  Gross profit per cent
  Net profit per cent

ROCE (Return on Capital Employed)
ROCI (Return on Capital Invested)
ROTA (Return on Total Assets).

2 *Efficiency ratios*
Expense percentages
Rate of stock turnover
Rate of debt collection
Sales to fixed assets
Sales to current assets.

3 *Liquidity ratios*
Current ratio (working capital ratio)
Acid test ratio (quick asset ratio).

4 *Structure ratios*
Proprietor's ratio
Liability ratio
Capital gearing.

5 *Investment ratios*
EPS (Earnings Per Share)
Cover
Yield
P/E (Price to Earnings) ratio.

This is not an exhaustive list by any means, but all the fundamental accounting ratios are included.

Example of accounting ratios and evaluation

The following information relates to G Johnson-Smith, an entrepreneur in sporting goods. At the financial year end 30 June 1989 his final accounts were as follows:

Trading and profit and loss statement

	£	£	£
Sales			210 000
Cost of sales			
Stock (1/7/88)	8 700		
Purchases	124 600		
	133 300		
Returns out	(2 000)		
	131 300		
Stock (30/6/89)	(5 300)		126 000
Gross profit			84 000

(Continues)

	£	£	£
Sales and distribution costs			
Motor expenses	5 870		
Advertising	580		
General expenses	1 650		
Salesmens' wages	18 900	27 000	
Administration expenses			
Rent and rates	9 005		
Wages, office	20 200		
Printing and stationery	495		
Interest	4 500		
Light and heat	1 800	36 000	63 000
Net profit			21 000

Balance sheet as at year end 30 June 1989

	£	£	£
FIXED ASSETS			
Equipment, tools		55 000	
Motor vans		17 400	72 400
CURRENT ASSETS			
Stock	5 300		
Debtors	4 800		
Bank/cash	2 430		
Pre-payments	310	12 840	
CURRENT LIABILITIES			
Creditors	6 000		
Accruals	740	6 740	
Net current assets			6 100
Capital employed			78 500
DEFERRED LIABILITIES			
9% loan			50 000
Net assets			28 500
FINANCED BY:			
Capital		20 000	
Profit		21 000	
Drawings		(12 500)	28 500

REQUIRED:

Using the final accounts of Johnson-Smith, calculate the accounting ratios which will test profitability, efficiency, liquidity and structure. Make brief comments relating to performance for the financial year. There are no previous figures for comparison purposes, therefore the evaluation will tend to be limited and not show the trends of the business.

1 *Profit ratios*

a) Gross profit % $= \dfrac{\text{Gross profit} \times 100}{\text{Net sales}}$

$= \dfrac{£84\ 000 \times 100}{£210\ 000}$

$= 40\%$

b) Net profit % $= \dfrac{\text{Net profit} \times 100}{\text{Net sales}}$

$= \dfrac{£21\ 000 \times 100}{£210\ 000}$

$= 10\%$

These two ratios indicate the gross and net margins of profit to sales. Is a 40 per cent gross margin adequate? Is it a more or less constant figure compared with previous years? The gross percentage tells us the difference between cost and selling prices. Every £100 of sales should bring in £40 gross profit. If the gross percentage falls, it could be due to a number of reasons, including:

increase in cost of purchases which have not been passed on to customers;
loss of stock from breakages, damage, stealing, or obsolete stock marked down in price;
poor buying policy, not taking advantage of bulk purchases and discounts.

The net profit margin indicates profit after all expenses have been taken into account. Therefore a 10 per cent return means that for every £100 of sales, £10 is net profit. How does this compare with previous years or with the type of business as a whole (in this case sporting goods)? If the net return was to fall, say to 8 per cent, this would need to be investigated to find out the reason for the decrease. Are the overheads more expensive? Have sales declined in recent years? If they have, what is behind the decrease? Is it a single cause, or are there a number of reasons which can explain what has happened?

c) ROCE (Return on Capital Employed) $= \dfrac{\text{Net profit} \times 100}{\text{Capital employed}}$

$= \dfrac{£21\ 000 \times 100}{£78\ 500}$

$= 26.75\%$

d) ROCI (Return on Capital Invested) $= \dfrac{\text{Net profit} \times 100}{\text{Capital invested (beginning)}}$

$$= \frac{£21\,000 \times 100}{£20\,000}$$

$$= 105\%$$

e) ROTA (Return on Total Assets) $= \dfrac{\text{Net profit} \times 100}{\text{Total assets}}$

$$= \frac{£21\,000 \times 100}{£85\,240}$$

$$= 24.64\%$$

These ratios relate profit or loss to the balance sheet and they are significant because profit is expressed in terms of returns on investment, either on the business or the owners.

The return on capital employed is one of the most fundamental and important accounting ratios measuring profit in relation to the available capital employed (fixed assets plus working capital). A ratio of 26.75 per cent appears to be a very adequate return indeed, but it needs to be compared with previous years to see if it is a constant return or whether, in fact, it is improving or falling. What could the business earn if it invested its capital elsewhere? What effect has inflation had on the figures? Could the business expect a higher return if it was to invest on the Stock Exchange or in property?

The return on capital invested indicates that Johnson-Smith had a capital of £20 000 at the beginning of his financial period and had made a profit of £21 000 at the period end, an admirable return of 105 per cent – a very impressive profitable investment on any terms. It would be difficult to have a similar return in any form of investment, perhaps with the exception of property during times of rising prices.

The return on the total assets of the business recognises profit to all assets and is a very similar ratio to that of capital employed.

2 *Efficiency ratios*

a) Expense percentages:

Cost of sales (per cent) $= \dfrac{\text{COS} \times 100}{\text{Net sales}}$

$$= \frac{£126\,000 \times 100}{£210\,000}$$

$$= 60\%$$

Sales and distribution (per cent) $= \dfrac{\text{Sales and distribution} \times 100}{\text{Net sales}}$

$$= \frac{£27\,000 \times 100}{£210\,000}$$

$$= 12.9\%$$

$$\text{Administration (per cent)} = \frac{\text{Administration} \times 100}{\text{Net sales}}$$

$$= \frac{£36\,000 \times 100}{£210\,000}$$

$$= 17.1\%$$

Total expenses (per cent) = 90%

Net profit (per cent) = 10%

Total = 60 + 12.9 + 17.1 + 90 + 10 = 100%

A breakdown of expenses may be indicated in relation to pence in the pound:

	Pence/£	
Cost of sales	60p	
Sales and distribution	13p	
Administration	17p	90p
Profit		10p
		100p

Is 10p/£ an adequate return? It appears so when taking all the profit returns into account. Could it be improved by a reduction in any one of the above costs? Could any of the selling prices be increased, thereby improving the margin of profit? Perhaps the administration costs could be more efficient – particular aspects to look at are office wages and interest payments which takes up about 60 per cent of administration. Again, comparisons need to be made with previous performances. (See the pie chart on the next page to show expenses/profit.)

Any individual expense could provide a ratio to sales. The office wages to sales ratio for example is 9.6 per cent, representing nearly 10p in the £.

b) The rate of stock turnover $= \dfrac{\text{Cost of sales}}{\text{Average stock}}$

$$= \frac{£126\,000}{*£7\,000} = \text{18 times per annum}$$

$$= \frac{52}{18} = \text{Every 2.88 weeks}$$

*Stock (beginning)	£8 700		
Stock (end)	£5 300	$\dfrac{£14\,000}{2}$	= £7 000

The speed of a business's stock turnover is a very important efficiency ratio, testing how fast a firm can sell its stock. The rate of turnover is dependent on the nature of goods

Breakdown of expenses to the number of pence profit in the £

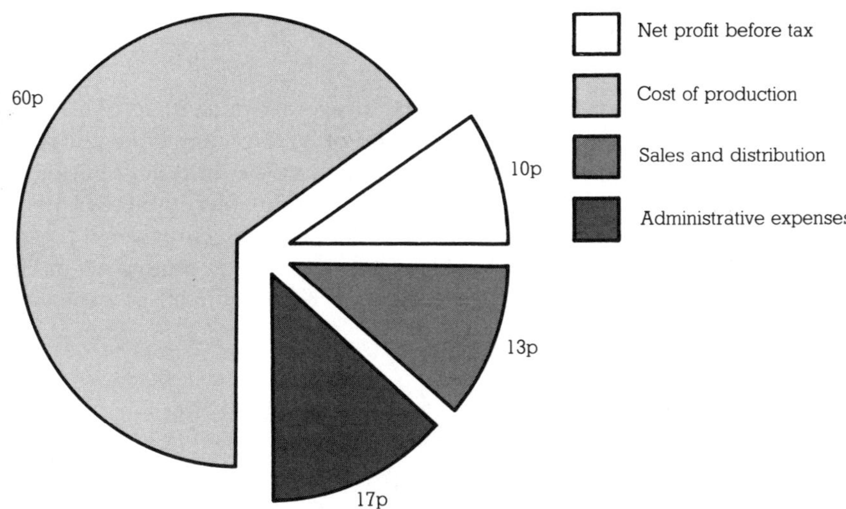

sold. A supermarket selling the essential day-to-day consumables is expected to have a fast turnover, whereas a furniture store would have a much slower rate. The faster the rate of turnover, the greater the potential profit is likely to be. It could be that a reduction to selling prices, reducing the margin of profit, could achieve a faster turnover and therefore greater profits in absolute terms. In this case, Johnson-Smith takes almost three weeks to move his stock which is a relatively fast turnover. Is this a constant figure or has it changed from previous years?

For example, which is best considering units which cost 80p each:

A 100 units @ selling price £1.00 each; or
B 200 units @ selling price £0.95 each?

	A	*B*
Sales	100	190
− Cost of sales	80	160
Gross profit	20	30

The gross profit percentage in A is 20 per cent and in B it is only 16 per cent. Clearly there is £10 more profit in B even though the margin of profit is less. Therefore, a reduction to selling price could increase profit in absolute terms because a higher turnover is achieved.

A higher stock turnover may also lead to more effective and economic buying, taking advantage of bulk purchasing and better trade discounts, thereby increasing the profit potential even more.

c) The rate of debt collection $= \dfrac{\text{Debtors} \times 365}{\text{Credit sales}}$

(Assume credit sales to be 30 per cent of total sales) $= \dfrac{£4\,800 \times 365}{£63\,000} = 27.8$ days

In this case, it takes about 28 days to collect the average debt. If we take a norm of 45 days to pay a monthly invoice, a collection period of 28 days may be regarded as being reasonably efficient. Some type of businesses need to give a far longer period of credit because of the nature of the goods. For expensive consumables, the credit period may need to be extended to allow for a reasonable time for payment. However, it is essential to monitor credit control and ensure that debtors do try to pay on time. Long debts can so easily turn into bad debts and assets then have to be written off as expenses to the business.

d) Sales/fixed assets $= \dfrac{\text{Sales}}{\text{Fixed assets}}$

$$= \frac{£210\,000}{£72\,400}$$

$$= 2.9:1$$

e) Sales/current assets $= \dfrac{\text{Sales}}{\text{Current assets}}$

$$= \frac{£210\,000}{£12\,840}$$

$$= 16.35:1$$

Both these ratios relate turnover to asset use. The higher the ratio, the more efficient the asset usage. It takes £1 of fixed assets to generate £2.90 of sales and £1 of current assets to generate a relatively high £16.35 of sales. Comparisons need to be made with past figures and, where possible, with competitors in the same line of business, to determine whether the use of assets is constant or fluctuating for any reason. These figures link with the attractive returns on assets indicated in the profit ratios and it appears that the business uses its resources efficiently.

3 Liquidity ratios

a) Current (working capital) ratio $= \dfrac{\text{Current assets}}{\text{Current liabilities}}$

$$= \frac{£12\,840}{£6\,740}$$

$$= 1.9:1$$

b) Acid test (quick asset) ratio $= \dfrac{\text{Current assets } (-\text{ stock})}{\text{Current liabilities}}$

$$= \frac{£7\,540}{£6\,740}$$

$$= 1.2:1$$

The current ratio has already been explained. It tests the ability of the business in paying its short-term debts and is essentially the relationship between current assets and current liabilities.

Fundamentally, a current ratio of 1 : 1 is seen by the accounting profession as the minimum required to be in a position to meet creditors. Any figure less than this means that the business, in effect, is trading whilst insolvent, that is, it is not in a position to meet its current debts. When a business is trading insolvently, it is always more vulnerable to the demand of creditors and is therefore more likely to stretch its resources in attempting to meet payments. It may be in a more risky and precarious financial position and creditors can get very annoyed when their bills are not paid on time. They may refuse to allow further stock sales and may take legal action to reclaim their debts. Bankruptcy proceedings could then be the next stage.

The acid test tends to be a more immediate test of liquidity. The business is being tested to see whether it can be in a position to meet payment for debts without resorting to stock sales. The significance of this ratio is linked to the rate of stock turnover. It follows that, in the majority of cases, the greater the turnover, the less important is the acid test. Sainsbury's, the supermarket, for example, has a very high rate of stock turnover and most of its current assets are stocks. It has a low acid test, well below the value of 1 : 1, but because the stock is almost like cash, due to its high turnover, its significance is diminished.

On the other hand, a business which has a low stock turnover, would be anxious if its acid test was also low, because if any immediate demands for payment were to be made by creditors, these may be difficult to satisfy with sales of stock being slow.

Johnson-Smith's liquidity position appears to be sound in that, even without resorting to stock sales, he could satisfy the demands of creditors. Ideally, a business should have at least a 1 : 1 ratio as its acid test and something like 2 : 1 for its current ratio. However, each business should be fully aware of what its own liquidity position must be in order to trade with reasonable comfort. It should monitor closely its position to ensure it stays within its own set of acceptable parameters.

4 *Structure ratios*

a) Proprietor's ratio (owner's stake) $= \dfrac{\text{Capital}}{\text{Total assets}}$

$$= \frac{£28\,500}{£85\,240}$$

$$= 0.33:1$$

b) Liability ratio $= \dfrac{\text{Total liabilities}}{\text{Capital}}$

$= \dfrac{£56\,740}{£28\,500}$

$= 2:1$

c) Gearing $= \dfrac{\text{Debt (fixed interest)}}{\text{Capital}}$

$= \dfrac{£50\,000}{£28\,500}$

$= 1.75:1$

These structural ratios relate the owner's capital to liabilities. The basic purpose of this is to recognise the extent of external financing against the proprietor's financing.

The proprietor's ratio, or owner's stake in the business, indicates that Johnson-Smith has a 33 per cent stake (or claim) on his business assets. The remaining 67 per cent is in the hands of the business's liabilities. In effect, the business owes Johnson-Smith $\frac{1}{3}$ and the liabilities $\frac{2}{3}$. In the event that the business was closed or sold off, the creditors would have to be satisfied to the extent of £56 740.

The liability ratio is virtually stating the same information. A 2 : 1 ratio indicates that the external financing by creditors is twice that of the owner's financing. A ratio of parity, 1 : 1, would indicate equal financing between the owners and liabilities. A ratio of less than 1 would indicate that financing is more in the hands of the owners relative to its creditors.

Capital gearing relates to the proportion of fixed interest capital (for limited companies this would include preference share capital), to that of the owner's capital. In Johnson-Smith's case, a gearing of 1.75 indicates relatively high gearing, where the proportion of fixed interest capital is high relative to the owner's capital. Low gearing refers to a situation where there is a greater proportion of the owner's capital to that of fixed interest capital. For example, if Johnson-Smith's capital was £200 000, gearing would be 0.25, which would indicate a relatively low dependency on external fixed interest funds.

Where liquidity ratios emphasise the need to have sufficient working capital to meet short-term debts, the structural ratios indicate longer term financing, taking into account creditors falling after 12 months. If a business ties up too much of its funds in fixed capital (fixed assets), it may be in danger of becoming over-capitalised and may need to resort to borrowing, whether on overdraft with the bank, or on a fixed interest loan over longer periods. In times of high interest rates, this could put a great deal of pressure, particularly on small businesses, to meet their debt commitments.

Company ratios. In the example relating to Johnson-Smith, company ratios do not apply because Johnson-Smith is a sole trader. However, company ratios are included in the next example.

Summary of Johnson-Smith's accounting ratios

Although no previous year's figures were available for comparison purposes, an assessment of performance for the financial year indicated the following:

1 *Profit ratios:*

	%
Gross profit	40.00
Net profit	10.00
ROCE	26.75
ROCI	105.00
ROTA	24.64

These are very promising returns, particularly 105 per cent return on the owner's investment.

2 *Efficiency ratios:*

	%
Cost of sales	60.0
Sales and distribution	12.9
Administration	17.1
	90.0
Net profit	10.0

Rate of stock turnover	Every 2.88 weeks
Rate of debt collection	27.8 days
Sales to fixed assets	2.9 : 1
Sales to current assets	16.35 : 1

This appears very sound, particularly when linked to profit returns. Turnover is relatively fast with only an average 28-day debt collection period which indicates good credit control. A very encouraging use of assets to sales, especially a high £16.35 to every £1 invested in current assets.

3 *Liquidity ratios:*

Current ratio	1.9 : 1
Acid test	1.2 : 1

Again very sound. Even without relying on stock sales, short-term (current liabilities) could be satisfied.

4 *Structure ratios:*

Proprietor's ratio	0.33 : 1
Liability ratio	2.00 : 1
Gearing	1.75 : 1

These ratios indicate a greater reliance on longer term financing by the business on its creditors rather than the owner's own capital resources. In times of good trading and when profits are sound, a high-geared business performs well. However, if trading becomes depressed and profits fall, a business whose gearing is relatively high, may be in a more unstable financial position because it must still find funds to pay its fixed interest to creditors, irrespective of profits.

In the following example, relating to the final accounts of Robert Andrew plc, accounting ratios will be calculated over two financial periods, including investment ratios.

Example

The following represents the accounts of Robert Andrew plc for the years ended 31 December:

Trading and profit and loss statement

	1989	*1990*
	£	£
Turnover (sales)	500 000	600 000
Cost of sales	300 000	390 000
Gross profit	200 000	210 000
Sales and distribution costs	50 000	70 000
Administration expenses	40 000	60 000
Net profit (before tax)	110 000	80 000
Provision for tax	34 000	22 000
Net profit (after tax)	76 000	58 000
Profit and loss account balance (1/1)	20 000	60 000
	96 000	118 000
Provision for dividends:		
Ordinary shares	20 000	12 000
8% preference shares	16 000	16 000
Profit and loss account balance (31/12)	60 000	90 000

Balance sheet as at 31 December

	£	£
FIXED ASSETS	412 000	472 000
CURRENT ASSETS	209 000	240 000
	621 000	712 000
CURRENT LIABILITIES	101 000	185 000
LONG-TERM LIABILITIES	60 000	37 000
	161 000	222 000
	460 000	490 000

(Continues)

	1989	*1990*
	£	£
ISSUED AND PAID-UP CAPITAL		
200 000 @ £1 ordinary shares	200 000	200 000
200 000 @ £1 preference shares (8%)	200 000	200 000
Profit and loss account balance	60 000	90 000
	460 000	490 000

REQUIRED:

a) Use the appropriate accounting ratios for both 1989 and 1990 to help evaluate financial performance.

b) Compare the financial performance of the company over the two periods. Note that the market value of the company's shares as quoted on the Stock Exchange was 225p in 1989 and 180p in 1990.

a) Robert Andrew plc – accounting ratios

	1989	*1990*
1 *Profit ratios:*		
Gross profit	40.0%	35.0%
Net profit (before tax)	22.0%	13.3%
ROCE (before tax)	21.2%	15.2%
2 *Efficiency ratios:*		
Cost of sales	60%	65.00%
Sales and distribution	10%	11.67%
Administration	8%	10.00%
	78%	86.67%
Net profit	22%	13.33%
3 *Liquidity ratio:*		
Current ratio	2.1 : 1	1.3 : 1
4 *Structure ratios:*		
Proprietor's ratio	0.74 : 1	0.69 : 1
Liability ratio	0.35 : 1	0.45 : 1
*Capital gearing	*1.00 : 1	0.82 : 1

$$\frac{\text{*Fixed interest debt + preference shares}}{\text{Ordinary shares + profit and loss account}} = \frac{260\,000}{260\,000}$$

5 *Investment ratios:*

Earnings per share (EPS) (ordinary shares) $= \dfrac{\text{Net profit (after tax)} - \text{Pref dividend}}{\text{Number of ordinary shares}}$

$= \dfrac{76\ 000\ (-16\ 000)}{200\ 000} \qquad \dfrac{£42\ 000}{200\ 000}$

$=$ 25p/share (1989) 21p/share (1990)

Dividend per ordinary share $= \dfrac{\text{Amount paid to ordinary shares}}{\text{Number of ordinary shares}}$

$= \dfrac{£20\ 000}{200\ 000} \qquad \dfrac{£12\ 000}{200\ 000}$

$=$ 10p/share (1989) 6p/share (1990)

Cover $= \dfrac{\text{Net profit (after tax)} - \text{Pref dividend}}{\text{Dividend paid to ordinary shares}}$

$= \dfrac{£60\ 000}{£20\ 000} \qquad \dfrac{£42\ 000}{£12\ 000}$

$=$ 3 times (1989) 3.5 times (1990)

Yield % $= \dfrac{\text{Dividend per share} \times 100}{\text{Market value per share}}$

$= \dfrac{10\text{p} \times 100}{225\text{p}} \qquad \dfrac{6\text{p} \times 100}{180\text{p}}$

$=$ 4.4% (1989) 3.3% (1990)

Price/earnings ratio $= \dfrac{\text{Market price per share}}{\text{Earnings per share}}$

$= \dfrac{225\text{p}}{25\text{p}} \qquad \dfrac{180\text{p}}{21\text{p}}$

$=$ 9 times (1989) $=$ 8.6 times (1990)

b) Evaluation of performance

The profit ratios in 1989 were all superior to 1990. The basic reason for this is that costs have increased from 78 per cent to 86. 6 per cent over the year, the most notable increase being the cost of sales, up by 5 per cent. Perhaps sale prices were marked too low in an effort to generate more sales. Sales did increase but perhaps not sharply enough to gain more gross profit – it could be that the buying of stock was simply not economic enough. The other expenses also increased and were not controlled sufficiently, with the result that the net margin fell by almost 9 per cent, a rather wide margin.

Liquidity has suffered at the same time, the current ratio falling from a respectable 2 : 1, to a more marginal 1.3 : 1. Creditors have increased rather substantially perhaps because of over-trading and this has weakened the company's ability to meet its short-term debts.

The structural ratios indicate that the company's shareholders finance the business by about 70 per cent although this has also fallen from the previous year (74 per cent). Company gearing is slightly on the high side because the preference share capital is grouped with long-term liabilities as part of the fixed interest capital.

The investment ratios indicate a deterioriation of performance over the year. One of the most common and significant indicators to a business's performance is the earnings per share and this has fallen by 4p in the year, or by 16 per cent, not a good sign of success. The shareholders ordinary dividend has been reduced by 4p per share (40 per cent) in an effort to retain funds in the company. This is reflected by the *cover* which indicates the number of times ordinary shareholders could have been paid from the available profits. The greater the cover, the more is retained in the business.

The price to earnings ratio is also very significant to the financial markets because it indicates the market value of the company's shares in relation to profits. A price to earnings ratio of 9 means that the current market price would take about nine years of profit and that the market is willing to pay the sum for the shares. Generally speaking, the higher the rate, the better the share prospects. This has marginally fallen over the year from 9 to 8.6 times. Is the company a good investment or not? Should shares be retained or sold? Although the Stock Exchange is a reliable source as far as reporting financial figures, nothing is ever certain as to which shares will be the most successful.

The limitations imposed by accounting ratios

Accounting ratios are only really useful if they can be compared with a business's past performances, with its competitors or with a given norm for its particular industry. Ratios used in isolation may not be of any value at all.

When making a study of performance comparisons, it is of critical importance to ensure that there is a consistent use of bases, for example, when measuring capital gearing it needs to be established exactly what items must be included in both debt and equity. By equity, are we to assume all organisations use the total of shareholders' funds (excluding preference share capital)?

Accounting ratios are unlikely to provide any really useful information unless several years of figures are calculated and trends can be observed. If these are compared with trends of companies in the same line of business, evaluation can become much more meaningful.

In some cases, accounting ratios may not reveal the true or realistic situation. For example, a company could have a very sound looking 2 : 1 current ratio yet, because of either stock or debtors being incorrectly accounted for, the real position could be that the business is close to insolvency.

Accounting ratios also fail to reveal the human side of business. What do they say of the company's employees? Are they reliable? Is the atmosphere at work positive? Are workers satisfied? What may appear good on paper, may be far from the case at the workplace.

Nevertheless, accounting ratios do have their value if they are measured on a consistent basis and there is an opportunity to study trends. The analysis of figures can give clues as to the business's profitability, liquidity, stability and general efficiency. This information could be of great importance to both owners and management and help them make better, more informed decisions.

Summary

1. Accounting ratios can assist both owners and management to make better, more informed decisions concerning their business.

2. Accounting ratios may be categorised in several different ways but the major headings tend to concern profitability, efficiency, liquidity, structural, and for companies, investment ratios.

3. Accounting ratios can help in the evaluation of the financial performance of the business. Ratios can provide a yardstick of measurement which could be useful for comparison purposes with previous performances or any other indicators.

4. Ratios cannot tell the whole story of a business. There are many other aspects to consider such as the morale of the workforce, the relationship which exists between management and workers, the future prospects of the business and the overall economic environment. Ratios have their limitations when financial information is to be evaluated.

QUESTIONS

1 The following information relates to the final accounts of Henry R David Co Ltd for the years ending 31 December 1989 and 1990.

Profit and loss account of Henry R David Co Ltd
for years ending 31 December

	1989	*1990*
	£	£
Retail sales	132 500	159 000
Net profit	19 875	23 850
Corporation tax	6 000	7 155
Net profit (after tax)	13 875	16 695
Provision for dividends:		
Ordinary shares	6 250	9 000
Retained profits	7 625	7 695

Balance sheet of Henry R David Co Ltd as at years ending 31 December

	1989	*1990*
	£	£
FIXED ASSETS (net)	65 000	79 735
CURRENT ASSETS		
Stock	8 750	12 150
Debtors	4 950	8 680
Bank	3 150	—
Cash	500	500
CURRENT LIABILITIES		
Creditors	4 350	4 875
Accruals	580	170
Taxation	6 000	7 155
Dividends	6 250	9 000
Bank	—	500
DEFERRED		
Loan ($1\frac{1}{2}$ years)	5 000	1 500
	60 170	77 865

REQUIRED:

From the information provided, prepare the appropriate accounting ratios which will test the company's profitability and liquidity over the two accounting periods.

(Institute of Bankers)

2 a) Give the definition of *working capital* and then describe its components.

b) **Balance sheet of Economy Ltd as at 30 September 1985**

	£		£
Ordinary shares	75 000	Land and buildings at cost	110 000
Reserves	25 700	Plant (book value)	24 000
		Vehicles (book value)	4 200
Long-term loan	60 000	Stock	18 600
Trade creditors	6 350	Debtors	15 700
Bank overdraft	9 600	Short-term investment	10 000
Taxation	4 100	Cash in hand	2 000
Dividend	3 750		
	184 500		184 500

Use this simplified balance sheet to calculate the value of working capital for Economy Ltd as at 30 September 1985. Also calculate the current working capital ratio and the liquidity ratio and comment on their values.
Note: Liquidity ratio is taken as the acid test ratio.

(Institute of Commercial Management)

3 a) Explain the meaning of the terms, 'profitability' and 'liquidity'.
b) Give two accounting formulae used to measure a firm's profitability.
c) Give one accounting formula used to measure a firm's liquidity.
d) Compare the figures given below, for two separate businesses taken over the same time period, in terms of profitability and liquidity.

Business A:		*Business B:*	
	£000		*£000*
Capital	100	Capital	80
Net profit	10	Net profit	20
Creditors	20	Creditors	40
Equipment	90	Premises	70
Bank	20	Debtors	5
Stock	10	Motor van	30
Debtors	10	Stock	10
		Equipment	20
		Bank	5

(AEB June '85)

4 The following information relate to two companies, both supermarkets, for the year ended 31 March 1987:

	Company Big Ltd	*Company Spiv Ltd*
	£000	*£000*
Revenue statement		
Sales	750	500
Cost of sales	450	325
Other costs	210	100
Net profit	90	75
Taxation	32	25
Net profit (after tax)	58	50

(Continues)

	Company Big Ltd £000	Company Spiv Ltd £000
Balance sheet		
Issued and paid-up capital:		
Ordinary shares	180	60
8% preference shares	20	—
Profit and loss account	30	10
10% debentures	—	80
	230	150
Bank overdraft	—	20
Other liabilities	105	50
	335	220
Fixed assets	146	129
Stocks	140	80
Debtors	29	11
Bank	20	—
	335	220

REQUIRED:

a) Calculate for both companies (to one decimal place) the following:
current ratio
liquid (or acid) ratio
capital gearing
net profit percentage to sales
earnings (after tax) as a percentage to ordinary shares
return on capital employed (after tax).

b) From the information gathered in a) above, briefly comment on the performance of the two supermarkets and state, giving reasons, which you consider is financially the safer investment of the two.

(Institute of Bankers)

5 *Situation*

Bourne Park commenced business 1 January 1983, and the company's accounts for the following four years made up annually to 31 December were as follows:

Year ended December 31	*Turnover*	*Purchases*	*Stock*	*Selling and distribution costs*	*Fixed costs*
	£	£	£	£	£
1983	45 000	42 500	12 500	5 500	6 500
1984	54 000	35 800	12 300	7 000	6 500
1985	72 000	57 500	15 800	9 000	7 500
1986	96 000	68 600	15 400	11 500	7 500

The directors have asked you, as the company's accountant, to provide an evaluation of profitability for the last four years.

TASKS:

a) Draw up in columnar form, the trading and profit and loss accounts of Bourne Park for each of the four years to 31 December.
b) Prepare a brief report outlining the implications of these figures and using any analysis ratios which may influence your findings.

(BTEC National)

6 Rocco Bank Ltd and Ball Bearings Ltd are two independent companies in the type of business activity their names suggest. As a young financial adviser, you are asked to assess the situation of both companies, by studying the figures given below:

	Ball Bearings Ltd		*Rocco Bank Ltd*	
	£000		*£000*	
Fixed assets (net)	39 000		4 000	
Intangibles	4 000		—	
Investments (long-term)	2 000	45 000	9 000	13 000
Stocks	27 000			
Debtors	25 000			
Advances			21 000	
Cash, liquid assets	—		59 000	
Investments	3 000	55 000	7 000	87 000
		100 000		100 000
Creditors	48 000			
Taxation	1 000		1 000	
Current and deposit accounts			91 000	
Bank	7 000	56 000		92 000
10% debenture stock		33 000		500
Shareholder's funds				
Ordinary shares @ £1	10 000		2 000	
Reserves	1 000		5 500	
		11 000		7 500
		100 000		100 000
Net profit (before tax)		2 500		2 600
Proposed ordinary dividends		700		400

REQUIRED:

Choose accounting ratios which you consider will reveal the differences between the two companies. Discuss your calculations from the point of view of profitability and financial stability.

(Institute of Bankers)

7 *Situation:*

The following figures relate to a retailing organisation which has expanded its business operations. Its premises were converted into a self-service style during the year 1987:

	1986	*1987*	*1988*
	£	£	£
Net sales	120 000	150 000	200 000
Gross profit (%)	30%	$33\frac{1}{3}$%	35%
Fixed expenses:	20 000	25 000	30 000
Variable expenses: (12% of sales)	?	?	?
Average stock held (cost):	8 000	8 500	10 000
Capital employed:	60 000	105 000	160 000

TASK A:

Prepare the trading and profit and loss accounts for each trading year, preferably in columnar format.

TASK B:

In tabular form, prepare the appropriate business profit returns and also the rate of stock turnover for each of the above years.

TASK C:

Briefly evaluate the business's progress over the three years in terms of its efficiency and profits.

(Institute of Bankers)

8 *Situation:*

Andrew David plc intends to expand its business activities and the board of directors are in agreement that an extra £500 000 will be required to meet their plans.

The schemes which have been put forward are:

Scheme A: To issue £500 000 10% preference shares @ £1 per share at par.
Scheme B: To issue £500 000 ordinary shares @ £1 per share at par.
Scheme C: To issue £500 000 10% redeemable debenture stock 1990/95 at par.

The company's current share capital consists of 3 000 000 @ £1 ordinary shares, issued and paid-up. Next year, it is estimated that a dividend of 12 per cent will be declared by the board.

The accountant of the company has estimated that the profit for the budget year ended 31 December 1989, will be £700 000, *before* the payment of interest or taxation. This year's interest payments on the company's overdraft is £5000 and it is estimated that the same payment will be made in 1989.

Corporation tax on the company's profits is at a rate of 35 per cent.

As the assistant to the accountant, you have been asked to prepare the following:

TASK A:

An estimated profit and loss appropriation account for each of the three schemes, in tabular form, relating to next year's figures. Commence your account with net profit *before* interest payments and taxation.

TASK B:

Calculate, for each of the three schemes, the earnings per share and capital gearing and state which scheme, in your view, is likely to be the most appropriate.

(Institute of Bankers)

9 The following trading results refer to the accounts of P Jackson & Co during the last three years, year ending 31 December.

	Year 1	*Year 2*	*Year 3*
	£	£	£
Trading and profit and loss account			
Sales:			
Cash	5 000	6 000	8 000
Credit	25 000	30 000	37 000
Cost of sales	20 000	24 000	31 950
Distribution costs	3 000	3 200	4 100
Administration expenses	3 150	3 750	4 275
Stock:			
1 Jan	1 950	2 050	2 950
31 Dec	2 050	2 950	5 050
Balance sheet (extract)			
Debtors	5 000	6 000	9 000
Capital invested (1 Jan)	26 500	30 000	31 750

REQUIRED:

a) The trading and profit and loss account of P Jackson & Co for each of the three years ending 31 December.
b) Accounting ratios to indicate:
   gross profit (%)
   net profit (%)
   expense (%'s)
   rate of stock turnover
   credit taken by debtors
   return on capital invested.
c) Brief comments using the accounting ratios to give some indication of the firm's performance over the three years. What limitations do the ratios impose?

(Institute of Bankers)

CHAPTER

24 Accounting for manufacturing organisations

- *What is the purpose of preparing a manufacturing account?*
- *How does it link to the final accounts?*
- *How are costs per unit calculated?*
- *What use are the mark-up and margins of profit?*
- *Why is it important to distinguish between fixed and variable costs?*

Introduction

The manufacturing account is prepared by those type of businesses which make their own products rather than purchasing them for resale. For example, Ford Motor Company makes their own cars to sell, it does not buy cars from another company like Nissan.

The purpose of preparing a manufacturing account is to find out how much it costs the company to produce their products, that is, its factory cost as distinct from other profit and loss costs such as selling and administration expenses. The factory cost of making the product is transferred to the trading account, recorded under the cost of sales.

The manufacturing account is basically in three parts:

direct costs
indirect costs
work-in-progress.

Direct costs

These costs are directly related to the making of the product, including factory labour, materials and direct expenses.

a) Direct labour: this represents the factory wages directly related to the workers making the product, such as assembly workers and machinists.
b) Direct materials: these represent the raw materials and component parts specifically used to make the product, such as the wheels, engine and brakes of a car.

c) Direct expenses: these include items such as direct power, which may be measured directly for producing the goods, the hiring or leasing of equipment or plant for production, or the payment of royalties for the use of patents or trade marks. Most expenses of the factory tend to be indirect and related to overheads.

Total direct costs = Prime cost of production

Indirect costs

These costs refer to the factory overheads. They are part of the factory cost, but not directly related to the actual making of the product. As in the case of direct costs, they include indirect labour, materials and expenses.

a) Indirect labour: these refer to the wages of factory workers who are not directly involved in making the product. Factory staff such as supervisors, foremen, production controllers, progress chasers, engineers and draftsmen are some examples.
b) Indirect materials: these are materials used in the factory although they are not the materials used in the product. Factory cleaning fluids, lubricants, stationery and safety clothing may be categorised as indirect.
c) Indirect expenses: these refer to the general class of expenses which come under factory overheads. Factory rates, rent and insurance, factory general expenses, depreciation of factory plant and equipment are some examples.

Work-in-progress

This relates to the stock of goods which are incomplete and therefore classed as *partly finished*. The stock of any work-in-progress at the beginning of the financial period is added to the factory cost as being part of the manufacturing expense, whilst any stock of work-in-progress at the end of the period is deducted from the factory cost because it will be used in the following financial period.

The presentation of the manufacturing account

The account is represented as:

Direct costs
\+ Indirect costs
\+ Work-in-progress (beginning)
− Work-in-progress (end)

= Factory cost

The *factory cost* is also commonly known as the *production cost* or the *manufacturing cost*. Some manufacturing organisations do not have any significant value for work-in-progress because there is little involvement in the assembly process or specific stages in production. The production of food or paints, for example, is more like a flow of production rather than stage production, therefore such organisations would have no material figure for partly finished goods.

Example of the manufacturing account layout

	£	£	£
DIRECT COSTS:			
Direct materials:			
Stock of RM* (1/1)	12 000		
+ Purchases of RM	45 000		
	57 000		
− Stock of RM* (31/12)	(13 000)	44 000	
Direct labour			
Factory wages (direct)	29 000		
Accrued wages (direct)	1 000	30 000	
Direct expenses			
Direct power		1 000	
Prime cost:			75 000
INDIRECT COSTS:			
Indirect materials		2 000	
Indirect factory wages		15 000	
Indirect expenses:			
Factory rates and insurance	3 500		
Factory maintenance	14 000		
Depreciation of plant and equipment	2 500		
Factory general expenses	3 000	23 000	
Factory overheads:			40 000
			115 000
WORK-IN-PROGRESS:			
+ Stock (1/1)			8 800
			123 800
− Stock (31/12)			7 800
Factory cost:			116 000

NOTE

*RM = Raw materials.

COST PER UNIT

If we assume that the factory produced 4000 units in the financial period, calculation of the unit costs are as follows:

a) Prime cost per unit $= \dfrac{\text{Prime cost}}{\text{Number of units (output)}}$

$= \dfrac{£75\,000}{4\,000} = £18.75$ per unit

b) Factory overheads per unit $= \dfrac{\text{Factory overheads}}{\text{Number of units}}$

$= \dfrac{£40\,000}{4\,000} = £10.00$ per unit

c) Factory cost per unit $= \dfrac{\text{Factory cost}}{\text{Number of units}}$

$= \dfrac{£116\,000}{4\,000} = £29.00$ per unit

Therefore (per unit):			
	Prime cost	=	£18.75
	Factory overheads	=	£10.00
	Adjustments for work-in-progress	=	£ 0.25
	Factory cost		£29.00

Factory cost does not include the business's profit and loss expenses, such as distribution and administration which may also be classified as a type of indirect costs. The factory cost is a guideline to indicate whether the business is cost effective in terms of manufacturing its products in relation to its competitors and the line of industry it is in.

Example

Davies & Green Ltd is a small manufacturing company producing electrical components for the computer industry. From the following details, prepare the manufacturing, trading and profit and loss account for the period ending 31 December 1990:

	£
Stocks (1/1):	
Raw materials	4 200
Work-in-progress	5 455
Finished goods	7 525
Stocks (31/12):	
Raw materials	4 875
Work-in-progress	5 855
Finished goods	9 675

(Continues)

	£
Purchases of raw materials	45 750
Wages: Factory direct	27 855
Factory indirect	10 440
Office	15 640
Rent, rates, insurance: ($\frac{4}{5}$ factory, $\frac{1}{5}$ office)	3 600
Sales of finished goods	121 565
Manufacturing general expenses	4 380
Selling and distribution expenses	3 895
Administration expenses	1 675
Depreciation: Factory machinery	4 500
Office equipment	1 850
Factory wages (direct) accrued	270

Based on an output of 10 000 units manufactured during the year, calculate:

1. The prime cost per unit.
2. The factory overheads per unit (adjust for work-in-progress).
3. The factory cost per unit.

Davies & Green Ltd –
Manufacturing account, year ended 31 December 1990

	£	£	£
DIRECT COSTS:			
Direct materials:			
Stock of RM (1/1)	4 200		
+ Purchases of RM	45 750		
	49 950		
− Stock of RM (31/12)	(4 875)	45 075	
Direct labour			
Wages (direct)	27 855		
Accrued	270	28 125	
Prime cost:			73 200
INDIRECT COSTS:			
Indirect labour			
Wages (indirect)		10 440	

(Continues)

	£	£	£
Indirect expenses			
Rent, rates and insurance	2 880		
Manufacturing expenses	4 380		
Depreciation of machinery	4 500	11 760	
Factory overheads:			22 200
			95 400
WORK-IN-PROGRESS:			
+ Stock (1/1)			5 455
			100 855
− Stock (31/12)			5 855
Factory cost:			95 000

Trading and profit and loss account, year ended 31 December 1990

	£	£	£
Sales			121 565
− Cost of sales:			
Stock of FG* (1/1)	7 525		
+ Factory cost	95 000	102 525	
− Stock of FG (31/12)		9 675	92 850
Gross profit			28 715
− Expenses:			
Selling and distribution expenses		3 895	
Administration expenses		1 675	
Office wages		15 640	
Depreciation of office equipment		1 850	
Office rent, rates, insurance		720	23 780
Net profit			4 935

NOTE

*FG = Finished goods.

Costs per unit based on an output of 10 000 units:

	£	
Prime cost per unit	7.32	$\frac{73\,200}{10\,000 \text{ units}}$
Factory overheads per unit	2.22	$\frac{22\,200}{10\,000 \text{ units}}$
	9.54	
Adjustment for work-in-progress	(0.04)	
	9.50	
Factory cost per unit	9.50	$\frac{95\,000}{10\,000 \text{ units}}$

The calculation of manufacturing profit

To see if the business is cost effective in its manufacturing process, an assessment of *profit* can be determined if it is possible to obtain a market value of the goods produced. In the example of Davies & Green Ltd, if the company could have purchased the finished goods from another producer at say, £13 per unit, of which £10 could be attributed to the factory cost, is the business cost effective in manufacturing? The answer must be 'Yes'.

	£
10 000 units produced × £10 per unit =	100 000
Davies & Green's factory cost	95 000
Profit	5 000

If the manufacturer wanted to show the profit made on the production side of the factory, the manufacturing account would need to show the market value of its goods:

	£
Market value	100 000
Factory cost	95 000
Manufacturing profit	5 000

In the trading account, the market value is shown in the cost of sales instead of the factory cost. This will then emphasise both the manufacturing profit, as well as the trading profit:

Davies & Green Ltd –
Trading account, year ended 31 December 1990

	£	£	£
Sales			121 565
– Cost of sales:			
Stock FG (1/1)	7 525		
Market value of factory cost	100 000	107 525	
– Stock FG (31/12)		9 675	97 850
Trading profit			23 715
Manufacturing profit			5 000
Gross profit			28 715

The calculation of stock of finished goods

In some examination questions, the value of any unsold stock of finished goods may not be given directly. Instead, the candidate may have to calculate its value on the basis of either its prime cost or its factory cost.

In the example above, the value of stock of finished goods on 31 December was £9675. If this figure was not given and the question asked 'Calculate unsold stock at factory cost', it would need to give:

a) the number of units left in stock
b) the basis of valuation (in this case at factory cost).

Suppose the number of units left in stock was 1000 calculated from:

Number of units manufactured during year:	10 000
Number of units in stock on 1 January:	750
	10 750
Number of units sold during year:	9 750
Number of units in stock (finished goods)	1 000

Stock FG on 31/12 valued at factory cost: 1000 × £9.50 per unit
= £9500

or Stock FG on 31/12 valued at prime cost: 1000 × £7.32 per unit
= £7320

Once a method of stock valuation has been adopted by the business, it should apply consistently that base from year to year in order to avoid any profit distortions (as required in SSAP No.2, Concepts in accounting).

The mark-up and margins of profit

The mark-up is usually given as a percentage based on the cost of the goods, and added on in order to arrive at a selling price.

Example

If the total cost of Davies & Green's product (per unit) came to £12 and they sold at £15 per unit, the profit is £3:

$$\text{Mark-up (\%)} = \frac{\text{Profit} \times 100}{\text{Cost price}}$$

$$= \frac{£3 \times 100}{£12} = 25\% \text{ mark-up}$$

Once a mark-up percentage is established by the company, it becomes a guideline to selling price. How much should an organisation mark-up the cost of their products? How much is the market willing to pay? How does their selling price compare with that of their competitors? If the market is willing to pay £15 per unit, the mark-up may well be adequate, but if competition becomes more intense, the company will have to review its prices in line with market forces.

$$\text{Margin (\%)} = \frac{\text{Profit} \times 100}{\text{Selling price}}$$

$$= \frac{£3 \times 100}{£15} = 20\% \text{ margin}$$

The margin percentage is the company's guideline to profits based on sales. Davies & Green should make £20 profit on every £100 sales, £200 on £1000 sales and so on. The margin percentage is an indicator of profit based on sales volume and may be compared with past performances in order to evaluate the company's profitability over periods of time, or with the margins of profit set by their competitors.

Fixed and variable costs

All the costs of a business may be classified in a variety of different ways. In the field of cost accounting where the emphasis lies in how things cost in relation to labour, materials and overheads, there is a need to differentiate between fixed and variable costs because they influence profit margins in relation to sales volume (or output).

Fixed costs

This type of cost is not sensitive to output change. For example, administration expenses would tend to be the same even if production levels fluctuated. Many of the company's overheads tend to be relatively fixed, regardless of levels of production. Factory rent and rates is another good example of a fixed cost.

Variable costs

This cost type does vary with output change because the cost is more sensitive to different levels of production. It refers to the *extra* costs incurred in producing one or more units over and above a given plan of production (or one or more fewer units). Direct materials and direct labour could be examples of variable costs.

For example, using the figures of Davies & Green Ltd, the costs may be classified as:

Variables:	Direct materials		£4.50	per unit
	Direct labour		£2.81	per unit
	Factory overheads (power)		£0.24	per unit
		Total:	£7.55	per unit
Fixed:	All other costs:			
	Factory overheads		£20 000	
	Profit and loss expenses		£24 500	
			£44 500	

Example questions

1 On an output of 10 000 units, what is the total cost?

Variable costs = 10 000 × £7.55 per unit
= £75 500
\+ Fixed costs = £44 500
£120 000

Total cost per unit = $\frac{£120\,000}{10\,000}$
= £12 per unit

2 On an output of 10 500 units, what is the total cost and how would it affect the total cost per unit?

Variable costs = 10 500 × £7.55 per unit
= £79 275
\+ Fixed costs = £44 500
£123 775

Total cost per unit = $\frac{£123\,775}{10\,500}$
= £11.79 per unit

Note that the total cost per unit on an improved output, has been reduced by 21p per unit (£12 − £11.79). This is because the fixed costs have been diluted by a greater output, therefore there is some achievement in economy.

3 On an output of only 9500 units, what is the total cost and how would it affect the total cost per unit?

Variable costs	=	9 500 × £7.55 per unit
	=	£71 725
+ Fixed costs	=	£44 500
		£116 225

Total cost per unit = $\frac{£116\ 225}{9\ 500}$

= £12.23 per unit

Note that the total cost per unit is 23p more costly on a reduced output. There are not as many units to dilute the fixed costs. For management purposes, it is very useful to know how variable costs affect the outcome of total cost because this will help them determine what the selling price should be.

Example of a manufacturing account illustrating the production of two major products

Tandem Co Ltd manufacture two major computer products for the electronics industry having an output of 10 000 units for ROM 'A' and 5000 units for ROM 'B'. The trial balance for the year ended 31 December 1990 was as follows:

Tandem Co Ltd –
Trial balance as on 31 December 1990

	£	£
Stocks of RM (1/1):		
ROM 'A'	8 000	
ROM 'B'	7 200	
Purchases of raw materials	80 000	
Direct wages	58 500	
Indirect factory wages	24 000	
Manufacturing expenses	18 600	
Provision for depreciation:		
Factory plant, equipment		6 000
Office equipment		3 000
Sales:		
ROM 'A'		108 000
ROM 'B'		120 000
Rent, rates and insurance:		
Factory	4 200	
Office	2 800	

(Continues)

	£	£
Debtors	18 200	
Creditors		16 800
Bank overdraft		12 200
Sales and distribution costs	8 400	
Administration expenses	18 900	
Plant and equipment (factory)	60 000	
Equipment (office)	10 000	
Capital:		
Issued and paid-up ordinary shares		20 000
Reserves		42 800
Stocks of finished goods (1/1):		
ROM 'A'	6 000	
ROM 'B'	4 000	
	328 800	328 800

NOTES

On 31 December 1990:

1 Stocks of RM: ROM 'A' £8200
ROM 'B' £6800
There were no stocks of work-in-progress.
2 Stocks of finished goods: value at factory cost per unit. There were 200 units of ROM 'A' and 400 units of ROM 'B' in stock.
3 Of the raw materials purchased, £44 000 was apportioned to ROM 'A'.
4 £1500 was owing for direct wages.
5 Direct wages are to be apportioned to each product, based on the number of production hours:
ROM 'A' 6000 hours
ROM 'B' 9000 hours.
6 Depreciation of all plant and equipment is 10 per cent of cost.
7 Of all factory overheads, including indirect wages, $\frac{2}{3}$ is apportioned to ROM 'A' and $\frac{1}{3}$ to ROM 'B'.
8 The directors of the company have decided to provide a dividend of 12p per share and a provision for tax of £700 should also be made.

REQUIRED:

a) Prepare the manufacturing account of Tandem Co Ltd for the year ended 31 December 1990 showing clearly the factory cost of each product in columnar form, as well as the total factory cost.
b) Prepare the company's trading and profit and loss account for the year ended 31 December 1990, showing the gross profit for each product in columnar form, as well as total gross profit.
c) Prepare the company's balance sheet as on 31 December 1990, in vertical format.

Tandem Co Ltd –
Manufacturing account, year ended 31 December 1990

	Products		*Total*
	ROM 'A'	*ROM 'B'*	
	£	£	£
DIRECT COSTS			
Direct materials:			
Stock of RM (1/1)	8 000	7 200	15 200
+ Purchases of RM	44 000	36 000	80 000
	52 000	43 200	95 200
− Stock of RM (31/12)	8 200	6 800	15 000
	43 800	36 400	80 200
Direct labour:			
Direct wages	24 000	36 000	60 000
Prime cost	67 800	72 400	140 200
INDIRECT COSTS			
Indirect wages	16 000	8 000	24 000
Indirect expenses:			
Manufacturing expenses	12 400	6 200	18 600
Depreciation of plant	4 000	2 000	6 000
Rent, rates, insurance	2 800	1 400	4 200
Factory overheads	35 200	17 600	52 800
WORK-IN-PROGRESS			
	—	—	—
Factory cost	103 000	90 000	193 000

NOTES

Factory cost per unit:	$\frac{103\,000}{10\,000}$	$\frac{90\,000}{5\,000}$ units
	= £10.30	£18
Stock value of finished goods (31/12)	× 200	× 400
	= £2060	£7200

Tandem Co Ltd –
Trading and profit and loss account,
year ended 31 December 1990

	Products		*Total*
	ROM 'A'	*ROM 'B'*	
	£	£	£
Sales	108 000	120 000	228 000
Cost of sales:			
Stock of FG (1/1)	6 000	4 000	10 000
Factory cost	103 000	90 000	193 000
	109 000	94 000	203 000
– Stock of FG (31/12)	2 060	7 200	9 260
	106 940	86 800	193 740
Gross profit	1 060	33 200	34 260
Sales and distribution costs			8 400
Administration expenses			18 900
Rent, rates, insurance			2 800
Depreciation of equipment			1 000
			31 100
Net profit (before tax)			3 160
Provision for tax			700
Net profit (after tax)			2 460
Provision for dividends (12p share)			2 400
Profit and loss balance c/f			60

Owing to the far greater profitability of ROM 'B' would it be better for the company to concentrate its resources in favour of this product? Is this just a poor year for ROM 'A'? Directors would need to investigate and decide the outcome.

Tandem Co Ltd –
Balance sheet as at 31 December 1990

	Cost	*Depreciation*	*Net*
	£	£	£
FIXED ASSETS			
Plant and equipment	60 000	12 000	48 000
Office equipment	10 000	4 000	6 000
	70 000	16 000	54 000

(Continues)

	Cost £	*Depreciation* £	*Net* £
CURRENT ASSETS			
Stocks:			
Raw materials	15 000		
Finished goods	9 260		
Debtors	18 200		
Bank/cash	—	42 460	
CREDITORS FALLING WITHIN 12 MONTHS			
Creditors	16 800		
Bank overdraft	12 200		
Accruals	1 500		
Provision for tax	700		
Provision for dividends	2 400	33 600	
Net current assets			8 860
Total assets less current liabilities			62 860
FINANCED BY:			
Issued and paid-up capital		20 000	
Reserves		42 800	
Profit and loss account		60	62 860

NOTES

1 There was no profit and loss balance at the beginning of the year, only £60 residue from the profit and loss appropriation account.

2 Working capital (or current ratio) = 1.26 : 1.

3 All stocks on 31 December, raw materials, work-in-progress and finished goods, entered as current assets. No stock of work-in-progress in this example.

Summary

1 The manufacturing account is prepared for manufacturing organisations for the purpose of calculating the factory cost of the firm's product or products.

2 Direct costs, indirect costs and work-in-progress make up the manufacturing account. Direct costs (prime cost), are related directly to the making of the product, mainly raw materials and direct labour. Indirect costs usually refer to all the factory overheads such as indirect wages, power, light, heat, depreciation of plant and general manufacturing expenses.

Work-in-progress refers to the stocks of partly finished goods. Some organisations do not have any material stocks of this because the method of production may be a continuous flow, for example, in food and drink industries.

3 A manufacturing profit may be indicated to show if the manufacturing process is cost effective in relation to the market value of the goods produced. Is it worth manufacturing some products if the goods are purchased more economically from another manufacturer?

4 The mark-up percentage is the business profit added to the cost price of the goods expressed as a percentage. The mark-up determines what the selling price will be.

5 The margin percentage is the business profit as a percentage of sales and is a guideline to profits in relation to sales. For example, a 15 per cent margin indicates that a profit of £15 is earned on £100 of sales.

6 Fixed costs are those costs which are not regarded as being sensitive to changes in output levels. Examples are rent, rates, insurance and administration expenses.

7 Variable costs are those costs sensitive to output changes. Examples are raw materials, direct wages and power. It is important to make the distinction between fixed and variable costs because, generally speaking, the greater the output, the more diluted fixed costs become, thereby making production more economic and cost effective.

QUESTIONS

1 From the following information, prepare the manufacturing and trading accounts of J Mason's Ltd for the year ended 31 December 1990:

	£
Stocks: (1 January)	
Raw materials	5 850
Work-in-progress	1 500
Finished goods	10 570
Purchases of raw materials	95 000
Stocks: (31 December)	
Raw materials	6 250
Work-in-progress	1 400
Finished goods	11 200

(Continues)

	£
Factory direct wages	24 550
Factory indirect wages	15 200
Factory general maintenance	2 500
Factory power, light and heat	1 750
Depreciation of plant	800
General factory expenses	2 550
Sales (finished goods)	185 000

NOTES

On 31 December 1990:

1 £250 was owing for factory power.

2 Rates of £150 were prepaid under general factory expenses.

REQUIRED:

If the factory had an output of 5000 units in the year, calculate the prime cost and factory cost per unit.

2 Harry is a manufacturer. From the following details relating to his business, prepare separate accounts to show:

i) the factory cost of goods

ii) the manufacturing profit

iii) the trading profit

iv) the net profit,

for the year ended 31 December.

		£
Stocks (1 January)		
Raw materials		6 757
Finished goods		10 560
Stocks (31 December)		
Raw materials		5 583
Finished goods		12 565
Wages:	factory (direct)	15 500
	office	12 765
Rent, rates and insurance ($\frac{4}{5}$ factory; $\frac{1}{5}$ office)		4 580
Sales of finished goods		101 500
Purchases of raw materials		40 875
Manufacturing expenses		5 945
Selling expenses		12 855
Administrative expenses		7 400
Depreciation:	machinery	2 150
	office furniture	500
	accounting machines (office)	150

Other information

a) (1/1) Stocks of work-in-progress, nil.
   (31/12) Stocks of work-in-progress, nil.

b) The market valuation of the cost of production is £78 000.

c) Calculate: on the basis of 2000 units produced in the year:
   i) Direct labour cost per unit.
   ii) Direct material cost per unit.
   iii) Factory overheads per unit.
   iv) Production costs per unit.

c) Was manufacturing cost effective? Compare the market value per unit cost with production cost per unit.

(Institute of Bankers)

3 You work in the accounts department of Georges Ltd, a manufacturing company. The following were some of the balances appearing in the books at 31 December 1985.

	£
Ordinary share capital	100 000
Stocks at 1 January 1985:	
Raw materials	22 000
Work-in-progress	32 000
Finished goods	40 180
Stocks at 31 December:	
Raw materials	34 000
Work-in-progress	36 810
Finished goods	36 080
Wages:	
Direct manufacturing	406 160
Factory supervisors	26 650
General office	59 000
Direct factory power	190 000
Heating and lighting	18 000
Purchase of raw materials	512 000
Carriage outwards	1 972
Plant and machinery	160 000
Premises	240 000
Returns inward	840
Office equipment	30 000
Rates	12 000
Administrative expenses	3 668
Debtors	28 000
Creditors	24 000
Cash in hand	7 324
Sales	1 600 580

NOTES

1 Heating and lighting rates are to be apportioned $\frac{2}{3}$ factory and $\frac{1}{3}$ office.

2 Depreciate plant and machinery by 5 per cent and office equipment by 10 per cent.
3 The total number of units completed in the year was 30 000.

TASKS:

a) Prepare the manufacturing account.
b) Prepare the trading and profit and loss account.
c) Compute the production cost of one item.

(Institute of Commercial Management)

4 *Situation*

Lindop Co Ltd is a small manufacturing company producing 12 000 units per annum. The accounts on 31 December were:

	£
Stocks (1 January):	
Raw materials	4 250
Work-in-progress	1 875
Finished goods (2050 units)	10 245
Purchases of raw materials	32 550
Sales (10 800 units)	86 400
Returns inward	105
Factory:	
Wages (direct)	14 242
Power	1 540
Indirect wages	4 250
Rent and rates	700
Indirect materials	4 480
Lighting and heating	590
Depreciation of plant and machinery	1 875
Office:	
Sales and distribution costs	4 875
Rent and rates	1 500
Administration expenses	4 950

NOTES

At 31 December 19 . . :

1 Stocks:
Raw materials £5 155
Work-in-progress £1 722
Finished goods: units in balance to be valued at production cost.
2 Wages owing: £625 (direct).
3 Depreciation of office equipment by 20 per cent of cost (cost £2500).
4 Create a provision for bad and doubtful debts to equal 5 per cent of debtors (debtors £7000).

5 Rent of office in advance £175. Factory in advance £100.
6 Bank charges accrued £300 (administration expense).

TASKS:

a) The preparation of the company's manufacturing account for the year ended 31 December.
   Calculate the cost of production per unit.
b) The preparation of the company's trading and profit and loss account for the year ended 31 December. Stock of finished goods to be calculated at production cost.
c) Based on the production capacity of 12 000 units, calculate:
   i) The prime cost per unit.
   ii) The production overheads per unit.
   iii) The mark-up percentage on cost of production given a selling price of £8 per unit.

(BTEC National)

5 The following information is taken from the accounts of Penny Jackson, a businesswoman producing science equipment to colleges:

Trial balance of P Jackson
as on 30 June 1990

	£	£
Stocks (1/7/89):		
Raw materials	6 885	
Finished goods	3 500	
Motor vehicle (cost)	8 750	
Premises (cost)	36 900	
Accumuled depreciation		
of vehicle (2 years)		1 750
Purchases		
(raw materials)	55 725	
Direct wages	45 780	
Sales		180 344
Discounts	855	1 044
Returns	548	
Salaries (assistants)	18 346	
Overheads (factory)	14 385	
Overheads (office)	7 044	
Creditors		6 755
Debtors	7 400	
Bank		2 045
Cash	400	
Drawings	10 420	
Capital		?

On 30 June, the following additional information was also available:

a) Stocks in hand were valued:
   raw materials £7432
   finished goods £4200
b) The motor vehicle is depreciated on a straight-line basis and is now three years old.
c) Of the factory overheads, £240 is prepaid and £600 is accrued.

REQUIRED:

Prepare the manufacturing account, trading and profit and loss account for the year ended 30 June 1990 and a balance sheet as on that date.

(BTEC National)

6 ACE Co Ltd is a company which manufactures electrical components for the car industry. Production is planned for 50 000 units in the financial year ended 31 December.

The trial balance extracted from the ledgers on 31 December is as follows:

	£	£
Authorised and issued share capital:		
70 000 @ £1 ordinary shares		70 000
Share premium		7 000
Premises (cost)	86 000	
Plant (cost)	12 000	
Provision for depreciation of plant		6 000
Debtors	10 498	
Creditors		58 409
Stock (1 Jan):		
Raw materials	5 892	
Finished goods (2500 units)	8 500	
Provision for bad debts		200
Bad debts	528	
Bank/cash	2 910	
Direct wages	56 804	
Raw materials, purchases of	156 820	
Sales (48 000 units)		204 000
General expenses ($\frac{1}{2}$ factory)	2 944	
Profit and loss balance (1 Jan)		5 830
Rates and insurance ($\frac{1}{2}$ factory)	610	
Office wages	5 220	
Delivery charges	2 400	
Discount	313	
	351 439	351 439

Further information available at 31 December:

a) Stocks: raw materials unused £20 893.
   50 000 units of finished goods were produced.
   the unsold stock to be valued at production cost/unit.

b) The provision for bad debts to be increased to £750.
c) The plant is to be depreciated 10 per cent on net value.
d) A taxation provision of £750 is to be made.
e) The directors have recommended a 5 per cent dividend on the share capital. A reserve is to be created of £3000.

REQUIRED:

Prepare the company's manufacturing, trading, profit and loss and appropriation account for the period ended 31 December, and a balance sheet as at that date.

(Institute of Bankers)

7 The following list of balances as at 31 July 1986 has been extracted from the books of Jane Seymour who commenced business on 1 August 1985 as a designer and manufacturer of kitchen furniture.

	£
Plant and machinery at cost on 1 August 1985	60 000
Motor vehicles at cost on 1 August 1985	30 000
Loose tools at cost	9 000
Sales	170 000
Raw materials purchased	43 000
Direct factory wages	39 000
Light and power	5 000
Indirect factory wages	8 000
Machinery repairs	1 600
Motor vehicle running expenses	12 000
Rent and insurances	11 600
Administrative staff salaries	31 000
Administrative expenses	9 000
Sales and distribution staff salaries	13 000
Capital at 1 August 1985	122 000
Sundry debtors	16 500
Sundry creditors	11 200
Balance at bank	8 500
Drawings	6 000

Additional information for the year ended 31 July 1986:

1 It is estimated that the plant and machinery will be used in the business for 10 years and the motor vehicles used for four years. In both cases it is estimated that the residual value will be nil. The straight-line method of providing for depreciation is to be used.
2 Light and power charges accrued at 31 July 1986 amounted to £1000 and insurance prepaid at 31 July 1986 totalled £800.
3 Stocks were valued at cost at 31 July 1986 as follows:
   raw materials £7000
   finished goods £10 000

4 The valuation of work-in-progress at 31 July 1986 included variable and fixed factory overheads and amounted to £12 300.
5 Two-thirds of the light and power and rent and insurance costs are to be allocated to the factory costs and one-third to general administration costs.
6 Motor vehicle costs are to be allocated equally to factory costs and general administration costs.
7 Goods manufactured during the year are to be transferred to the trading account at £95 000 as the market value.
8 Loose tools on hand on 31 July 1986 were valued at £5000.

REQUIRED:

Prepare a manufacturing, trading and profit and loss account for the year ended 31 July 1986 of Jane Seymour.

(AAT)

8 W J & G Ltd of Wakefield, manufacture cricket bats in three qualities, one star, two star and three star. The following information relates to the company's financial year end 31 December 1990:

	£
Stock of raw materials (1/1/90)	4 200
Stock of finished goods (1/1/90)	
One star	2 200
Two star	3 000
Three star	5 500
Purchase of raw materials	228 200
Carriage of raw materials	1 200
Returns out raw materials	400
Factory direct wages:	
One star	28 400
Two star	36 300
Three star	42 500
Factory light and heat	2 800
Factory rent and rates	1 800
Factory general expenses	5 400
Depreciation of plant	2 000
Sales:	
One star	120 000
Two star	160 000
Three star	190 000

(Continues)

	£
Stock on 31 December 1990:	
Raw materials	4 000
Finished goods:	
One star	1 650
Two star	2 300
Three star	1 000

The factory records show that of the raw materials actually consumed in production are, one star £64 000, two star £76 000 and the rest allocated to three star.

All factory costs are to be allocated $\frac{1}{4}$ each to one star and two star and $\frac{1}{2}$ to three star.

REQUIRED:

On 31 December, 1990:

a) A manufacturing account to show the prime cost and factory cost of each product.
b) A trading account showing the gross profit of each product.
c) The gross margin percentage of each product.

(AEB)

CHAPTER

25 Looking ahead: budgets and spreadsheets

- *What is a budget?*
- *Why are they used?*
- *Can they assist management?*
- *What advantages can the use of a spreadsheet provide?*

Introduction

The purpose of preparing a well planned budget is to make the best possible use of business resources. It is the financial planning ahead in terms of where funds are going to come from and how funds are going to be allocated. Budgets are a management device to assist in decision making.

At the national level, the Chancellor of the Exchequer plans the Government's income and expenditure for the year in the preparation of his budget to the nation. How much in taxes must he raise and from which sources? How is this income to be spent? How are the funds to be allocated to the various Government departments? The budget is not all about raising funds and spending money. Budgets can influence the major policy decisions of an organisation.

The Chancellor, for example, can use his budget to influence the economy by way of regulating the demand for goods and services. He can make it easier or more difficult for us to buy the things we want. Look at what the level of interest rates can do.

A business can use its budget to plan its objectives. It can plan for adequate returns on capital and targets can be set for the organisation to achieve.

A budget can help to optimise the use of business resources by forecasting what can be done and establishing objectives. For example, can a sales target of £50 000 per week be achieved? What plan of action will be needed? How much marketing and sales promotion will be required? Are production and manpower facilities adequate? Plans are then made and objectives agreed. A yardstick for management to achieve objectives is established.

Once targets for both revenue and expenditure have been set, profits can be estimated for the financial period (or periods) ahead. The budget will provide management with some means by which to measure business performance. Will the actual results match the budgeted plan? How much difference (or variance) will occur between these figures?

Management will be able to use the information by comparing the budget with actual results to help them to make better decisions about how to use the resources of the business. Will they have to increase production to meet a higher than expected demand or will they have to scale down activities because targets have not been met? Budgets should help management decide what plan of action to take. Budgetary control is a tool of management and includes the following.

Stages of the budget

1 Management objectives should be stated clearly. How should the resources of the business be used?
2 Plans are drawn up and the appropriate budgets prepared. Targets for sales and expenditure are drafted.
3 All personnel should be aware of budgets; they need to know what the plans and forecasts are and the targets which have been set.
4 Actual results should then be regularly checked with budget figures, identifying any differences between them and analysing the possible reasons for the variances.
5 Any amendments or modifications to the budget can be taken into consideration and new initiatives can be taken by management if changes to plans are required.

Realistic objectives should be set by management otherwise staff morale may suffer. Careful consideration in setting targets is essential. If targets are too optimistic, staff may soon give up or be put under severe stress. If they are set too low, staff motivation may diminish once the targets have been achieved.

Types of budget

There are a number of different types of budget which may be used by management. Smaller businesses may not prepare any budget and simply conduct their affairs in direct response to the market, without planning too much ahead. Larger organisations however, may adopt one or more of the following types of budget:

sales budget
production budget
manpower budget
cash budget
operating budget.

Sales budget

The sales aspect is the life-blood of any organisation and therefore an accurate assessment of future sales is required because this provides the basic framework of what the business activity is going to be. Sales provides income by which expenditure can be met. Expenditure plans can then be prepared. If a 20 per cent increase is predicted, management will need to ensure that the business is ready in every respect to meet this target.

Production budget

The production budget must ensure it has the resources in terms of labour, materials and equipment to meet the sales target. It would be of little use predicting a 20 per cent increase in sales if production is unable to meet this demand because it is under-resourced.

Manpower budget

The manpower (personnel) budget must ensure that the organisation has the right labour force at the right time. Manpower planning is essential, particularly in larger organisations, to prepare for management, educational and training needs. The labour force must be efficiently and effectively employed, and given the right opportunities to motivate them to their best efforts. If there is a labour shortage and staff are overworked or there is under-financing of training needs, morale will decline and staff will fail to produce their best. Any organisation is only as good as its staff.

Cash budget

The cash budget is an essential budget because it predicts the future cash flow of the business. Will it have sufficient cash resources to meet payments at the right time? Will any overdraft or specific loans be required? All other budgets will be involved in this budget because the cash budget must include all aspects concerning the receipts and payments of monies. The business must have adequate cash resources to meet its day-to-day needs otherwise it can soon be in financial difficulties. A cash shortage can lead to disaster if creditors cannot be paid on time. The business needs to know, month by month, the cash it requires so that it can organise the finances well ahead of time.

Operating budget

The operating budget (sometimes referred to as the financial budget), is the culmination of all the other budgets. It represents the forecast of the trading and profit and loss account and the balance sheet. Profit is the key figure in management thinking. Will the business improve its performance? Will return on capital be satisfactory?

Profit can be broken down into monthly periods, so that actual results can be measured against those of the budget. Variances (differences) can then be analysed and evaluated which will help management in their decisions. Budgets need not be static or inflexible in their use. They can be modified to meeting changing events. They can be updated to suit new circumstances as these arise.

The following examples will illustrate accounting's two significant budgets: the cash budget and the operating budget.

The cash budget example

The following information relates to a businessman, D Balfour, who has started business on 1 January with £5000. He has made a forecast for the next six months concerning receipts and payments of cash:

a) Production will involve the making of an electrical component for the computer industry. His plan is to produce 500 units per month in the first six months.
b) Sales: each unit has a selling price of £12.50. The sales estimate for six months to 30 June is:

Jan	Feb	Mar	Apr	May	June	
400	480	480	560	640	400	(Units)

c) Variable overheads (based on output), will be £1.50 per unit, payable in the month of production
d) Fixed costs will be £1000 per month payable *after* the month of production.
e) Production wages (direct) will be £3 per unit payable in the month of production.
f) Salaries will be £500 per month until April, but expected to rise by 10 per cent in the following months.
g) Equipment costing £8000 will be purchased in March. A 25 per cent deposit will be paid in March, with the balance to be paid equally in April and May.
h) Materials will cost £2 per unit and suppliers will be paid in the month *after* the purchase.

All unit sales are on credit. Debtors are expected to pay in the month *following* their purchase. £5000 was deposited in the business bank account on 1 January.

REQUIRED:

a) A schedule of payments for the six months to 30 June and a cash budget covering the same period.
b) A brief analysis of the cash budget.
c) An operating budget which will show the trading and profit and loss forecast for the six months to 30 June and a forecast balance sheet as on that date.

The schedule of payments

	Jan £	*Feb* £	*Mar* £	*Apr* £	*May* £	*June* £	*Total* £
Fixed costs	—	1 000	1 000	1 000	1 000	1 000	5 000
Variable overheads (500 × £1.5)	750	750	750	750	750	750	4 500
Production wages (500 × £3.0)	1 500	1 500	1 500	1 500	1 500	1 500	9 000
Salaries	500	500	500	500	550	550	3 100
Materials (500 × £2.0)	—	1 000	1 000	1 000	1 000	1 000	5 000
Equipment			2 000	3 000	3 000		8 000
	2 750	4 750	6 750	7 750	7 800	4 800	34 600

The cash budget

	Jan	*Feb*	*Mar*	*Apr*	*May*	*June*	*Total*	
	£	£	£	£	£	£	£	
Bank balance b/f	5 000	2 250	2 500	1 750	—	(800)	5 000	(1/1)
+ Receipts	—	5 000	6 000	6 000	7 000	8 000	32 000	
(£12.5 unit)	5 000	7 250	8 500	7 750	7 000	7 200	37 000	
− Payments (above)	2 750	4 750	6 750	7 750	7 800	4 800	34 600	
Bank balance c/f (to next month)	2 250	2 500	1 750	—	(800)	2 400	2 400	

ANALYSIS OF THE CASH BUDGET

From the forecast of cash flow, it appears that D Balfour may be a little short of liquidity in the months of April and May. This is not surprising because part of his expenditure is capital expenditure, purchasing equipment in March of £8000 and finishing the payment for it in May. He could ask the bank to tide him over during these months by arranging for an overdraft facility. He could, if he wanted, finance the asset purchase in other ways, probably by simply extending the period of credit over 12 months or even longer.

In June, however, the cash flow is back in surplus and certainly appears sound. Cash flow forecasts a business's liquidity. Can sales generate sufficient receipts of money to be able to finance labour, materials, overheads and capital expenditure?

Budgets are an important management tool if they are taken seriously. They can help plan and control the business because they assist in management decision making. When actual results are recorded, they can be carefully monitored against the budget forecast. How will D Balfour's budget compare with his first six months trading? Will he have about £2500 in the bank in June? If he has not, what factors have occurred to have caused the difference? These are the questions which help make accounting more dynamic; a little more involved in making things happen and not just recording what has already happened.

The operating budget example

The operating budget relates to the forecast of the trading and profit and loss account and the balance sheet. The sales forecast for the six months to June was:

Total of 2960 units × £12.5 per unit = £37 000 (Sales)

The first six production months at 500 units per month would cost:

				£	
Wages	£3.0	per unit × 3000	=	9 000	
Variable overheads	£1.5	per unit × 3000	=	4 500	
Materials	£2.0	per unit × 3000	=	6 000	
	£6.5	Total cost:		19 500	(Production)

There was no opening stock because it was a new business and therefore there will be no closing stock carried forward from the previous period. If the closing stock was to be valued at production cost per unit then:

Units produced:	3 000 units
Units sold:	2 960 units
	40 units in stock × production cost per unit
Value of closing stock:	40 × £6.5 per unit
	= £260

As far as any adjustments are concerned, D Balfour decided to depreciate the equipment by 20 per cent per annum and a full 10 per cent for the six months, even though it was to be purchased in March.

D Balfour –
Budgeted trading and profit and loss account for six months ending 30 June

	£	£	£
Sales			37 000
– Cost of sales:			
Stock (1/1)	—		
Production cost	19 500		
Stock (30/6)	(260)		19 240
Gross profit			17 760
– Expenses:			
Fixed costs	5 000		
+ Accrued (1 month)	1 000	6 000	
Salaries		3 100	
Depreciation of equipment		800	9 900
Net profit			7 860

D Balfour –
Budgeted balance sheet as on 30 June

	£	£	£
FIXED ASSETS			
Equipment	8 000	800	7 200
CURRENT ASSETS			
Stock	260		
Debtors			
(400 × £12.5)	5 000		
Bank	2 400	7 660	

(Continues)

	£	£	£
CURRENT LIABILITIES			
Creditors			
(500 × £2)	1 000		
Accruals	1 000	2 000	
(1 month fixed cost)			
Working capital			5 660
			12 860
FINANCED BY:			
Capital (1/1)	5 000		
+ Net profit	7 860		12 860

D Balfour's prospects look very sound for a period covering the first six months' trading. It may be that his sales forecast is a little optimistic and his expenditure may be greater than predicted. He will be able to compare his actual trading results with the budget and see if his targets have been met. Will the demand for his product be maintained? Has he arranged any firm contracts with clients? Can he hold his own against other competitors? These are the type of questions D Balfour will need to answer.

Example

Situation

You work as an assistant to a firm of accountants who deal with a wide variety of financial and management accounts. One of their clients, a partnership called Smith & Jones, have submitted data for your preparation. The information has been placed with you to prepare the draft documents before they are passed on to the client.

Information

Smith & Jones wish to form a new private limited company in the name of S & J Co Ltd. The new company is to commence its operations with effect from 1 July 1989. The data estimated for the period from 1 July 1989 to 31 December 1989 is as follows:

1 Smith is to put £50 000 into the business bank account on 1 July 1989 and will be issued with 50 000 £1 ordinary shares.

Jones will put £100 000 into the business bank account on the same date and will be issued with 50 000 £1 ordinary shares and £50 000 of debenture stock at 12 per cent interest.

2 The sales will be on a credit basis and are estimated to be:

July	£25 000	Oct	£50 000
Aug	£45 000	Nov	£45 000
Sep	£65 000	Dec	£60 000

All debtors are expected to settle their accounts two months after the month in which the goods are bought.

3 The purchases will be on a credit basis and are estimated to be:

July	£65 000	Oct	£45 000
Aug	£35 000	Nov	£30 000
Sep	£50 000	Dec	£45 000

Creditors payments are arranged to be paid in the month following the purchase.

4 Wages and salaries are estimated to be £1750 per month payable on the last weekday of each month.

5 Smith and Jones will each draw directors' fees of £1000 per month payable on the same date as in **4** above.

6 Debenture interest is to be paid half-yearly, the first payment is due in December 1989.

7 Premises are to be purchased for £85 000 and paid for in August 1989.

8 Fixed costs are estimated to be £1500 per month for the first three months of business and then increase by 20 per cent thereafter. These costs are payable one month in arrears.

9 Equipment is to be purchased on 1 July 1989 for £30 000, half of which is to be paid in July and the other in October. It is also to be depreciated by 20 per cent per annum on the straight-line basis.

10 Stock is estimated to be valued at £40 000 on 31 December 1989.

TASK A:

Prepare a cash flow budget for the period July to December 1989 (inclusive).

TASK B:

Prepare a budgeted profit and loss account and a balance sheet for the half year to 31 December 1989.

TASK C:

a) Using a disk with spreadsheet software, input your data as presented in Task A and obtain a printout of the result.
b) Assume that a change has occurred in your estimated cost of the equipment from a value of £30 000 to £40 000 (as in **9** above) and also an increase of £100 in wages for November and December. Input this data in your budget program for the purpose of producing a further printout indicating the changes it will affect.
(The answer to Task C is shown in the following section, beginning on page 364, which deals with spreadsheets.)

S & J Co Ltd

Schedule of payments	*July*	*Aug*	*Sep*	*Oct*	*Nov*	*Dec*	*Total*	
	£	£	£	£	£	£	£	
Creditors	—	65 000	35 000	50 000	45 000	30 000	225 000	
Wages and salaries	1 750	1 750	1 750	1 750	1 750	1 750	10 500	
Directors' fees	2 000	2 000	2 000	2 000	2 000	2 000	12 000	
Premises		85 000					85 000	
Debenture interest						3 000	3 000	
Fixed costs	—	1 500	1 500	1 500	1 800	1 800	8 100	
Equipment	15 000			15 000			30 000	
	18 750	155 250	40 250	70 250	50 550	38 550	373 600	
Cash budget	£	£	£	£	£	£	£	
Bank balance b/f	150 000	131 250	(24 000)	(39 250)	(64 500)	(50 050)	150 000	(1/7)
+ Receipts	—	—	25 000	45 000	65 000	50 000	185 000	
	150 000	131 250	1 000	5 750	500	(50)	335 000	
− Payments	18 750	155 250	40 250	70 250	50 550	38 550	373 600	
Bank balance c/f	131 250	(24 000)	(39 250)	(64 500)	(50 050)	(38 600)	(38 600)	

NOTE

The company will need substantial overdraft facilities from the bank in its first six months and possibly through to the next six. This was caused by the delay in the receipt of debtors' payments; debtors enjoy two months' credit. In the second six months, the receipts should be flowing in each month to help diminish the overdraft.

S & J Co Ltd –
Budgeted trading and profit and loss account
six months ending 31 December 1990

	£	£	£
Sales			290 000
− Cost of sales:			
Stock (1/7)	—		
Purchases	270 000		
Stock (31/12)	(40 000)		230 000
Gross profit			60 000
− Expenses:			
Wages and salaries		10 500	
Directors' fees		12 000	
Debenture interest		3 000	
Fixed costs	8 100		
+ Accrued	1 800	9 900	
Depreciation (equipment)		3 000	38 400
Net profit			21 600

Budgeted balance sheet as on 31 December 1990

	£	£	£
FIXED ASSETS			
Premises	85 000		85 000
Equipment	30 000	3 000	27 000
			112 000
CURRENT ASSETS			
Stock	40 000		
Debtors (Nov/Dec)	105 000		
Bank	—	145 000	
CURRENT LIABILITIES			
Creditors (Dec)	45 000		
Bank O/D	38 600		
Accruals	1 800	85 400	
Net current assets			59 600
			171 600
LONG-TERM LIABILITIES			
Debentures			50 000
			121 600
ISSUED AND PAID-UP CAPITAL			
100 000 @ £1 ordinary shares			100 000
Profit and loss account			21 600
			121 600

Computer-based accounts: The use of a spreadsheet

A spreadsheet program contains a matrix or grid, which displays a series of rows and columns.

A program would normally display around 60 columns across (not all visible on screen at the same time of course) and about 250 rows down.

The matrix is often referred to as a *worksheet* which may be used as a tool to solve a range of business problems. Once a spreadsheet has been set up, for example, to prepare cash budgets, it can be used over and over again, incorporating any changes which may be required. Figures can be changed to try out different ideas and to see their effect on the overall plan, assisting management to make their decisions.

The matrix

← Columns →

	A	B	C	D	E	F	G	H
1	*Income*	*July*	*Aug*	*Sept*	*Oct*	*Nov*	*Dec*	*Total*
2	Debtors	500	500	600	600	700	800	3 700
3	Other (cash)	100	150	150	200	200	400	1 200
4	Total:	600	650	750	800	900	1 200	4 900
5	*Payments*							
6	Creditors	400	500	500	500	600	700	3 200
7	Wages	80	80	85	85	85	85	500
8	Overheads	100	100	100	100	100	100	600
9	Fixed assets			40		40		80
10	Total:	580	680	725	685	825	885	4 380
11	*Balance* b/f	50	70	40	65	180	255	50
12	+ Total (4)	600	650	750	800	900	1 200	4 900
13	− Total (10)	580	680	725	685	825	885	4 380
14	*Balance c/f*	70	40	65	180	255	570	570

Rows ↕

Commands: Copy/Delete/Edit/Format/Insert

NOTE

If it was decided to change debtors, for example, in July and August to 600 in each month, all relevant figures on the grid would instantly be updated, ending with a final balance of 770 in December.

Cells

The columns across and the rows down form cells. These are the locations on the grid. For example, B2 locates the cell for the receipts of debtors in July (500) and F8 locates the overheads in November (100). Each individual cell is identified by its column and row position in the same way as a grid reference on an ordinance survey map. Columns in this example are all identified by a letter and rows by a number.

The cells may be used to enter three distinct types of information:

1 The text: the headings for rows and columns.
2 Numbers: whole numbers, decimals or currency.
3 Formulae: relating to numbers for adding, subtracting, multiplying, dividing, etc.

The size of a cell may vary, but will normally hold about 8 to 10 characters. This can be modified if more spaces are required by using a command such as Format.

Formulae may be set up in any of the cells to instruct the computer to do the necessary calculations. For example, in cells B across to G, a total of these must be made in column H, for each of the rows from 2 to 3, 4, 6, 7, 8, 9, 10, 12 and 13.

Method:	+ Sum [B2 : G2]	to be entered in column H2
	+ Sum [B3 : G3]	to be entered in column H3, etc.

The same principle is applied to the columns down. The totals of income in row number 4 must be calculated for each month including the final total in column H. The same applies to payments in column 10 for each of the months across, including the final total.

Method:	B2 + B3	to be entered in B4 (income)
	C2 + C3	to be entered in C4, etc.
	+ Sum [B6 : B9]	to be entered in B10 (payments)
	+ Sum [C6 : C9]	to be entered in C10, etc.

This procedure may sound a little tedious, although the command Replicate has the facility of making the same formulae across a number of cells and does save time. However, once the formulae are in place, any figures may be entered and calculations are instantly updated!

The symbols for the use of formulae are:

+ Add
− Subtract
* Multiply
/ Divide

By using these basic symbols, any row or column can be totalled, subtracted, divided, averaged, multiplied, percentaged, etc. Once a formula is set to a particular cell, it will calculate the relevant figures. Formulae can also be changed to suit the circumstances. It is then a straightforward matter of entering the appropriate figures in the appropriate cells, entering the calculation command and all figures are instantly updated.

Moving from cell to cell

The arrow keys on the keyboard allow the movement from cell to cell, either across or down. The cell cursor identifies the cell to be used. If the arrow keys are held down, the cursor moves across or down more rapidly. If the cursor is moved beyond the column visible on the screen (in our case, H), then the worksheet automatically scrolls past the screen window to the next section, I onwards, so that the cursor is always on view. If the cursor was moved down beyond row 14, the worksheet would scroll past the screen window to the next section, that is, from 15 downwards.

The prompt line is at the bottom of the screen and allows the operator to select the option he or she requires. For example, commands may be entered to copy, delete, calculate, etc. The prompt line lists the set of options for the operator to choose from.

Uses of the spreadsheet

The spreadsheet has a wide range of uses in all sorts of different organisations. A wide spread of calculations can be performed automatically within the basic framework of the matrix. An operator can test any number of variations to check on the outcome, in order to discover what the effects of these changes might be. For example, if another £50 000 was spent on equipment, payable in March and June, what effect would it have on cash flow in the budget period?

In business, the spreadsheet is particularly useful in the preparation of all types of budgets for the purpose of forecasting cash flow, profits, sales, production costs, stocks, etc. Mistakes can be corrected quite easily and new figures inserted. A wide range of calculations can be performed instantly and the operator may try out a number of different variables to see what the effects might be. Spreadsheets may be stored on disks and called up when needed. Printouts of the spreadsheet may also be obtained. Some spreadsheet packages are integrated with other programs and can provide graphics to produce charts and diagrams.

The following is an example of a spreadsheet being used to calculate a cash flow budget: it refers to Task C of S & J Co Ltd on page 362.

Task C: The spreadsheet of S & J Co Ltd

Details	July	August	Sept	Oct	Nov	Dec	Total
INCOME							
Debtors	0	0	25000	45000	65000	50000	185000
S.Cap	150000	0					150000
TOTAL	150000	0	25000	45000	65000	50000	335000
PAYMENTS							
Creds.	0	65000	35000	50000	45000	30000	225000
Wages	1750	1750	1750	1750	1750	1750	10500
Dir.Fees	2000	2000	2000	2000	2000	2000	12000
Deb.Int	0					3000	3000
Premises	0	85000					85000
F.Costs	0	1500	1500	1500	1800	1800	8100
Eqpt.	15000			15000			30000
Sundries							
TOTAL	18750	155250	40250	70250	50550	38550	373600
Bal.b/f	0	131250	−24000	−39250	−64500	−50050	0
+Income	150000	0	25000	45000	65000	50000	335000
	150000	131250	1000	5750	500	−50	335000
Payments	18750	155250	40250	70250	50550	38550	373600
Bal.c/f	131250	−24000	−39250	−64500	−50050	−38600	−38600

Task C: The spreadsheet of S & J Co Ltd showing the effect of changes in wages and equipment costs

Details	July	August	Sept	Oct	Nov	Dec	Total
INCOME							
Debtors	0	0	25000	45000	65000	50000	185000
S.Cap	150000	0					150000
TOTAL	150000	0	25000	45000	65000	50000	335000
PAYMENTS							
Creds.	0	65000	35000	50000	45000	30000	225000
Wages	1750	1750	1750	1750	1850	1850	10700
Dir.Fees	2000	2000	2000	2000	2000	2000	12000
Deb.Int	0					3000	3000
Premises	0	85000					85000
F.Costs	0	1500	1500	1500	1800	1800	8100
Eqpt.	20000			20000			40000
Sundries							
TOTAL	23750	155250	40250	75250	50650	38650	383800
Bal.b/f	0	126250	−29000	−44250	−74500	−60150	0
+Income	150000	0	25000	45000	65000	50000	335000
	150000	126250	−4000	750	−9500	−10150	335000
Payments	23750	155250	40250	75250	50650	38650	383800
Bal.c/f	126250	−29000	−44250	−74500	−60150	−48800	−48800

Example

The following information relates to the finances of Davies & Smith Ltd, a small manufacturing enterprise, for the year ended 31 December 1990:

Budget year: 1991

Sales target:	52 000 units
Production schedule:	50 000 units
Finished goods carried forward to 1/1/91	7 000 units @ £8 each
Costs per unit:	
Direct materials	£5.0
Direct labour	£3.0
Factory variables	£1.0
Sales and distribution variables	£1.5
Fixed costs	£180 000

The unsold stock of finished goods on 31/12/91 is to be valued at factory cost. The selling price per unit is to be based on a 40 per cent *margin* on the factory cost.

REQUIRED:

a) A forecast of the manufacturing account for the year ended 31 December 1991.
b) Calculations to show how the mark-up and margin percentage is arrived at, based on the factory cost.
c) A forecast trading and profit and loss account for the year ended 31 December 1991.

Forecast of manufacturing account for the year ended 31 December 1991

	£	£
DIRECT COSTS		
Direct materials (50 000 × £5)	250 000	
Direct labour (50 000 × £3)	150 000	
		400 000
INDIRECT COSTS		
Factory variables (50 000 × £1)		50 000
FACTORY COST =		450 000

Mark-up and margins of profit

$$\text{The factory cost per unit} = \frac{\text{Factory cost}}{\text{No of units produced}}$$

$$= \frac{£450\ 000}{50\ 000\ \text{units}}$$

$$= £9 \text{ per unit}$$

What is the selling price based on a *margin* of 40 per cent? (Margin is based on selling price, not cost.)

Call the selling price:	100
Deduct margin	40
Cost price	60

Therefore 'profit' is £40 on a cost price of £60.

$$\textit{The mark-up percentage} = \frac{\text{Profit} \times 100}{\text{Cost price}}$$

$$= \frac{40 \times 100}{60}$$

$$= 66\tfrac{2}{3}\%$$

$$\textit{Selling price} = \text{Factory cost} + 66\tfrac{2}{3}\%$$

$$= £9 + £6 = £15$$

$$\text{SALES} = 52\,000 \text{ units} \times £15$$
$$= £780\,000$$

If the question stated that the selling price is £15 per unit and the *mark-up percentage* is $66\frac{2}{3}$, how is the margin percentage found?

Call the cost price:	100
Add mark-up	$66\frac{2}{3}$
Selling price	$166\frac{2}{3}$

Therefore 'profit' is £$66\frac{2}{3}$ on a selling price of £$166\frac{2}{3}$.

$$\textit{The margin percentage} = \frac{\text{Profit} \times 100}{\text{Selling price}}$$
$$= \frac{£66\frac{2}{3} \times 100}{166\frac{2}{3}}$$
$$= 40\% \text{ (Check: } £15 - 40\% = £9\text{).}$$

Davies & Smith Ltd –
Forecast trading and profit and loss account
31 December 1991

	£	£
Sales (52 000 × £15)		780 000
– Cost of sales:		
Stock (1/1) (7 000 × £8)	56 000	
Factory cost (50 000)	450 000	
	506 000	
– Stock (31/12)		
(5 000 × £9)	45 000	461 000
Gross profit		319 000
– Expenses:		
Sales and distribution costs		
(52 000 × £1.5)	78 000	
Fixed costs	180 000	258 000
Net profit		61 000

Summary

1 A budget is a prepared forecast of a business's resources. It is a management tool to help them in their objectives and to assist them in their decision making.

2 Budgets need to be well-planned and communicated to all key members of staff. Realistic targets need to be set.

3 Actual results need to be carefully monitored with the budget. Variances which may arise can then be evaluated by management to assist them in their decisions.

4 There are several different types of budget. Accounting concerns itself with the cash and operating budgets which involve all other budgets.

5 The spreadsheet is computer-based accounting and is very convenient when preparing cash budgets in particular. Any changes can easily be updated by simply pressing the appropriate keys.

6 The mark-up and margins of profit help to determine the selling price. The mark-up is always based on the cost, whereas the margin is always based on the sales.

QUESTIONS

1 The following information relates to Downing & Co Ltd concerning the preparation of its six-monthly budget:

	Mar	*Apr*	*May*	*June*	*July*	*Aug*	*Sept*	*Oct*
	£	£	£	£	£	£	£	£
Sales on credit	20 000	30 000	35 000	34 000	36 000	25 000	26 000	27 000
Purchases on credit	20 000	22 000	23 000	17 000	18 000	19 000	22 000	20 000

Rent, rates	Paid half yearly, in advance; first payment in March; £12 000 per year.
Salaries	£2 000 per month, payable in the same month.
Wages	£1 000 per month, payable in the same month, but having a 10 per cent increase in September.
Fixed costs	£1 000 per month payable in the same month.
Depreciation on equipment	£75 per month.
Bank balance	1st April £5 000.
Debtors	To pay in the *following* month of sale.
Creditors	To be paid in the month *after* the purchase.
Corporation tax	£12 000 to be paid in June.

REQUIRED:

a) Prepare a schedule of payments for the months April to September, inclusive.
b) Prepare a cash budget for the same period.
c) Make any brief comment on your findings.

2 *Situation*
You work for a firm of accountants, who have just taken on a client, Small & Co. In addition to the year-end accounts the client requires a cash forecast and has supplied various data.

Information

i) Opening cash (including bank) balance £2000.
ii) Production in units:

(1986)									*(1987)*	
April	*May*	*June*	*July*	*Aug*	*Sept*	*Oct*	*Nov*	*Dec*	*Jan*	*Feb*
480	540	600	640	700	740	760	680	620	520	500

iii) Raw materials used in production cost £10 per unit, payable in the month of production.
iv) Direct labour costs of £17 per unit are payable in the month of production.
v) Variable expenses are £3 per unit, payable $\frac{2}{3}$ in month of production and $\frac{1}{3}$ in the month following production.
vi) Sales at £40 per unit:

Mar	*April*	*May*	*June*	*July*	*Aug*	*Sept*	*Oct*	*Nov*	*Dec*
520	400	640	580	800	600	700	800	780	800

Debtors to pay their accounts in the month following the sale.
vii) Fixed expenses of £1200 per month payable each month.
viii) Machinery costing £21 000 to be paid for in August.
ix) Receipt of an investment grant of £7000 is due in November.
x) Drawings to be £800 per month.

REQUIRED:

a) Prepare a schedule of payments for the six months to 31/12/86.
b) Prepare a cash budget for the six months to 31/12/86.
c) Prepare a draft memorandum to the client commenting on the results of your cash budget.

(BTEC National)

3 You are employed by a consultancy firm and are working on the cash flow budget of a new client, Forbes & Co Ltd.

i) On 1/4/88 Forbes plan to set up in business by depositing £120 000 in the business bank account.
ii) On 2/4/88 to buy and pay for premises £80 000; shop fixtures £10 000; and a motor van £8000.
iii) To employ three sales assistants – monthly wages £1500 (total) payable at the end of each month (ignore tax and insurance).
iv) To buy the following goods:

	April	*May*	*June*	*July*	*Aug*	*Sept*
(Units)	1000	600	600	700	700	700

v) To sell the following goods:

	April	*May*	*June*	*July*	*Aug*	*Sept*
(Units)	400	500	500	600	700	700

vi) Units will be sold for £30 each and customers will be expected to pay their accounts in the month following that in which they buy the goods.
vii) Units will cost £17 each and suppliers expect to be paid in the same month as supply.
viii) General expenses are estimated at £600 per month payable in the month following.
ix) The directors will draw monthly salaries totalling £2000 per month – but they will *not* draw such salaries in the first two months.
x) Variable costs are £5 per unit for sales distribution payable in the month following.

REQUIRED:

a) A schedule of payments for the six months ending 30 September 1988.
b) A cash budget for the same period.

4 You are employed by a small firm of accountants and one of their clients, P Jackson & Co Ltd requires a cash flow forecast leading up to the financial year ending 31 March 1987.

Information available

Client: P Jackson & Co Ltd

		1986			1987	
Number of units	*Oct*	*Nov*	*Dec*	*Jan*	*Feb*	*Mar*
produced per month:	650	700	550	500	450	400

a) Direct materials cost £4 per unit paid for one month after production.
b) Direct labour costs are £2.50 per unit paid in the same month of production.
c) Sales revenue is £15 per unit. All production is sold but debtors pay in the second month following production.
d) Variable overheads are £2 per unit paid half in the month of production and the other half in the following month.
e) Fixed overhead costs are £1000 per month paid by the month.
f) Other wages are £600 per month payable in the month.
g) Taxation due to be paid in March 1987 is £3500.
h) New machinery costing £35 000 in January 1987 is to be paid by a 20 per cent deposit in January and followed by equal instalments over 14 months commencing in February.
i) The bank balance on 1 December 1986 is estimated at £1000 rounded up in Jackson's favour.

REQUIRED:

a) Produce a cash flow plan for P Jackson & Co Ltd for the final four months of their financial year (December–March).

b) Prepare a memorandum to the client commenting on the basic difference between fixed and variable costs.

(Institute of Bankers)

5 The following information relates to a businessman, E Allan, who will be starting his enterprise on 1 July 1990 with £10 000. He has made a forecast for the next six months concerning his cash flow:

a) Production will concern the making of an electrical component for the computer industry. His plan is to produce 600 units (output) per month in the first six months.
b) Sales: each unit has a selling price of £20.00. The sales estimate for six months to 31 December is:

July	*Aug*	*Sept*	*Oct*	*Nov*	*Dec*	
300	680	680	600	540	400	(units)

c) Variable overheads (based on output), will be £2.50 per unit, payable in the month of production.
d) Fixed costs will be £2000 per month payable *after* the month of production.
e) Production wages (direct) will be £5 per unit payable in the month of production.
f) Salaries will be £700 per month until October but expected to rise by 20 per cent in the months following.
g) Equipment, to cost £12 000 will be purchased in September. A 25 per cent deposit will be paid in September with the balance to be paid equally in October and November. Depreciation is 25 per cent per annum.
h) Materials will cost £4 per unit and suppliers will be paid in the month *after* the purchase.

All unit sales are on credit. Debtors are expected to pay in the month *following* their purchase. £10 000 was deposited in the business bank account on 1 July.

TASK A:

A schedule of payments for the six months ending 31 December 1990 and a cash budget to cover the same period.

TASK B:

An operating budget which will show the trading and profit and loss forecast for the six months ending to 31 December 1990 and a forecast balance sheet as on 31 December 1990.

Note: Closing stock to be valued at £11.50 per unit.

TASK C:

A statement which briefly analyses the cash budget.

(BTEC National)

6 Clare Jones must submit a six month cash budget plan and forecast final accounts for her bank manager. The details are as follows:

a) Opening cash balance £12 000 to be used as her business bank account. She also has a motor van valued £5000 to be used in the business.
b) Her production (in units) per month is as follows:

Jul	*Aug*	*Sept*	*Oct*	*Nov*	*Dec*
700	720	760	680	700	750

c) Direct materials used in production will cost £10 per unit, payable in the month of production.
d) Direct labour will cost £18 per unit payable in the month of production.
e) Variable overheads will cost £5 per unit payable half in the month of production and half in the following month.
f) Sales per unit will be £50. Estimates sales are:

Jul	*Aug*	*Sept*	*Oct*	*Nov*	*Dec*
300	700	720	750	800	800

Debtors are expected to pay in the month after the sale.

g) Fixed costs are estimated at £1250 per month, payable each month.
h) Machinery costing £20 000 is to be paid for, 50 per cent in August and 50 per cent in September.
i) The bank loan expected, £10 000 over five years, should be through in August.
j) Personal drawings to be £600 per month.
k) Depreciation of machinery at 25 per cent per annum, the van is revalued to £2000. The interest of £175 per month is accrued from 1 September.

REQUIRED:

a) A schedule of payments and a cash budget for the six months to 31 December. The closing value of stock is to be calculated on the factory cost of £33 per unit.
b) A budgeted profit and loss account for the period of six months to 31 December and a balance sheet as at that date.

7 The following information relates to a forecast for Jim Smith, of revenue and costs for the year ending 31 December:

Sales target is expected to reach 35 000 units.
Selling price per unit, £8.00

Costs forecast:	£
Direct materials	1.50 per unit
Direct labour	2.00 per unit
Factory variables	1.25 per unit
Distribution variables	1.75 per unit
Factory fixed cost	28 500 per annum
Administrative fixed cost	15 000 per annum

Stock of finished goods at 31 December to be valued at the factory cost per unit.

The production target is 38 000 units.

REQUIRED:

a) A forecast of the manufacturing cost based on 38 000 units produced in the year to 31 December.
b) A forecast of the trading and profit and loss account for the year ending 31 December.
c) The mark-up and margins of profit based on the factory cost on 31 December (as percentages).

(AEB)

8 Jones is a teacher of accounting and he has decided to produce a book of accounting exercises. He has enlisted the help of his senior class and the headteacher has kindly agreed to the use of school typing and duplicating facilities.

For the first year target production is 5000 books and target sales 4900 books. The senior class agreed to be responsible for sales in return for a fixed fee of £80 and a further 5p for each book sold.

The additional forecasts covering the year ending 31 May 1988 were:

Materials
Paper and stencils £500 for the 5000 books.
Cover 3p per book.
Binding 10p per book.

Direct labour
Typing of stencils 50p each (50 stencils required, first year).
Duplication 10p per book.
Binding 15p per book.

Fixed expense of £75 to be paid to the school fund for use of typewriters, duplicating and binding equipment used in producing the books.

Estimated stock on 31 May 1988: 100 books to be valued at factory cost. The selling price per book is to be determined by adding 50 per cent to the factory cost of finished output.

REQUIRED:

a) the forecast manufacturing account showing both prime cost and factory cost of goods manufactured;
b) the forecast trading and profit and loss account.

(AEB)

9 Julie Watt has started her own factory producing toy trains. Her production target for the year is 20 000 and she hopes to achieve a sales target of 90 per cent of her output.

The additional forecasts she has made are as follows:

	£
Direct materials	2.5 per unit
Direct labour	2.0 per unit
Factory variables	0.5 per unit
Fixed factory cost	12 000 per annum
Variable selling and distribution costs	1.75 per unit
Office overheads	4 500 per annum

Julie will determine a selling price by a *margin* of $33\frac{1}{3}$ per cent (one third), based on her factory cost.

REQUIRED:

a) A forecast manufacturing account for the year. Stock unsold is to be valued at factory cost per unit.
b) A forecast trading and profit and loss account for the year.
c) A statement to clearly define the difference between fixed and variable costs and its importance to business.

(AEB)

CHAPTER

26 The trial balance and its limitations

- *Why is the trial balance not a foolproof system in checking the double-entry principle?*

Introduction

In Chapter 5, the trial balance was seen as a checking device of the ledger system. It is not an account in itself, merely a listing of all the relevant ledger accounts in their respective debit and credit balances. If the totals should agree, then it may be assumed that ledger recording has been correct. Yet it is not a foolproof system. Are the ledger accounts 100 per cent correct? If a computer program is used, the input of transactions are virtually certain to have a built-in double-entry system to ensure that the trial balance does balance. Yet even so, errors can still be made within the system and the trial balance will still balance, failing to disclose any discrepancy between the total debits and credits. As a checking device, the trial balance has its limitations.

Errors in the accounting system

Essentially, there are five basic type of errors which the trial balance fails to disclose. These are:

an error of original entry
an error of omission
an error of principle
an error of commission
an error of compensation.

An error of original entry

This refers to an error which may have been made in an original document such as an invoice or credit note. For example in the sales invoice to J Jack:

	£
Sales (net)	350.00
Vat (15%)	42.50
	392.50

Error: Vat should be £52.50

The invoice has been sent, the entry is already recorded.

Double entry:

Debit	J Jack (debtor)	£392.50	
Credit	Sales		£350.00
	Vat		£42.50

Both debit and credit entries equal the same value and therefore the trial balance could not disclose the error in Vat.

If a person such as an auditor, cross-checking the accounts, found the error in Vat, the correction in the ledgers would be:

Double entry:

Debit	J Jack (debtor)	£10.00	
Credit	Vat		£10.00

Ledger

		Debit £	*Credit* £	*Balance* £
J Jack account				
5/7	Sales	350.0		350.0 Dr
5/7	Vat	42.5		392.5
21/7	Vat (error)	10.0		402.5
Sales account				
5/7	J Jack			350.0 Cr
Vat account				
5/7	J Jack		42.5	42.5 Cr
21/7	J Jack (error)		10.0	52.5

An error of omission

This type of error is quite similar to that of the above example. It refers to a transaction that has been omitted altogether, neither the debit nor credit entries being made. Suppose for example, a credit note to a customer had somehow been misplaced and no entry had been made. Subsequently, by examining the sequence of credit note numbers, it was revealed that a credit note had not been recorded, and on investigation the note was discovered. In the credit note to H Smith:

	£
Goods returned (damaged)	20
Vat (15%)	3
	23

This information now needs to be recorded because no transaction has been entered in the books and the trial balance could not have disclosed it.

Double entry:

Debit	Returns inward	£20	
	Vat	£3	
Credit	H Smith		£23

Ledger

		Debit	Credit	Balance
		£	£	£
Returns inward account				
22/7	H Smith	20		20 Dr
Vat account				
22/7	H Smith	3		3 Dr
H Smith account				
22/7	Returns in		20	
	Vat		3	23 Cr

An error of principle

This is a type of error concerning posting a transaction to the wrong group of accounts. The double entry is correct as far as debit and credit goes, but the choice of account is in error. For example:

	£
Purchased equipment from Office Services Ltd	500
Vat (15%)	75
	575

The entry was posted to the purchases account instead of the office equipment account. An *expense account* instead of an *asset account*.

Double entry:

Debit	Purchases	£500	
	Vat	£75	
Credit	Office Services Ltd		£575

On cross-checking the accounts, the accountant located the error and made the necessary correcting entry. The error of principle was that an expense (purchases) was wrongly debited with £500 which clearly should have been debited to an asset account (office equipment). The correction would be:

Double entry:

Debit	Office equipment	£500	
Credit	Purchases		£500

Ledger

		Debit	Credit	Balance
		£	£	£
Purchases account				
5/7	Office Services Ltd	500		500 Dr
15/7	Office equipment		500	—
Vat account				
5/7	Office Services Ltd	75		75 Dr
Office Services Ltd account				
5/7	Purchases		575	575 Cr
Office equipment account				
15/7	Purchases	500		500 Dr

An error of commission

This is a similar error to that of an error of principle, with the exception that, although the transaction has been posted to the wrong account, it has been posted within the same group. For example:

A gas bill of £75, paid by cheque, has been wrongly posted to the stationery account.

Double entry:

Debit	Stationery	£75	
Credit	Bank		£75

Again, both debit and credit entries record the same value and the trial balance would fail to disclose the error. On finding such an error, the correcting entry would be:

Double entry:

Debit	Light and heat	£75	
Credit	Stationery		£75

Ledger

		Debit £	*Credit* £	*Balance* £
Stationery account				
10/7	Bank	75		75 Dr
22/7	Light and heat		75	—
Light and heat account				
22/7	Stationery	75		75 Dr
Bank account				
10/7	Stationery		75	75 Dr

An error of compensation

This type of error refers to the *same* mistake made on *both* sides to the transaction, thereby ensuring that both debit and credit sides are equal. For example:

A cheque was sent to H Brown (creditor) in settlement of his account, £359, but was entered incorrectly as £395, an error of £36.

Double entry:

Debit	H Brown (creditor)	£395	
Credit	Bank		£395

Because both debit and credit entries are equal, the trial balance could not disclose this 'compensating' error. To correct this mistake, the entry is:

Double entry:

Debit	Bank	£36	
Credit	H Brown		£36

Ledger

		Debit £	*Credit* £	*Balance* £
H Brown account				
1/7	Balance			359 Cr
7/7	Bank	395		36 Dr
21/7	Bank		36	—
Bank account				
7/7	H Brown		395	395 Cr
21/7	H Brown	36		359

All these five basic types of error will not be disclosed by the trial balance. It is therefore not a foolproof system and cannot guarantee the absolute accuracy of the ledger.

Example

The following information relates to the accounts of George Ralston on 28 February 1990:

George Ralston–
Trial balance as on 28 February 1990

	Dr	*Cr*
	£	£
Bank	3 010	
Premises	12 000	
Equipment	3 000	
Mortgage		9 500
Vat		215
Capital		10 000
Wages	125	
Light and heat	115	
Purchases	750	
Sales		1 035
Creditor: J Jones		250
Debtor: R Smith	2 000	
	21 000	21 000

The accountant, checking the figures at the end of the month, located a number of errors which the trial balance has failed to disclose:

a) The purchase of goods for resale £800, had wrongly been posted to the equipment account.
b) A sales invoice to R Smith had omitted to charge £15 Vat.
c) A telephone bill £35, had in error been posted to light and heat.
d) A purchase invoice to J Jones £200 + Vat 15 per cent had not yet been entered in the books.
e) Wages on the paysheet were £152 and were entered as £125 in the ledger.
f) A gas bill of £45, paid by cheque, had not been recorded.

REQUIRED:

a) For each of the above, state the type of error which was located by the accountant.
b) Make the necessary correcting entries in the ledger.
c) Extract a new trial balance, incorporating the corrections, as on 28 February 1990.

1 *Type of error located*

a) An error of principle.
b) An error of original entry.
c) An error of commission.
d) An error of omission.
e) An error of compensation.
f) An error of omission.

2 **Ledger entries**

		Debit £	*Credit* £	*Balance* £
Purchases account				
28/2	Balance			750 Dr
	Equipment	800		1 550
	J Jones	200		1 750
Equipment account				
28/2	Balance			3 000 Dr
	Purchases		800	2 200
Vat account				
28/2	Balance			215 Cr
	R Smith		15	230
	J Jones	30		200
R Smith account				
28/2	Balance			2 000 Dr
	Vat	15		2 015
J Jones account				
28/2	Balance			250 Cr
	Purchases		200	
	Vat		30	480
Wages account				
28/2	Balance			125 Dr
	Bank	27		152
Light and heat account				
28/2	Balance			115 Dr
	Telephone		35	80
	Bank	45		125
Telephone account				
28/2	Light and heat	35		35 Dr

(Continues)

		Debit £	*Credit* £	*Balance* £
Bank account				
28/2	Balance			3 010 Dr
	Wages		27	2 983
	Light and heat		45	2 938

3 **Trial balance as on 28 February 1990 (reconstructed)**

	Dr £	*Cr* £
Bank	2 938	
Premises	12 000	
Equipment	2 200	
Mortgage		9 500
Vat		200
Capital		10 000
Wages	152	
Light and heat	125	
Telephone	35	
Purchases	1 750	
Sales		1 035
Creditor: J Jones		480
Debtor: R Smith	2 015	
	21 215	21 215

Summary

1 The function of a trial balance is to check the arithmetical accuracy of the double-entry principle.

2 If a trial balance does balance, that is, Total debits = Total credits, it is likely that transactions in the ledgers have been recorded correctly.

3 The trial balance however, is not a foolproof system. It fails to disclose certain types of error. Basically these are: errors of original entry; errors of omission; errors of principle; errors of commission; and errors of compensation.

QUESTIONS

1 The following errors have been found in the books of K Jackson on 31 March:

a) A sum of £550 has been included in the wages account for repairs to the owner's property, not the business's.

b) The purchase of an office typewriter for £180 has been posted to the purchases account.
c) A cheque from R Smith (debtor) £200 has been posted to the account of J Smith, another customer.
d) An invoice from the Wessex Water Authority for £85 has just been discovered and no entries have yet been made.
e) A purchase invoice from K Welland had £7.50 Vat included but this had been excluded in both supplier's and Vat accounts.

REQUIRED:

a) List the type of errors which have been found.
b) Explain briefly why the trial balance would have failed to disclose them.
c) State the relevant double entries required to correct the above errors.

2 What is the role of the trial balance? Why is it not a foolproof system? Explain your answer by using your own examples to clarify your meaning.

3 The following errors have been discovered by J Jones on 31 July:
a) Purchases of £180 + 15 per cent Vat had been posted to David Brown Ltd instead of Joe Brown Ltd in the purchases ledger.
b) New office equipment costing £2250 bought on credit from Nelson's Ltd has been entered in the purchases journal and included in the purchases account.
c) Sales totalling £185 had been posted in error as £158 both to the customer's and sales accounts.
d) An electricity bill for £36, paid by cheque, had not gone through the books.

REQUIRED:

Make the necessary correcting entries in the ledger of J Jones.

4 The following errors have been located in the books of Jack Jones as on 31 March:
a) A supplier in the returns outward day book, Jane Rawlins, £20 + 15 per cent Vat, had not yet been entered in the ledgers.
b) A sales invoice of £220 + 15 per cent Vat had been misplaced, no entries having been made. It was addressed to Sam Jones.
c) A purchase invoice of £317 from Rebecca Smith had in error been posted as £371.
d) A private purchase of £435 by the owner, had been included as a business purchase.
e) A commission of £42 received by Jack Jones had not yet been recorded.
f) A purchase of equipment of £200 had been entered under purchases.
g) A sale of office furniture, £300 had been entered in the sales account.

REQUIRED:

a) Show the correcting entries for the above entries.
b) Although all the entries are not disclosed by the trial balance would any of these affect profit? Comment on your findings.

CHAPTER

27 The journal and use of the suspense account

- *Why use the journal?*
- *When is a suspense account used?*
- *What is the link between the trial balance, suspense account and journal?*

Introduction

The function of the journal is to provide an original entry for those type of transactions which do not readily 'fit into' the other subsidiary books such as the sales and purchases journal and the cash book. In the early days of accounting, the journal was the only book of prime entry in use. All financial transactions were entered in the journal prior to posting to the ledger system. As accounting developed and was applied to different kinds of business organisations, the use of the journal alone was inadequate. Many repetitious types of entry such as sales and purchases required separate journals to be used.

The use of the journal

There is still a place for the journal as a record of prime entry even though direct entries could be made to the ledger. The more common uses of the journal include the following:

the correction of errors,
the opening entries in a new accounting period,
the purchase of fixed assets on credit,
the transfer of balances between accounts, for example, writing off a bad debt or transferring revenue and expense accounts to trading and profit and loss account,
the making of balance-day adjustments to the final accounts, for example, providing for depreciation or for bad debts.

The presentation of the journal reflects the double-entry principle; that for every debit entry there is a corresponding credit entry. Thus the journal has two columns, precisely to emphasise this point. The debit entry is always recorded first and the credit entry, on a separate line, second. The credit entry is also slightly indented for effect. A brief comment usually accompanies a transaction, offering some very limited explanation why the entry has been made.

Example

Bought £5000 of plant and machinery on credit from Dave McKee Ltd.

Journal

		Debit £	*Credit* £
1/7	Plant and machinery,		
	Dave McKee Ltd	5 000	
	Bought fixed asset on credit over five years		5 000

Example using the journal

In Chapter 26, a number of errors were not disclosed by the trial balance. These errors could have all been *journalised* first, as a record of prime entry, prior to ledger posting. The errors disclosed in the books of George Ralston, 28 February 1990 were:

a) The purchase of goods for resale £800, had wrongly been posted to the equipment account.
b) A sales invoice to R Smith had omitted to charge £15 Vat.
c) A telephone bill £35, had in error, been posted to light and heat account.
d) A purchase invoice to J Jones £200 + Vat 15 per cent, had not yet been entered in the books.
e) Wages entry on the paysheet was £152 and was entered as £125 in the ledger.
f) A gas bill of £45, paid by cheque, had not been recorded.

REQUIRED:

Make the necessary journal entries to correct the above errors. Posting to the ledger has already been made in Chapter 26.

Journal – G Ralston

		Debit £	*Credit* £
Feb 28	Purchases	800	
	Equipment		800
	(Error of principle, an expense posted as an asset)		
28	R Smith (debtor)	15	
	Vat		15
	(Error of original entry, invoice omitted Vat)		
28	Telephone	35	
	Light and heat		35
	(Error of commission, telephone bill charged to light and heat)		

(Continues)

		Debit	Credit
		£	£
28	Purchases	200	
	Vat	30	
	J Jones		230
	(Error of omission, invoice from supplier temporarily mislaid)		
28	Wages	27	
	Bank		27
	(Error of compensation; wages £152 misread as £125)		
28	Light and heat	45	
	Bank		45
	(Error of omission, gas bill temporarily mislaid)		

Further examples using the journal in the books of G Ralston are:

a) On 1 February, G Ralston had the following accounts in his books:

 Premises, £12 000; Bank £2500; Equipment £2200; Stock £500; Debtors £1800; Mortgage £9500; Creditors £500.

 Make the appropriate journal entry, showing the capital of G Ralston.

b) On 28 February, G Ralston decided to write off £1000 of R Smith's account as 'bad' in response to Smith's financial difficulties.

c) On 28 February, G Ralston decided to depreciate his equipment by 20 per cent.

Journal – G Ralston

		Debit	Credit
		£	£
1/2	Premises	12 000	
	Bank	2 500	
	Equipment	2 200	
	Stock	500	
	Debtors	1 800	
	Mortgage		9 500
	Creditors		500
	Capital: G Ralston		10 000
	(Being assets, liabilities and capital of G Ralston at commencement of year)		

(Continues)

		Debit £	Credit £
28/2	Bad debts	1 000	
	R Smith		1 000
	(£1000 written off as 'bad')		
28/2	Profit and loss depreciation	440	
	Provision for depreciation of equipment		440
	(Equipment depreciated by 20 per cent)		

The use of the suspense account

The purpose of using a suspense account is to ensure that the trial balance *will agree* until the error or errors have been located and corrected. When errors produce an incorrect trial balance, where total debits fail to agree with total credits, the suspense account may be used to make up the difference between the two sides.

In computer-based accounts, there is usually a suspense account written into the trial balance in the event that the program cannot find an appropriate debit or credit account to enter.

If a suspense account is necessary, it is entered in the nominal ledger, with the balance taken from the trial balance. The account is written off when the errors are located, using the journal to make the relevant entries.

The following is an example of using the suspense account in conjunction with the trial balance and journal. It also shows how to correct the profit and loss account and balance sheet, if these had already been prepared.

Example

The following represent the accounts of G Balfour as on 30 June:

Trial balance as on 30 June

	Debit £	Credit £
Bank	1 245	
Stock (30/6)	3 400	
Premises	20 000	
Furniture and fittings	900	
Wages and salaries	5 400	
Office expenses	1 060	
Purchases	23 900	
Sales		31 900

(Continues)

	Debit	*Credit*
	£	£
Drawings	3 800	
Debtors	2 600	
Creditors		3 230
Capital (1/6)		24 900
Suspense account		2 275
	62 305	62 305

The net profit for the month of June was £1540 before it was subsequently discovered that the following errors had been revealed on 30 June:

a) The bank account was overdrawn by £1245.
b) £200 drawn by G Balfour for his personal expenses had been charged to office expenses.
c) Purchases of £1000 on credit had not yet been recorded in the books.
d) The balance of £160 discount allowed had been omitted.
e) £2400 included under wages and £600 included under purchases represented, in error, figures which should have been included in premises.
f) The balance of £55 in cash, had also been omitted from the list of accounts.

REQUIRED:

1 Journal entries to make the necessary corrections to the above errors.
2 A suspense account in the ledger to show the effect of these entries.
3 A corrected profit and loss account and a balance sheet as on 30 June.

1 **Journal entries**

		Dr	*Cr*
		£	£
June 30	Suspense account	2 490	
	Bank account		2 490
30	Drawings account	200	
	Office expenses account		200
30	Purchases account	1 000	
	Creditors' account		1 000
30	Discount allowed account	160	
	Suspense account		160
30	Premises account	3 000	
	Wages and salaries account		2 400
	Purchases account		600
30	Cash account	55	
	Suspense account		55

2 **Suspense account**

Dr					*Cr*
		£			£
June 30	Bank	2 490	June 30	Trial balance	2 275
				Discount allowed	160
				Office cash	55
		2 490			2 490

3 **Profit and loss correction**

	£	£
Net profit (before errors)		1 540
Add		
Increases to profit:		
Office expenses	200	
Wages	2 400	
Purchases	600	3 200
		4 740
Less		
Decreases to profit:		
Purchases	1 000	
Discount allowed	160	1 160
Net profit (adjusted)		3 580

Balance sheet as at 30 June

	£	£	£
FIXED ASSETS			
Premises	23 000		
Fixtures and fittings	900		23 900
CURRENT ASSETS			
Stock	3 400		
Debtors	2 600		
Bank	—		
Cash	55	6 055	

(Continues)

	£	£	£
Less			
CURRENT LIABILITIES			
Creditors	4 230		
Bank overdraft	1 245	5 475	
Working capital			580
			24 480
FINANCED BY:			
Capital	24 900		
+ Net profit	3 580	28 480	
− Drawings		4 000	24 480

The location of errors

If the trial balance fails to balance the first thing to do is to find out the difference between the total debits and total credits. It is then a matter of checking all the relevant places. Remember that the trial balance has its limitations and that some errors could have been made which the trial balance could not have disclosed.

If control accounts are used and these have been cross-checked with the personal ledgers (sales and purchases ledgers), it may then be assumed that all debtors' and creditors' accounts are correct.

It will then be necessary to comb through the nominal ledger to check for any arithmetical inaccuracies or any obvious errors in double entry. For example, a cheque from a customer posted on the debit side instead of the credit, in his account, or a discount received posted on the debit side instead of the credit, etc.

It may be necessary to look back to the subsidiary books such as the journals and cash book to ensure that the correct figures were posted to the relevant accounts in the ledgers. It may have been an incorrect addition to the columns of figures. Some item in the cash book may have been entered on the wrong side, for example, a payment for a receipt or vice versa.

Therefore, before the entry of any figures to the accounting system, they should be absolutely arithmetically correct and then the precise debit and credit entries made to the relevant accounts.

Summary

1 The journal is a subsidiary book of prime entry to record those type of transactions outside the scope of the other journals and cash book.

2 It is used to record correction of errors, opening entries in a new financial period, the purchase of fixed assets on credit, the transfer of balances and adjustments to the final accounts.

3 The format of the journal reflects the double-entry principle in that there are two columns, one for the debit entry, the other for the credit.

4 The suspense account may be used as a temporary device where there is a discrepancy between total debits and total credits in the trial balance. It should be written off as soon as the errors have been located.

5 The location of errors may involve a thorough checking of accounts either in the ledgers or the subsidiary books.

QUESTIONS

1 Draft the journal entries required to correct the following errors discovered on 12 July:

a) Purchases of £170 credited in error to W Brown instead of Willis & Brown.
b) New office equipment costing £2000 had been bought on credit. The item was entered in the purchases journal and included in the purchases total.
c) J Elliot, a customer, had paid his account taking £7 cash discount which he was not entitled to do. This had been entered in the books.
d) An account of £20 for repairs to the owner's car (private use) had been posted to delivery expenses account.
e) An electricity bill for £42 had not yet been entered in the books and had been paid by cheque the previous month.

(RSA)

2 The following trial balance relating to Len Shackleton's business, failed to agree. One of the major causes of this disagreement appeared to be the failure to post the following day book totals to the ledger: purchases £1562; sales £2941; returns inward £98; and returns outward £46. In addition, the petty cash balance £18 was omitted and some of the items inadvertently placed on the wrong side of the trial balance.

Trial balance of Len Shackleton as at 31 May 1983

	Debit	*Credit*
	£	£
Premises	25 000	
Purchases	1 398	
Sales		3 975
Bank overdraft	621	
Discount allowed		45
Rates	91	
Lighting and heating	96	
Bank charges	14	
Stock at 1 May 1983	823	
Debtors	960	
Creditors		840
Capital		21 682
	29 003	26 542

REQUIRED:

a) Preparation of a corrected trial balance as at 31 May 1983.
b) i) Two types of error which would not prevent trial balance totals from agreeing.
   ii) An explanation, using an example in each case, why the trial balance totals would still be in agreement, despite the existence of such errors.

(AEB Nov '84)

3 The following information has been extracted from the trial balance of J Smith as on 30 June:

	Dr	*Cr*
	£	£
Suspense account		247

Subsequently the following errors were found:

a) Goods £285 to R Smith had been posted to J Smith in error.
b) Accounting equipment sold for £600 credited to sales account.
c) Cash discount of £8 allowed to J Jones and credited to him, but no entry was made to the discount account.
d) The addition of the sales day book was undercast by £200.
e) Salaries accrued £55 at the end of the previous year had not been brought forward to the new accounting period.
f) A sales invoice of £275 had been misplaced. No entries had been made.
g) A standing order £55 for insurance had been omitted from the cash book.

REQUIRED:

a) Journal entries necessary to correct the books.
b) The suspense account entries.

(Institute of Bankers)

4 D McForan's trial balance, extracted at 31 October 1984, failed to agree and the difference was recorded in a suspense account. In early November the following errors were discovered:

1 the sales day book had been overcast by £220;
2 goods valued at £121 returned by A Wilkinson had been correctly recorded in the returns inward account but had not been entered in the personal account;
3 a payment for repairs to the motor van £41 had been entered in the vehicle repairs account as £14;
4 when balancing the account of B Heath in the ledger, the credit balance had been brought down in error as £32 instead of £23;
5 the total of the discounts received column of the cash book £120 had been incorrectly debited to the discounts allowed account and no entry had been made in the discounts received account.

REQUIRED:

a) i) Journal entries to correct each of the above errors (narrations are *not* required).
   ii) A suspense account indicating the nature and extent of the original difference in the books.

b) Name and explain *four* types of error that would not affect the agreement of the trial balance. Illustrate your answer by giving an example of *each* type of error.
(AEB Nov '85)

5 The draft trial balance of James McLippie and Son as at 30 April 1986 did not agree and the difference was posted to a suspense account. Subsequent investigation of the accounts revealed the following errors of £1352 debit.

1 The discount received column in the cash book had been overcast by £100.
2 J Stanley, a customer, had not been credited with £8 discount although this had been correctly entered in the cash book.
3 The sales book had been overcast by £900.
4 An invoice made out (correctly) for £45 in respect of sales made to H Purcell had been recorded in the sales book as £54. (This is quite apart from the error in the sales book referred to above.)
5 The purchases book had been undercast by £360.
6 Goods returned from J Blow, a customer, had been recorded in the returns inward book as £108. In fact, the value of the goods returned had been subsequently agreed with the customer at £88 but no adjustment had been made in the accounting records.
7 Value added tax (at 15 per cent) amounting to £15 collected on cash sales of £100 had not been entered in the Vat column in the cash book. Instead the sales had been recorded in the cash column as £115.

REQUIRED:

a) Prepare journal entries to show how the above errors would be corrected.
b) The suspense account entries.
c) If the profit had been calculated at £13 564 before the errors were disclosed, what is the profit for the year after correcting the above errors?

(AAT)

6 *Situation*

XYZ Co had prepared its trading, profit and loss account and balance sheet which included a suspense account of £188.

The balances were as follows on 31 December 1985:

	Dr	*Cr*
	£	£
Equipment	1 406	
Furniture and fittings	826	
Stock	1 218	
Debtors, creditors	1 548	1 200
Bank	145	
Capital		5 339
Drawings	2 000	
Profit		792
Suspense	188	
	7 331	7 331

On checking the records, your researches reveal:

a) A purchase invoice for £64 had not been entered in the books.
b) A desk valued £82 had been wrongly debited to repairs of fittings account instead of furniture and fittings.
c) The bank account should have been entered as a credit balance.
d) Interest charges of £50 had not been included in the cash book and no posting had been made to the ledger.
e) The sales account balance had been overstated by £378 in error.
f) A credit note from a supplier of £110 had been entered correctly in the returns book but as £10 in the supplier's account.

REQUIRED:

a) Journal entries to correct each of the above errors (no need for narration).
b) A suspense account showing the appropriate correcting errors.
c) A statement showing the revised profit for the year ended 31 December 1985.
d) A brief comment regarding the effectiveness of the trial balance as a testing device.

(Institute of Bankers)

7 *Situation*

The trial balance of J Sharp, a retailer, does not balance. You are asked to look through his accounts and subsequently you do find the errors below. The trial balance of the proprietor on 30 June was as follows:

	Dr	*Cr*
	£	£
Premises	20 000	
Motor van	500	
Equipment	2 100	
Stock	1 860	
Debtors	675	
Creditors		1 155
Capital, J Sharp		12 500
Bank		455
Sales		35 750
Purchases	20 195	
General expenses	1 250	
Wages	3 970	
Suspense		690
	50 550	50 550

Errors found:

a) A piece of equipment £500 had wrongly been posted to purchases account.
b) A gas bill of £85 had been paid but had not gone through any of the books.
c) Discount allowed £68 had not been posted to the ledger.
d) Sales were undercast by £800.

e) A cheque from a debtor (R Smith) £150 had been recorded as £105 in his account but correctly in the corresponding account.
f) The total from the returns inward account £87 had not been posted to the ledger.

TASK A:

Prepare suitable journal entries to correct the above errors and write up the suspense account.

TASK B:

Prepare a corrected trial balance for J Sharp as on 30 June.

TASK C:

State which of the above errors were not found by the trial balance and explain briefly to J Sharp why such a device has its limitations.

(AEB)

8 An extract of the trial balance was taken from the books of Simon Buckley on 30 June:

	Dr	*Cr*
	£	£
Premises	13 000	
Sales		38 600
Purchases	22 500	
Equipment	4 200	
General expenses	150	
Discounts	40	85
Returns	130	420
Suspense		915
	40 020	40 020

The following errors were located:
a) Sales were undercast by £315 in the sales journal.
b) General expenses £85 had been overlooked when posting from the cash book.
c) Purchases had been overcast in the purchases journal by £500.
d) Discount from suppliers £90 had not been posted to the relevant discount account.
e) Returns to suppliers £95 had been posted to the personal accounts but not the nominal account.

REQUIRED:
a) Prepare the appropriate journal entries to correct the above errors.
b) Prepare the suspense account.
c) If the calculated net profit was £12 420 before the above errors were located, compute the corrected net profit.

(Institute of Bankers)

CHAPTER

28 The sale and purchase of a business

- *How are accounts recorded when a business is sold?*
- *What part does the journal play?*

Introduction

The journal may be usefully employed as a book of original entry to record the sale of a business in the vendor's books and also to record the purchase of a business, from the vendor, in the buyer's books.

The sale price of a business is dependent on, and influenced by, a number of factors including the market value of the assets for sale, the demand for the particular type of business, the general economic conditions prevailing at the time and a price agreed for goodwill (the good name and reputation of the business).

The prospective buyer will want to make a study of the financial accounts of the business he wishes to purchase. He would want to study the final accounts of the vendor over a number of years and certainly the last three financial periods. Is the business a profitable venture? Has it got potential? How keen is the purchaser to buy? These are significant questions which will help determine the final purchase price.

Estate agents normally act on behalf of a vendor's business, particularly where an assessment of property values are concerned. The agents assess the value of the business's assets and in conjunction with the seller, calculate a suitable figure for goodwill. A further consideration concerns the liabilities of the business. Will the buyer take on the liabilities, or will the seller settle the accounts himself?

Over recent years, the demand for certain type of businesses has been high. Post offices have sold well because there is usually a good level of demand for them. On the other hand, some small high street businesses have suffered because of the stiff competition from the large retail organisations and consequently their value has fallen.

The sale of a business in the vendor's books

Mike Walker, owner of a small business selling gifts and general items, decided to sell and retire. On 1 June his balance sheet showed his financial position to be as follows:

M Walker –
Balance sheet as on 1 June

	£	£	£
FIXED ASSETS			
Premises	50 000		
Equipment	2 000		52 000
CURRENT ASSETS			
Stock	5 000		
Bank	3 000		
Debtors	1 000	9 000	
CURRENT LIABILITIES			
Creditors		5 000	4 000
			56 000
LONG-TERM LIABILITIES			
Mortgage			14 000
			42 000
CAPITAL: M Walker			42 000

The estate agents, Goadsby & Harding, had already updated the value of the property to £50 000 and the net assets, *excluding the bank account of £3000*, had a value of £39 000. This represented the net worth of M Walker, less his bank account.

The purchase was negotiated and M Walker agreed to sell the business to P Jackson for a sum of £50 000. The value of *goodwill* was therefore assessed at £11 000, (£50 000 – £39 000).

All the accounts in the books of M Walker would be closed off against the *realisation account*, except for the bank and capital accounts. This took place on 21 June.

M Walker's (the vendor's) Journal

		Debit	*Credit*
		£	*£*
21/6	Realisation account*	58 000	
	Premises		50 000
	Equipment		2 000
	Stock		5 000
	Debtors		1 000
	Assets closed off on sale of business to P Jackson	58 000	58 000
21/6	Creditors	5 000	
	Mortgage	14 000	
	Realisation account		19 000
	Liabilities closed off on sale of business to P Jackson		
21/6	P Jackson (buyer)	50 000	
	Realisation account		50 000
	(Being the agreed sum to be paid by the buyer)		
21/6	Realisation account	11 000	
	Capital account		11 000
	(Being price agreed for goodwill)		

NOTE

*The realisation account is used to close off the accounts of the business against the price it will sell for.

Ledger – M Walker

		Debit	*Credit*	*Balance*
		£	*£*	*£*
Premises account				
1/6	Balance			50 000 Dr
21/6	Realisation		50 000	—
Equipment account				
1/6	Balance			2 000 Dr
21/6	Realisation		2 000	—
Stock account				
1/6	Balance			5 000 Dr
21/6	Realisation		5 000	—

(Continues)

		Debit £	Credit £	Balance £
Debtors' account				
1/6	Balance			1 000 Dr
21/6	Realisation		1 000	—
Creditors' account				
1/6	Balance			5 000 Cr
21/6	Realisation	5 000		—
Mortgage account				
1/6	Balance			14 000 Cr
21/6	Realisation	14 000		—
Bank account				
1/6	Balance			3 000 Dr
Capital account: M Walker				
1/6	Balance			42 000 Cr
21/6	Realisation		11 000	53 000
P Jackson (Buyer)				
21/6	Realisation	50 000		50 000 Dr
Realisation account				
21/6	Premises	50 000		
	Equipment	2 000		
	Stock	5 000		
	Debtors	1 000		
	Capital (profit)	11 000		69 000 Dr
	P Jackson		50 000	
	Creditors		5 000	
	Mortgage		14 000	—

NOTES

1 All the accounts in M Walker's books have been closed off to realisation account, except the bank and capital accounts. £11 000 has been credited to his capital account as the 'profit' from goodwill.

2 The realisation account acts something like 'the disposal of the business accounts', closing off the relevant assets and liabilities, using the realisation as the corresponding double entry.

Final payment by the buyer

When the buyer eventually settles the purchase on completion day, his cheque will be debited to the bank account and credited to the buyer's account, thereby clearing the debt.

The cheque for £50 000 was settled on 30 June. The final closing off of the accounts would be:

Ledger

		Debit £	Credit £	Balance £
Bank account				
1/6	Balance			3 000 Dr
30/6	P Jackson (buyer)	50 000		53 000
P Jackson account				
21/6	Realisation	50 000		50 000 Dr
30/6	Bank		50 000	—

The final double entry would be to withdraw the £53 000 from the business bank account and debit this to the capital account. This last transaction effectively closes off the business:

Ledger

		Debit £	Credit £	Balance £
Bank account				
1/6	Balance			3 000 Dr
30/6	P Jackson	50 000		53 000
30/6	Capital		53 000	—
Capital account: M Walker				
1/6	Balance			42 000 Cr
21/6	Realisation		11 000	53 000
30/6	Bank	53 000		—

NOTE

Walker received a total of £53 000 by selling his business. His net worth in the balance sheet was £42 000. He profited by £11 000 because of the goodwill value.

The purchase of a business in the buyer's books

When Peter Jackson bought the shop from his old friend, Mike Walker, for the sum agreed, £50 000, he added to his property, equipment, stock and debtors. He also took over the responsibility for the payment of debt to creditors and the outstanding mortgage on the property. Part of the agreed price was the sum of £11 000 for goodwill.

Peter Jackson already had a business and with this new acquisition, he will be able to merge the values of the two businesses together.

The following figures relate to his balance sheet as on 21 June:

P Jackson –
Balance sheet as on 21 June

	£	£	£
FIXED ASSETS			
Premises	85 000		
Equipment	3 500		
Motor vehicle	6 500		95 000
CURRENT ASSETS			
Stock	8 600		
Debtors	3 750		
Bank	42 500		
Cash	250	55 100	
CURRENT LIABILITIES			
Creditors		4 700	
Net current assets			50 400
LONG-TERM LIABILITIES			145 400
Mortgage			48 400
			97 000
CAPITAL: P Jackson			97 000

On 21 June, when the buyer and seller exchanged contracts on the purchase of the business, P Jackson would enter the details in his journal. M Walker would be credited with £50 000 because this would represent the sum owing to him until the sum was paid. The journal entry is as follows:

P Jackson's (the buyer's) journal

		Debit	*Credit*
		£	£
21/6	Premises	50 000	
	Equipment	2 000	
	Stock	5 000	
	Debtors	1 000	

(Continues)

	Debit	Credit
	£	£
Goodwill	11 000	
Creditors		5 000
Mortgage		14 000
M Walker (vendor)		50 000
	69 000	69 000
(Being the purchase of a business from M Walker)		

Before P Jackson enters these in his books, he may decide to revalue some of the above items. On 30 June, the completion date of the purchase, when he hands over the £50 000 to M Walker, Jackson decided to:

a) Mark-down the value of the equipment to £1500 and the stock to £4000.
b) Increase the value of the property to £60 000.

How would this affect the value of goodwill?

P Jackson's journal

		Debit	Credit
		£	£
30/6	Premises	60 000	
	Equipment	1 500	
	Stock	4 000	
	Debtors	1 000	
	Goodwill	2 500	
	Creditors		5 000
	Mortgage		14 000
	M Walker		50 000
		69 000	69 000
	(Being the revaluation of assets on acquisition)		
30/6	M Walker	50 000	
	Bank		50 000
	(Settlement of purchase of business)		

NOTE

The new figure for goodwill is simply the total of the revaluation of the assets less the liabilities and purchase price agreed, (£69 000 − £66 500).

The journal entries would be posted to the relevant accounts in P Jackson's ledger, merging the two businesses together. The balance sheet extracted on 30 June would appear as follows:

P Jackson –
Balance sheet as on 30 June

	£	£	£
FIXED ASSETS			
Premises	85 000		
+ New	60 000		145 000
Equipment	3 500		
+ New	1 500		5 000
Motor vehicle	6 500		6 500
			156 500
Goodwill			2 500
			159 000
CURRENT ASSETS			
Stock	8 600		
+ New	4 000	12 600	
Debtors	3 750		
+ New	1 000	4 750	
Bank		—	
Cash		250	
		17 600	
CURRENT LIABILITIES			
Creditors	4 700		
+ New	5 000		
	9 700		
Bank overdraft			
(£42 500 – £50 000)	7 500	17 200	
Net current assets			400
			159 400
LONG-TERM LIABILITIES			
Mortgage	48 400		
+ New	14 000		62 400
			97 000
CAPITAL: P Jackson			97 000

Summary

1 The journal is used as the book of original entry for the recording of the sale or purchase of a business.

2 The realisation account is used to close off the assets and the liabilities of a business which has been sold. It acts as the double entry against the value of the net assets, including the goodwill price.

3 Any sum paid for goodwill is credited as 'profit' to the seller's capital account and the corresponding debit is in the realisation account.

4 On completion of the sale of the business, the final transactions include debiting the owner's capital to clear the account and crediting the appropriate asset(s) which the proprietor takes with him.

5 In the buyer's books, a journal entry is used to list the assets and liabilities acquired, including goodwill, if any. The vendor's account (seller) is credited with the agreed purchase price of the business. The buyer may wish to revalue any of the assets purchased and reassess the goodwill figure.

6 If the purchaser of a business already has an existing enterprise, the assets and liabilities acquired will be merged and a new balance sheet or journal entry can list these.

QUESTIONS

1 On 1 April 1990, J Jackson purchased the business of J Davies. It was agreed that Jackson should take over all the assets of the business with the exception of the bank account.

It was also agreed that the debtors should be allowed a 10 per cent provision against bad and doubtful debts. The equipment and motor vehicle should be depreciated by 20 per cent respectively.

An additional figure to be paid for goodwill was to be based on 10 per cent of the average annual sales over the last three years, which were: £65 000, £63 000 and £68 500.

Jackson was to finance the purchase by providing 50 per cent of the purchase price from his own personal funds and the balance from the bank as a fixed loan over a number of years.

The balance sheet of J Davies, on 1 April 1990, before negotiation, was as follows:

	£	£	£
FIXED ASSETS			
Premises	30 000		
Equipment	5 000		
Motor vehicle	1 000		36 000
CURRENT ASSETS			
Stock	4 500		
Debtors	3 500		
Bank	3 000	11 000	
CURRENT LIABILITIES			
Creditors		7 000	4 000
			40 000
FINANCED BY:			
Capital: J Davies			40 000

REQUIRED:

a) Show the journal entries in the books of the *buyer* as on 1 April, 1990.
b) If the completion date of the purchase was on 20 April 1990, show the journal entry in the books of the *buyer* on this date.
c) Prepare the opening balance sheet of J Jackson as on 20 April 1990.

2 A Donald, a sole trader, has arranged to sell his business to D Smith, already in business as a sole trader. The balance sheet of A Donald, on 1 January 1990 was as follows:

	£	£	£
FIXED ASSETS			
Premises	50 000		
Equipment	8 000		
Motor van	2 000		60 000
CURRENT ASSETS			
Stock	12 000		
Debtors	7 500		
Bank/cash	8 500	28 000	

(Continues)

	£	£	£
CURRENT LIABILITIES			
Creditors		8 000	20 000
			80 000
FINANCED BY:			
Capital: A Donald			80 000

D Smith has agreed to purchase the business for a sum of £85 000, although this does not include the bank/cash balance.

For the purpose of Smith's own records, she valued the premises at £65 000, equipment at £5000 and stock at £9000.

To finance the purchase, D Smith took out a loan at a fixed rate of interest for ten years for 80 per cent of the agreed purchase price. The balance is financed by her own business funds. The completion date was settled on as 25 January 1990.

The balance sheet of D Smith on 1 January 1990 was as follows:

	£	£	£
FIXED ASSETS			
Premises	20 000		
Equipment	5 000		25 000
CURRENT ASSETS			
Stock	5 000		
Debtors	2 000		
Bank	18 000	25 000	
CURRENT LIABILITIES			
Creditors		5 000	20 000
			45 000
CAPITAL: D Smith			45 000

REQUIRED:

a) The journal entries to show the purchase of the business in the books of D Smith both on 1 January and 25 January 1990.
b) The balance sheet of D Smith as on 25 January 1990, after she has acquired the purchase.

3 This question relates to the details found in Question 2 above, where the sole trader, A Donald (the vendor), has sold his business to D Smith (the buyer). Details are required in the books of the vendor.

REQUIRED:

a) In the books of the vendor, A Donald, prepare the journal entries as to the sale of the business, as completed up to 25 January 1990.
b) Prepare the realisation account as on 1 January 1990.
c) Show the capital account of A Donald on 25 January 1990 when the business was wound up.

4 *The amalgamation of two sole traders*
Johnson and Taylor had agreed to amalgamate their businesses (mutual joining) into a partnership where they had agreed to share profit or loss equally, irrespective of their final capital account balances.

Before the amalgamation took place, they decided on 5 January to:

a) Depreciate all their fixed assets by 25 per cent.
b) To make a provision against their debtors of 5 per cent for possible loss of debts.
c) That Taylor should inject money from his own personal funds to clear his bank overdraft and provide the same bank balance as Johnson on 1 January 1990.

The balance sheets of the two sole traders, on 1 January 1990, were as follows:

	Johnson	*Taylor*
	£	£
FIXED ASSETS		
Plant and equipment	8 000	6 000
Motor vans	2 000	4 000
	10 000	10 000
CURRENT ASSETS		
Stocks	3 590	2 980
Debtors	1 800	1 600
Bank/cash	1 500	—
	6 890	4 580
CURRENT LIABILITIES		
Creditors	2 800	1 500
Overdraft		500
	2 800	2 000
Working capital	4 090	2 580
CAPITAL ACCOUNTS	14 090	12 580

REQUIRED:

a) Show the capital account of each partner as on 5 January, using the accounting equation.
b) Prepare the amalgamated balance sheet of the new partnership as on 5 January.

CHAPTER

29 Stock valuation

- *How can the value of stock affect profits?*
- *On what bases can stock be valued?*
- *Why is it important to use a base consistently?*

Introduction

In most business organisations there are three main areas of cost:

the purchase of stock,
the cost of wages and salaries,
the payment for overheads such as light and heat, rent, rates and general expenses.

Many businesses can spend at least half of their financial budgets on the procurement of materials and therefore the buying of stock is of essential importance to a business.

The optimum level of stock should be purchased, that is, just the right quantity required, neither excessive nor too little. An organisation cannot afford to tie up too much of its working capital in stock otherwise it may have difficulty financing other important aspects of the business such as research, design, development and marketing. If it carries too little stock, a sudden large demand would mean running out of stock and possibly losing vital orders.

A good purchaser of stock needs to know the market well, have a ready and available list of suppliers and ensure that prices are competitive. He or she should be aware of new sources of supply, changes in prices and delivery times.

When stocks arrive from suppliers, they should be checked carefully to ensure that they are satisfactory and that details comply with the instructions sent with the original order. When the invoice is received from the supplier, it should be checked thoroughly for details relating to quantity, discount, type of goods, Vat and any other significant points.

Stock is an important asset to a business. Its value at the financial year-end will influence how much profit has been made. If stock is over-valued, for example, it will have the effect of over-stating profit in the current period and also carry over to the next period; an over-inflated stock value distorting the calculation of profit in both periods.

Methods of stock valuation

There are different methods to value stock (SSAP No. 9, Part 24), the important point to note is that once a particular method is adopted, it should be used consistently (SSAP No. 2), otherwise distortions to profits will occur. Basically, there are three methods to value stock:

historical cost
selling price
lower of cost and net realisable value.

Historical cost

Many organisations, both large and small, tend simply to itemise all their stock and value it at its historical cost, that is, the price they purchased it for at the time. This is straightforward and simple depending on how many different types of stock are purchased and whether the price fluctuates or remains relatively stable.

Selling price

The selling price could be used but it would tend to give a rather optimistic value of stock. The business would need to be quite confident of its market and its customers. The selling price of stock should take into account some of the processing cost of getting the goods into a saleable condition. A prudent approach must be taken in calculating the stock figure in case demand should suddenly fall, otherwise the loss could be greater than anticipated. Conservatism in accounting needs to anticipate possible losses.

Lower of cost and net realisable value (NRV)

SSAP No. 9: Stock and Work-in-Progress, specifies that stocks should be valued 'at the lower of cost and net realisable value (NRV)'. The NRV is defined as the selling price *less* the costs of getting the goods into a saleable condition (marketing, selling and distribution costs). If the NRV is *less* than its cost value, then the NRV should be used to value a particular stock. Again, the concept of conservatism is adopted to anticipate any possible losses arising from old or obsolete stock.

There are computer programs available to maintain stock records for an infinite number of different stock types. Companies like Wadham Stringer, which deals with motor vehicle parts, require an absolutely effective system of stock control to ensure that all their stock parts are up-to-date in relation to minimum and maximum levels, reorder levels and current balances actually in stock. From time to time, computer records should be checked with physical records of stock to ensure effective stock control and to avoid cases of pilfering or fraud.

Materials at cost price

At the end of the financial year, when stock-taking occurs, many organisations simply count up the quantity of different stock types and these are valued at the supplier's price, that is, the historical cost.

Example

Code no.	*Quantity in stock*	*Cost/unit £*	*Amount £*
4215	500	2.5	1 250
4216	400	1.0	400
4217	50	4.2	210
4218	50	1.5	75

In manufacturing, many direct materials may have a *low value* per unit. Items such as bins of nuts, bolts, washers, pins, screws, etc. could be purchased in large quantities from time to time and the cost of these may fluctuate. If prices for these items do change, which price is chosen to value the remaining stock?

The cost of these items may be valued in three distinct ways:

FIFO (first in, first out) assumes that the first stock in is the first stock out and therefore the stock on hand will be valued at the most recent prices.
LIFO (last in, first out) assumes that the stock in last is the first out and therefore the stock on hand will be valued at the earlier prices.
AVCO (average cost) the stock on hand is valued at the weighted average of the unit price.

In physical terms, it does not matter whether the stock left in hand is the most recent or not, what does matter is how the stock is to be valued. Once a method is adopted, it should of course be used consistently to avoid any distortion of profit calculation. Most manufacturing organisations tend to use FIFO because the stock in hand is valued at the most recent prices. LIFO values stock at the lowest value in times of rising prices and would have the effect of understating profits.

The following pages illustrate the stock record cards, using the same item of stock and adopting the three alternative methods of valuation:

Example

Unit:	Code 4235 Bracket	
January:	Balance in stock	2000 units @ £1.00
January:	Purchases	1000 units @ £1.00
January:	Purchases	2000 units @ £1.20
February:	Issues of stock	1500 units
March:	Purchases	2000 units @ £1.35
March:	Issues of stock	2000 units

The FIFO method

STOCK RECORD CARD									
Unit: Bracket Code: 4235 Supplier: Johnson's							Quantity levels: Minimum: 2 000 Maximum: 6 500 Reorder: 3 500		
	RECEIVED			ISSUED			BALANCE		
Date	**Qty.**	**Unit price £**	**Cost £**	**Qty.**	**Unit price £**	**Cost £**	**No. in stock**	**Unit price £**	**Stock value £**
1/1	Balance						2 000	1.00	2 000
10/1	1 000	1.00	1 000				{ 3 000	1.00	3 000
25/1	2 000	1.20	2 400				{ 2 000	1.20	5 400
10/2				1 500	1.00	1 500	{ 1 500	1.00	
							{ 2 000	1.20	3 900
8/3	2 000	1.35	2 700				{ 2 000	1.35	6 600
25/3				1 500	1.00	1 500	{ 1 500	1.20	
				500	1.20	600	{ 2 000	1.35	4 500

In stock: 31/3, 3500 units valued at £4500.

LIFO method

STOCK RECORD CARD									
Unit: Bracket Code: 4235 Supplier: Johnson's							Quantity levels: Minimum: 2 000 Maximum: 6 500 Reorder: 3 500		
	RECEIVED			**ISSUED**			**BALANCE**		
Date	**Qty.**	**Unit price £**	**Cost £**	**Qty.**	**Unit price £**	**Cost £**	**No. in stock**	**Unit price £**	**Stock value £**
1/1	Balance						2 000	1.00	2 000
10/1	1 000	1.00	1 000				3 000	1.00	3 000
25/1	2 000	1.20	2 400				2 000	1.20	5 400
10/2				1 500	1.20	1 800	3 000	1.00	
							500	1.20	3 600
8/3	2 000	1.35	2 700				2 000	1.35	6 300
25/3				2 000	1.35	2 700	3 000	1.00	
							500	1.20	3 600

In stock: 31/3, 3500 units valued at £3600.

AVCO method

STOCK RECORD CARD

Unit: Bracket
Code: 4235
Supplier: Johnson's

Quantity levels:
Minimum: 2 000
Maximum: 6 500
Reorder: 3 500

	RECEIVED			ISSUED			BALANCE		
Date	**Qty.**	**Unit price £**	**Cost £**	**Qty.**	**Unit price £**	**Cost £**	**No. in stock**	**Unit price £**	**Stock value £**
1/1	Balance						2 000	1.000	2 000
10/1	1 000	1.00	1 000				{3 000	1.000	3 000
25/1	2 000	1.20	2 400				{2 000	1.200	2 400
							*5 000	1.080	5 400
10/2				1 500	1.080	1 620	{3 500	1.080	3 780
8/3	2 000	1.35	2 700				{2 000	1.350	2 700
							*5 500	1.178	6 480
25/3				2 000	1.178	2 356	3 500	1.178	4 124

NOTE

$$\text{*Calculation of average unit price} = \frac{\text{Stock value}}{\text{No. of units}} = £\frac{5\,400}{5\,000} = £1.08.$$

In stock: 31/3, 3500 units valued at £4124.

Value of stock on 31 March

	£
Using the FIFO method of stock valuation:	4 500
Using the LIFO method of stock valuation:	3 600
Using the AVCO method of stock valuation:	4 124

Clearly, because prices increased between January and March, FIFO's stock value was the highest because the stock in hand was valued at the latest prices. LIFO's stock value was the lowest because the stock in hand used the earlier lower prices in January. AVCO's stock value was somewhere between the two, taking the average cost value in terms of units purchased.

It does not matter which of these methods is adopted as long as the same method is consistently applied from one financial period to the next. Over the accounting periods, the discrepancies between stock valuations arising from the different bases used will be eliminated because the stock value at the end of one financial period becomes the initial stock value in the next period.

For example, if the FIFO method was used as a base, it would have a greater value of stock at the year end, but its opening stock would also be greater, thereby having the effect of increasing the cost of sales. This apparent advantage would then be nullified in the following final accounts at the end of the period.

The effect on the trading account

Assume that sales for the period were £75 000 and that opening stock plus purchases were £64 000. The effect of using these alternative methods in this period would be:

	FIFO	*LIFO*	*AVCO*
	£	£	£
Sales	75 000	75 000	75 000
– Cost of sales:			
Stock (beginning) + purchases	64 000	64 000	64 000
– Stock (31 March)	4 500	3 600	4 124
	59 500	60 400	59 876
Gross profit	15 500	14 600	15 124

As the value of stock under FIFO was of the highest value, it has the highest gross profit. Using LIFO, with its lowest stock value, the gross profit is the lowest. AVCO falls between FIFO and LIFO. On 1 April, in the new financial period, the stock (beginning) values will be the same as on 31 March. LIFO's opening stock value will be £3600 giving it the advantage of a lower opening cost of sales than either FIFO or AVCO. Discrepancies in future calculations of gross profit should therefore cancel each other out.

The lower of cost and net realisable value (NRV)

If the NRV is judged to have a lower value than the cost of some items of stock (because the stock is old, damaged or obsolete), then the NRV will be used to value the stock rather than the cost price. Again, this emphasises accounting's concept of prudence.

Stock valuation at 31 March

Code No.	*Units in stock*	*Cost price* £	*Value at cost* £	*NRV* £	*Lower of cost + NRV* £
DX 421	100	1.5	150	175	150
422	20	5.0	100	25	25
423	120	4.2	504	600	504
424	5	10.0	50	10	10
425	210	1.0	210	252	210
			1 014	1 062	899

For these stocks valued on 31 March, the lower of cost plus NRV, which equals £899, would be taken as the stock end-value. Code numbers 422 and 424 value the stock items as well under the cost price, perhaps because the stock is damaged or out-of-date.

Many different types of businesses have adopted this method of stock valuation as a base for valuing many of their stock items, following the guidelines laid down in SSAP No. 9, Stock and Work-in-Progress.

Summary

1 Stock is an important asset to a business and therefore great care should be taken to value its worth.

2 At the end of a financial period, the value of stock influences the cost of sales and therefore the gross profit of the business.

3 There are different ways (or bases) to value stock, the most common being either at cost price or lower of cost and net realisable value (NRV).

4 Stock could be valued at its selling price, although this method is rarely adopted because it tends to over-optimise the value of stock and therefore over-estimates profit.

5 In manufacturing organisations, direct materials which have a low unit price may be valued at cost in alternative ways, using FIFO, LIFO and AVCO as the bases for calculation of stock.

QUESTIONS

1 At stock-taking time on 31 December, the following items were compiled and valued at lower of cost and NRV:

Code no.	*No. of units in stock*	*Unit value* £	*Amount* £
Z421	300	2.50	
Z422	10	2.95	
Z423	25	5.00	
Z424	55	1.20	
Z426	—		
Z427	160	1.50	

REQUIRED:

a) Calculate the total stock value of items coded from Z421 to Z427.
b) Explain briefly what is meant by the term 'lower of cost and NRV'.

2 On 1 December, the stock item Z427 had a balance of 150 units. The stock card recorded the following:

Dec 5	Received	200 units
10	Issues	125 units
15	Issues	150 units
19	Received	200 units
21	Issues	125 units
23	Issues	50 units
29	Received	175 units
31	Issues	110 units

REQUIRED:

a) Calculate the number of units which should be in stock on 31 December.
b) Does your answer reconcile with the stock-taking figure in Question 1? Suggest what may have occurred.

3 The words FIFO, LIFO and AVCO relate to the valuation of stock.

a) Give a brief explanation what these terms mean.
b) Use an example to show which *one* of these methods will produce a higher value of stock in times of rising prices. How would profit be affected?

(RSA)

4 The goods listed below were in stock at Jack's Store on 31 December. Record the items on a stock card/sheet and calculate the value of stock at the end of the year, 31 December.

Code no.	*Items*	*Quantity*	*Cost per unit*	*NRV per unit*	*Lower of cost or NRV*
			£	£	£
427	Jeans	50	10.50	12.50	
428	Jeans	10	15.20	14.00	
859/1	Sweaters	120	8.75	7.50	
859/2	Sweaters	60	12.50	15.95	
859/3	Sweaters	15	9.95	12.50	
870	Men's socks	50	1.15	1.50	
870/1	Men's socks	5	3.90	1.00	

(BTEC National)

5 **Stock issues – June, July, August**

		Quantity (units)	*Cost per unit*	*Value of stock*
			£	£
1/6	Balance	200	2.00	400
15/6	Purchases	100	1.95	
30/6	Purchases	200	2.10	
		500		
30/6	Issues	150		
1/7	Balance	350		
21/7	Purchases	200	2.15	
		550		
30/7	Issues	200		
1/8	Balance	350		
10/8	Purchases	150	2.20	
21/8	Purchases	100	2.20	
		600		
31/8	Issues	250		
1/9	Balance	350		

REQUIRED:

Write up a stock record card for the months June to August and calculate the value of stock on 1 September in terms of both FIFO and LIFO order issues.

(Institute of Bankers)

6 The following information relates to a stock code X445 (bags of washers):

Jan	2	Received 150 bags at £12 each bag
	4	Received 125 bags at £10 each bag
	8	Issued 175 bags
	12	Received 200 bags at £14 per bag
	16	Issued 120 bags
	20	Received 500 bags at £16 per bag
	25	Issued 200 bags
	28	Issued 80 bags.

REQUIRED:

a) Prepare a stock record card from the above information using the AVCO method of valuation.

b) If the LIFO method had been used for stock value, what effect would it have on both the value of this stock item and in the trading account?

CHAPTER

30 Accounting for clubs and societies

- *What financial statements may be prepared for social organisations?*
- *Do the same principles of accounting apply?*

Introduction

In every town and village, there is virtually always some sort of social organisation, either a club or society, which has been set up for a specific purpose. It may be a sports club, to run cricket, football, netball or tennis, or an amateur society to put on dramas or operatic events. These organisations are not normally profit motivated and are run for the benefit and enjoyment of their members.

The finance required to run these social clubs comes from the annual subscriptions paid by their members. Other sources of finance may come from fund raising activities or donations from sponsors. Finance is needed to pay for the running expenses and upkeep of the club including any new equipment.

A club treasurer is normally appointed by the members to take charge of their finances. All monies coming in and going out should be controlled and properly accounted for to safeguard the interests of the members. It is therefore necessary for the treasurer to keep basic records of the receipts and payment of monies and to take charge of the club's bank account.

Accounting reports

It would be rare to find a full accounting system operating ledgers and trial balance in a club or society. The treasurer may not have the time or expertise to record the accounts in a formalised way. However, the position demands that a reasonably tight control of cash and other resources ought to be made and that at committee meetings, the treasurer would be expected to advise members of the club's financial position.

The treasurer is expected to produce some form of financial reporting to the members at the end of the club's social year. These usually consist of:

the receipts and payments account
the income and expenditure account
the balance sheet.

The receipts and payments account

This statement is the equivalent of a simple cash book. It is a summary of all the receipts and payments of the club for the year. Its purpose is to show the club's members where the cash has come from and where it has gone and the balance in hand at the year-end.

The income and expenditure account

This statement is the equivalent of a business's trading and profit and loss account. The principles of the matching of revenue with expenses, including adjustments, apply exactly in the same way. It will not be unusual therefore to find accruals, prepayments and depreciation in this account. A club does not usually use the words 'profit' or 'loss' to indicate the difference between revenue and expenses. The adopted wording is *'surplus or deficit'*.

Some clubs operate a bar or refreshment counter for the use and benefit of their members and visitors and the treasurer can prepare a special *bar account* to indicate whether it has made either a surplus or deficit in the social year.

The balance sheet

This statement is prepared in the same way as any other type of organisation. The capital of the club is generally known as its *accumulated funds*, representing its assets less liabilities. Any surplus or deficit from the income and expenditure account is transferred to this account.

Example

Broadstone Bowls Club begins its financial year on 1 January. Its accumulated funds on 1 January 1990 were £29 200:

Assets	£	Liabilities	£
Club house	25 000	Creditors	500
Bank account	2 300	(bar)	
Stock (bar)	800		
Equipment	1 600		
	29 700		

The treasurer at the financial year-end, 31 December 1990, prepared the receipts and payments account for the year, for the benefit of the members as follows:

Broadstone Bowls Club –
Receipts and payments account year ended
31 December 1990

	Receipts	£	*Payments*	£
1/1	Balance (bank)	2 300	Equipment	900
	Members' subscriptions	1 500	Hire of courts	280

(Continues)

Receipts	£		*Payments*	£
Subscriptions in advance	50		Hire of halls	1 000
Bar sales	2 185		Light and heat	135
Dances	425		General expenses	255
Donations	150		Bar purchases	1 160
Tournament fees	270		Club house extension	1 850
		31/12	Balance (Bank)	1 300
	6 880			6 880
Balance (bank)	1 300			

The treasurer has also prepared a club bar account and the surplus for the year has been transferred to the income and expenditure account. Other information on 31 December 1990 included:

a) Bar stock, £290.
b) Subscriptions owing by members for the year, £150.
c) Gas bill still due to be paid, £85.
d) Equipment, including new purchases, to be depreciated by 20 per cent.
e) Bar purchases still to be paid, £350.

Broadstone Bowls Club –
Bar Account, year ended 31 December 1990

	£	£
Sales		2 185
– Cost of sales:		
Stock (1/1)	800	
+ Purchases	1 160	
	1 960	
– Creditors due (1/1)	500	
	1 460	
+ Creditors due (31/12)	350	
	1 810	
– Stock (31/12)	290	1 520
Bar account surplus for year (Transferred to income side of income and expenditure account)		665

NOTE

Creditors due on 1 January (accrual) is deducted from cost of sales because the expense related to last year's bar account. The creditors due on 31 December for bar stock is added as an accrual in the normal way.

Broadstone Bowls Club –
Income and expenditure account year ended
31 December 1990

Expenditure		£	*Income*	£
Hire of courts		280	Subscriptions	1 500
Hire of halls		1 000	Subscriptions owing	150
Light and heat	135		Bar surplus	665
+ Accrued	85	220	Dance receipts	425
General expenses		255	Donations	150
Deprecation of equipment		500	Tournament fees	270
Surplus		905		
(income – expenditure)		3 160		3 160

NOTES

1 The surplus of £905 is transferred to the accumulated funds (in the balance sheet).
2 Subscriptions owing from members is revenue accrued, which belongs to the current financial year and is added to income.
3 Subscriptions in advance £50, in the receipts and payments account are not included because they belong to the next accounting period, 1991.

Broadstone Bowls Club –
Balance sheet year ended
31 December 1990

	£ Cost	£ Depreciation	£ Net
FIXED ASSETS			
Club house	25 000		
+ Extension	1 850		26 850
Equipment	1 600		
+ New purchases	900	500	2 000
			28 850
CURRENT ASSETS			
Bar stock	290		
Subscriptions owing	150		
Bank	1 300	1 740	

(Continues)

	£	£	£
– CURRENT LIABILITIES			
Subscriptions in advance	50		
Accruals (350 + 85)	435	485	
Working capital			1 255
			30 105
ACCUMULATED FUNDS			
Balance (1/1)	29 200		
+ Surplus	905		30 105

Example (Institute of Bankers)

The following information has been submitted by the Corfe Mullen Social Club, for the year ended 31 March 1988:

Corfe Mullen Social Club – Receipts and payments account, year ended 31 March 1988

Receipts		£	*Payments*		£
1/4/87	Balance (bank)	2 000		Insurance, rates	480
	Subscriptions	5 575		Wages	5 650
	Surplus (bingo)	850		Bar purchases	6 500
	Bar takings	10 225		General expenses	275
				Light and heat	480
				New furniture	500
				Club repairs, maintenance	1 275
			31/3/88	Balance (bank)	3 490
		18 650			18 650

Other information:

1/4/87	£	31/3/88	£
Club premises at cost	25 000	Bar stock	850
Furniture and equipment	2 000	Subscriptions: in arrears	480
Bar stock	1 600	in advance	50
Bank balance (as above)	2 000	Furniture and equipment valued	1 950
Subscriptions: in arrears	150	Bar purchases owing	500
in advance	100	Insurance prepaid	35
Insurance prepaid	80	Light and heat owing	50
Light and heat owing	130		

REQUIRED:

a) The club's bar account for the period ended 31 March 1988.
b) The club's income and expenditure account for the same period.
c) The club's balance sheet as at 31 March 1988.

1 **Corfe Mullen Social Club – Bar account, year ended 31 March 1988**

	£	£
Sales		10 225
– Cost of sales:		
Stock (1/4/87)	1 600	
+ Purchases	6 500	
	8 100	
+ Purchases due	500	
	8 600	
– Stock (31/3/88)	850	7 750
Surplus t/f to income and expenditure account		2 475

2 **Corfe Mullen Social Club – Income and expenditure account, year ended 31 March 1988**

Expenditure	£	£	*Income*	£	£
Insurance and rates	480		Surplus from bar		2 475
+ Prepaid (1/4/87)	80		Surplus from bingo		850
	560		Subscriptions	5 575	
– Prepaid (31/3/88)	35	525	+ In advance (1/4/87)	100	
Wages		5 650		5 675	
Light and heat	480		– In arrears (1/4/87)	150	
– Owing (1/4/87)	130			5 525	
	350		+ In arrears (31/3/88)	480	
+ Owing (31/3/88)	50	400		6 005	
General expenses		275	– In advance (31/3/88)	50	5 955
Maintenance and repairs		1 275			
Depreciation of furniture and equipment		550			
Surplus t/f to accumulated fund		605			
		9 280			9 280

3 **Corfe Mullen Social Club – Balance sheet as at 31 March 1988**

	£	£		£	£
FIXED ASSETS			Accumulated fund		
Premises	25 000		(1/4/87)	30 600	
Furniture and equipment	1 950	26 950	+ Surplus	605	31 205
			Stock creditors	500	
CURRENT ASSETS			Light and heat (accrual)	50	
Stock (bar)	850		Subscriptions (advance)	50	600
Subscriptions (arrear)	480				
Bank	3 490				
Insurance (prepaid)	35	4 855			
		31 805			31 805

NOTES

1 The Accumulated fund on 1 April 1987 was calculated as:

	Assets	–	*Liabilities*
	£		£
Premises	25 000		
Furniture and equipment	2 000		
Bar stock	1 600		
Bank account	2 000		
Subscriptions: arrears	150		
advance			100
Insurance (prepaid)	80		
Light and heat (owing)			130
	30 830	–	230

Accumulated fund was £30 830 – £230 = £30 600.

2 Adjustments at the beginning of the accounting year as well as at the end.

When accruals and prepayments appear at the beginning of an accounting year (1 April 1987) they are treated in the reverse way as to how they are treated at the end (31 March 1988). Therefore:

	1/4/87	*31/3/88*
Accrued expenses	deducted	added
Prepaid expenses	added	deducted
Subscriptions: arrears	deducted	added
advance	added	deducted

3 The balance sheet has been presented in the horizontal format with assets on the left and capital and liabilities on the right.

Summary

1 Clubs and societies are social organisations set up for the benefit of their members. They are normally non-profit motivated. Any surplus or deficit arising from the year's activities, is transferred to the balance sheet (or statement of affairs), under the club's accumulated funds.

2 A treasurer is normally appointed by the club's members to take responsibility for its finances. Accounting tends to be informal and the treasurer's task is generally to keep control of the club's cash, bank receipts and make the appropriate payments.

3 At the end of the club's financial year, the treasurer will be expected to prepare for the members, accounting reports. These are accounts for receipts and payments, income and expenditure and the balance sheet.

4 The accounting reports for clubs and societies follow exactly the same accounting principles as for any other type of organisation. For example, adjustments such as accruals, prepayments and provisions need to be included for matching revenue against expenses.

5 In cases where a club runs a bar or refreshment counter, the treasurer may prepare a special bar account to calculate whether it is in surplus or deficit for the year. A surplus is transferred to the income side of the income and expenditure account, a deficit to the expenditure side.

QUESTIONS

1 From the following receipts and payments account of the Mid-Town Golf Club and the further particulars provided below prepare an income and expenditure account for the year ended 31 March 1986 and a balance sheet as at that date.

Receipts and payments account for the year ended 31 March 1986

Receipts	£	*Payments*	£
Balance from last year	640	Wages	1 080
Entrance fees	400	Payment for new lockers	140
Subscriptions:		Printing and stationery	145
Current year	820	Postages	135
In advance	40	Lighting and heating	280
Profits from refreshments	165	Insurances	140
Locker rents	75	Balance c/d	280
Interest on deposit account	60		
	2 200		2 200
Balance b/d	280		

Additional information

i) £50 is owing for subscriptions for the year, to March 1986.
ii) £15 is owing by members for locker rents.
iii) Printing and stationery, value £28, is still unpaid.
iv) £1000 is on deposit at the bank, from 1 April 1985.
v) The club house and equipment appear in the books on 1 April 1985 at a value of £10 000.

(RSA)

2 The following statement has been submitted to you by the Keyworth Bowls Club whose financial year ended on 31 March 1988.

Receipts and payments account

	£		£
Balance b/f	2 000	Rent and rates	460
Subscriptions	5 600	Wages	2 650
Profit from dances	825	Light and heat	240
Bar takings	10 200	Bar purchase	6 400
		Sundry expenses	185
		New furniture	200
		Club maintenance	270
		Balance c/f	8 220
	18 625		18 625

You are asked to prepare an income and expenditure account for the year under review and a balance sheet at 31 March 1988. Your enquiries produce this information:

i) £400 subscriptions are still in arrear.
ii) £60 of the rent is in advance.
iii) At the end of the previous year the furniture and equipment was valued at £2000. £400 of this amount is to be written off.
iv) The bar stock was valued: on 1 April 1987 at £600; on 31 March 1988 at £800.
v) £600 was owed for bar purchases.
vi) Of the subscriptions received, £80 were for the 1 April 1988 season.

(RSA adapted)

3 The following were the assets and liabilities of the Fitorama Sports Club on 1 July 1983:

ASSETS	£
Premises at cost	28 000
Fittings and equipment	4 200
Deposit in building society	2 700
Cash and bank balance	2 027
LIABILITIES	
Electricity bill outstanding	168

The club's cash book for the year to 30 June 1984 showed the following:

Receipts	£	*Payments*	£
Balance b/f	2 027	Rates	1 250
Subscriptions for year	4 870	Groundsman	2 200

(Continues)

Receipts	£	*Payments*	£
Competition entry fees	2 700	Purchase of sports	
Sale of dance tickets	450	equipment	1 650
		League entry fee	20
		Dance expenses	300
		Prizes for competitions	3 050
		Electricity	740
		Balance c/f	837
	10 047		10 047

REQUIRED:

a) Calculate the accumulated fund at 1 July 1983.
b) Prepare the club's income and expenditure account for the year ended 30 June 1984, and a balance sheet on that date after taking into account the following points:
   1 An electricity account of £194 was outstanding at the end of the year.
   2 The amount paid for rates included £200 paid in advance.
   3 During the year interest of £107 had been received from the building society. The interest has been reinvested in the society.

(RSA)

4 On 1 November 1984 The Kingsley Bowling Club had the following assets and liabilities.

ASSETS	£
Club house	12 500
Fixtures and fittings	1 750
Sports equipment	340
Bank and cash	1 195
LIABILITIES	
Sundry creditors	235

During the year ending 31 October 1985 the following amounts were received and paid.

Receipts	£	*Payments*	£
Subscriptions	760	Postage and stationery	175
Sales of refreshments	1 575	Groundsman's wages	550
Dance tickets	240	Purchase of refreshments	960
Competition fees	375	Repairs to equipment	100
		Sundry creditors	100
		Purchase of lawn mower	140
		General expenses	150
		Competition expenses	360

REQUIRED:

a) Calculate the accumulated fund as at 1 November 1984.
b) Prepare the club's receipts and payments account for the year ending 31 October 1985.
c) Prepare the club's income and expenditure account for the year ending 31 October 1985 and a balance sheet as at that date. The following points are to be taken into consideration:
   i) The general expenses included rates, insurance and electricity. At 31 October 1985 there was an unpaid electricity account of £50 and a payment in advance of £25 for rates.
   ii) There was an unpaid invoice for competition expenses £10.
   iii) Equipment revalued to £200 (excluding lawn mower).

(RSA)

5 The following is a summary of the receipts and payments of the Miniville Rotary Club during the year ended 31 July 1986.

Miniville Rotary Club –
Receipts and payments account for the year ended 31 July 1986

	£		£
Cash and bank balances b/f	210	Secretarial expenses	163
Sales of competition tickets	437	Rent	1 402
Members' subscriptions	1 987	Visiting speakers' expenses	1 275
Donations	177	Donations to charities	35
Refund of rent	500	Prizes for competitions	270
Balance c/f	13	Stationery and printing	179
	3 324		3 324

The following valuations are also available:

As at 31 July	*1985*	*1986*
	£	£
Equipment	975	780
(original cost £1 420)		
Subscriptions in arrears	65	85
Subscriptions in advance	10	37
Owing to suppliers of competition prizes	58	68
Stocks of competition prizes	38	46

REQUIRED:

a) Calculate the value of the accumulated fund of the Miniville Rotary Club as at 1 August 1985.
b) Reconstruct the following accounts for the year ended 31 July 1986:
   i) the subscription account,
   ii) the competition prizes account.

c) Prepare an income and expenditure account for the Miniville Rotary Club for the year ended 31 July 1986 and a balance sheet as at that date.

(AAT)

6 The following is a summary of the receipts and payments of the Technicians Club during the year ended 31 December 1986.

Technicians Club –
Receipts and payments account
for the year ended 31 December 1986

	£		£
Cash and bank balances b/f	358	Secretary's expenses	150
Sales of disco tickets	632	Rent	800
Members' subscriptions	2 108	Meeting expenses	722
Donations	250	Heating and lighting	269
		Disco expenses	515
		Purchase of equipment	400
		Stationery and printing	287
		Cash and bank balances c/f	205
	3 348		3 348

The following valuations are also available as at 31 December:

	1985	*1986*
	£	£
Equipment written down value	1 300	1 460
Subscriptions in arrears	80	110
Heating and lighting accrued	37	41
Stocks of stationery	54	46
Rent pre-paid	200	240

REQUIRED:

Prepare an income and expenditure account for the Technicians Club for the year ended 31 December 1986 and a balance sheet as at that date.

(AAT)

7 The following figures were taken from the records of the Riverside Club for the year ended 31 December.

Receipts	£
Members subscriptions	690
Sale of refreshments	2 021
Sundry receipts	140

(Continues)

Payments	£
Suppliers of refreshments	1 424
Wages	650
Rent, rates, and insurance	250
Repairs and renewals	213
Purchase of new furniture for lounge	205
Sundry expenses	129

NOTE

All receipts and payments were passed through the club's bank account.

Other information:

	£
Members' subscriptions in arrear at 1 January and paid during the year	60
Members' subscriptions in arrear at 31 December	35
Cash at bank, 1 January	131
Rates paid in advance at 31 December	26
Estimated depreciation on club furniture and fixtures for the year	72
Purchases of refreshments during the year	1 540
Stocks of refreshments at 1 January	138
Stocks of refreshments at 31 December	156

REQUIRED:

a) A receipts and payments account and a refreshment account for the year ended 31 December.

b) An income and expenditure account for the year ended 31 December and a balance sheet as at that date.

(AEB)

8 Wentworth Cricket Club had the following assets and liabilities at 1 January 1984:

	£
Ground and pavilion	250 000
Equipment	2 300
Fixtures and fittings	3 900
Subscriptions in arrears (from 1983)	92
Subscriptions received in advance (for 1984)	106
Light and heat owing	81
Insurance prepaid	209
Bar stocks	943
Members' long-term (interest free) loans	50 000
Accumulated fund	210 549

**Wentworth Cricket Club –
Receipts and payments account for year ending
31 December 1984**

	£		£
Balance b/d	3 292	Bar purchases	7 306
Subscriptions	809	Equipment	860
Bar sales	10 243	Lottery tickets and prizes	821
Sales of monthly lottery tickets	4 391	Ground maintenance	4 202
Net proceeds from fruit machines	5 002	Light and heat	320
Loans from members	5 000	Insurance	609
		Extension to pavillion	11 500
		Affiliation fees	30
		Balance c/d	3 089
	28 737		28 737

At 31 December 1984, the following matters were outstanding:

1 subscriptions in arrears (for 1984) £23 and subscriptions received in advance (for 1985) £86;
2 subscriptions still outstanding for 1983, £22 were to be written off;
3 equipment, including additions, had depreciated by 10 per cent;
4 insurance prepaid £220 and light and heat owing £90;
5 bar stocks at 31 December 1984 were valued at £1100.

REQUIRED:

a) An income and expenditure account of the Wentworth Cricket Club for the year ended 31 December 1984, including a bar account.
b) A balance sheet as at 31 December 1984. An explanation of the difference, in accounting treatment at year-end, between: (i) subscriptions in arrears and light and heat owing; and (ii) subscriptions in advance and insurance prepaid.

(AEB June '85)

CHAPTER

31 Accounting for incomplete records

- *How are final accounts prepared without a ledger system?*
- *What method can be used to value sales and purchases?*
- *How can the loss of stock be valued?*

Introduction

The sole trader, in charge of a small business, often does not have the time or expertise to prepare a formal set of accounting books such as ledgers and trial balance.

It is essential however, for tax purposes at least, to keep significant accounting records and documents relating to the business's finances, so that the accountant can prepare the final accounts at the end of the financial year. The business may also have to prepare Vat records and returns if its turnover is greater than a certain level set by the Chancellor each year.

The businessman (or woman) therefore, needs to retain essential information concerning the business, on a day-to-day level. He needs to know the cash resources he has available, how much his customers owe him, how much he owes his suppliers, what his sales figures are, when to pay his Vat and other bills, and many other diverse aspects of the business.

Even if accounting records are not prepared on a formal basis, information still needs to be kept so that an accountant can use it to prepare the final accounts at the financial year-end. From records regarded as 'incomplete' it is still possible to reconstruct certain accounts to enable the financial reports to be prepared.

Preparation of accounts

In business practice, an accountant would require all the available records kept by the business throughout the financial period, including all relevant documents such as:

invoices to customers and from suppliers,
credit notes to customers and from suppliers,
bank receipts,
bank payments,
bank statements,
Vat returns,
bills paid or unpaid.

The accountant would organise this informtion in chronological order where necessary, and prepare the following:

a) Establish the owner's capital at the commencement of the financial year (assets less liabilities).
b) Prepare a summary of cash receipts and payments for the year, identifying the monies in and out of the business and calculating the balance of cash in hand.
c) Reconstructing accounts for debtors and creditors, where relevant, to calculate sales and purchases for the year (on credit).
d) Ensure all relevant adjustments are included such as accruals, prepayments and provisions.
e) Prepare the trading and profit and loss account for the financial year ended and a balance sheet as at that date.

Example

Tina Smith is a sole trader in business as a computer engineer and supplier of computer hard- and software. She has a small workshop attached to her residence and most of her business is with local clients. On 1 January, the start of her financial year, her statement of affairs (or balance sheet) was as follows:

Assets:	£	£
Workshop (cost)	8 000	
Equipment	2 250	
Motor vehicle	1 500	
Debtors	550	
Bank	800	
Stock	3 350	16 450
Less Liabilities:		
Creditors		1 350
Capital (1/1/90)		15 000

Owner's capital: £15 100

Preparation of bank/cash summary

From the necessary documents including cheque book records, bank statements, till rolls and other sources, a simplified cash book may be drawn up. Tina Smith's summary was as follows:

Tina Smith – Bank summary

	Receipts	£	*Payments*	£
1/1	Balance (bank)	800	Payments to suppliers	33 400
	Customer receipts	48 575	Drawings by Smith	8 800
	Cash sales	2 400	Wages	4 500
	Commission received	500	Motor costs	1 300
			General expenses	850
			Insurance and rates	595
			Telephone	325

(Continues)

	Receipts	£		*Payments*	£
				Light and heat	280
				Advertising	450
				New equipment	285
				Workshop extension	590
			31/12	Balance (bank) c/d	900
		52 275			52 275
	Balance b/d	900			

NOTE

This type of accounting, in its organisation, is similar to that of Chapter 30 – Accounting for clubs and societies. The receipts and payments of monies listed above, are used to help prepare the trading and profit and loss account. The accountant will also need to list further information, including the balance day adjustments.

Other information available on 31 December 1990:

a) Cash discounts: discount allowed to customers, £780.
discount received from suppliers, £565.

b) Returns inward, £255 and returns outward, £950.

c) Stock valued at cost £4250.

d) Debtors balance, £740; creditors balance, £1855.

e) Provision for depreciation: motor vehicle and equipment, by 20 per cent.

f) A garage bill on the motor vehicle was owing, £211.

Reconstruction of debtors and creditors to establish credit sales and purchases

It may be reasonably straightforward to establish cash sales if the owner of the business retains all till rolls or cash receipts. Some traders religiously keep a tally of daily sales records and the accountant has little problem in summing up a total figure. The same may apply for cash purchases.

To arrive at credit sales or credit purchases for the year, the accountant may get his information from invoices sent to customers or received from suppliers. Credit notes will also help to establish details concerning returns inward and returns outward. If cash discount has been taken advantage of, the details are usually found on the invoice.

Debtors: to establish credit sales

	DEBIT			CREDIT	
1/1	Balance b/d	550	31/12	Bank/cash	48 575
31/12	Sales	49 800		Discount allowed	780
				Returns inward	255
				Balance c/d	740
		50 350			50 350
	Balance b/d	740			

NOTE

The sales figure of £49 800 was calculated by deducting the opening debtor's balance of £550 from the total of the credit column, £50 350.

Creditors: to establish credit purchases

	DEBIT			CREDIT	
31/12	Bank/cash	33 400	1/1	Balance b/d	1 350
	Discount received	565	31/12	Purchases	35 420
	Returns outward	950			
	Balance c/d	1 855			
		36 770			36 770
				Balance b/d	1 855

NOTE

The purchases figure of £35 420 was calculated by deducting the opening creditor's balance of £1350 from the total of the debit column, £36 770.

The credit sales and credit purchases figures are then transferred to the trading account.

Preparation of the trading and profit and loss account for Tina Smith, year ended 31 December 1990

	£	£	£
Sales (credit)	49 800		
(cash)	2 400		
	52 200		
− Returns inward	255		51 945
− Cost of sales:			
Stock (1/1)	3 350		
Purchases	35 420		
	38 770		
− Returns outward	950	37 820	
− Stock (31/12)		4 250	33 570
Gross profit			18 375
− Expenses			
Wages		4 500	
General expenses		850	
Motor costs	1 300		
+ Accrued	211	1 511	
Insurance and rates		595	
Telephone		325	
Light and heat		280	
Advertising		450	
Discount allowed		780	

(Continues)

	£	£	£
Depreciation: Equipment	507		
Motor	300	807	10 098
			8 277
+ Other revenue			
Commission	500		
Discount received	565		1 065
Net profit			9 342

Preparation of the balance sheet for Tina Smith, as at 31 December 1990

	Cost £	*Depreciation* £	*Net* £
FIXED ASSETS			
Workshop premises	8 000		
+ Extension	590	—	8 590
Equipment	2 250		
+ New	285		
	2 535	507	2 028
Motor vehicle	1 500	300	1 200
	12 625	807	11 818
CURRENT ASSETS			
Stock	4 250		
Debtors	740		
Bank/cash	900		
Prepayments	—	5 890	
– CURRENT LIABILITIES			
Creditors	1 855		
Accruals	211	2 066	
Working capital			3 824
			15 642
FINANCED BY:			
Capital (1/1)	15 100		
+ Net profit	9 342	24 442	
– Drawings		8 800	15 642

NOTE

Tina Smith has increased her net worth by £542 during her financial year. Most of her

£9342 profit has been used up because of the owner's personal drawings throughout the year, £8800. Tina's balance sheet is also referred to as her 'statement of affairs' when dealing with incomplete records.

Tina Smith will be assessed for tax. The Inland Revenue will base the tax payable on her profit for the year less the appropriate taxable allowances. For example:

		£
Profit for the year		9 342
− Allowances		4 500
Taxable income	=	4 842
		4 842 × 25 per cent tax rate
	=	1 210.5 tax payable

The calculation of profit from the owner's net worth

It should be possible to assess a businessman's or woman's financial position at a specific point in time by preparing a statement of affairs, i.e. a balance sheet, to calculate net worth (his or her capital).

The accounting equation to establish capital is:

Capital = Assets − Liabilities

If the net worth of the owner is calculated at both the beginning and end of an accounting period, then it is possible to determine profit or loss for the year.

If net worth has increased (without further investment of capital by the owner), then a profit has been made. If net worth has decreased, the owner has either personally withdrawn too much from the business, or the business has made a loss, or it may be a combination of the two.

In Tina Smith's case, her net worth had increased by £542 over the year:

1/1/90:

Capital	=	Assets	− Liabilities
£15 100	=	£16 450	− £1 350

31/12/90:

Capital	=	Assets	− Liabilities
£15 642	=	£17 708	− £2 066

Tina's capital (net worth) was £15 100, this equalled her net assets on 1 January. On 31 December, her net worth was £15 642, an increase in capital of £542.

Information has indicated that her total drawings for the year were £8800 and that she had not invested any further new capital in the business. What is her profit for the year?

Using the business equation, $P = NA + D - NC$, where NA = net asset change; D = Drawings; NC = New capital invested; and P = Profit then

P	=	NA	$+ D$	$- NC$
£9342	=	£542	+ £8800	− 0

The valuation of stock following loss through fire or theft

If stock is lost because of fire on the premises or is stolen due to theft or burglary, the loss must be assessed as accurately as possible particularly if it is insured and compensation is required for the loss.

If adequate stock records are not kept it is still possible to value the stock loss if the gross profit margin is known and the trading account can be constructed.

Example

Jack owns a shop in the local high street and on 18 May there was a fire which destroyed most of his stock. He could salvage about £500 worth and the insurance assessor wanted an accurate assessment of stock loss on the claim form.

At the start of the financial year Jack had an opening stock value of £6000. His purchases to 18 May had been £28 000. His sales to this date were £40 000, Jack having a margin of 25 per cent on sales.

How much stock was lost in the fire? His financial year runs from 1 January to 31 December.

Construction of trading account to value stock loss to 18 May

	£	£
Sales		40 000
less		
Cost of sales:		
Stock (1/1)	6 000	
+ Purchases	28 000	
	34 000	
− Stock (18/5)	4 000	30 000
Gross profit		10 000

Working backwards: 25 per cent of sales = a gross profit of £10 000 therefore cost of sales is £30 000. The difference between £34 000 (stock + purchases) and £30 000 is the stock which should be a value of £4000.

If Jack salvaged £500 stock from the fire, the assessment of loss for the insurance claim must be for £3500.

Answer: Stock loss valued at £3500.

Example

You work for a firm of accountants which prepares the accounts for Murry Ltd.

During the night of 2 June 1987, Murry Ltd suffered a fire. The fire, in fact, destroyed all the company's stock records and a quantity of stock. The stock was covered by insurance against loss by fire. You have been asked by your firm to assist with preparing the insurance claim for Murry Ltd.

Data available:

a)

	On 1/1/87	*On 2/6/87*
	£000	*£000*
Stock at cost	264	?
Trade debtors	78	94
Trade creditors	90	106

b) The following transactions took place between 1/1/87 and 2/6/87.

	£000
Cash purchases	34
Payments to creditors	548
Cash received from debtors	628
Cash sales	160
Discount received	20
Discount allowed	16

c) The physical stocktake taken first thing in the morning on 3/6/87 showed the remaining stock (undamaged) to have a cost value of £182 000.

d) Murry Ltd operate a standard margin of 30 per cent, i.e. a gross profit of 30 per cent on selling price.

TASKS:

1 Calculate the total value of purchases for the period.

2 Calculate the total value of sales for the period.

3 Use the information in tasks 1 and 2 to calculate the cost of the damaged stock.

1 Value of purchases

Creditors:

	DEBIT	£		*CREDIT*	£
2/6	Bank/cash	548 000	1/1	Balance b/d	90 000
	Discount received	20 000			
	Balance c/d	106 000	2/6	Purchases	584 000
		674 000			674 000
			3/6	Balance b/d	106 000

Credit purchases	=	584 000
Cash purchases	=	34 000
Total	=	618 000

2 Value of sales

Debtors:

		£			£
1/1	Balance b/d	78 000	2/6	Bank/cash	628 000
2/6	Sales	660 000		Discount allowed	16 000
				Balance c/d	94 000
		738 000			738 000
3/6	Balance b/d	94 000			

Credit sales	=	660 000
Cash sales	=	160 000
Total	=	820 000

3

Trading account –
Murry Ltd from 1 Jan–2 June 1987

	£	£	£
Sales			820 000
− Cost of sales:			
Stock (1/1)	264 000		
+ Purchases	618 000	882 000	
− Stock (2/6) (undamaged)		182 000	
		700 000	
Loss of stock		126 000	
			574 000
Gross profit (30%)			246 000

Cost of damaged stock: £126 000

Summary

1 Sole traders of small businesses generally do not keep formal records of their accounting. Rather they retain essential records of the business for the accountant to piece together at the end of the financial year for the purpose of preparing the final accounts.

2 The procedure for this type of accounting is not unlike the preparation of accounts for clubs and societies found in Chapter 30. It includes establishing the owner's net worth, summarising cash/bank receipts and payments, preparing adjustments and drafting the final accounts.

3 There may be a need to reconstruct debtors' and creditors' accounts in order to determine the credit sales and credit purchases for the period. Sales and purchases can be calculated by deducting one side of entries from the other.

4 Profit for the year can be calculated by using the business equation ($P = NA + D - NC$). The difference in net worth (or net assets) from one financial period to the next, indicates whether the owner's stake in the business has increased or decreased.

5 It is possible to calculate the loss of stock through reasons such as fire or theft by working backwards from gross profit in the trading account. Once the sales and cost of sales figures are known, the missing figure for stock loss can be entered in the cost of sales.

QUESTIONS

1 *Situation*

You have just completed a two year BTEC Business Studies Course and have been asked by an old school friend, J Starky, to have a look at his books. J Starky has been running a retailing business for the past year and needs to know what his state of affairs is for taxation purposes.

Information

J Starky's summary cash book for the year ended 31/3/88 is as follows:

	£		£
1/4 Balance b/f	10 000	Payments to suppliers	157 340
Cash sales	50 000	Cash purchases	7 880
Cash received from debtors	219 500	Rent	22 500
		Rates	900
		Salaries	13 080
		Wages	30 500
		General expenses	22 000
		Drawings	15 000
		31/3 Balance c/f	10 300
	279 500		279 500

His assets and liabilities were:

	1/4/87	*31/3/88*
	£	£
Creditors for goods	28 400	30 010
Rent owing		500

(Continues)

	1/4/87	*31/3/88*
	£	£
Stock	54 000	53 000
Debtors	46 600	55 700
Prepaid rates	—	295
Fixtures and fittings	10 000	10 000
Vehicle	7 500	7 500

In preparing the accounts you decide:

i) To depreciate the vehicle by $33\frac{1}{3}$ per cent.
ii) To depreciate the fixtures and fittings by 10 per cent.
iii) To make a provision for bad debts of 5 per cent.
iv) To assume (based on J Starky's estimate) that J Starky has taken £1000 worth of goods from the business for his own use.

REQUIRED:

Prepare the trading and profit and loss account for the year ended 31 March 1988 and a balance sheet as at that date.

(BTEC National)

2 D Bazen's assets and liabilities on 1 January 1984 and 31 December 1984 were:

	(1/1/84)	*(31/12/84)*
	£	£
Cash in hand	420	490
Cash at bank		96
Bank loan (repayable in 1990)	3 000	3 000
Bank overdraft	6 000	
Stock in trade	2 100	3 600
Trade debtors	3 420	3 561
Trade creditors	2 916	1 696
Equipment	5 000	4 800
Premises	25 000	25 000
Expenses paid in advance	231	360
Rent received in advance	96	89
Expenses accrued	41	52
Rent receivable	67	161

During the year ended 31 December 1984, Bazen had withdrawn cash £8000, for private use, and had paid the proceeds of selling his private car, £6220, into the business.

REQUIRED:

a) An opening statement of affairs as at 1 January 1984, to find the opening capital.
b) A closing statement of affairs as at 31 December 1984, to find the closing capital.
c) A statement showing the calculation of the net profit for the year ended 31 December 1984.

(AEB Nov '85)

3 On 30 November 1986 A Mole's balances were: premises £76 000; fittings £2320; stock £4060; bank overdraft £3515; trade debtors £2500; trade creditors; £5100; capital £?.

A Mole does not keep full accounting records, but the following information, relating to the half year ended 31 May 1987, is available.

Bank account

	£		£
Sales	5 060	Balance b/d	3 515
Debtors	14 021	Drawings	3 610
Balance c/d	23 728	Expenses	2 444
		Creditors	13 240
		Premises	20 000
	42 809		42 809

Cash discount allowed amounted to £52 and cash discount received was £65.
Depreciation on fittings is at the rate of 10 per cent per annum.
On 31 May 1987 the following figures are available: stock £5012; trade creditors £2341; trade debtors £4323.

REQUIRED:

a) For the six months ended 31 May 1987:
   i) the trade debtors' total account and the trade creditors' total account, showing the calculation of credit sales and credit purchases;
   ii) the trading and profit and loss account.
b) The balance sheet as at 31 May 1987.
c) An explanation of the meaning of cash discount. How does cash discount affect the proprietor's capital?

(AEB June '87)

4 *Situation*

Ted Albeury is a retailer who does not keep the appropriate accounting books. He keeps records of receipts and payments through the bank and also other significant documents such as invoices and general bills attributed to his business. He seeks assistance from a firm of accountants where you work as a junior assistant.

At the commencement of his financial year, 1 January 1988 his statement of affairs showed he had the following balances:

	£	£
Premises	100 000	
Fixtures, fittings and equipment	10 000	
Motor vehicle	3 500	
Debtors	2 750	
Creditors		2 600

(Continues)

	£	£
Stock	4 780	
Bank loan (10 years) 12% p.a.		40 400
Capital		80 000
Rates in advance	70	
Wages owing		100

His summarised bank statement for the year:

Receipts	£	*Payments*	£
Balance (1 Jan)	2 000	Payments to suppliers	38 550
Receipts from sales	47 250	Light and heat	295
Rent received	1 510	Advertising	300
		Wages to assistant	1 550
		Drawings	2 875
		Rates	250
		Motor expenses	750
		Equipment purchases	1 300
		General expenses	1 705
		Balance (31 Dec)	3 185
	50 760		50 760

NOTES

Discount given to customers, £225.
Discount from suppliers, £550.

Further information at 31 December 1988:

		£
a)	Debtors	1 800
	Creditors	2 465
	Stock	4 190

b) The motor vehicle is revalued at £3000.
Fixtures to be depreciated by 25 per cent on 1 January 1988 value.
c) The rates were £90 paid in advance and wages still outstanding were £75.
d) A full year's interest is owing on the bank loan.

TASKS:

Prepare the following:

a) A computation of sales and purchases figures for the year.
b) Ted Albeury's trading and profit and loss accounts for the year ended 31 December 1988.
c) Ted Albeury's balance sheet as at 31 December 1988, clearly showing working capital and the current ratio in brackets.
d) A brief report to your immediate supervisor including the accounting ratios relating to profit for the financial year ended 31 December 1988.

(Institute of Bankers)

5 Julie Jones, a retailer, did not keep proper books of account. However, it had been possible to provide the following financial information on her activities for the year ended 30 September 1988.

Summarised statements

	Cash	*Bank*		*Cash*	*Bank*
	£	£		£	£
Balances (1/10/87)	178	2 580	Wages and salaries	1 300	
Rate rebate after			Lighting and heating		190
appeal		50	Advertising	35	
Shop takings			Rent and rates		550
(including receipts			Payments to self		2 500
from credit sales)	1 580	16 990	Creditors for goods	170	12 270
Surrender of			Repairs to shop		
private national			window		25
savings bonds		550	Running expenses		
			motor van	32	170
			Additional shop		
			shelving		350
			Purchase of new		
			motor van		1 700
			Balances at (30/9/88)	221	2 415
			c/d		

NOTES

Discounts allowed, £125.
Discounts received, £247.

1 Balances other than cash or bank as at 1 October 1987 were:

	£
Premises	15 000
Fixtures and fittings	2 580
Rent owing	75
Motor van	350
Trade debtors	750
Prepaid advertising	70
Stock	3 000
Trade creditors	1 433

2 Balances other than cash and bank as at 30 September 1988:

	£
Trade debtors	1 870
Trade creditors	2 400
Stock	4 350

3 The proprietor took £130 of goods for her own use during the year.

4 The existing motor van was disposed of early in the year for £200; settlement had not been received for this amount.
The new van was to be depreciated at 20 per cent on cost.

5 Fixtures and fittings were depreciated at 10 per cent per annum on the reducing balance method including any additions.

6 At 30 September 1988: rent in arrears, £120; advertising paid in advance, £15.

REQUIRED:

a) Prepare a trading and profit and loss account for the year ended 30 September 1988.
b) A balance sheet as at that date.

(AEB)

6 R Smithers runs a retail store in the local village. After a fire on the night of 20 June, he lost most of his stock. He needed to make an assessment of the stock lost in the fire for insurance purposes.
Information:

	£
Sales to 20 June	26 800
Margin on sales 20 per cent	
Purchases to 20 June	20 500
Stock salvaged at cost	400
Stock 1 January	3 850
Returns out	90

REQUIRED:

a) A constructed trading account on 20 June to indicate the stock position at this date.
b) The amount of stock lost in the fire for insurance purposes.

7 During the night of 17 June 1983 the premises of Match Ltd were damaged by a fire which also destroyed a quantity of stock and all of the company's stock records. The destroyed stock was covered by insurance against loss by fire and the company wishes to calculate the amount to claim. The following information is available:

i)	*(On 1/1/83)* £000	*(On 17/6/83)* £000
Stock at cost	132	
Trade creditors	45	53
Trade debtors	39	47

ii) The following transactions took place between 1 January and 17 June 1983

	£000
Cash purchases	17
Payments to creditors	274
Cash received from debtors	314
Cash sales	80
Discounts received	10
Discounts allowed	8

iii) A physical stock take carried out first thing in the morning on 18 June 1983 showed the remaining stock to have a cost of £91 000.

iv) Match Ltd earns a gross profit of 30 per cent of selling price on all of its sales.

REQUIRED:

Calculate the cost of the stock destroyed by the fire.

(RSA)

8 *Situation*

You work for a firm of accountants which prepares the accounts for R Powell Ltd. During the night of 2 June 1990 the company suffered a fire which destroyed all the company's stock records and a quantity of stock. The stock was covered by insurance against loss by fire. You have been asked by your firm to assist with preparing the insurance claim and have ascertained the following information:

a)

	On 1/1/90	*On 2/6/90*
	£	£
Stock at cost	64 500	?
Trade debtors	78 250	94 725
Trade creditors	90 100	106 400

b) The following transactions took place between 1/1/90 and 2/6/90:

	£
Cash purchases	34 200
Payments to creditors	184 500
Cash received from debtors	282 250
Cash sales	60 900
Discount received	2 000
Discount allowed	1 600

c) The physical stocktake, carried out first thing in the morning on 3/6/90, showed the remaining stock (undamaged) to have a cost value of £105 000.

d) The company operates a standard margin of 40 per cent on gross profit.

REQUIRED:

Calculate the cost of the stock destroyed by the fire.

(BTEC National)

CHAPTER

32 Accounting for wages

- *How are wages of an employee calculated, after taking into account income tax and National Insurance contributions?*
- *What is understood by the different terms associated with the wages of an employee, such as taxable income, gross and net pay, etc.?*

Introduction

Most people have to work for a living and earn an income to pay for the things they need and want. A minority of people are self-employed; they run their own businesses and are sole traders or are in partnership. An accountant would normally be engaged to take charge of their financial affairs at the year-end and prepare the final accounts on their behalf. The accountant would probably prepare their income tax returns for the Inland Revenue and advise them on how much tax they would be liable for.

The self-employed must also pay their share of National Insurance contributions to ensure that they too can claim benefits from the State, in the event of sickness or unemployment.

The majority of people earn their wages or salaries by working for an employer. Wages are usually paid on a weekly basis to non-office staff, whereas salaries are more often associated with monthly payments, most commonly through a bank or post office giro system.

Gross and net pay

The gross pay of an employee refers to the total sum earned before any deductions are made from pay, that is, before income tax and National Insurance contributions, or any other items are taken from pay.

Example

A man earns £14 560 per annum gross pay which is £280 per week. From this sum, the Inland Revenue will take an appropriate amount for taxation and the Department of Social Security (DSS) will take its share of National Insurance contributions.

Deductions

Income tax and National Insurance contributions are both statutory deductions from pay, demanded by law, and paid to the Exchequer (the Government's account). The rates levied by the Chancellor of the Exchequer tend to vary each year in his annual Budget during March. Tax and National Insurance tables are made available to employers to enable them to make the correct deductions from pay.

There may also be some items deducted from pay which are non-statutory, such as pensions or superannuation contributions, voluntary savings, trade union or other subscriptions. All these items may be deducted from an employee's gross pay to arrive at the net pay.

Income tax

Income tax in the UK is a progressive form of tax which means that the higher the person's income, the more tax is paid. In the last few years, the Chancellor reduced the tax bands to two levels:

a) earnings to the first £20 700 per annum, at 25 per cent rate.
b) earnings from £20 701 and above this figure, at 40 per cent rate.

All employees are liable to pay income tax through the PAYE (Pay As You Earn) system, where employers deduct the tax charge directly from their employee's pay.

Tax is not levied on gross pay. Each person is entitled to a personal allowance from pay, which may be deducted from gross pay, to arrive at what is known as the *taxable income*, that is, the income which is taxed.

In 1990–1 the allowance rates applicable were:

single person's allowance: £3005 per annum.
married couples' allowance: £4725 per annum.

Examples

a) A married person, earning a gross income of £14 560 per annum, will have a taxable income of:

£14 560 − £4725 = £9835
tax due = £9835 × 25 per cent
= £2458.75 per annum
or £47.28 per week.

b) A single person earning a gross income of £14 560 per annum, will have a taxable income of:

£14 560 − £3005 = £11 555
tax due = £11 555 × 25 per cent
= £2888.75 per annum
or £55.55 per week.

In addition to personal allowances decided by the Exchequer, a person may be entitled to other taxable deductions such as pension fund contributions, subscriptions to professional bodies and mortgage interest relief. When interest relief is not deducted at source, that is, the payment of the mortgage is net of the interest relief, as in the MIRAS (Mortgage Interest Relief At Source) scheme, the interest payable has a relief of tax. In other words, the interest payable acts as a further tax allowance. If the mortgage interest in a year is £750, then £750 can be used as a deductible tax allowance.

Example

A married man earning £14 560 per annum, contributes to a pension fund paying 6 per cent of his gross salary. He also has a mortgage which he pays £750 in interest payments and is not part of the MIRAS scheme. How much tax is he liable to pay?

Allowances	£
Married allowance	4 725.00
Pension (6 per cent)	873.60
Mortgage interest relief	750.00
	6 348.60
Taxable income	
Gross pay	14 560.00
Less allowances	6 348.60
	8 211.40

Tax at 25 per cent = £2052.85 per annum or £39.47 per week.

Tax tables

The Inland Revenue provide employers with two books of tables for them to make the appropriate calculations for income tax. Table A gives the amount of weekly 'free pay' an employee is entitled to in order to get to his taxable income. Table B is linked to Table A and gives the weekly amount of tax payable.

National Insurance contributions

An employee pays National Insurance towards his sick pay and unemployment benefit. It is, in fact, another form of direct tax which is statutory. The DSS provide employers with Contribution Tables to enable them to make the appropriate deductions. At the time of publication, the 1990–91 rates for an employee were:

Lower limit: up to the first £46 per week at 2 per cent of gross pay.
Upper limit: from £46.01 to a maximum of £350 per week, 9 per cent of gross pay.

Example

A person earns £100 per week, how much National Insurance would he pay?

On £46 × 2 per cent = £0.92
On £54 × 9 per cent = £4.86
£5.78

The employer must also pay a proportion of National Insurance for each of his employees. This sum may change occasionally, depending on what the Chancellor decides. Usually, the amount paid correlates by about twice the sum the employee pays. In the above example, the employer's contribution would be about £11.56.

In the event that employees are sick and absent from their work, the employer must pay the employee the appropriate sum called Statutory Sick Pay (SSP). This payment is normally for up to 28 weeks of sickness for full-time workers. Whilst receiving sickness benefit, employees must still pay the same rates for tax and insurance, the employers recover SSP by deducting the sum payable to the DSS from the National Insurance contributions they forward each month.

The pay slip (or pay advice)

This is the employee's individual pay details which will indicate his gross pay, deductions and net pay. Other details are also shown such as earnings, tax, insurance and superannuation totals to date.

PAY ADVICE

Details	Period	Tax Period	Tax Code	Dept/Works No.
A0074	30.0.90	01 91	O472H	4560

	Pay & Allow.	Deductions	
Gross	1 280.75	Supn.	76.85
Less	(59.54)	NIC	79.65
SSP	59.54	Tax	209.50
Total	1 280.75		366.00

Totals to Date	Pay	Supn.	Taxable Pay	Tax	NIC	O/Time	SSP
	1 280.75	76.85	1 203.90	209.5	79.65		59.54

A payroll of a business is simply the total details of each employee indicating their gross pay, all deductions, amount of free pay and their net pay.

In those businesses which keep a ledger system, the payroll is used to transfer details, in total, of gross pay, National Insurance contributions, income tax and other deductions, to the accounting records.

Cash book payments (30/6)	*Credit*
	£
Net pay	9 600.75
Pension fund	860.25
Income tax	2 960.50
National Insurance	1 846.50
	15 268.00

Ledger

		Debit	Credit	Balance
		£	£	£
Wages account				
30/6	Gross pay	15 268		15 268 Dr

Summary

1 Wages are made up of gross pay less deductions for taxation and National Insurance contributions. Other items such as pension schemes and subscription payments may also be deducted in arriving at the net pay.

2 Employees pay tax and National Insurance as statutory deductions to the Inland Revenue.

3 Taxable income is that part of income which is taxed, that is, after deducting personal and other allowances.

4 The Chancellor of the Exchequer reviews the Nation's income and expenditure for the year in his March budget. He may wish to incorporate changes to tax rates, National Insurance and personal allowances as part of the Government's economic and social policies.

5 The pay advice slip is the personal information of an employee which indicates details of his gross and net pay. The payroll is the listing of all employees' pay, as indicated on their pay advice slips.

QUESTIONS

1 Calculate the gross pay for each of the following employees:
a) Tom 40 hours
b) Dick $38\frac{1}{2}$ hours
c) Harry 45 hours
The basic working week is 36 hours and the pay is £3 per hour. For any overtime above 36 hours, the rate is at time and a half per hour.

2 Calculate the net pay of Jack Jones from the following:

Gross pay	£120 per week.
Deductions	
Pension fund	£12.50
National Insurance	£7.58
Trade union	£0.65
PAYE (to calculate)	?

Allowances
Personal allowance £57.79 'free pay'
Pension fund £12.50

3 Calculate the net pay of Freddie from the following:

Basic pay: 36 hours at £5 per hour
Overtime: 4 hours at time and a quarter per hour.

Deductions:
National Insurance: Use 1990–1 rates
Taxable allowance: Freddie is allowed £57.79 tax free pay
Basic tax rate: 25 per cent.

4 A single person works a basic 36-hour week and earns £144. All overtime is paid at one and a quarter. In a week where he works 43 hours, calculate his net pay, using 1990–1 rates for tax and National Insurance contributions.

5 A married couple earn the following rates of pay:
One earns a salary of £14 820 per annum and pays 4 per cent of the salary towards a pension fund;
The other person earns £120 per week.
Calculate their separate net incomes per week, using the 1990–1 rates for tax and National Insurance contributions. Assume the married couples' allowance to be taken on the annual salary.

CHAPTER

33 Accounting for departments

- *How can accounting be adapted to assist management?*

Introduction

This particular aspect of accounting is most useful to those retail stores which may have many different departments, each department really a store in its own right. In some of the large departmental stores like Boots, Debenhams and Dingles, the size of some of their departments is far larger than many individual shops, with huge turnovers, numbers of employees and budgets of thousands of pounds.

For such stores, it is an immediate advantage to know how successful or otherwise, each of their departments is and therefore, it is of great value to be able to assess the individual profit or loss of each department as well as for the store as a whole.

Comparisons can be made inter-departmentally to see if each of their activities are up to the targets set for them by the management. Results can then be analysed and evaluated and those departments whose figures are different from the budgeted figures, can then be called upon to explain the reasons behind the variances which may have occurred.

Example

A store makes a profit of £35 000 overall, the break-down being as follows:

	Profit	*Loss*
	£	£
Ladies wear	15 000	
Mens wear		(18 000)
Footwear	10 000	
Furnishings	6 000	
Household	22 000	
	53 000	(18 000)

If the total of the store's profit only had been calculated, it would have hidden the significant fact that mens wear had made a loss of £18 000. By calculating individual profit or loss for each of the departments, it becomes easier to analyse the financial performance of separate departments and helps management to make better decisions relating to all aspects of the store, sales, purchasing, staff and costs.

Costs

As far as costs are concerned, a cost incurred by a specific department, directly attributed to it such as wages or materials, is known as an *allocation* of cost.

If a cost is incurred for the benefit of a number of departments and is not so easily traceable to any specific one, it is known as an *apportion* of cost. For example, rent, rates and insurance may cost a store £5000 per month but how should this be apportioned to each of the departments? The size of a department in terms of floor area, the number of staff employed or the value of sales, can be used as the basis for distribution of the cost.

Example

The following information relates to the monthly figures of three departments:

	Mens wear	*Ladies wear*	*Footwear*	*Total*
	£	£	£	£
Sales	24 000	60 000	12 000	96 000
Cost of sales	16 000	24 000	3 600	43 600
Wages	3 800	4 200	2 600	10 600
Rent, rates, insurance				4 200
Sales and distribution				8 000
Administration				12 000
Total cost				78 400

How much profit did each department make?

The policy of the management is to apportion those costs not specific to any one section, according to the following criteria (or base):

a) Rent, rates, insurance and administration should be distributed in relation to floor area:

Mens wear	$\frac{1}{3}$
Ladies wear	$\frac{1}{2}$
Footwear	$\frac{1}{6}$

b) Sales and distribution costs should be distributed in relation to sales value:

Mens wear	$\frac{24}{96}$	$(\frac{2}{8})$
Ladies wear	$\frac{60}{96}$	$(\frac{5}{8})$
Footwear	$\frac{12}{96}$	$(\frac{1}{8})$

Departmental trading and profit and loss account, month ending, 31 May

	Mens wear	*Ladies wear*	*Footwear*	*Total*
	£	£	£	£
Sales	24 000	60 000	12 000	96 000
Cost of sales	16 000	24 000	3 600	43 600
Gross profit	8 000	36 000	8 400	52 400
Wages	3 800	4 200	2 600	10 600
Rent, rates, insurance	1 400	2 100	700	4 200
Sales and distribution	2 000	5 000	1 000	8 000
Administration	4 000	6 000	2 000	12 000
	11 200	17 300	6 300	34 800
Net profit/loss	(3 200)	18 700	2 100	17 600

The outcome of these figures indicate that ladies wear obviously carries the store, having the greatest profit of £18 700, against a poor performance by mens wear, which suffered a loss of £3200. Footwear had a relatively small profit of £2100.

These figures only relate to the month of May. What has been the trend? Is this just a poor month for mens wear or is the department showing signs of becoming a liability to the store as a whole? Management should investigate and research these performances and try to evaluate what is needed to turn mens wear back into a profitable department.

Summary

1. Departmental accounting helps management to identify the performance of each department or product in the organisation.

2. Costs may be allocated and apportioned to the relevant departments (or cost centres) according to bases such as floor area, sales value or the number of employees working in a department.

3. Individual figures for profit or loss may be calculated for each department as well as the overall profit of the organisation.

4. This form of accounting can help management in their decision making and in the evaluation of a department's (or cost centre's) individual performance.

QUESTIONS

1 Jake's store has two major departments, electrical and furnishings. The financial figures for the month of August were:

	Electrical	*Furnishings*	*Total*
	£	£	£
Sales	50 000	75 000	125 000
Stock (1/9)	8 400	6 500	14 900
Purchases	34 500	40 000	74 500
Stock (30/9)	10 900	8 500	19 400
Wages	8 000	12 000	20 000
Administration			8 000
Sales and distribution			6 000
Rent and rates			10 000
Depreciation charges			6 000

The apportioning of expenses is as follows:

a) Administration and depreciation costs on the basis of floor area: $\frac{1}{4}$ (electrical) and $\frac{3}{4}$ (furnishings).
b) Rates, rent and insurance on the basis of floor area and number of employees: $\frac{2}{5}$ (electrical) and $\frac{3}{5}$ (furnishings).
c) Sales and distribution costs on the basis of sales value.

REQUIRED:

a) Prepare a trading and profit and loss account of Jake's Store for the month of August, in columnar form, to show both gross and net profit for each department as well as the overall total profit.
b) Briefly comment on your findings.

2 a) What is the basic difference between the allocation of a cost and the apportioning of a cost? Give examples to clarify your answer.
b) On which kind of bases can expenses be apportioned? Suggest on what bases the following expenses could be distributed:
rent and rates
light and heat
advertising and selling
canteen costs
administration
depreciation of motor vehicles (representatives)
depreciation of fixtures and fittings (store).

3 Carlingford Ltd is a large store and the following information relates to the year ended 31 December:

		£
Sales:		
Department	A	21 400
	B	33 600
	C	24 800
	D	18 600
Purchases:		
Department	A	17 900
	B	24 700
	C	21 100
	D	14 900
Returns outward:		
Department	A	350
	B	560
	C	320
	D	810
Stock (1 Jan):		
Department	A	2 940
	B	3 760
	C	4 100
	D	1 670
Stock (31 Dec):		
Department	A	3 490
	B	1 900
	C	2 880
	D	1 760

Purchases of £1000 were transferred from department A to department C.

REQUIRED:

You are asked to prepare a departmental trading account in columnar form for the period ended 31 December. You should also calculate the gross profit percentage of each department.

(RSA)

4 Jacksons & Walker is a store which has three departments, A, B and C. The following information relates to the business's financial year ended 31 December 1990:

		£
Stocks on 1/1/90:		
Department	A	4 400
	B	6 000
	C	11 000

(Continues)

	£
Stocks on 31/1/90:	
Department A	3 300
B	4 600
C	7 500
Purchases:	
Department A	64 000
B	84 000
C	102 000
Wages and salaries:	
Department A	30 600
B	33 500
C	42 000
Light and heat	3 300
Rent, rates, insurance	4 800
General administration	6 000
Distribution costs	8 500
Sales:	
Department A	120 000
B	180 000
C	200 000

Those expenses not directly attributed to any one department are to be apportioned:

a) Light and heat to be borne equally between departments.
b) Rent, rates and insurance and general administration according to space: department A, $\frac{1}{5}$, departments B and C $\frac{2}{5}$ each.
c) Distribution costs to be distributed in relation to the sales value.

REQUIRED:

a) Prepare the trading and profit and loss account for each department in columnar form, including a column for totals.
b) Calculate the gross and net margins of each department and briefly state your findings.

5 The following information relates to the activities of A Parrish, a wholesaler, selling two distinct products, X and Y, for the year ended, 31 March 1981.

Balances as at 1 April 1980

	£
Freehold premises at cost	36 000
Capital	118 700
Motor vehicles at cost	20 000
Fixtures and fittings at cost	25 000
Stocks: X	6 500
Y	26 000
Provisions for depreciation:	
Motor vehicles	3 500
Fixtures and fittings	4 500

Balances as at 31 March 1981

	£
Purchases: X	35 000
Y	158 000
Sales: X	43 500
Y	201 950
Sales return: X	3 500
Y	11 950
Purchases return: X	4 300
Y	14 900
Drawings	9 000
Trade creditors	21 000
Trade debtors	22 950
Balance at bank	18 900
Cash	3 050
Administration expenses	15 000
Selling expenses	21 500

The following further information had not yet been taken into account:

i) during the year he had taken £450 of good X for his own use; the goods taken were valued at cost price;

ii) depreciation was to be provided as follows:
motor vehicles 20 per cent on cost
fixtures and fittings 10 per cent on cost;

iii) stocks at 31 March 1981:

	£
X	7 750
Y	31 200

iv) commissions owing to sales team as at 31 March 1981 were £1350;

v) administration expenses paid for 1981–82 were £1500.

REQUIRED:

a) Separate trading accounts for each of the products X and Y (columnar presentation may be used) for the year ended 31 March 1981.

b) A profit and loss account for the whole business for the year ended 31 March 1981.

c) A detailed statement of the working capital as at 31 March 1981.

(AEB)

CHAPTER

34 Examination techniques

- *How should students prepare for their examinations?*
- *What factors can help them to be successful?*

Introduction

Many candidates waltz into examination rooms without any thought to pre-planning or having much idea what to expect. They hope for the best. If candidates are serious about wanting to pass their examinations, they should of course be thoroughly prepared for them.

Part of this examination preparation includes knowing the full extent of the syllabus of the subject that they are taking and to have attempted a reasonable number of past examination questions in order to get the feel of what is to come.

The syllabus, or scheme of work, should be covered more than adequately and this means that leaving convenient chunks out of it should not be left to chance. It is too much of a risk to say, 'This or that part will not be in because it was in last year'. So many students have come out of an examination wishing they had done some revision on a particular topic because they had neglected to revise it with any thoroughness, if at all.

Revision

A revision list should be drawn up well before an examination is due. A list of topics should be completed which adequately covers the major features of a course. From these topics, the basic underlying principles should be understood. For example:

Balance sheets

Check list: the accounting equation
types of assets, liabilities and capital
format – vertical or horizontal
calculation of working capital
capital employed
liquidity ratios.

Once a check list has been completed, questions on balance sheets, including past examination questions if possible, should be attempted.

Revision time varies from one student to the next but it should commence in sufficient time so that all the broad areas of a course syllabus are covered.

It should be the aim of every accounting student to practise so many practical questions as possible on all areas of the course, rather than to specialise in an inadequate number of areas. Just practising your favourite type of questions may not be sufficient to be awarded a pass.

The examination

Can a student complete the whole paper in reasonable time? Correct timing is very important in any type of examination. A student should be alert to how long each question is given and therefore how long he or she should take to do it. Some questions are awarded more marks than others and it is necessary to allocate the right proportion of time to the right question. For example:

> A paper has three hours allowed with a total of six questions. Part A requires the student to attempt two questions from three.
> Part B is the same. The student must, therefore, attempt two questions from each part.
> There are 30 marks allotted to each question in A.
> There are 20 marks allotted to each question in B.
>
> Time suggested: allow about 50 minutes per question in A.
> Allow about 35 minutes per question in B. (Total 170 minutes.)
> This leaves a balance of 10 minutes for reading and final checking.

Too many students spend a totally disproportionate length of time attempting to balance their accounts, particularly the balance sheet or trial balance. Only a little time should be spent searching for a balance. As long as the main structure of the accounts is correct and the basic principles have been followed, this should be adequate to succeed in the question.

Students should always keep a steady eye on the clock and make sure they do not stay on the same question too long. Once the allotted time is up, every attempt must be made to close the question and start the next one. Unfortunately, it is little use attempting two very good questions out of a possible five. Every attempt should be made to complete the paper.

In the examination room, try to relax, breath deeply and off you go. Find a seat where you think you will be comfortable and make sure you have sufficient light. Ensure that you have your watch on the desk in front of you or that you can easily see a clock.

Procedure

a) When you are allowed to commence the exam, read over the paper briefly but carefully. Make sure you only answer the number of questions you are required to do.

b) Try to make a choice as soon as you can and tick the questions you want to do.

c) Always attempt what you consider to be the easiest question first. This should give you some early confidence and get you started.

d) If any errors are found, you could, in pencil, lightly cross them through and correct them, or it may be better to correct perhaps the final figures and make a note to the examiner pointing out the errors you have located.

e) Although you will need to write rather quickly in examinations, try not to sacrifice presentation altogether for speed. You still need to present accounts quite legibly and always allow yourself plenty of space for each question. Nothing is worse for the examiner than accounts all crammed into a limited space.

f) Use a fresh sheet of paper for the start of a new question. This is sound organisational practice, both for you and the examiner. You can always go back to finish a question more easily if each question is separated by its own sheet of paper.

g) Try to use a ruler, at least to underline headings and side headings. Major totals should also be underlined. It makes your work look organised and competent.

h) Most of the practical accounting questions require three columns for figures. Try to use these effectively. For example, in the trading and profit and loss account make the adjustment in the first column and net off in the second:

Less expenses

	£	£	£
Wages	1 500		
+ Accrued	200	1 700	
Light and heat		550	
Overheads		1 800	
Rates	420		
– Prepaid	30	390	4 440

i) Try to complete the whole paper. Do not spend all your time on only half the questions. Otherwise you will not stand much of a chance of success.

Prepare for your examinations thoroughly. Like a conductor in an orchestra giving a performance, all the hard work has already been done prior to the performance. The musicians can then concentrate on giving their best. Whether you revise up to the very last minute or have an evening off just before the day, is simply a matter of choice.

When Nick Faldo (the golfer) was interviewed after winning the USA Masters, it was pointed out that he was rather lucky. His reply was 'Yes, I find the more I practise, the luckier I get.'

Work hard and good luck in all your examinations.

CHAPTER

35 Projects

1 The balance sheets of different business organisations

Situation

Study the balance sheets provided below. They are of three distinct business organisations from the private sector (that is, businesses owned and controlled by private individuals and not the State).

TASK 1:

Identify the status of each of the three organisations (that is, sole traders, partnerships and limited companies). Explain how you were able to identify their respective categories, using figures from the respective balance sheets to clarify your answer.

TASK 2:

From the balance sheets provided, calculate the working capital ratios of each organisation over the two financial periods. Briefly comment on each organisation's ability to cover its debts.

TASK 3:

Prepare a balance sheet, using your own figures, of any business organisation of your choice. Ensure the business has a working capital ratio close to what is generally accepted as the ideal ratio.

Business A –
Balance sheet as at 31 October 1990

	1990		*1989*
	£000	*£000*	*£000*
FIXED ASSETS			
Investments		33 020	33 020
CURRENT ASSETS			
Stocks	10 380		7 907
Debtors	44 000		27 080
Cash/bank	2		2
	54 382		34 989

(Continues)

	1990 £000	1990 £000	1989 £000
CREDITORS FALLING WITHIN ONE YEAR			
Creditors/accruals	33 096		32 496
NET CURRENT ASSETS		21 286	2 493
Total assets, less current liabilities		54 306	35 513
CREDITORS FALLING AFTER ONE YEAR			
Loan stock		16 667	16 667
		37 639	18 846
CAPITAL AND RESERVES			
Issued and paid-up capital		10 000	8 333
Reserves		24 859	7 447
Profit and loss account		2 780	3 066
		37 639	18 846

Business B –
Balance sheet as at 31 December 1990

	1990 £	1990 £	1989 £
FIXED ASSETS			
Land and buildings	50 000		
Fixtures and fittings	12 000		
Motor vans	6 150	68 150	60 800
CURRENT ASSETS			
Stock	28 050		
Debtors	21 600		
Bank/cash	6 900		
Prepayments	700	57 250	49 300
CURRENT LIABILITIES			
Creditors	26 000		
Accruals	2 100	28 100	17 200
Working capital		29 150	32 100
Capital employed		97 300	92 900

(Continues)

	1990		1989
	£	£	£
DEFERRED LIABILITIES			
Bank loan		10 000	11 400
		87 300	81 500
FINANCED BY:			
Capital accounts:	35 000		
	35 000	70 000	70 000
Current accounts:	8 500		
	8 800	17 300	11 500
		87 300	81 500

Business C –
Balance sheet as at 31 June 1990

	1990		1989
	£	£	£
FIXED ASSETS			
Premises	20 000		
Motor vehicle	4 230	24 230	24 110
CURRENT ASSETS			
Stock	76 170		
Debtors	8 184		
Cash	1 190	85 544	46 569
CURRENT LIABILITIES			
Trade creditors		30 631	11 962
Net current assets		54 913	34 607
Capital employed		79 143	58 717
LONG-TERM LIABILITIES			
Mortgage on premises		23 354	25 417
		55 789	33 300
FINANCED BY			
Capital:	33 300		30 000
Profit	28 500		16 500
Drawings	(6 011)		(13 200)
		55 789	33 300

2 Input of information

Situation

The following information relate to the accounts of Jenkins Jeans Ltd as on 1 January 1990:

Balance sheet as on 1 January 1990

		£	£
FIXED ASSETS			
Premises		20 000	
Plant and equipment		4 500	
Motor vehicle		4 000	28 500
CURRENT ASSETS			
Stock		1 000	
Debtors:			
Davies	800		
Smith	450		
Jones	250	1 500	
Bank		750	
		3 250	
CURRENT LIABILITIES			
Creditors:			
Harries	1 250		
Brown	250	1 500	
Net current assets			1 750
			30 250
FINANCED BY			
Capital			30 250

TASK A:

Enter the above accounts in the books of Jenkins Jeans Ltd using sales and purchases ledgers for personal accounts and the nominal ledger for all other accounts, as on 1 January 1990.

During the month of January, the following invoices were sent to customers:

	Name	*Invoice*	*Amount* £
5/1	Davies	2334	200 +15%
12/1	Smith	2335	80 +15%
17/1	Davies	2336	120 +15%
21/1	Forbes (new)	2337	400 +15%
28/1	Smith	2338	300 +15%
30/1	Jones	2339	180 +15%

Invoices received from suppliers during the month of January were:

	Name	*Invoice*	*Amount*
			£
11/1	Harries	8875	360 +15%
17/1	Brown	33391/4	120 +15%
25/1	Harries	9320	400 +15%
28/1	James (new)	1212	160 +15%

Credit note sent to customer:

24/1	Davies	c/n 42	60 +15%

TASK B:

Prepare the sales and purchases day books for the month of January. The credit note may be included in the sales day book as a negative figure.

If computer-based accounts are to be prepared, give each account an appropriate account number and also ensure that the opening customer and supplier balances are entered in the sales and purchases ledger programs.

Cheques received during January were:

	Name	*Amount*
		£
28/1	Davies	760 (discount allowed £40)
30/1	Smith	500 on account
30/1	Forbes	250 on account
31/1	Jones	250 on account
31/1	Cash sales	3 220 (into bank) (Vat £420 included)

Cheques paid during January were:

	Name	*Amount*
		£
25/1	Harries	1 000 on account
28/1	Brown	235 (discount received £15)
30/1	Wages	400
30/1	Overheads	500

TASK C:

Post all cheques received and paid to their appropriate accounts in the personal and nominal ledgers.

If computer-based accounts are prepared, enter all debtors and creditors details in their respective sales and purchases ledger programs.

If a nominal ledger program is used, given an appropriate ledger account for the nominal accounts: sales, purchases, Vat, discounts, wages and overheads.

TASK D:

Prepare a schedule of debtors and creditors for the month of January. If control accounts are used, these should verify the totals of the schedules.

Extract a trial balance as on 31 January 1990.

3 Forecast of final accounts

Situation

The following information relates to G Johnson-Smith, an entrepreneur in sporting goods.

At the financial year end 30 June 1989 his final accounts were:

Trading and profit and loss statement

	£	£	£
Sales			210 000
Cost of sales			
Stock (1/7/88)	8 700		
Purchases	124 600		
	133 300		
Returns out	(2 000)		
	131 300		
Stock (30/6/89)	(5 300)		126 000
			84 000
Sales and distribution costs			
Motor expenses	5 870		
Advertising	580		
General expenses	1 650		
Salesmens' wages	18 900	27 000	
Administration expenses			
Rent and rates	9 005		
Wages, office	20 200		
Printing and stationary	495		
Interest	4 500		
Light and heat	1 800	36 000	63 000
Net profit			21 000

Balance sheet as at year end 30 June 1989

	£	£	£
FIXED ASSETS			
Equipment, tools		55 000	
Motor vans		17 400	72 400
CURRENT ASSETS			
Stock	5 300		
Debtors	4 800		
Bank/cash	2 430		
Pre-payments	310	12 840	
CURRENT LIABILITIES			
Creditors	6 000		
Accruals	740	6 740	
Net current assets			6 100
Capital employed			78 500
DEFERRED LIABILITIES			
9% loan			50 000
Net assets			28 500
FINANCING:			
Capital		20 000	
Profit		21 000	
Drawings		(12 500)	28 500

Mr Smith has *forecast* the following information for the financial year ending 30 June 1990:

a) Sales are expected to increase by 10 per cent.
b) Cost of sales should be held to a 7.5 per cent increase.
c) Sales and distribution costs should increase by 10 per cent largely due to extra spending on advertising.
d) Administration to increase by 5 per cent.
e) Commission received on an expected sports venture should earn £500.
f) Purchases of new fixed assets should increase these to £80 000.
g) Current assets are estimated to increase by 25 per cent but current liabilities by 50 per cent due to an increase in trade creditors.
h) The outstanding loan will be reduced by £45 000.
i) The forecast of drawings for the year will represent the balancing figure under the 'financed by' section in the balance sheet.

TASK A:

From the information given above, draw up a forecast of the trading and profit and loss account and balance sheet for the year to 30 June 1990.

TASK B:

Calculate the following accounting ratios for *both* years, that is 1989 and the forecast to 1990:

a) Gross profit percentage
b) Net profit percentage
c) Return on capital employed
d) Working capital (current ratio)
e) Acid test
f) Any expense ratios you feel significant.

TASK C:

From your findings in Task B, give an outline of Mr Smith's business performance over the current year's trading and the forecasted figures.

4 An evaluation of two companies

Situation

Allied Components plc makes electrical components used in the production of electrical appliances. Because of intense competition, especially from the Far East, the board has taken a decision to diversify Allied's business interests.

Two plans are put forward:

1 To produce other products using existing plant and equipment. This plan is favoured by the production director because his research and development team has devised new plans for other products.

2 To purchase another manufacturing organisation in order to give Allied a wider product range and diversify its markets. This plan is favoured by the finance and sales directors who would like to use the company's funds to acquire subsidiaries. Particular interest has been shown in purchasing one of two private companies which specialise in producing circuit boards used in a wide variety of products. Both companies appear to be sound financial investments.

The companies are:

Arrowsmith Ltd An older, well established company having a stable record of production and profits over a number of years, and a good labour relations record.

Hardcastle Ltd A relatively new company which has rapidly become established. Only a few years trading figures are available but early trend shows rising profits. Young and more aggressive management but more strained labour relations.

Information

The financial director has been able to secure the most recent figures of both of these organisations and you have been asked as one of his assistants to prepare a draft of the final accounts of the two companies and to give a reasoned assessment of them. You have also acquired accounting ratios from Inter-Firm Comparison Ltd provided by the British Institute of Management.

Below information is made available to you relating to Arrowsmith Ltd and Hardcastle Ltd.

Accounting data to year ended December 1989

	Arrowsmith Ltd	*Hardcastle Ltd*
	£	£
Turnover	356 000	327 000
Stock (1/1/89)	62 000	58 750
Cost of production	256 500	201 500
Stock (31/12/89)	84 000	68 750
Sales and distribution costs	28 100	44 800
Administration expenses	44 400	38 700
Interest payable	4 000	5 500
Taxation provision	15 500	14 500
Transfer to reserves	20 000	25 000
Dividends proposed	9 000	2 500
Fixed assets (net values)	156 500	135 100
Debtors	84 200	76 750
Bank/cash	4 800	(10 800) o/d
Prepayments	—	500
Accruals	500	4 900
Creditors	86 500	89 400
Loans (long-term)	40 000	52 000
Issued and paid-up capital		
Ordinary @ £1 shares	100 000	50 000
Reserves (1/1/89)	78 000	27 500

Accounting ratios are provided by the British Institute of Management on electronic industries 1988. The median figures have been supplied for guidance as to financial performance.

	Accounting ratios
	%
Gross margin	40.00
Net profit (b/t)/sales	14.50
Net profit (a/t)/capital employed	20.75
Net profit (a/t)/net worth	29.55
Production cost/sales	60.50
Sales and dist cost/sales	9.50
Administration exp/sales	11.00
Current ratio	Deci 1.85 : 1
Acid test	Deci 0.95 : 1
Capital gearing	80%

(Continues)

	Accounting ratios
Current assets/sales £1000	£450
Fixed assets/sales £1000	£421
Earnings per share	£0.55
Cover	8 times
Dividend per share	£0.05
Yield	Not available
P/E ratio	Not available

The current market value per share for Arrowsmith is 174p and for Hardcastle 256p.

TASKS:

a) Prepare a draft copy of the trading and profit and loss accounts of the two companies for the year ended 31 December 1989.
   Prepare the balance sheets as at that date.
b) Using the inter-firm comparison ratios as a guide, prepare accounting ratios of both companies on which to form your assessment. Include investment ratios for both companies, as listed.
c) Evaluate the case for and against the company which appears to be the better of the two investments. Draw attention to the limitations accounting ratios tend to impose on the assessment of financial performance.

5 Be your own boss

Situation

A number of years after leaving college you and a small group of friends want to start your own business enterprise. When drawing up your personal finances you find that you can invest something in the region of £100 000 between you.

You will need to research thoroughly the kind of business venture you want to undertake and ensure there is sufficient demand for your product or service. You will need answers to the following questions:

Is there an adequate market for your product or service?
What is the competition like?
Who are the potential customers?
What prices are you likely to charge?

You must also decide what type of business organisation you want to set up and whether you need to acquire business premises. You will need to take into consideration:

the relevant Acts; legal implications such as health and safety, contracts of employment, dismissal procedure; the tax authorities to be notified.

You will need to know what kind of stock you require if you decide to produce or trade in products, also what quantities to buy, where to buy and what prices to pay.

If further capital sums are required you will want to know where extra funding may be found.

TASK 1:

Formulate your own business plan which will outline clearly how you propose to establish, organise and control your new business venture. This may be done in groups of not more than five.

TASK 2:

Your business plan is not likely to include any real detail with regard to the day-to-day running of the business.

You are required to supplement the plan and, after due consideration, design and/or give details of the following:

a) Documentation system and procedures.
b) Layout of your business premises, i.e. office, factory etc., giving due regard to the relevant legislation.

The above information will depend on the nature of your business and its requirements.

Present your answer in a suitable format as a supplement to your business plan.

TASK 3:

The law requires that you keep accurate financial records and it is necessary for any successful venture to have adequate finance and to be able to forecast figures ahead of time.

You will need to prepare budgets to indicate your financial plans. You are required to forecast *two* sets of figures, one for the first six months of trading and a second for the first year's trading, i.e. from January to June 1990 and then from January to December 1990. The figures are to flow naturally from one period to the next.

You will need to forecast for six and 12 months each:

a) Cash budgets
b) Trading and profit and loss
c) Balance sheet.

You should also take into consideration:

i) the volume of sales (from market research);
ii) for manufacturing concerns, figures indicating the factory cost;
iii) allowing appropriate sums for depreciation of any fixed assets;
iv) the calculation of stock figures, where appropriate, for both six and 12 months.

d) From the findings of the information above, you are asked to prepare a report which will indicate a forecast of the financial performance of your new business.

Answers

Chapter 1 Accounting information

1 All businesses need to record financial information to help in the control of the business and to allow financial statements to be prepared such as the profit and loss account. The Inland Revenue require accounts so that tax can be charged.
2 The profit and loss account and the balance sheet.
3 Accounting has five groups: assets, liabilities, capital, revenue and expenditure.
4 To record financial transactions, for example buying and selling goods and services.
5 Recording accurately financial information on a day-to-day basis. Software: sales purchase and nominal ledgers, payroll, stock control, invoicing, costing, etc.

Chapter 2 Sources of capital

1 If a sole trader invested his or her own capital, it is likely to be a small sum and this limits the resources of the business. A plc, issuing £1 million shares has the potential to purchase far greater resources.
2 Short-term: creditors, bank overdraft, loans less than 12 months, bills outstanding.
Long-term: loans payable longer than 12 months, debentures, mortgages, hire-purchase agreements.
3 The accounting equation separates the resources of a business (assets) from whoever finances the business (capital and liabilities). The equation is $C = A - L$, or alternatively, $A = C + L$.
4 Shares relate to share capital or ownership capital (equity). Debentures relate to loan capital.
5 Probably with the bank to arrange overdraft facilities or a short-term loan repayable within 12 months. This would normally be used to finance day-to-day expenditure such as wages, purchases of stock, light and heat, etc.
6 What the owner is worth in the business; an owner being a sole trader, partner or shareholder.

Chapter 3 The balance sheet

Note: FA = fixed assets, CA = current assets, CL = current liabilities, WC = working capital, LTL = long-term liabilities.

1 a) Capital £17 740. FA £18 100, CA £54 775, CL £34 382, WC £20 393, LTL £20 753 = £17 740. Capital £15 000 add net profit £4000 less drawings £1260 = £17 740. b) Stock would lose value and both working capital and profit would fall.
2 a) Capital £30 000. b) FA £39 700, CA £10 350, CL £7550, WC £2800, LTL £12 500 = £30 000. Capital £30 000. c) C £30 000 = A £50 050 − L £20 050.

3 a) Capital £40 000. FA £73 100, CA £6645, CL £4745, WC £1900, LTL £35 000 = £40 000. Capital £35 000 add profit £10 000 less drawings £5000 = £40 000. b) 1.4. c) 9%.

4 a) Capital £47 000. FA £81 000, CA £8000, CL £7000, WC £1000, LTL £35 000 = £47 000. Capital £40 000 add profit £7000 = £47 000. b) C £47 000 = A £89 000 − L £42 000. c) Yes, only just.

5 a) Capital (1/1) £2449 less loss and drawings £676 = capital £1773 (31/12). b) FA £1809, WC £2039, LTL £2075 = £1773. c) A poor trading year, a loss of £385.

6 i) Capital £5500. FA £4325, CA £3805, CL £630, WC £3175, LTL £2000 = £5500. Capital £5500. WC ratio = 6.04: 1. ii) C £5500 = A £8130 − L £2630.

7 a) Capital £12 740. FA £11 323, CA £8070, CL £2653, WC £5417, LTL £4000 = £12 740. Capital £10 000 add profit £2990 add £2000 less drawings £2250 = £12 740. b) 3.04. Yes.

8

		Year 1	Year 2	Year 3
a)	WC	£700	£920	£1720
b)	WC ratio	1.5	1.8	1.9
c)	Year 2 (no overdraft).			

9 Profit £11 500. Check: Capital £10 000 add new £2000 add profit £11 500 less drawings £8500 = Capital £15 000 as on 31/12.

10 Capital £11 000. FA £34 050, CA £7370, CL £6420, WC £950, LTL £24 000 = £11 000. Capital £12 000 less drawings £1000 = £11 000. a)–d) Liabilities are excessive. Check: C £11 000 = A £41 420 − L £30 420.

Harry's cash resources are very limited. Relatively small amount of current assets to fixed assets.

Chapter 4 The profit and loss account

Note: FA = fixed assets, CA = current assets, CL = current liabilities, WC = working capital, LTL = long-term liabilities.

1 Gross profit £10 950 net profit £5485. FA £73 750, CA £9260, CL £6525, WC £2735, LTL £30 000 = £46 485. Capital £41 000 add profit £5485 = £46 485.

2 i) Gross profit £86 200 net profit £45 470. ii) FA £16 000, CA £54 100, CL £4200, WC £49 900, LTL £18 000 = £47 900. Capital £16 630 add profit £45 470 less drawings £14 200 = £47 900.

3 i) Gross profit £95 500 net profit £48 600. ii) FA £60 500, CA £21 400, CL £5200, WC £16 200, LTL £10 000 = £66 200. Capital £29 900 add profit £48 600 less drawings £11 800 = £66 200.

4 a) Gross profit £74 900 net profit £22 360. FA £31 370, CA £21 430, CL £6300, WC £15 130, LTL £16 000 = £30 500. Capital £20 500 add profit £22 360 less drawings £12 360 = £30 500. b) 3.4 : 1.

5 Gross profit £7150 net profit £500. FA £61 900, CA £8830, CL £13 055, WC (£4225) negative, LTL £37 175 = £20 500. Capital £20 000 add profit £500 = £20 500. b) WC ratio = 0.68: 1 (insolvent).

6 a) Gross profit £64 619 net profit £32 275. FA £45 650, CA £16 405, CL £8800, WC £7605 = £53 255. Capital £31 400 add profit £32 275 less drawings £10 420 = £53 255. b) WC ratio = 1.86: 1 (sound).

Chapter 5 The ledger system

1 Debit balances: premises, fixtures, debtors, cash, wages, purchases.
Credit balances: creditors, bank overdraft, sales, capital, bank loans, mortgage.

2 Balance c/d £350 Dr. Balance b/d £350 Cr.
Balance c/d £1510 Dr. Balance b/d £1510 Cr (overdraft).
Balance £4775 Cr.

3 Trial balance totals: £27 600. Credit balances: sales, creditors, loan, interest due and capital accounts.

4 Trial balance totals: £7175. Debit balances: bank £2255, Baker £100, purchases £4000, rent £125, general expenses £80, light and heat £80, advertising £35, motor van £500.
Credit balances: capital £2000, sales £2175, T Smith £3000.

5 a) Dr assets £2100, Cr capital £2100.
b) Dr assets £1800, Cr liability £1800.
c) Dr asset £300, Cr asset £300.
d) Dr liability £500, Cr asset £500.
e) Dr asset £2500, Cr liability £2500.
f) Dr asset £1500, Cr asset £1500.
g) Dr asset £500, Cr capital £500.
h) Dr asset £600, Cr asset £600.
$C = A - L$; £2600 = £6400 − £3800.

6 a) Dr expenses £400, Cr liability £400.
b) Dr asset £750, Cr revenue £750.
c) Dr expenses £650, Cr asset £650.
d) Dr expenses £120, Cr asset £120.
e) Dr expenses £35, Cr asset £35.
f) Dr asset £85, Cr revenue £85.
g) Dr asset £60, Cr revenue £60.
h) Dr liability £150, Cr asset £150.
i) Dr expenses £369, Cr liability £369.
j) Dr asset £672, Cr revenue £672.
k) Dr asset £50, Cr asset £50.
l) Dr expenses £15, Cr asset £15.
h) and k) would not affect profit in the profit and loss account.

7 Trial balance totals £3910. Debit balances: David £300, Jones £740, bank £125, purchases £1500, rent £300, wages £125, overheads £70, equipment £750.
Credit balances: capital £650, Robert £650, sales £1010, Andrew £850, Brown £750.

8 Trial balance totals £28 968. Debit balances: drawings £3100, fixtures £2500, stock £2386, purchases £13 255, Gibson £555, bank £1828, general expenses £5344.
Credit balances: capital £7228, sales £21 255, Lowe £485.

9 Trial balance totals £22 800. Debit balances: Round £500, light and heat £670, printing and stationery £590, rent and rates £950, wages £6100, vehicle £1500, equipment £600, discount £300, purchases £11 000, bank £590.
Credit balances: capital £5600, discount received £200, sales £17 000.

10 Nominal ledger: sales, purchases, rent, bank, capital, cash, wages, premises, van.
Sales ledger: Smith.
Purchases ledger: Marks.
Real accounts: bank, cash, premises, van.
Personal accounts: Smith, Marks.
Nominal accounts; sales, purchases, rent, wages.

Chapter 6 The sales journal

1 a) Sales journal value £2260.
b) Sales ledger: Dr side of customer's a/c (asset).
c) Sales a/c (revenue). Cr side.

2 a) Sales journal: sales £1240, Vat £186, total £1426.
b) Sales ledger (all debits): Goldney £414, Capel £391, Carlton £345, Wood £426. Total debtors £1576.
Nominal ledger: sales £1240 Cr, Vat £186 Cr. Sales ledger control £1576 Dr.

3 a) Invoice £65.60, Vat £9.84, total £75.44.
b) Sales journal: Creese £75.44 Dr, sales £65.60 Cr, Vat £9.84 Cr.
c) As a cross-checking device with the sales ledger.

4 a) Sales journal: Product A £840, Product B £220, Vat £159, total £1219.
b) Sales ledger (all debits): Jones £526, Smith £713, Brown £1250.
c) Nominal ledger: sales A £840. Cr, sales B £220 Cr, Vat £159 Cr, S/L control £2489 Dr.
d) Debtors schedule: £526, £713, £1250 = £2489.

5 a) Sales journal: sales S161 £500, S162 £200, S163 £560, Vat £189, total £1449.
b) Sales accounts (all credits): S161 £500, S162 £200, S163 £560.
c) Sales ledger (all debits): Davies £1168, Smith £887, Forbes £644.

Chapter 7 The purchases journal

1 a) Purchases journal: purchases £1800, Vat £270, total £2070.
b) Purchase ledger: credit creditors.
c) Nominal ledger: purchases £1800 Dr, Vat £270 Dr, P/L control £2070 Cr.

2 a) Invoice: Goods £165, Vat £23.51, total £188.51.
b) Purchases ledger: Sports Ltd £188.51 Cr.
c) Nominal ledger: purchases £165 Dr, Vat £23.51 Dr.

3 a) Purchases journal: purchases £2780, Vat £417, total £3197.
b) Purchases ledger (all credits): Metro £1180, Auto £972, Dunlop £345.
c) P/L control £2497 Cr.
d) Purchases £2780 Dr, Vat £417 Dr.

4 a) Sales invoices: £300 + Vat £45 = £345; £540 + Vat £81 = £621.
Purchase invoices: £312 + Vat £46.80 = £358.80; £110 + Vat £16.50 = £126.50.
b) Sales £840, purchases £312, fittings £110, Vat £62.70.

5 a) Purchases journal: purchases £3365, Vat, £504.75, total £3869.75.
b) Purchases ledger: each supplier a/c Cr £1207.5, £1466.25 and £1196.
Nominal ledger: purchases £3365 Dr, Vat £504.75 Dr, P/L control £3869.75 Cr.

6 a) Purchases journal: purchases £2360, Vat £346.80, total £2706.80.
b) Purchases ledger (all credits): Slazenger £596.80, Metro £509, Auto £601.
Nominal ledger: purchases £2360 Dr, Vat £346.80 Dr, P/L control £1706.80 Cr.

7 i) Yes. ii) Purchases (all) Dr, Vat Dr, P/L control Cr. iii) Purchases ledger (all credits): Footwear Ltd £983.25; FH&W £327.75, Country Casual £86.25, Jones Leather £310.50.

8 a) Purchases journal: purchases £3117, Vat £444.17, P/L control £3561.17. Invoices corrected: 4367 £60.56, 34420 £60.42, 2321 £29.07
b) Nominal ledger: purchases and Vat accounts Dr. P/L control Cr.

Chapter 8 The returns journals

1 a) RO journal: returns out, £180, Vat £27, total £207.
b) Purchases ledger (all debits): Slazenger £69, Auto £23, Metre £115.
c) Nominal ledger: returns out, £180 Cr, Vat £27 Cr.
P/L control £207 Dr.

2 a) RI journal: returns in, £200, Vat £30, total £230.
b) Sales ledger (all credits): Lewis £69, Smith £138, Taylor £23.
c) Nominal ledger: returns in, £200 Dr, Vat £30 Dr.
S/L control £230 Cr.

3 a) RO journal: returns out, £174, Vat £26.10, total £200.10.
b) Purchases ledger (all debits): Slazenger £816, Auto £315.50, Metre £541.40.
c) Nominal ledger: returns out, £1154 Cr, Vat £250.10 Cr.
P/L control £1672.90 Dr.

4 a) RI journal: returns in, £100, Vat £15, total £115.
b) Sales ledger (all debits): Lewis £657, Smith £969.40, Taylor £378.60.
c) Nominal ledger: returns in, £100 Dr, Vat £209 Cr.
S/L control £2005 Dr.

5 a) Purchases journal: purchases £440, Vat £66, total £506.
Sales journal: sales £820, Vat £123, total £943.
RO journal: returns out, £40, Vat £6, total £46.
RI journal: returns in, £20, Vat £3, total £23.
Stationery £120, Vat £18, total £138.
Office furniture £320, Vat £48, total £368.
b) Nominal ledger: purchases £440 Dr, sales £820 Cr; returns out, £40 Cr; returns in, £20 Dr, Vat £6 Dr, stationery £120 Dr, office furniture £320 Dr.

6 Sales ledger (all debits): Appleby £230, Shuttleworth £320, Vincent £651.
Purchases ledger: Morton £460 Cr, Pierce £180 Cr.

7 a) Purchases journal: total £9500. Sales journal: total £10 200.
b) Trial balance totals: £47 480.
Debits: cash £2658, bank £16 758, fixtures £6200, advertising £56, rent £6000, wages £170, insurance £400, printing and stationery £38, drawings £500, purchases £9500, Redhill £3100, Shaw £2100.
Credits: capital £30 000, sales £11 480, Green £3500, Black £2500.
c) To help organise accounts more efficiently, particularly if there are many accounts for debtors and creditors.

Chapter 9 Computer-based accounts: sales and purchases ledger programs

1 Keyboard, monitor (screen) disk drive and printer.

2 The software is the 'brains' enabling programs to operate. In accounting, programs available include ledgers, payroll, stock control, invoicing and job costing.

3 Where businesses have relatively large numbers of repetitive transactions, such as sales and purchases, the computer is ideal because information can instantly be stored in memory, updated, analysed and retrieved when required.

4 A programs menu system offers a range of functions which an operator can use. For example, a sub-section of the sales program, ledger transactions, would have a number of functions such as posting and accounts update, to enable accounts to be processed.

6 Small types of businesses, like retailers, who would benefit more by using a cash book or other system to record their takings and expenditure and those enterprises which do not have a sufficient number of accounts of a repetitive nature.

7 Check the options compared to a manual system and note how a computer program offers greater analytical information.

Chapter 10 Computer-based accounts: the nominal ledger program

1 The recording of all accounts including the totals from the sales and purchases ledger programs, the preparation of the trial balance and the financial statements.
2 In the menu 'Ledger Transactions', No. 2 Journal Entries. For example:
Cash sales £500 into bank.
C005 Bank £500 Dr.
S161 Sales £500 Cr.
3 Details from the sales and purchases ledger programs may be transferred by means of the function 'sales & purchase analysis' which become journalised in the nominal ledger and the appropriate accounts are updated such as sales, purchases, Vat, bank, discounts and the control accounts.
4 Check individual accounts.
5 The function in the nominal ledger menu No. 4 'Special Reports'.
6 The computer may give a warning sound or signal.
7 Not really, if the running balance method is used in the manual system.

Chapter 11 The cash book

1 a) Balances b/d: cash £540, bank £2143, discount allowed £25, discount received £45.
b) Sales ledger: bank and discount allowed Cr, (e.g. Barnes).
Bought ledger: bank and discount received Dr (e.g. Rawlings).
2 a) Balances b/d: cash £305, bank £1490, discount allowed. £35, discount received £10.
b) Nominal ledger: sales £2175 Cr, general expenses £230 Dr.
3 a) Balances b/d: cash £145, bank £2087, discount allowed £28, discount received £44. b) Sales and purchases ledgers: each personal account would have a nil balance.
4 Balance b/d: bank £195 Cr (overdrawn). Totals: discount allowed £20, debtors £1020, sales £1725, bank £3230 (receipts); discount received £30, creditors £1820, drawings £600, wages £240, other expenses £765, bank £3425 (payments).
5 a) Balances b/d: cash £88, bank £291 Cr (overdrawn), discount allowed £5, discount received £9. b) R/D returned to drawer (person who signed cheque). Account may have insufficient funds, cheque not accepted by bank.
6 a) Analysis: wine £830; beer £1030; spirits £290; other sales £134; total £2284. Vat £342.60; bank £2626.60. b) Each sale account credited. c) Better for control and organisation of stocks.
7 Balances b/d: cash £28, bank £22 Cr (overdrawn), discount received £7.
8 a) Balances b/d: cash £85.30, bank £201, discount allowed £50.65, discount received £28.60.
b) Sales £863.30 Cr. Salaries £237, Advertising £42.24, Delivery expenses £25.25 and Petty expenses £8.50, all Dr.

Chapter 12 The bank reconciliation statement

Note: BRS = bank reconciliation statement.
1 Bank b/d £2112. BRS £2592 + £615 − £1110 = £2097 (bank).
2 Bank b/d £11 164. BRS £13 236 + £716 − £2788 = £11 164 (bank).
3 Bank b/d £697. BRS £3189 + 0 − £2492 = £697 (bank).
4 Bank b/d £563. BRS £590 + £40 − £10 = £620 (bank).

5 Bank b/d £838. BRS £1270 + £210 − £642 = £838 (bank).
It is necessary to reverse procedure from £838 bank to calculate the £1270 bank statement balance.
6 Bank b/d £213. BRS £203 + £39 − £29 = £213 (bank).
7 Bank b/d £285 Cr (overdrawn). BRS £190 Dr (overdrawn) + £528 = £338 − £623 = £285 (bank Cr) overdrawn.
8 a) Bank b/d £2850. BRS £1935 + £1800 − £1535 = £2200 (bank).
Cash book debits: £600 £420 £122; credits: £79, £1353 £90 £200 and £70. b) To ensure that the cash book and bank statement entries cross-check correctly.

Chapter 13 The petty cash book

1 a) Cash balance £12.05. Totals: cleaning £16, refreshments £13.70, travel £34.75, postages £21.15, Vat £7.80, sundries £44.55, total £137.95. b) Each expense group is posted as debit entries in the ledger, as expenses.
2 a) Cash balance £16. b) Totals: stationery £68.20, Vat £10.65, travel £19.55, refreshments £20.45, sundries £15.15, total £134. All debits.
3 a) Cash balance £13.33. b) Totals: cleaning £20.80, travel £8, newspapers £3.50, stationery £34.80, post £21.50, refreshments £4.85, Vat £8.22, sundries £10, total £111.67. Each expense group posted as a debit entry in the ledger. c) Vouchers are proof that cash has been authorised and the recipient has signed for the sum received.
4 a) Cash balance £19.25. Totals: Vat £7.65, travel £18, stationery £18, post £10.25, cleaning £20, refreshments £15.60, sundries £16.25, total £105.75. b) Reinbursement £105.75 as per total cash spent.
5 a) £84.35. b) Cash balance £39.26. Totals: Vat £4.30, travel £8.35, cleaning £16.30, post £13.28, stationery £12.40, refreshments £3.76, sundries £2.35, total £60.74. c) Each expense total a debit balance.

Chapter 14 Control accounts

1 S/L control: debits £41 220, £37 350, £790, £40 and £300.
Credits £500, £27 800, £950, £675 and £800.
Balance £48 975 Dr. Agrees with the sales ledger.
2 P/L control: debits £58 200, £2450, £11 285.
Credits: £6432, £81 360, £125.
Balance £15 982 Cr. Agrees with purchases ledger.
3 a) S/L control: debits £5000, £103 000, £300.
Credits: £81 000, £1500, £400, £200.
Balance £25 200 Dr. Sales ledger £25 110. Discrepancy £90. b) P/L control: debits £74 000, £1200, £600.
Credits: £9000, £72 000.
Balance £5200 Cr. Agrees with purchases ledger.
4 a) S/L control: debits £35 000, £36 000, £200, £100, £50 and £200.
Credits: £400, £500, £200, £30 400, £400 and £1000.
Balance £38 650 Dr. Sales ledger £39 050. Discrepancy £400. b) P/L control: debits £200, £600, £100, £11 400 and £400.
Credits: £12 000, £24 000, £20 and £100.
Balance £23 420 Cr agrees with purchases ledger. c) Control accounts are used as a cross-checking device. A measure of control is maintained. Totals of debtors and creditors from the control accounts are posted to the trial balance.

5 a) S/L control: debits £18 776, £231 and £55.
Credits: £3112, £125 050, £460, £661 and £3150.
Balance £17 040 Dr. Sales ledger £16 940. Discrepancy £100.
P/L control: debits £2097, £139 830, £460, £3227.
Credits: £13 199, £155 603.
Balance £23 188 Cr agrees with purchases ledger. b) Error of £100 could be from any item posted from the subsidiary books such as the journals or cash book.

6 a) Sales ledger: Durban £893 Dr, Elliott £2122 Dr.
Nominal ledger: sales £2975 Cr, returns in £32 Dr. b) S/L control balance £51 138 Dr. c) To cross-check with the personal ledgers.

7 S/L control: £38 324 Dr, £456 Cr.
Sales ledger £38 124. Discrepancy £200.
P/L control: £12 484 Cr, £150 Dr agrees with the purchases ledger.

Chapter 16 The final accounts of sole traders

Note: FA = fixed assets. CA = current assets. CL = current liabilities. WC = working capital. LTL = long-term liabilities.

1 a) Gross profit £785, net profit £200. b) FA £17 000, CA £4535, CL £1435, WC £3100, LTL £10 000 = £10 100.
Capital £10 000 + profit £200 − drawings £100 = £10 100.
WC ratio 3.2:1.

2 a) Gross profit £6285, net profit £5230. b) FA £63 150, CA £4720, CL £1180, WC £3540, LTL £42 000 = £24 690.
Capital £20 000 + profit £5230 − drawings £540 = £24 690.
WC ratio 4:1.

3 a) Gross profit £108 300, net profit £67 570. b) FA £56 500, CA £59 700, CL £4230, WC £55 470, LTL £38 000 = £73 970.
Capital £16 600 + profit £67 570 − drawings £10 200 = £73 970.
WC ratio 14:1.

4 a) Gross profit £7535, net loss £1053. b) FA £6225, CA £7252, CL £3580, WC £3672, LTL £4050 = £5847. Capital £11 000 − loss £1053 − drawings £4100 = £5847. c) WC ratio 2:1. A very sound ratio to meet current debts despite net loss of £1053.

5 a) All entries in trial balance correct. Estimated value of closing stock £800. b) Gross profit £13 925, net profit £11 430. FA £34 290, CA £1515, CL £1525, WC (£10), LTL £12 350 = £21 930. Capital £10 500 + profit £11 430 = £21 930.

6 a) Gross profit £7150, net profit £500. FA £61 900, CA £8830, CL £13 055, WC (£4225), LTL £37 175 = £20 500. Capital £20 000 + profit £500 = £20 500. b) 0.68:1 (insolvent).

Chapter 17 Adjustments to final accounts

Note: FA = fixed assets. CA = current assets. CL = current liabilities. WC = working capital. LTL = long-term liabilities.

1 a) Gross profit £15 430, net profit £6237. b) FA £8375, CA £13 032, CL £2625, WC £10 407 = £18 782.
Capital £18 000 + profit £6237 − drawings £5500 = £18 782.

2 Gross profit £7770, net profit £1373. FA £15 010, CA £33 750, CL £35 587, WC (£1837) insolvent, = £13 173. Capital £16 000 + profit £1373 − drawings £4200 = £13 173.

3 Gross profit £10 000, net profit £8000. FA £73 000, CA £11 670, CL £2670, WC £9000 = £82 000. Capital £80 000 + profit £8000 − drawings £6000 = £82 000.

4 Gross profit £12 500, net profit £7000. FA £72 500, CA £18 200, CL £3700, WC £14 500 = £87 000. Capital £85 000 + profit £7000 − drawings £5000 = £87 000.

5 a) Provision for bad debts: debit £550. Credits: £600, £660. Balance £710 Cr. b) 1990: P & L expenses £600; BS debtors £11 400. 1991: P & L expenses £660; BS debtors £13 490.

6 Gross profit £29 500, net profit £16 400. FA £50 000, CA £6700, CL £3900, WC £2800, LTL £21 000 = £31 800. Capital £20 850 + profit £16 400 − drawings £5450 = £31 800.

7 Gross profit £32 125, net profit £4250. FA £21 500, CA £25 500, CL £18 100, WC £7400 = £28 900. Capital £29 250 + profit £4250 − drawings £4600 = £28 900.

8 a) Group A errors: filing cabinet, petty cash, office desk, chair, drawings.
Group B errors: carriage outwards, advertising, new staples, gun, dividends, transfer to reserve, new light bulbs.
Pocket calculators and painting of building could be classed as either depending on value and time. Both likely to be revenue expenditure items.
b) Profits would either be over- or understated, having the same effect on the assets of the business.

9 Capital expenditure: vehicle, fittings, seats and covers.
Revenue expenditure: tax, insurance, petrol, maintenance, tyre and exhaust (running expenses).
The vehicle at cost may have included tax and insurance as part of capital expenditure.

10 To ensure that the profit and loss statement is 'true and fair' and an accurate reflection of the business activities. If capital expenditure items were treated as revenue expenditure, profits would be understated as would assets. The reverse would be true if revenue items were treated as capital items.

Chapter 18 The depreciation of fixed assets

Note: FA = fixed assets. CA = current assets. CL = current liabilities. WC = working capital. LTL = long-term liabilities.

1 Gross profit £9787, net loss £28 883. FA £125 320, WC £1907 = £127 227. Capital £170 350 − loss £28 883 − drawings £14 240 = £127 227.

2 i) Gross profit £110 615, net profit £16 667. FA £104 400, CA £54 340, CL £26 020, WC £28 320 = £132 720. Capital £131 653 + profit £16 667 − drawings £15 600 = £132 720.
ii) Mitchell has ample working capital and could use some funds to expand or improve her business.

3 Gross profit £56 141, net profit £5888. FA £30 300, CA £27 560, CL £6681, WC £20 879 = £51 179. Capital £53 091 + profit £5888 − drawings £7800 = £51 179.

4 Capital £27 908. Gross profit £65 409, net profit £31 632. FA £43 025, CA £15 495, CL £9400, WC £6095 = £49 120. Capital £27 908 + profit £31 632 − drawings £10 420 = £49 120.

5 Gross profit £32 600. Net profit £20 578. (Depreciation £512.)

6 a) Gross profit £130 000, net profit £57 100. b) FA £65 000, CA £181 100, CL £86 500, WC £94 600 = £159 600. Capital £127 500 + profit £57 100 − drawings £25 000 = £159 600.

7 a) Premises £1 500 000 Dr. Plant and machinery £900 000 Dr. Depreciation of plant and machinery £423 500 Cr. Asset disposal a/c £10 000 (P & L a/c). b) Balance sheet: FA £2 400 000 (cost), depreciation £423 500, net value £1 976 500. c) Details of the revaluation such as name of valuers, date valued, basis of valuation.

8 Balances 1987: a) plant £4500 Dr. b) Depreciation of plant £1350, c) Asset disposal a/c £100 (P & L a/c). d) Balance sheet: FA £4500 (cost), depreciation £1350, net value £2150. e) Revaluation and reducing balance methods.

9 a) Stationery: debits £110, £406; credits £125, £391 (P & L). Rent: debit £768; credits: £96, £96, £576 (P & L). Provision for bad debts: debits £49, £200 (P & L); credit £249. b) Profit & Loss a/c: stationery £391, rent £576, provision for bad debts £49 (Cr). c) Balance sheet: prepayments–rent £96, stationery £125. Debtors £4000 – provision for bad debts £200, = £3800. Adjustments must be indicated to give a true and fair picture of the accounts for the accounting period.

Chapter 19 Accounting for partnerships

1 i) a) Share of profits £10 415 each. b) Current accounts: Trevalyn £4550 Cr, Curtis £2265 Cr. Balance sheet: capital £45 000, current accounts £6815 = £51 815. ii) A limited partner has no right to control, only general partners. He is only liable up to the amount of his capital, not personal wealth.

2 a) Share of profits: Robert £9900, Susan £7425, Thomas £2475. b) Current accounts: Robert £81 Cr, Susan £100 Cr, Thomas £328 Dr.

3 Share of profits: Alan £18 000, Bill £12 000, Charles £6000. Current accounts: Alan £13 000 Cr, Bill £5000 Cr, Charles £0.
FA £112 000, CA £47 400, CL £21 400, WC £26 000 = £138 000. Capital £120 000, current accounts £18 000 = £138 000.

4 a) Share of profits £8900 each. Current accounts: Fairway £2500 Cr, Rough £7060 Dr. b) FA £51 500, WC £3940 = £55 440 – LTL £15 000 = £40 440. Capital £45 000, current accounts (£4560) = £40 440.

5 a) Gross profit £10 012, net profit £5690. Share of profits: Smith £3036, Jones £2024. b) Current accounts: Smith £101 Dr, Jones £824 Cr. FA £27 500, WC £3222 = £30 722. Capital £30 000, Current accounts £722 = £30 722.

6 a) Share of profits £2242 each. Current accounts: Stevenson £11 392 Cr, Little £1558 Dr. b) FA £63 790, WC £6044 = £69 834. Capital £60 000, current accounts £9834 = £69 834. c) Employees' salaries an expense in profit and loss account. Partners' salaries in appropriation account to show profit/loss which excludes owners' salaries.

7 a) Share of profits: Wooldridge £6540, James £4360. Current accounts: Wooldridge £7990 Cr, James £2660 Cr. b) FA £114 000, WC £5650, LTL £29 000 = £90 650. Capital £80 000, current accounts £10 650 = £90 650. c) Under Section 24 of the 1890 Partnership Act, profits or losses must be borne equally if no agreement exists in the event of partners in disagreement.

8 i) Gross profit £25 000, net profit £9000. Share of profits £2500 each. Current accounts: Dick £1870 Cr, Tom £2960 Cr. ii) FA £11 250, CA £29 580, CL £6000, WC £23 580 = £34 830. Capital £30 000, current accounts £4830 = £34 830.
Note: £350 purchases lost are deducted from cost of sales and entered as a current asset. iii) NP% 12, ROCE 25.8 returns on profit.

9 i) Share of profits: Smith £2050, Jones £2050, Rodgers £1025. Current accounts: Smith £1095 Cr, Jones £1075 Cr, Rodgers £370 Dr. ii) FA £30 700, WC £50, LTL £4950 = £25 800. Capital £24 000, current accounts £1800 = £25 800. iii) Working capital very marginal.

10 a) Share of profits £8500 each. Current accounts: French £2100 Cr, Saunders £7160 Dr. b) FA £61 000, WC (£1060), LTL £20 000 = £39 940. Capital £45 000, current accounts (£5060) = £39 940. c) WC ratio = 0.87:1 (insolvent). Insufficient funds to cover debts. Improve by reducing future drawings, particularly Saunders. Increase sales. d) The profit of £19 800 would be reduced to £19 300 and French's current account would also be reduced by £500.

Chapter 20 Accounting for limited companies

1 Net profit £108 000 (before tax), £78 000 (after tax) + P & L £22 000 − dividends £64 000 − reserves £20 000 = P & L £16 000. FA £554 000, (depreciation £256 000), WC £16 000 = £570 000. Capital £500 000, premium a/c £20 000, reserves £34 000, P & L £16 000 = £570 000.

2 Gross profit £135 500, net profit £46 500 (before tax), £32 000 (after tax) − dividends £2500 − reserves £25 000 = P & L £4500. FA £135 100, WC £23 900, LTL £52 000 = £107 000. Capital £50 000, premium a/c £10 000, reserves £42 500, P & L £4500 = £107 000.

3 a) Net profit £40 600 (before tax), £30 600 (after tax) + P & L £19 200 − dividends £14 400 − reserves £10 400 = P & L £25 000. b) FA £165 000, CA £39 960, CL £34 560, WC £5400 = £170 400. Capital £130 000, reserves £15 400, P & L £25 000 = £170 400.

4 a) Net profit £10 300 + P & L £9600 − dividends £7200 − reserves £12 000 = P & L £700. b) FA £75 000, WC £2700 = £77 700. Capital £65 000, reserves £12 000, P & L £700 = £77 700. c) Interim dividend: part payment, usually half-yearly. Ordinary shares (equities) true shares, carry greater risk, no fixed dividends. Preference shares paid at fixed rate of dividend, carry less risk.

5 a) Net profit £300 (before tax), £290 (after tax) + P & L £10 − dividends £230 − reserves £40 = P & L £30. b) FA £1380, WC £140 = £1520. Capital £1400, reserves £90, P & L £30 = £1520. Equity £1020.

6 Gross profit £151 800, net profit £43 033 (before tax), £23 833 (after tax) + P & L £7780 − dividends £22 400 − reserves £4000 = P & L £5213. FA £322 330, CA £102 169, CL £110 286, WC (£8117) insolvent, LTL £40 000 = £274 213. Capital £240 000, reserves £29 000, P & L £5213 = £274 213.

7 a) Assets: premises £75 000, fittings £14 300, debtors £18 600, stock £6861, bank £13 679 = £128 440. Liabilities: creditors £10 300, dividends £7500 = £17 800. Capital £110 640, (A − L). Capital £100 000 P & L £10 640 = £110 640. b) Insufficient WC, danger of insolvency. Too much WC, funds should be optimised to make best use of resources.

8 a) Net profit £8964 + P & L £3200 − dividends £7200 − reserves £2000 = P & L £2964. b) FA £82 904, CA £25 870, CL £13 810, WC £12 060, LTL £30 000 = £64 964. Capital £60 000, reserves £2000, P & L £2964 = £64 964.

9 a) Gross profit £121 500, net profit £45 000 (before tax), £29 500 (after tax) − dividends £9000 − reserves £20 000 = P & L £500. FA £156 500, WC £61 500, LTL £40 000 = £178 000. Capital £100 000, reserves £77 500, P & L £500 = £178 000. b) 1.6:1, working capital appears adequate.

10 Net profit £80 000 (before interest and tax), £47 500 (after tax) + P & L £40 000 − dividends £55 000 − reserves £25 000 = P & L £7500. FA £355 000, CA £419 000, CL £296 500, WC £122 500, LTL £100 000 = £377 500. Capital £300 000, reserves £70 000, P & L £7500 = £377 500.

Chapter 21 The statement of sources and application of funds

1 Sources £5780, application £4590. WC £770, NLF £420 = surplus £1190.

2 Sources £6450, application £6850. WC £400, NLF (£800) = deficit £400.

3 Sources £27 750, application £21 100. WC £7070, NLF (£420) = surplus £6650.

4 a) Reconstruct the appropriation a/c to find net profit £37 000 (before tax). b) Sources £105 000, application £80 000. WC £19 000, NLF £6000 = surplus £25 000. c) WC ratio 1.1 (1988), 1.9 (1989).

5 a) Sources £88 460, application £97 520. WC £4140, NLF (£13 200) = deficit £9060. b) WC ratio 2.7 each year. Return on capital employed = 17.6%.

6 a) Sources £28 400 + sale of FA £4200 = £32 600. Application £33 000. WC £5600 NLF (£6000) = deficit £400. b) WC ratios: 1.77 and 1.88.

7 Sources £11 300 + sale of FA £3500 = £14 800. Application £15 000. WC £800, NLF (£1000) = deficit £200.

8 a) Sources £79 000, application £163 300. WC (£82 400), NLF (£1900) = deficit £84 300. b) Capital expenditure on FA was financed in a number of ways including £60 000 issue of shares. The WC has declined by £84 300 and this was the major financing. The WC ratio is 1.6 (sufficient) and excess WC has been used for capital expenditure.

9 a) Sources: £198 100 − profit on sale of FA £6000 = £192 100. Other sources £213 000 = total £405 100. Application £183 000. WC £338 300, NLF (£116 200) = surplus £222 100. b) Large increase in WC although the bank balance has been reduced, helping to support a great increase in debtors.

Chapter 22 Statements of Standard Accounting Practice (SSAPs)

1 Accounts would be prepared more subjectively without the SSAP guidelines and anomalies would appear more frequently in the final accounts.

2 SSAP No. 2 (Disclosure of Accounting Policies) outlines the four basic concepts upon which the final accounts are prepared: going concern, accruals, consistency and conservatism.

3 Final accounts could easily give the wrong impression and profit distortions would occur. For example, changing the method of stock value or depreciation from one period to the next.

4 Concepts identified include: historical cost, consistency (depreciation items), conservatism (stock value), realisation (sales on contract date), accruals (interest and other payments), conservatism (provision for loss), going concern (assumption that the firm will continue in the next financial period).

Chapter 23 Accounting ratios

1 a)

	1989	1990
Net profit%	15	15
ROCE	30.5	30.1
ROTA	24.1	23.6
WC ratio	1.01	0.98
Acid test	0.5	0.42

b) Profit returns taken before tax. All ratios marginally inferior in 1990. The company is insolvent in 1990 and perhaps the dividends should be reduced to ensure solvency.

2 a) WC is the ability of a business to meet its short-term debt. The minimum ratio should be 1:1, a figure less than this means insolvency. Each business should identify its own margin of safety. b) WC ratio 1.95, acid test 1.16. These appear adequate as a test of the business's liquidity.

3 a) Profitability: tests returns on profit before or after tax.
Liquidity: tests ability to meet debt.

b) Gross profit %, net profit % (profit to sales).

c) WC ratio, CA/CL

d) 'A' ROCI 10%, ROCE 9.1%, WC ratio 2:1.
'B' ROCI 25%, ROCE 20%, WC ratio 0.5:1.
Business A moderate profitability and sound liquidity.
Business B good profitability but poor liquidity.

4 i)

	Big	Spiv
WC ratio	1.8	1.3
Acid test	1.1	0.72
Gearing	11%	133%
NP %	12%	15%
EPS	31.3p	83.3p
ROCE	25.2%	33.3%

ii) Big has low gearing and sound liquidity. Spiv has higher gearing and relies more on outside finance and has more attractive returns, especially EPS (earnings per share).

5 a)

	1983	1984	1985	1986
Gross profit (£)	15 000	18 000	18 000	27 000
Net profit (£)	3 000	4 500	1 500	8 000
GP%	33.33	33.33	25.00	28.00
NP%	6.67	8.33	2.08	8.33

b) The poor year was 1985. GP% inferior, identify what went wrong with buying or selling. Recovery in 1986, improving GP return.

6

	Ball Bearings	Rocco
Net Profit (a/t)	£1.5 m	£1.6 m
EPS	15p	80p
Dividend	7p	20p
Cover	2.1	4
WC ratio	0.98	0.95
Acid test	0.5	0.95
Capital gearing	300%	6.67%

The bank is far more profitable and stable, even though its WC ratio is 0.95, as a bank it should not have a liquidity problem.

7

	1986	1987	1988
Gross profit	36 000	50 000	70 000
Net profit	1 600	7 000	16 000
GP%	30%	33.33%	35%
NP%	1.3%	4.6%	8%
ROCE	2.67	6.67	10
Stock turnover	10.5	11.8	13

Sound improvement although 8% net return in 1988 still looks low. Stock turnover has gained each year as sales have expanded and the trend looks promising.

8

	A	B	C
Net profit (b/t)	695 000	695 000	645 000
Net profit (a/t)	451 750	451 750	419 250
Dividends	410 000	420 000	360 000
P & L balance	41 750	31 750	59 250
EPS	13.4p	12.9p	13.9p
Gearing	16.6%	0%	16.6%

Plan C may be the best to pursue because it has the highest retained profits and marginally better EPS. In times of high interest rates it may be better to opt for Plan A.

9

		Year 1	Year 2	Year 3
		£	£	£
a)	Gross profit	10 000	12 000	13 050
	Net profit	3 850	5 050	4 675
b)	GP%	$33\frac{1}{3}$%	$33\frac{1}{3}$%	29%
	NP%	12.8%	14%	10.4%
	Dist. %	10%	8.9%	9.1%
	Admin. %	10.5%	10.4%	9.5%
	Stock turnover	10	9.6	8
	Credit days	73	73	89
	ROCI	14.5%	16.8%	14.7%

c) Year 3 inferior primarily because of fall in GP% from $33\frac{1}{3}$% to 29% indicating trading problems. Accounting ratios may fail to reveal the true or realistic situation.

Chapter 24 Accounting for manufacturing organisations

1 Prime cost £119 150. Prime cost/unit £23.83. Factory OH's £22 900. Factory cost £142 150. Factory cost/unit £28.43. Gross profit £43 480.

2 a) Prime cost £57 549. Factory OH's £11 759. Factory cost £69 308. Factory profit £8692. Total gross profit £34 197. Net loss £389. b) DL/unit £7.75, DM/unit £21.02, FOH's/unit £5.88, FC/unit £34.65. c) Yes, by £4.35 per unit.

3 a) Prime cost £1 096 160. Factory OH's £54 650, factory cost £1 146 000. FC/unit £38.20. b) Gross profit £449 640. Net profit £372 000.

4 i) Prime cost £46 512. Factory OH's £13 335. Factory cost £60 000. ii) Gross profit £32 300. Net profit £20 000. iii) Prime cost/unit £3.88. FOH's/unit £1.11. FC/unit £5. Value of finished goods £16 250. Mark up 60%.

5 Prime cost £100 958. Factory OH's £14 745. Factory cost £115 703. Gross profit £64 793. Net profit £38 717. FA £43 025, CA £19 672, CL £9400, WC £10 272 = £53 297. Capital £25 000 + profit £38 717 − drawings £10 420 = £53 297.

6 Prime cost £198 623. Factory cost £201 000. FC/unit £4.02. Value of finished goods £18 090. Gross profit £12 590. Net profit £1802. P & L balance £382. FA £91 400, WC (£11 018), insolvent = £80 382. Capital £70 000, premium a/c £7000, reserves £3000, P & L £382 = £80 382.

7 Prime cost £75 000. Factory OH's £40 550. Factory cost £103 250. Manufacturing loss £8250. Gross profit £85 000 − £8250 = £76 750. Net profit £8400.

8

		Star 1	**Star 2**	**Star 3**	**Total**
a)	Prime cost	92 400	112 300	131 500	336 200
	Factory cost	95 400	115 300	137 500	348 200
b)	Gross profit	24 000	44 000	48 000	116 000
c)	Gross profit%	20%	27.5%	25.2%	

Chapter 25 Looking ahead: budgets and spreadsheets

1 a) and b) Cash budget

	April	**May**	**June**	**July**	**Aug**	**Sept**
Balance b/f	5 000	1 000	5 000	1 000	14 000	28 000
Receipts	20 000	30 000	35 000	34 000	36 000	25 000
Payments	24 000	26 000	39 000	21 000	22 000	44 100
Balance c/f	1 000	5 000	1 000	14 000	28 000	8 900

c) Banking limits may be tight during the first three months but improve in last three.

2 a) and b) Cash budget.

	July	Aug	Sept	Oct	Nov	Dec
Balance b/f	2 000	4 040	(7 900)	(8 060)	(4 840)	11 680
Receipts	23 200	32 000	24 000	28 000	39 000	31 200
Payments	21 160	43 940	24 160	24 780	22 480	20 660
Balance c/f	4 040	(7 900)	(8 060)	(4 840)	11 680	22 220

c) Small needs overdraft facility for months August to October.

3 Cash budget

	April	May	June	July	Aug	Sept
Balance b/f	120 000	3 500	1 200	(600)	(4 100)	(5 100)
Receipts	—	12 000	15 000	15 000	18 000	21 000
Payments	116 500	14 300	16 800	18 500	19 000	19 500
Balance c/f	3 500	1 200	(600)	(4 100)	(5 100)	(3 600)

4 i) Cash budget

	Dec	Jan	Feb	Mar
Balance b/f	1 000	3 725	1 125	1 700
Receipts	9 750	10 500	8 250	7 500
Payments	7 025	13 100	7 675	10 750
Balance c/f	3 725	1 125	1 700	(1 550)

ii) Fixed costs are insensitive to output change, for example, rent, rates, insurance. Variable costs change relative to output and are sensitive to changes in levels of production. Examples, materials and direct labour.

5 a) Cash budget

	July	Aug	Sept	Oct	Nov	Dec
Balance b/f	10 000	4 800	1 200	2 200	1 700	(540)
Receipts		6 000	13 600	13 600	12 000	10 800
Payments	5 200	9 600	12 600	14 100	14 240	9 740
Balance c/f	4 800	1 200	2 200	1 700	(540)	520

b) Trading a/c: sales £64 000 − cost of sales £36 800 = gross profit £27 200. Net profit £9220. FA £10 500, CA £13 120, CL £4400, WC £8720 = £19 220. Capital £10 000 + profit £9220 = £19 220. Note: value of stock 400 units × £11.5 = £4600.

c) The owner may need a bank overdraft facility as his cash flow reduces to an overdraft in November.

6 a) Cash budget

	July	Aug	Sept	Oct	Nov	Dec
Balance b/f	12 000	(11 200)	(21 760)	(23 590)	(12 080)	520
Receipts		25 000	35 000	36 000	37 500	40 000
Payments	23 200	35 560	36 830	24 490	24 900	26 475
Balance c/f	(11 200)	(21 760)	(23 590)	(12 080)	520	14 050

b) Trading a/c: sales £203 500 − cost of sales £134 310 = Gross profit £69 190. Net profit £55 490. FA £19 500, CA £61 965, CL £2575, WC £59 390, LTL £10 000 = £68 890. Capital £17 000 + profit £55 490 − drawings £3600 = £68 890.
Note: stock value 240 units × £33 = £7920.

7 a) Prime cost £133 000, factory cost £209 000. FC/unit £5.5. b) Gross profit £87 500. Net profit £11 250. c) Mark-up 45.45%. Margin 31.25%.

8 a) Factory cost £2500. FC/unit 50p. SP/unit 75p. b) Gross profit £1225, expenses £325, net profit £900.

9 a) Prime cost £90 000, factory cost £112 000. FC/unit £5.60. SP/unit £8.40. b) Gross profit £50 400, net profit £14 400. Note: mark-up 50%, margin 33.33%. c) Variable cost: sensitive to output change. Fixed cost: insensitive to output change. Greater output dilutes fixed costs.

Chapter 26 The trial balance and its limitations

1 a) Errors of: principle, principle, commission, omission and original entry. b) In each case, a debit has a corresponding credit, not disclosed by the trial balance. c) Drawings £550 Dr, wages £550 Cr, office equipment £180 Dr, purchases £180 Cr, rates and water £85 Dr, accrued expenses £85 Cr, Vat £7.5 Dr, Welland £7.5 Cr.

2 The trial balance is an arithmetical check on the accuracy of the recording of double entry. If each transaction has an equal Dr and Cr any error will not be disclosed.

3 D Brown £207 Dr, J Brown £207 Cr, office equipment £2250 Dr, purchases £2250 Cr, debtors £27 Dr, sales £27 Cr, light and heat £36 Dr, bank £36 Cr.

4 a) Rawlins £23 Dr, returns out £20, Vat £3 Cr, Jones £253 Dr, sales £220, Vat £33 Cr, Smith £54 Dr, purchases £54 Cr, drawings £435 Dr, purchases £435 Cr, bank £42 Dr, commission £42 Cr, equipment £200 Dr, purchases £200 Cr, sales £300 Dr, equipment £300 Cr.

b) Each item which affects either revenue or expenses affect the profit of a business.

Chapter 27 The journal and use of the suspense account

1 D Brown Dr, W Brown Cr, office equipment Dr, purchases Cr, Elliott Dr, discount allowed Cr, drawings Dr, delivery expenses Cr, light and heat Dr, bank Cr.

2 a) Trial balance totals £30 105.
Debits: purchases £2960, returns in £98, petty cash £18, discount allowed £45, rates £91, bank charges £14, stock £823, debtors £960, premises £25 000.
Credits: sales £6916, returns out £46, bank overdraft £621, creditors £840, capital £21 682.
b) Errors of principle, compensation, etc.

3 a) R Smith £285 Dr, J Smith £285 Cr, sales £600 Dr, equipment £600 Cr, discount allowed £8 Dr, suspense £8 Cr, suspense £200 Dr, sales £200 Cr, suspense £55 Dr, salaries £55 Cr, debtors £275 Dr, sales £275 Cr, insurance £55 Dr, bank £55 Cr. b) Suspense a/c: debits – sales £200 and salaries £55; credits – balance £247 and discount allowed £8.

4 a) Sales £220 Dr, suspense £220 Cr, suspense £121 Dr, Wilkinson £121 Cr, vehicle repairs £27 Dr, suspense £27 Cr, Heath £9 Dr, suspense £9 Cr, suspense £240 Dr, discount allowed £120 and discount received £120 Cr. Suspense a/c: debits – Wilkinson £121 and discounts £240; credits – balance £105, sales £220, vehicle repairs £27 and Heath £9. b) Errors of principle, commission, omission and compensation.

5 i) Discount received £100 Dr, suspense £100 Cr, suspense £8 Dr, Stanley £8 Cr, sales £900 Dr, suspense £900 Cr, sales £9 Dr, Purcell £9 Cr, purchases £360 Dr, suspense £360 Cr, Blow £20 Dr, returns in £20 Cr, sales £15 Dr, Vat £15 Cr. ii) Suspense a/c: debits – balance £1352 and Stanley £8; credits – discount received £100, sales £900 and purchases £360. iii) The adjusted profit £12 200.

6 i) Purchases £64 Dr, creditors £64 Cr, furniture £82 Dr, repairs £82 Cr, suspense £290 Dr, bank £290 Cr, sales £378 Dr, suspense £378 Cr, interest charges £50 Dr, bank £50 Cr, creditors £100 Dr, suspense £100 Cr. ii) Suspense a/c: debits – balance £188 and bank £290; credits – sales £378 and creditors £100. iii) The adjusted profit £382.

7 a) Equipment £500 Dr, purchases £500 Cr, Light and heat £85 Cr, bank £85 Cr, discount allowed £68 Dr, suspense £68 Cr, suspense £800 Dr, sales £800 Cr, suspense £45 Dr, Smith £45 Cr, returns in £87 Dr, suspense £87 Cr. Suspense a/c: debits – sales £800 and Smith £45; credits – balance £690 discount allowed £68 and returns in £87. b) Trial balance totals £50 705.

8 Suspense £315 Dr, sales £315 Cr, general expenses £85 Dr, suspense £85 Cr, suspense £500 Dr, purchases £500 Cr, suspense £90 Dr, discount received £90 Cr, suspense £95 Dr, returns out £95 Cr. Suspense a/c: debits – sales £315, discount received £90, purchases £500 and returns out £95; credits – balance £915 and general expenses £85. Adjusted profit £13 335.

Chapter 28 The sale and purchase of a business

1 a) Jackson's (buyer's) journal: debits – premises £30 000, equipment £4000, motor £800, debtors £3500, stock £4500 and goodwill £6550; credits – provision for bad debts £350, creditors £7000, Davies (vendor) £42 000. Totals £49 350. b) Bank £42 000 Dr, capital £21 000 Cr, bank loan £21 000 Cr. On settlement: Davies £42 000 Dr, bank £42 000 Cr. c) Balance sheet: FA £34 800, goodwill £6550, WC £650, LTL £21 000 = £21 000. Capital = £21 000.

2 a) Smith's (buyer's) journal: debits – premises £65 000, equipment £5000, motor £2000, stock £9000, debtors £7500, goodwill £4500; credits – creditors £8000, Donald (vendor) £85 000. Totals £93 000. Bank £68 000 Dr. Loan £68 000 Cr.
On settlement: Donald £85 000 Dr, bank £85 000 Cr. b) Balance sheet: FA £97 000, goodwill £4500, CA £24 500, CL £13 000, WC £11 500 = £113 000, LTL £68 000 = £45 000. Capital £45 000.

3 a) Donald's (vendor's) journal: debits – realisation £85 000 and creditors £8000; credits – premises £50 000, equipment £8000, van £2000, stock £12 000, debtors £7500 and capital (profit) £13 500. Totals £93 000. Smith £85 000 Dr. Realisation £85 000 Cr. Bank £85 000 Dr. Smith £85 000 Cr. b) Realisation a/c: debits – premises £50 000, equipment £8000, van £2000, stock £12 000, debtors £7500, capital £13 500; credits – creditors £8000 and Smith £85 000. Totals £93 000. c) Capital a/c: debit bank £93 500; credit balance £80 000; profit £13 500.

4 a) Accounting equation Johnson: capital £14 090 = assets £16 890 − liabilities £2800. Taylor: capital £12 580 = assets £14 580 − liabilities £2000. b) Balance sheet: FA £15 000, CA £12 800, CL £4300, WC £8500 = £23 500. Capital: Johnson £11 500, Taylor £12 000 = £23 500.

Chapter 29 Stock valuation

1 a) Value of stock £1210.50. b) If the net realisable value is less than the cost price, the lower price will be used to value stock rather than its cost. This would probably apply to old or obsolete stocks.

2 a) 165 units should be in stock. b) This is five less than the stock take figure of 160 units. The difference could arise from the miscounting of units, or units lost, stolen or damaged, or entries inaccurately recorded.

3 a) FIFO – it is assumed that the stock of units received first are issued first (irrespective of how the stock is issued).
LIFO – it is assumed that the last stock received is the first to be issued.
AVCO – the costing of the stock is averaged according to volume and price of units.
b) FIFO because the unused stock will be valued at the most current (higher) value. The higher the closing value of stock, the greater the gross profit. The following period will show the closing stock as the opening stock at the higher value, therefore profit will not be distorted if a method is adopted consistently.

4 Final column: £525, £140, £900, £750, £149.25, £57.50 and £5. Total stock value £2526.75.

5 *FIFO*. Stock value 1/7 £715, 1/8 £745, 1/9 £765, Balance 100 units × £2.15 = £215. 250 units × £2.20 = £550. Total £765 in stock.
LIFO. Stock value 1/7 £700, 1/8 £700, 1/9 £700. Balance 200 units × £2 = £400. 100 units × £1.95 = £195. 50 units × £2.10 = £105. Total £700 in stock.

6 a) *AVCO*. Stock value 4/1 £3050, unit price £11.09, 12/1 £3909, unit price £13.03, 20/1 £10 345, unit price £15.21. 28/1 balance 400 units × £15.21 = £6084 in stock. b) LIFO would give a lower stock value than either AVCO or FIFO, using the earliest prices to value stock. The cost of sales would show a higher expense using LIFO, thereby reducing the gross profit.

Chapter 30 Accounting for clubs and societies

1 Expenditure £1808, income £1585, deficit £223. FA £10 140, CA £1345, (including £1000 bank), CL £68, WC £1277 = £11 417. Accumulated fund £11 640 − deficit £223 = £11 417.

2 Expenditure £4145, income £10 145 (bar profit £3400). Surplus £6000. FA £1800, CA £9480, CL £680, WC £8800 = £10 600. Accumulated fund £4600 + surplus £6000 = £10 600.

3 a) Accumulated fund £36 759. b) Expenditure £7386, income £8127, surplus £741. FA £33 850, bank investment £2807, CA £1037, CL £194, WC £843 = £37 500. Accumulated fund £36 759 + surplus £741 = £37 500.

4 a) Accumulated fund £15 550. b) R & P a/c: balance £1195 + receipts £2950 − payments £2535 = closing balance £1610. c) Expenditure £2470, income £2950, surplus £480. FA £14 590, WC £1440 = £16 030. Accumulated fund £15 550 + surplus £480 = £16 030.

5 a) Accumulated fund £1220. b) Subscriptions a/c: debits – £65, £37; credits – £10, £1987, £85, balance £1980. Prizes a/c: COS £272. Surplus = £165. c) Expenditure £3249, income £2822, deficit £427. FA £780, CA £131, CL £118, WC £13 = £793. Accumulated fund £1220 − deficit £427 = £793.

6 Accumulated fund £1955. Expenditure £2955, income £3020, surplus £65. FA £1460, CA £601, CL £41, WC £560 = £2020. Accumulated fund £1955 + surplus £65 = £2020.

7 a) R & P a/c: payments £2871, receipts £2842 = £29 (overdrawn). Refreshment a/c surplus £499. b) Expenditure £1288, income £1164, deficit £124. FA £133, CA £217, CL £145, WC £72 = £205. Accumulated fund £329 − deficit £124 = £205.

8 a) Bar a/c: sales £10 243, COS £7149 surplus £3094. Expenditure £6318, income £13 269, surplus £6951. Subscriptions a/c £782. (subscriptions £22 w/o: Dr expense, Cr subscriptions). b) FA £268 244, CA £4432, CL £176, WC £4256 = £272 500 − LTL £55 000 = £217 500. Accumulated fund £210 549 + surplus £6951 = £217 500.

Chapter 31 Accounting for incomplete records

1 Sales £278 600, purchases £166 830, gross profit £111 770, net profit £16 300. FA £14 000, WC £86 000 = £100 000. Capital £99 700 + profit £16 300 − drawings £16 000 = £100 000.

2 a) 1/1 FA £30 000, CA £6238, CL £9053, LTL £3000 = capital £24 185. b) 31/12 FA £29 800, CA £8268, CL £1837, WC £6431, LTL £3000 = £33 231. Capital £33 231.
c) Profit = Net asset change + drawings − new capital
£10 826 £9046 £8000 £6220

3 a) Sales £29 956, purchases £10 546, gross profit £11 362, net profit £8699. b) FA £98 088, CA £9335, CL £26 069, WC (£16 734) insolvent = £81 354. Capital £76 265 + profit £8699 − drawings £3610 = £81 354.

4 a) Sales £46 525, purchases £38 965. Gross profit £6970, net loss £2232. b) FA £118 800. CA £9265, CL £5772, WC £3493, LTL £40 400 = £74 893. Capital £80 000 − net loss £2232 − drawings £2875 = £74 893.

5 a) Sales £19 815, purchases £13 654, gross profit £7641, net profit £4628. b) FA £18 997, CA £9071, CL £2520, WC £6551 = £25 548. Capital £23 000 + profit £4628 − drawings £2630 = £25 548.

6 a) Sales £26 800 COS (before stock loss) £23 860. Stock loss £2420 COS (including stock loss) £21 440. Gross profit £5360. (Margin 20%.) b) Stock loss £2420.

7 Sales £410 000, purchases £309 000. COS (before stock loss) £350 000. Stock loss £63 000. COS (after stock loss) £287 000. Gross profit £123 000. (Margin 30%.)

8 Sales £361 475, purchases £237 000. COS (before stock loss) £296 500. Stock loss £79 615. COS (after stock loss) £216 885. Gross profit £144 590. (Margin 40%.)

Chapter 32 Accounting for wages

1 Gross pay: Tom £126, Dick £119.25, Harry £148.50.

2 Gross pay: £120. Deductions £33.16 (tax £12.43). Net pay £86.84.

3 Gross pay: £205. Deductions NIC £15.23, tax £36.80 = £52.03. Net pay £152.97.

4 Gross pay: £179. Deductions NIC £12.89, Tax £30.30 = £43.19. Net pay £135.81.

5 Gross pay: £285 per week. Deductions: pension £11.40, NIC £22.43, tax £45.68 = £79.51. Net pay £205.49. (Pay with marriage allowance.) Gross pay £120 per week. Deductions NIC £7.58, tax £15.55 = £23.13. Net pay £96.87. (Pay with single allowance.)

Chapter 33 Accounting for departments

1 a)

	Elect	**Furn**	**Total**
Gross profit	18 000	37 000	55 000
Net profit	100	4 900	5 000

b) The furnishings department carries the store, Electrical barely break-even. An evaluation is needed as to why profitability is a low £100.

2 a) Allocation: a cost specifically allotted to a department or cost centre, for example, wages and cost of materials. Apportion: a cost incurred for the benefit of two or more sections which must be divided on some basis such as floor space or number of staff.

b) Likely bases: a) floor space; b) meter readings or floor space; c) sales volume or value; d) number of staff; e) floor space or number of staff; f) sales volume or value; g) floor space or value of fixtures in each department.

3

	Dept A	**Dept B**	**Dept C**	**Dept D**
Gross profit	5 400	7 600	1 800	4 600
Gross profit%	25.2%	22.6%	7.26%	24.7%

Obviously Dept C requires some evaluation as having a disproportionately low gross margin.

4 a)

	Dept A	**Dept B**	**Dept C**	**Total**
Gross profit	54 900	94 600	94 500	244 000
Net profit	19 000	52 620	43 680	115 300

b)

Gross profit (%)	45.75%	52.60%	47.25%
Net profit (%)	15.8%	29.2%	21.8%

Dept B appeared to be the most successful. Was it the most efficient in terms of buying and cost effectiveness? Were the overheads apportioned on a fair basis?

5

		Product X	**Product Y**	**Total**
a)	Gross profit	11 000	52 100	63 100
b)	Net profit			20 250

c) FA £66 500, WC £63 000 = £129 500. Capital £118 700 + profit £20 250 − drawings £9450 = £129 500.

Index